Money
Management
Information
Source Book

CONSUMER INFORMATION SERIES

The Consumer Health Information Source Book
By Alan M. Rees and Blanche A. Young

Developing Consumer Health Information Services
Edited by Alan M. Rees

Money Management Information Source Book
By Alan M. Rees and Jodith Janes

The Travel Book: Guide to the Travel Guides
By Jon O. Heise

Money Management Information Source Book

Alan M. Rees & Jodith Janes

R. R. BOWKER COMPANY
New York & London, 1983

Published by R. R. Bowker Company
205 East Forty-second Street, New York, NY 10017
Copyright © 1983 by Xerox Corporation
All rights reserved
Printed and bound in the United States of America

Library of Congress Cataloging in Publication Data

Rees, Alan M.
   Money management information source book.

   (Consumer information series)
   Includes bibliographies and indexes.
   1. Finance, Personal—Bibliography. I. Janes, Jodith.
II. Title. III. Series: Consumer information series
(R. R. Bowker Company)
Z7164.T4R43 1983 [HG179]   016.332024   83-9258
ISBN 0-8352-1738-8

Contents

	Preface	ix
1	**Money Management, Financial Planning, and the Consumer**	1
2	**Bibliographies and Selection Guides**	9
	Popular Literature	10
	Professional/Technical Literature	16
3	**Money and the Consumer**	23
	General	23
	Money-Saving Strategies and Tips	30
	Consumer Redress	37
	Inflation and Financial Survival	38
	Money and the Family	45
	Women and Money	46
	Children and Money	49
	Making Money at Home	50
	Psychology of Money	51
	Credit and Borrowing Money	53
	Student Financial Aid	55
	Bartering and the Underground Economy	57
	Couponing and Refunding	59
	Saving on Travel	60
	Striking It Rich	61
	Banks and Banking	62
	Unemployment Benefits	63
	Debt and Bankruptcy	63

4 Investments and the Stock Market — 67

Investments: General	67
Stock Market: General	75
Stock Market: Strategy	78
Stock Market: Technical Analysis	86
Stock Market: Psychology	89
Options	90
Futures Trading	90
Penny Stocks	94
Bonds	94
Mutual Funds	95
Gold and Silver	96
Strategic Metals	99
Diamonds and Gems	100
Collectibles: Art, Automobiles, Coins, Stamps	101

5 Real Estate — 105

Buying and Selling a Home	105
Mortgages and Creative Financing	111
Condominiums	114
Mobile Homes	115
Resort Time Sharing	116
Investing in Real Estate	116

6 Taxes — 125

General	125
The 1981 Tax Law	132
Tax Deductions	133
Tax Shelters	134
Tax Havens	137
Tax Audits	137
Real Estate Taxes	138

7 Financial Planning — 141

Personal Finance	141
Retirement Planning	145
IRA and Keogh Retirement Accounts	150
Estate Planning	152
Trusts	156
Insurance	157
Social Security and Medicare	159

8	**Consumer Magazines, Business Periodicals, and Newspapers**	**163**
	Popular Women's Magazines	164
	Other Audiences Magazines	167
	Preretirement and Retirement Magazines	167
	Consumer Concerns Magazines	168
	Weekly Newsmagazines	168
	Personal Money Management Magazines	169
	Business and Investment Magazines	170
	Newspapers	172
	Special Topic Newspapers	173
9	**Investment Newsletters**	**177**
	General Advisory and Reporting Services	178
	Growth Stocks	183
	Low-Priced Stocks	184
	Newsletter Digests and Performance Ratings	185
	Mutual Funds	186
	Commodities	187
10	**Pamphlet Resources**	**189**
11	**Investments and Securities Reference Sources**	**217**
	Fundamental Industry and Company Information	217
	Fixed-Income Securities	220
	Chart Services	220
	Directories	221
	Encyclopedias, Handbooks, and Guides	222
	Almanacs	224
	Dictionaries and Glossaries	224
	Glossary	**227**
	Directory of Pamphlet Resource Organizations	**239**
	Subject Index	**247**
	Author Index	**255**
	Title Index	**279**

Preface

The objective of the *Money Management Information Source Book* is to bring together, organize, and evaluate sources of money management and financial planning information that will be useful to the layperson. The prime focus is on the large amount of literature now existing on personal money management, personal financial planning, personal finance, and personal investment, terms used interchangeably by many authors. The scope of this book lies in the domain of personal financial planning as defined by Frederick Amling and William Droms (*The Dow Jones-Irwin Guide to Personal Financial Planning*, Dow Jones-Irwin, 1982, p. 3): "the interrelated topics of . . . budgeting, taxes, savings, housing, credit, insurance, investments, retirement and estate planning." Personal finance planning, according to G. Victor Hallman and Jerry S. Rosenbloom (*Personal Financial Planning*, 3rd ed., McGraw-Hill, 1983), is consumerism applied to one's financial affairs. Francis Albin (*Consumer Economics and Personal Money Management*, Prentice-Hall, 1982, p. xx) considers money management to include "the topics of food, shelter, transportation, insurance, budgeting, banking, saving, investing, and the inevitable death and taxes." Harold A. Wolf (*Personal Finance*, 6th ed., Allyn & Bacon, 1981, p. 2) notes that "people are consumers, and personal finance is the finance of and for the consumer." Preoccupation with financial well-being and survival is a paramount consumer concern.

This book provides organization and structure to the popular literature of financial planning and personal investment. Rather than a guide to sources primarily oriented to professionals, such as stockbrokers, security dealers, tax attorneys, accountants, bankers, real estate brokers, insurance underwriters and investment advisers, here are relevant and useful information resources for the financial and economic interests of lay individuals. The materials included are those judged by the authors to be useful to consumers in making intelligent decisions regarding spending and saving, coping with inflation, credit, budgeting, banking, investments, taxes, insurance, real estate, estate planning, and retirement.

The distinction between the information concerns and needs of laypeople and business professionals must be emphasized in that two fairly distinct bodies of literature exist: one professional/technical and the other popular. Much of the content

x   Preface

may be common to both, yet the level of presentation, complexity of subject, and terminology are vastly different. Most libraries and major indexing services do not distinguish between these two literatures. Professional books are shelved together with popular volumes. *Readers' Guide to Periodical Literature*, the *Magazine Index*, and most bibliographic compilations mix professional with popular entries.

This differentiation between popular and professional books is reflected in the scope of this work. Comprehensive coverage is provided of popular books, pamphlets, magazines, journals, newspapers, and other information resources. However, a selective and representative listing of professional works is also included. This decision stems from the fact that many professional publications concerned with investment, banking, credit, insurance, real estate, and retirement planning are also of interest to the sophisticated private investor. For example, Standard and Poor's *Stock Reports* and *Value Line* are clearly of concern to both professional and individual investors. Although the primary emphasis here is on popular literature, a secondary focus is on those resources the authors believe will be of interest to the more advanced lay investor. In this manner, included are technical books likely to interest those individuals who wish to probe further, research more deeply, substantiate theories, or extend their conceptual framework; for example, both *The Complete Book of Bonds: How to Buy and Sell Profitably* (Holt, 1981) and *The Handbook of the Bond and Money Markets* (Darst, 1981), and both *Playboy's Investment and Financial Planning Guide for Singles* (Rutberg, 1981) and *Elliott Wave Principle: Key to Stock Market Profits* (Frost and Prechter, 1981).

Chapter 1 discusses the need for information on money management by many people confronted with a changing and increasingly complex economic environment. The demand for reliable and comprehensive information stems from the pressures placed on individuals by inflation, higher taxation, international competition, and technological change. Accurate information is required to make judicious decisions in relation to consumer concerns such as spending and saving, credit, shelter, insurance, investment, taxes, and retirement. The characteristics and extent of the large body of literature that has appeared in response to these needs of the layperson are discussed in detail.

Chapter 2 brings together bibliographies and selection guides. Most are quite old and primarily concerned with listing professional publications and specialized information sources. Very few bibliographies exist in the field of personal finance and money management. Of these, most are fragmentary and nonevaluative, published for the most part in popular magazines.

The book literature is annotated and evaluated in Chapters 3 through 7, covering the major topics relating to money management, investment, real estate, taxes, and financial planning. From the large number of books available, more than 600 titles of some significance and interest to the general reader are selected and evaluated. Apart from a few early classics, most of these books have publication dates of 1978 or later. This restriction is due to the fact that information on investments, taxation, real estate, and inflation-coping strategies becomes rapidly obsolescent as economic conditions change. The criteria used to evaluate titles are reputation of author and publisher, comprehensiveness and credibility of content, clarity and level of presentation appropriate for a lay audience, and inclusion of lists of resource organizations, bibliographies, and recommended readings for further study.

Chapter 3, devoted to money and the consumer, covers general money management, financial planning, credit, banking, women and money, children and money, money-saving strategies and tips, and debt and bankruptcy. Chapter 4 brings together books on investment strategies, operation of the stock market, technical analysis and timing, penny stocks, options, bonds, commodities market and futures trading, mutual funds, gold and silver, diamonds and gems, and investment in collectibles such as art, automobiles, coins, and stamps.

Chapter 5 assembles publications on home ownership, buying and selling a home, mortgages and creative financing, condominiums, mobile homes, vacation time sharing, and investing in real estate. Chapter 6 is a compilation of literature available on taxes and taxation, recent revisions in the tax laws, tax shelters, tax havens, how to avoid or cope with tax audits, and real estate taxes. The rumblings of a taxpayer's counterattack can be discerned in this literature. Financial planning, which has assumed much importance recently, is covered in Chapter 7, reflecting major topics such as retirement planning, IRA and Keogh accounts, estate planning, trusts and wills, insurance, Social Security, Medicare, and pension benefits.

Chapter 8 covers consumer magazines, business periodicals, and newspapers. Listed are those publications most likely to contain popular information on personal finance and money management. Both the range and number of publications concerned with these subjects are extensive. These include general consumer magazines, women's magazines, weekly newsmagazines, personal money management magazines, investment and business periodicals, general newspapers, and special topics newspapers. The major publications are listed and discussed to illustrate the range of information contained in each of the principal types of publication.

The investment newsletters covered in Chapter 9 offer a blend of statistics, commentary, analysis, advice, and specific recommendations covering various areas of investment opportunity. As such, they are strongly flavored with statistical compilations, computer-generated charts, prognostication, pure speculation, and self-congratulation. Although specialized in nature, and fairly costly, these newsletters are of interest to individuals concerned with investment strategy, market conditions and trends, market indicators and timing, stock selections, growth companies, high technology opportunities, options, mutual funds, commodity futures, gold, and so on. The newsletters range from the well-known Standard and Poor's *The Outlook* and *Granville Market Letter* to the lesser known *Penny Stock Preview* and *Switch Fund Advisory*. Descriptions are provided for 56 representative newsletters out of the more than 1,000 presently published.

The fairly large pamphlet literature is described in Chapter 10, which lists some 600 relevant pamphlets covering 56 major topics from annuities to women and money. These pamphlets, booklets, and brochures are derived from 120 organizations, such as banks, insurance companies, the Federal Reserve system, credit associations, professional associations, trade groups, stock and commodities exchanges, and so on. A few tend to be technical, but most are comprehensible and useful to the layperson. Titles are arranged alphabetically by subject to permit rapid identification of relevant publications.

Chapter 11, Investments and Securities Reference Sources, provides a select list of technical works useful in supplementing a popular collection. Many of the titles included contain essential data on stock prices and bond ratings not available in the popular literature.

Following Chapter 11 is a glossary that defines technical terms used in the book.

These definitions include basic terms used in investment, the stock market, real estate, taxation, and financial planning and should be helpful for those unfamiliar with this specialized terminology. Following the Glossary is a Directory of Pamphlet Resource Organizations.

This book is perhaps the first of its kind focusing on literature relating to new consumer concerns with personal money management. The authors believe that as the individual becomes increasingly sophisticated and more responsible for his or her financial future, the amount of, and demand for, this literature will continue to grow. Already, the production of the literature has outstripped available access.

The essential orientation of existing bibliographic compilations on finance, banking, investment, estate planning, real estate, taxation, and so on is professional. "Business" information exists for businesspeople and bibliographic access is provided for their purposes. This book gathers, assesses, and describes sources of money management information likely to assist the layperson in effective decision making in relation to his or her financial health and prosperity. It is the authors' hope that this guide will be a valuable tool for both those seeking relevant information and for those concerned with selection and collection development.

The authors wish to thank the many publishers who contributed materials for review. Acknowledgments are also due to Professor Miranda Pao for advice and constructive critique, to Susan Peck and colleagues of the Cuyahoga County Public Library for both publications and helpful suggestions, to Syrinthia White and Gloria Verbec for their perseverance in transforming our handwriting into a typed manuscript, and to the numerous practitioner-librarians who urged and encouraged the production of this book.

1

Money Management, Financial Planning, and the Consumer

For those living in the United States in the 1980s, it is difficult to be unaware of the economic, fiscal, and monetary realities of our time. The mass media have sensitized us to a painful awareness of the state of the national economy. A steady flow of information reports the size of the national debt, fluctuations in unemployment figures, the rise and fall of the Dow Jones Industrial Average, increases and decreases in the money supply, balance of payments deficits, the price of gold in London, percentage increases in the cost of living at the retail and wholesale levels, prime rates, discount rates, tax increases, auto sales for the first ten days of the month, housing starts, and amount of anticipated federal borrowing. These economic indicators are carefully scrutinized on a daily basis to diagnose recession or prosperity and to detect improvement or deterioration of the economy.

The daily newspapers and the parade of commentators on the nightly news programs engage in endless speculation over the possibility of runaway global inflation, disintegration of OPEC, default of Third World countries on their debts, collapse of the international banking system—all of which may severely affect the standard of individual citizens.

Financial and economic matters are featured prominently on television programs, such as "Good Morning America" (ABC), "Today" (NBC), and "CBS News" (Kurtis/Sawyer). "Business Times" is offered daily on the ESPN cable network, and the "Nightly Business Report" on PBS provides an in-depth summary of market activity and commentary on economic trends. Louis Rukeyser's "Wall Street Week" features interesting discussions of investment opportunities.[1] Good radio coverage exists in the form of "Wall Street Journal Report," Leonard Sloane's "Personal Finance" features, and Gordon Williams's syndicated radio reports.

2 Money Management

The widespread public interest in business and finance is more than academic. In many instances it reflects profound concern about the stability of savings, retirement benefits, social security, and the future of the economy. The ravages of inflation, reindustrialization, structural unemployment, technological change, shifting markets for job skills, and international trade competition combine to create individual concern.

A rapidly changing economic environment forces people into important decisions concerning employment, shelter, investment, and retirement. Economic pressure in the form of inflation and increased taxation places heavy demands on individuals to take firmer control of their personal finances. Although one may choose to ignore global or national economic problems, sheer financial survival dictates that close attention be paid to one's financial future. The specter of unemployment lingers despite the allure and promise of high technology. Not surprisingly, an increasingly large number of persons have been shocked into considering and planning their financial future. Neither the poor nor the affluent can afford to neglect their financial well-being. A 1983 advertisement of Prudential-Bache in *Time* (February 21) captures this feeling:

> Once upon a time . . . you could get ahead just by working hard and saving your money. Not anymore. Today, it's a lot more complicated. How do you keep your savings ahead of taxes and inflation . . . and still provide for mortgage payments, college tuitions, insurance, investments, and retirement? . . . How do you cope with a financial world that has suddenly become infinitely more complex?

Andrew Tobias notes that money and personal finance "have captured the national attention ever since the national pie stopped growing and people became increasingly concerned, understandably, over the size of their slice."[2]

The increasing willingness to accept more responsibility for financial planning reflects the prudence of many people who are necessarily concerned with achieving a solid career, building a secure future, providing for their children, adjusting to inflation, and laying the foundation for retirement. With few exceptions, people are concerned with money—whether earning, saving, conserving, spending, or investing it. A very small minority of affluent individuals can delegate responsibility to such professionals as investment advisers, tax specialists, and accountants, whereas those living in abject poverty are preoccupied more with daily survival rather than purposeful planning for the future. But for the majority of people, increasing financial concern and anxiety have outpaced the capacity of most individuals to cope.

Robert Rosefsky describes the shifting and confusing financial scene:

> In recent years changes have started taking place with shocking rapidity. Interest rates have gyrated like an out-of-control roller coaster. New investments have come at us like an artillery barrage: NOW Accounts, IRA's, All-Savers, money market funds, repurchase agreements, variable certificates, and more. New tax laws, new credit legislation, new investment regulations have poured out of Washington like a waterfall. . . . Confusion reigns supreme! So how do you cope?[3]

Personal financial planning in the 1980s is difficult and continues to elude many people. Sylvia Porter aptly describes the plight of many people:

You have only a vague notion of how much money you spend each month and even less an idea of precisely where it goes. Your reluctance to look hard at your own financial habits feeds on itself; you end up frightened, guilty, and confused. Since you feel neither trained nor qualified to deal with money, you procrastinate, sometimes crashing head over heels into debt. . . . And often you muddle through hoping that you can make it through life before your ignorance catches up with you.[4]

At the same time that economic conditions have become so competitive and adverse, the financial system has become more complex. A new set of skills has to be learned in order to pick one's way through the labyrinth of the modern financial structure. The tax system is now so complicated that it is almost beyond the competence of the average individual to complete the most simple tax return.

A new vocabulary has to be learned: IRAs, Keoghs, tax shelters, electronic banking, mutual funds, penny stocks, Super-NOW accounts, zero coupon securities, CATS and TIGERS, unit investment trusts, Cash Management Accounts, stock index futures, salary reduction plans, certificates of deposit, "wild card" certificates, Ginnie Maes, Fannie Maes, creative financing, tax-exempt bonds and notes, municipal bonds, universal life insurance, commodities, Eurodollars, repurchase agreements, sweep accounts, Medicare Parts A and B, T-bills, vacation time sharing, Chapter 13, and so on.

Having mastered the vocabulary, the more sophisticated financial shopper faces an almost infinite array of opportunities. In this connection William Shepherd notes:

> For investors in 1983, a new era will offer an enormous array of possibilities—not just new industries, but a vast number of investment vehicles, from financial futures and puts and calls to life insurance with equity kickers, from venture capital funds to all sorts of tax shelter limited partnerships.[5]

William Donoghue and Thomas Tilling point out that "Buy, hold and pray is dead. It's been buried in the shifting sands of a rapidly changing marketplace. Today you must be prepared to move intelligently and skillfully, in and out of new investments, in a new market."[6]

The need for basic advice on money management, credit rights, debt repayment, and family budgeting is reflected in the emergence of nonprofit debt and budget counseling services in metropolitan areas. Many schools have introduced courses in the curriculum on economics and consumerism covering personal finances, budgets, tax forms, and prudent use of credit.[7] Merrill Lynch and Hutton are now offering individualized personal finance services to the more affluent. Clients complete questionnaires that are reviewed by staff members and processed by computer. Customized advice is then provided on investment planning, insurance, college financing, and retirement. Computerized personal finance reports are also supplied by some banks and such organizations as the Consumer Financial Institute and United Economic Services.[8]

The advent of money market funds in the mid-1970s ended the simple distinction between passive savings and active investment. Banking became equated with saving as individuals moved their assets from banks to money market funds earning high rates of interest with check-writing privileges. Investors were enticed by a smorgasbord of opportunities ranging from stocks and bonds to annuities, gold, collectibles, diamonds, commodities futures, and options. Mutual fund families offered to individuals a cafeteria of investment opportunities in growth funds, income funds, high-yield bond funds, tax-exempt bond funds, and a variety of other vehicles.

The sophisticated, aggressive consumer now plays the financial game by switching money from one form of investment to another by tracking interest rates and other leading economic indicators. In this manner, savings and investment have become an extension of the consumer market, requiring the same sort of shrewdness that shoppers bring to the marketplace in purchasing televisions or toothpaste. Consumers now shop, not just for products and services, but also for financial yields offered by competing banks, savings and loan associations, insurance companies, stockbrokers, and mutual funds. The essential factors sought by consumers are liquidity, safety, and yield.

The financial consumer has been assisted by the arrival of the one-stop financial conglomerate offering investment, banking, saving, real estate, insurance, and other services under one roof in the form of Cash Management Accounts and variations combining saving, investing, credit, and banking. These financial supermarkets include Prudential-Bache, Dean Witter Reynolds/Sears, Shearson/American Express, and Merrill Lynch.[9] Bankers are becoming stockbrokers and stockbrokers are becoming bankers.

In the same manner that the more affluent investors have sought to combine banking with saving and other investments in an effort to cope with inflation and plan for a more secure financial future, the less affluent have also developed their own set of money-saving strategies. These include bartering, swapping, exchanging, and trading in the underground economy. Considerable interest also exists in moonlighting, taking in tenants to share expenses, turning a house into a money factory by working at home, renovating houses for profit, and attracting and ensnaring a wealthy marriage partner.

Other innovative individuals have developed imaginative methods of cutting costs, locating sources of saving, eliminating wasteful spending, shopping at discount outlets and auctions, organizing garage sales, and joining food cooperatives. Ingenious money-saving practices include using thread instead of dental floss, purchasing disposable razors rather than refill blades, snipping facial tissues in half, using plastic bags instead of disposable gloves, and so on. Yet others have developed a mastery of refunding and couponing, saving countless dollars at the supermarket checkout by taking advantage of the 7,000 refund offers and more than 80 billion cash-off coupons distributed annually.

Money management, financial planning, and coping with inflation are of interest to all segments of society: to those with money seeking to maximize and conserve it; to those with modest incomes buffeted by inflation and rising taxes; to those with little money, cleverly developing techniques to economize, pinch pennies, and save for the future; to young married couples striving to purchase a home, care for children, and lay the foundation for a lifetime of financial security; to those in midlife endeavoring to build assets for eventual retirement and to finance college educations for their children; to the elderly struggling to live on fixed incomes and dwindling social security benefits.

Preoccupation with money and financial planning is both a necessary and very worthy human activity. Money can represent an important bridge to the future. Yale Meltzer speaks of humanizing money:

> You can humanize money when you take pride in the fruits of your labor. You humanize money when you draw satisfaction from hard work, strenuous efforts, and accomplishments, when you see them show up in even greater value and then see that value transmitted into money terms. . . . When you think in these terms, money then becomes saturated with a sense of human vitality, human significance, and human values. Money is not then something cold, unfeeling, and inhuman.[10]

Money management, formerly believed to be of concern only to those in business, investment advisers, and a few affluent individuals, is now a subject of widespread interest and is viewed as essential for fulfilling our life's goals, for providing for our needs and those of our families, and for achieving independence. Effective money management requires an ability to establish goals and to work toward their fulfillment. For effective financial decision making, access to reliable and relevant information is essential. Information can, in fact, be translated into monetary gain.

The need for such information is seen in the large number of reference requests in libraries on investment, taxation, real estate, retirement planning, and related subjects. Heavy circulation of books on money topics is also very apparent. It is clear that large numbers of library users are seeking information and advice from the published literature.

The available literature of personal finance and investment is varied, rich in diversity, and at times opinionated, pessimistic, impassioned, wildly optimistic, mystical, simplistic, religious, academic, seditious, speculative, practical, and political. The tone of the publications varies from flights of fancy (from rags to riches in real estate in six steps on other people's money) to gloomy prognostications predicting the collapse of the financial markets. Several popular doomsayer authors have produced best-sellers predicting crisis and calamity in the form of runaway global inflation, erosion of savings, collapse of private and government pension programs, bank failures, panic in the streets, black markets, rationing, and social chaos. The prophets of the coming apocalypse recommend purchase of gold and silver, selling all fixed-income investments, and the storing of food, water, seeds, ammunition, and durable clothing in a rural hideaway to escape the coming social breakdown.

The literature is also replete with authors advocating get-rich schemes: how to make a million dollars in real estate/gold/diamonds; how to make a "killing" in the stock market as advocated by expert "pickers" and "timers"; how to invest successfully in commodities futures trading (the "fastest game in town"), growth stocks, penny stocks, high-technology stocks, strategic metals, condominiums, house recycling; how to spend less for everything. Yet other authors urge one to think like a tycoon, outwit the IRS, live without a salary, open a Swiss bank account, save $50 a week by using coupons at the supermarket, buy only at discount outlets, make love to your money (fondle your funds and indulge in money lust), and marry into money.

The problem of quality is not easily resolved. In evaluating popular books on, for example, medical or legal topics, one can refer to the knowledge and opinion of the medical or legal establishment. Criteria for evaluating consumer health books can be constructed with the assistance of medical experts. Any book can be scrutinized to determine whether it contains the most accurate and comprehensive statement of current thinking on topics such as cancer or heart disease. Unfortunately, no such authoritative establishment exists in relation to personal finance and investment. Although one may identify "experts" who write, lecture, and even invest their own money (practice what they preach), there is no consensus. One seeks in vain for the body of agreement that exists in medicine or law. There is no consensus as to whether interest rates will rise or fall, whether to purchase gold or diamonds, or how to detect market peaks and troughs.

However, much of the literature is eminently sensible and practical, providing a most interesting insight into current consumer concerns with financial planning and money management. The range of topics discussed in the literature is extensive and covers many current interests. One can expect to find reliable information on:

- The Economic Recovery Act of 1981 and the Tax Equity and Fiscal Responsibility Act of 1982
- Selling a home without a real estate broker
- Financing a college education
- Financial arrangements for people who live together
- International investment opportunities
- Medicare benefits and eligibility
- The Christian view of money and family life
- Swiss bank accounts and tax havens
- Pitfalls of plastic money (credit card usage)
- Bartering and the underground economy
- Understanding Wall Street
- The "roaring 80s": Dow 2,000 or Dow 3,000?
- Opportunities in penny stocks
- Financial savvy for the independent woman
- Money market funds
- Money and divorce
- Financial privacy
- Tax shelters
- Use of home computers for managing investments
- How to invest in options/futures/gold/diamonds/mutual funds
- Making money from fads, crazes, and trends
- Penny pinching and money-saving techniques
- Art of couponing and refunding
- Chapter 13 and bankruptcy
- Retirement planning
- IRA and Keogh plans
- Wills and estate planning
- Income tax audits
- Term and whole life insurance

Such information is highly relevant and useful to large numbers of library users concerned with problems relating to investment, taxation, real estate, retirement planning, and other money matters. Financial health and well-being is at present of almost equal importance to physical health and well-being.

Most libraries purchase books on personal finance and investments in response to the perceived public demand. No attempt has, however, been made to establish money management or personal finance information services similar to those provided in consumer health. Many library users are directed to the business section or specialized stock market reports oriented primarily to the business community. Library services to the layperson would be considerably improved by segregation of the popular materials from such technical books and materials. If this is not feasible, then displays of materials on high-interest topics would be highly desirable.

By way of example, a collection of materials on income tax in the several months prior to the April 15 filing date would be particularly helpful. Such a display would contain books, IRS pamphlets, forms, and brochures, and the IRS audiocassette tapes containing step-by-step instructions on the preparation of tax returns. Presentations by a certified public accountant and an IRS official would focus attention on the available library materials. Similar displays and programs would be highly useful on other key topics, such as buying and selling homes, retirement planning, investment opportunities in the stock market, insurance, travel, and banking. Such programs, highlighting relevant library materials, could be organized with the cooperation and support of local realtors, stockbrokers, insurance agents, travel representatives, and bankers. Most of these professionals are able to differentiate between their educational responsibilities and salesmanship.

In the future, there is little doubt that more sophistication will be required on the part of individuals to function successfully and profitably within the economic system. As one author remarks: "Downturns in the economy, deregulation, electronic transfer and credit systems, and inflation require customers to be informed of future money management systems. It is more important than ever before that consumers get the best return and service for their money."[11] Interest in information sources in this area will continue to grow in order to respond to the emerging public demand.

A small minority of individuals are now pointing the way to the future. The increasing popularity and use of home computers opens up new vistas in personal money management. The Source, a general-purpose information utility available to those with personal computers, offers such business and financial services as stock and bond prices, financial news and headlines, foreign exchange rates, and stock market average and closing statistics. The Dow Jones News/Retrieval Service makes available yet more extensive information resources: Dow Jones News, *Wall Street Journal* Highlights, Dow Jones Quotes on stocks, options, and bonds, Wall Street Week Online, and free text searching of articles from the *Wall Street Journal, Barrons*, and the Dow Jones News Service. Moreover, software exists for portfolio analysis, income projections, and record keeping on home computers. The electronic age will doubtless extend consumer involvement in financial planning.

NOTES

1. Andrew Tobias, "Want the Bottom Line on TV's Business Reporting?" *TV Guide*, November 20, 1982, pp. 5–8.
2. Ibid., p. 5.

3. Robert Rosefsky, *Money Talks: Bob Rosefsky's Complete Program for Financial Success* (New York: Wiley, 1982), p. vii.
4. Sylvia Porter, *Sylvia Porter's New Money Book for the 80's* (New York: Avon, 1980), p. xi.
5. William G. Shepherd, "Variety, New Risks, Complicate Decisions," *New York Times*, December 12, 1982, Sect. 12, Personal Investing '83, p. 11.
6. William Donoghue and Thomas Tilling, *William E. Donoghue's No-Load Mutual Fund Guide* (New York: Harper & Row, 1983), p. xiii.
7. Consumer Saturday, *New York Times,* February 5, 1983, p. 29.
8. "Personal Finance: Peddling Advice to the Middle Class," *New York Times*, November 7, 1982.
9. Bonnie Siverd, "Financial Supermarkets," *Working Woman*, July 1982, pp. 51–53.
10. Yale Meltzer, *Putting Money to Work: An Investment Primer for the 80's* (Englewood Cliffs, NJ: Prentice-Hall, 1982), p. ix.
11. Gerald Gibbs, *The Complete Guide to Credit and Loans* (New York: Playboy Paperbacks, 1982), p. 135.

2

Bibliographies and Selection Guides

A number of guides to the professional and technical literature of business, finance, and investment facilitate access to information sources relating to the needs of money managers, bankers, investment specialists, stockbrokers, and corporate executives. Unfortunately, very few assist the layperson in identifying popular information sources. Although the bibliographies and guides to the technical literature contain many items of interest to the layperson, it is unrealistic to expect that compilations designed for professional specialists would satisfy the needs of those seeking popular information sources.

In this chapter, a clear differentiation is made between bibliographic compilations of professional and popular literature. Bibliographies of the professional literature tend to be comprehensive and scholarly, whereas guides to the popular literature are most often highly selective and fragmentary. Most of the popular compilations have appeared in magazines and newspapers, prepared for individuals who wish to read further or explore some aspect of money management, financial planning, or investment. In some instances, the recommended reading list is extracted from the bibliography section of the author's book on the same subject. Bibliographies of professional information publications are included and described in this chapter because the more sophisticated layperson may well be interested in using these more specialized publications and resources.

The lack of bibliographies and guides to the popular literature of personal finance and money management is perhaps due to the widespread unwillingness or inability to differentiate between the money management information needs of professionals and those of laypeople, as pointed out in Chapter 1. Consequently, the layperson has been expected to use professional publications to satisfy his or her personal information needs.

POPULAR LITERATURE

Appelbaum, Judith. "The 1040 Form and All That." Paperback Talk. *New York Times Book Review*, March 13, 1983, pp. 27-38.
A comprehensive list of a dozen of the best-selling paperback tax books that are so popular from about January 1 until April 15 each year. This is a very useful compilation in that the publications cited can answer the most common questions about taxes.

Arenson, Karen. "What to Do with Money." *New York Times Book Review*, October 17, 1982, pp. 15-23.
Arenson, a financial reporter for the *Times*, believes that one indicator of current financial anxiety is the mushrooming of books on personal finance and money management. From recently published books, she provides brief descriptions and evaluations of 22 titles in three categories—How Things Work, General Strategies for Investing, and Books with Formulas. Arenson warns against books offering painless solutions to money problems. These should be "eyed every bit as warily as those that offer ways to shed pounds painlessly or to improve your sex life in three lessons." A limited but good selection of the popular literature.

Bettner, Jill (ed.). "What to Read on How to Invest During Shaky Times." *Business Week*. Personal Business Column. December 31, 1979, pp. 129-130.
A very brief review of books popular in 1979. "The best selling books," according to Bettner, "were the ones that read like survival manuals." Against a backdrop of inflation-recession, Bettner lists and reviews eight recommended books, including Quinn's *Everyone's Money Book* (see p. 26), Cobleigh's *The Dowbeaters* (p. 80), and *Sylvia Porter's New Money Book for the 80's* (p. 25). Hardly an extensive or representative compilation.

Brownstone, David, and Sartisky, Jacques. "Sources of Information." In their *Personal Financial Survival: A Guide for the 1980's and Beyond*. New York: Wiley, 1981.
A fairly extensive compilation of sources of information drawn from Brownstone and Carruth's *Where to Find Business Information* (see p. 16). In one alphabetical array, the authors mingle books, magazines, newsletters, information services, and reports with no distinction made between technical and popular information sources. Consequently, *Changing Times* is listed with *Chartcraft Weekly Service*. Not very helpful as a guide to popular materials.

Business Information from Your Public Library. San Francisco: Business Information (Box 993, South San Francisco, CA 94080). 3 times per year.
This is a brief, four-page newsletter, published three times per year, containing a short lead article on a business-related topic; "Some New Books You Might Like to Meet" (one-sentence annotations on approximately nine or ten books); "One Man's Reading" (short annotations of interesting magazine or newspaper articles); and "They're Asking" (listing of popular questions and answers). This publication is sold to public libraries and can be customized with a specific library's name and ad-

dress. In this manner, "it purports to come from YOUR PUBLIC LIBRARY and its recipients will assume that it was prepared there." The publisher claims that: "You spend no thought, time, or money preparing the copy—and you get a publication that is all yours." The cost is 14 cents on orders less than 300 copies per issue; 13 cents on orders of 300 to 599; and 12 cents on orders of 600 or more. Although designed to enhance the image of the library in the community, its content is of poor quality. Most professional librarians can do much better by preparing their own publication.

Carter, Malcolm N. "There's Help Out There: Knowing You Don't Have to Do It Alone Can Make the Difference between Success and Not Even Getting Started." *Money*, October 1982, pp. 91–94.

Provides evaluative descriptions of books, pamphlets, and financial planning services designed to help readers with personal financial planning. Venita Van Caspel's *The Power of Money Dynamics* (see p. 28) is described as "the most comprehensive book on personal finance." The strengths and weaknesses of a number of other books—including works by Quinn, Porter, and Rosefsky—on personal money management are discussed. The author does not, however, state his criteria for assessment. Noting that financial institutions publish helpful material, he cites examples of pamphlets and booklets available from Merrill Lynch and the Bank of America. A great deal of attention is devoted to the promises and pitfalls of educational programs and materials offered by adult education departments, banks, brokers, and insurance companies and the assistance available from financial planners. Carter concludes: "You alone must make the commitment to assess your situation, determine your priorities and decide on your goals." Of limited use as a collection development tool for librarians.

Davis, Joann, and Smith, Wendy. "Books on Money Matters: A Current Checklist." *Publishers Weekly*, March 5, 1982, pp. 31–42.

Published as "an aid to booksellers and libraries trying to assist consumers in their quest for information about money books," this annotated checklist can also help consumers find their way among the increasing number of such books. The extensive compilation is an update of a checklist published in 1979. Brief, nonevaluative descriptions are provided for each title with entries arranged alphabetically by publisher and title within 15 different categories. Titles listed under Taxes, Real Estate, Psychology of Money, Stock Market/Investments, Retirement, Credit/Borrowing, Personal Finances, Consumer Advice, Salaries, Estate Planning, and Women and Money offer practical advice. Those listed under Reaganomics, Inflation, Fund Raising, Economic Analysis, and History are of a more theoretical and analytical orientation. Most of the books listed have imprint dates of 1980 or later, although a few are dated as early as 1973. Despite the lack of evaluative judgment, this compilation is useful to librarians as a checklist of new titles and to consumers searching for recent publications on a wide range of topics.

DiMattia, Susan S. "Business Books of 1981: A Selection of Recommended Books Published during the Past Year." *Library Journal*, March 1, 1982, pp. 519–525.

A short overview of the major characteristics of business, economic, and finance

12 Bibliographies and Selection Guides

books published during the preceding year. The list of 86 books was chosen from more than 400 titles found in reviews, publishers' catalogs, and advertisements. The selection reflects the author's "personal choices, based on reviews by others and on the holdings of three large business libraries." Although many of the selections are technical, covering aspects of corporate finance, companies and executives, business abroad, and advertising and marketing, there is a good representation of consumer-oriented books on financial planning and taxation, investments, and real estate. DiMattia has labeled only a few titles as being for a particular size and kind of library. "Only you, based on a thorough knowledge of the constituency your library serves, can build a collection appropriate to unique local needs."

DiMattia, Susan S. "Business Books of 1982: A Selection of Recommended Books Published during the Past Year." *Library Journal*, March 1, 1983, pp. 451–459.
In this annual update, DiMattia provides short descriptions with evaluative comments on 87 books selected from the 400 titles considered. The publications selected reflect considerable interest in currently popular topics—tax law changes, new mortgage options, investment in strategic metals, job search and career strategy, unemployment, and making money by working for yourself. Only 19 of the 87 books listed are related to personal financial management and related topics. The rest of the titles are concerned with economics and business, corporate strategies and planning, corporate life, marketing and communications, and productivity. This is an interesting annual literature review, of considerable use in evaluating library collections.

Dunn, Donald (ed.). "The First Risk in Investing: Reading about It." *Business Week*. Personal Business Column. December 19, 1980, p. 135–136.
Short comments on some 25 books on investing and the stock market, presumably published during 1979 and 1980 (no publication dates given). The authors note how a rapidly changing economic climate presents unforeseen problems for the writers of books containing investment advice. They warn that events can quickly undo advice written many months before actual publication. As no criteria for selection are discussed, one presumes that personal choice determined which books were reviewed. Readers are warned "not to base all your investment activity on a single writer's advice."

Financial Planning Bibliography: A Selected List, Resources. Denver: College for Financial Planning, 1982. 12 pp.
A listing of some 60 titles on financial planning, risk management, investments, tax planning and management, and retirement and estate planning. Very brief, one- or two-sentence descriptions are given for each item. Most titles are popular in nature, while several are required texts for the Certified Financial Planner Program of the College for Financial Planning. A good selection of representative titles of value as an abbreviated checklist for collection development purposes.

Gitman, Lawrence J., and Joehnk, Michael D. "Resources: Financial News." *Working Woman*, March 1982, pp. 24, 26.
A summary of the wealth of information available in newspapers, business periodicals, news magazines, annual reports of companies, subscription services, and in-

dustrial reports that can be used by the individual investor. This short bibliographic essay provides a valuable insight into the types of information that can be gleaned from these sources. Reprinted from Gitman and Joehnk, *Fundamentals of Investing* (see p. 70).

Gupta, Udayan. "Market Publications: Guide Posts on the Investment Landscape." *Black Enterprise*, June 1982, p. 68.
The listing of 11 sources of financial information is aimed at showing readers "where to get financial information, how to separate the good advice from the bad, and how to use the knowledge efficiently." The author provides comments on one periodical, one book, two market letters, a directory, four other publications that describe trends on market activity, a newsletter that monitors the performance of the leading market letters, and a company offering trial subscriptions to financial magazines and newsletters for a nominal fee. A brief description is given of the kind of information to be found in each publication or source. A useful listing for the uninitiated seeking guidance through the maze of publications in investments, although many of the items listed are technical.

Hardy, C. Colburn. "Bibliography." In his *Dun and Bradstreet's Guide to Your Investments*. 28th Edition. New York: Harper & Row, 1983, pp. 190-200.
In this annual reference book, Hardy offers an extensive list of recent publications by principal authors in the investment field (Casey, Cobleigh, Dreman, Malkiel, Rolo, Rukeyser, Schultz, Sokoloff, Tuccille, and others). Titles are recommended on Technical Analysis; Special Securities/Speculations/Collectibles; Commodities; Information on Investment Companies; Chart Services; Real Estate; Sources of Investment Information; Investment Services and Advisory Reports; and Investment Trading Information. Despite the absence of annotations, this is a comprehensive and valuable listing.

Hazard, John. "Managing Your Money: Where to Research That Stock." *U.S. News & World Report*, November 29, 1982, p. 87.
A number of information sources are suggested for serious investors who wish to select their own stock. The sample of publications provided is intended to supply information on stock prices, earnings, dividends, buy-and-sell recommendations, and market trends. Recommended works include Standard and Poor's *New York Stock Exchange Reports* and its *Stock Guide* and *Bond Guide*; *United Business and Investment Report*; *Better Investing* magazine; and *Trendline's Current Market Perspective*. Fragmentary and incomplete.

Hazard, John. "A Reading List for Investors." Managing Your Money Column. *U.S. News & World Report*, August 23, 1982, p. 68.
This is a very short list of only 14 titles for readers wishing "to brush up on their investment techniques," selected from the "hundreds of books about the stock market." The titles are arranged in four categories: General How-to Books, More Specific Techniques, How Fortunes Have Been Made, and Good General Reading. Some of the classics cited are out of print, and no publication dates are given. Of very limited use.

14 Bibliographies and Selection Guides

Liebman, Walter H. "Buyer's Guide: When You Wish upon a Stock." The Bookshelf Column. *Wall Street Journal*, May 18, 1982, p. 29 (w), p. 30 (e).

Liebman, a senior official at the American Stock Exchange, offers some penetrating comments on six recent books on the stock market. He believes that although the books "don't help much in the acquisition of wealth," they do contain some valuable, practical information. Comparing these books to those published 60 to 70 years ago, he comments that "the genre hasn't changed much. The charts and illustrations may be a bit more sophisticated, but the promise of success, the eleemosynary instinct to impart great wealth to anonymous readers, and the structure of advice remain the same."

Mechanic, Sylvia. *Investment Bibliography: A Selected List of Books, Services, Newspapers, Periodicals and Financial Organizations*. New York: New York Stock Exchange, 1981.

This list will assist neophyte and experienced investors, as well as librarians and students, seeking information on both the basic concepts of investing in the market and sophisticated techniques of speculating. Very brief descriptive annotations are provided for some 50 books in six categories: Introduction to Investing, Some Classics, Learning to Invest, Textbooks on Theory and Practice, For the Experienced Investor, and Selected Reference Works. A selection of newspapers, investment periodicals, financial services, and national and regional financial organizations is also listed. Mechanic, who is business librarian at the Brooklyn Public Library, believes that "most of the general titles included will be available in local libraries; those of a more technical or research nature should be found in the business sections of larger public libraries."

Raphaelson, Elliot. "Low Cost Investment Information." Money Column. *Working Woman*, September 1981, pp. 52-53.

A useful overview of sources of information for anyone wishing to learn more about the stock market or seeking to diversify investments. Sources of information are given for finding out about stocks, mutual funds, annual reports of corporations, commodities, options, municipal bonds, and the Federal Reserve banks. Good bibliographic information is mingled with advice. For those with "substantial net worth (not less than $50,000), have liquidity and . . . can accept short-term losses without experiencing a great deal of anxiety," then commodities may be appropriate. The Commodity Exchange, Inc. (COMEX), can supply information on this investment alternative. Also listed are the names and addresses of a number of brokerage firms that provide free information about investing in municipal bonds. Publications from the Federal Reserve explain how to buy treasury notes, bonds, and bills directly from the Federal Reserve rather than through securities dealers and commercial banks, which usually charge a fee. A helpful listing. Raphaelson is the author of *Planning Your Financial Future* (see p. 149).

A Selection of 1982 Internal Revenue Service Tax Information Publications. 3 volumes. Washington, DC: Internal Revenue Service, Department of the Treasury, 1982.

An indispensable reference tool for the reference desk, especially prior to April 15. This three-volume set contains, in numerical sequence, the full text of the IRS's 43 most frequently requested publications. Volume 1 contains the text of 19 publications, including those on Travel Expenses, Credit for the Elderly, Charitable Contributions, and Tax Information for Homeowners. Volume 2 reproduces ten publications, ranging from Business Expenses, Sales and Other Disposition of Assets to Examination of Returns, Appeals Rights, and Claims for Refunds. Volume 3 contains 14 publications on topics such as Investment Credit, Tax Information for Survivors, Executors and Administrators, and Tax Information for Individual Retirement Arrangements. Access to the contents is through an alphabetical subject index in the back of each volume. Users are cautioned that the subject index refers to all publications issued by the IRS, not just the ones reproduced in these three volumes. Ordering instructions and an order form are included. Photocopying of any pages is encouraged. A most useful tool, especially at tax time.

Sideris, Georgia. "Free Booklets on Smart Money Management." *Woman's Day*, October 5, 1982, p. 66.

This list of 23 free pamphlets was "carefully chosen for accuracy, usefulness, and objectivity (although some stress the sponsor's products or point of view)." Most of the items listed are free, but some have a small handling and postage charge ($1 maximum) or require a self-addressed envelope. Topics covered include annuities, credit, pensions, and taxes. Short descriptions of the contents provide the reader with sufficient information on which to decide whether particular pamphlets will answer his or her needs. Typical titles include "An Introduction to NOW Accounts," "What to Do When Debts Pile Up," and "Consumer Credit Terminology Handbook." Very useful for consumers but of limited use for collection development.

Small, Linda. "Want to Curl Up with a Good Money Book? Our No-Frills Guide Tells Which Ones Are Worth It." *Working Woman*, February 1979, p. 28.

Evaluative reviews of eight books published between 1974 and 1978, on money management for women. The selections identify books that explore the money needs of working women. Small has a strong feminist point of view and criticizes Lumb's *What Every Woman Should Know about Finances* (see p. 47) because it says nothing about credit or the laws that affect women or the economics of marriage and divorce. *Sylvia Porter's Money Book* is recommended with reservation, since it is "geared to that ever-shrinking American entity—the nuclear family, which accounts for only a small percentage of today's family living styles."

Taxpayer's Guide to IRS Information and Assistance. IRS Publication 910. Washington, DC: Internal Revenue Service, Department of the Treasury, October 1982.

In addition to listing and describing the free publications most often requested by taxpayers, with an index of taxpayer information publications, this pamphlet describes the numerous assistance programs available from the IRS. These include toll-free telephone service, Tele-Tax (dial-up service with 140 recorded topics on tape), and special services for deaf, hearing-impaired, and blind taxpayers. A valuable listing of IRS tax publications and other information services.

16 Bibliographies and Selection Guides

PROFESSIONAL / TECHNICAL LITERATURE

Bibliography and Information Source List: Financial Futures. Chicago: International Money Market, Chicago Mercantile Exchange.
A compilation of information sources relating to futures markets and the factors influencing them. Coverage includes commodity markets, interest rates, currencies and metals, futures trading (spreading, technical analysis, commodity prices, commodity options), and International Money Market (IMM) publications. Books, periodicals, government reports, and IMM publications are listed.

Brealey, Richard A., and Pyle, Connie (comps.). *A Bibliography of Finance and Investment.* Cambridge, MA: MIT Press, 1973, $18.50. O.P.
More than 3,600 entries are arranged in 150 subject areas, covering all aspects of corporate finance, securities, and financial markets. Approximately one-sixth of the references are dated before 1960, with the latest published in 1972. No annotations are provided, but a short introduction to each subject category defines its scope. Where the compilers feel it necessary, they suggest "initial readings for the incognoscenti."

Brownstone, David M., and Carruth, Gordon. *Where to Find Business Information: A Worldwide Guide for Everyone Who Needs the Answers to Business Questions.* 2nd Edition. New York: Wiley, 1982. 632 pp. $45.
An alphabetical listing of more than 5,000 English publications, mainly American and British. Coverage includes books focusing on current business information (including yearbooks and directories), periodicals and magazines, newsletters, newspapers, computerized data bases, and government business publications. Access is provided by means of a "Source Finder" or subject index, a "Publishers Index," and a listing of "Sources of Business Information." The Source Finder is an alphabetical listing of more than 2,500 subject headings covering most aspects of business and finance. If a particular publisher is already known as producing relevant publications, the Publishers Index lists the titles published by that organization. The third and largest section, Sources of Business Information, is arranged alphabetically by title of publication. Each title has a unique number to which one is referred from the other two indexes. Each citation includes title, author, publisher, address, telephone number, frequency, short description of source, and price, if available. The very abbreviated descriptions of the titles are not evaluative and do not adequately indicate the content. The major focus is on professional and technical sources rather than lay materials.

Business Literature. Leslie P. Rupprecht, Business Librarian, Editor. Public Library of Newark, Business Library (34 Commerce Street, Newark, NJ 07102). $3/year: 10 issues September-June.
Each issue of *Business Literature*, a compilation of books and periodical articles, is devoted to a single topic. The contents of most issues are aimed at professional investors, business managers, and theoreticians rather than individual investors. Each listed item has a very brief annotation describing the title. Occasionally, an issue will be of interest to individual investors. For example, the September-October 1981

issue is devoted to commodities and is designed to appeal also to the less sophisticated investor.

Coman, Edwin. *Sources of Business Information*. Berkeley: University of California Press, 1970. 330 pp. $8.50. O.P.

A compilation of information on statistical sources, real estate, insurance, accounting, foreign trade, and the business scene, covering books, journals, handbooks, encyclopedias, and bibliographies. This bibliography is extensive but out of date, and little attention is given to personal finance.

Commodity Futures Trading Bibliography Cumulative through 1976 and Updates. Chicago: Chicago Board of Trade, 1976.

This comprehensive list of materials can provide anyone interested in commodity futures trading with access to information sources on most aspects of this specialized field. The publication incorporates material from an extensive bibliography published through the University of Illinois and from bibliographies compiled by the Chicago Board of Trade for 1967–1974, 1975, and 1976. Sources of information are given for trading, commodity exchanges, economic impact of federal regulation, taxation, trading techniques, technical analysis, commodity funds, and commodity options. Annual supplements keep track of current writings in the field. Sources cited include books, general and trade periodicals, professional journals, academic theses, reports, pamphlets, and legislative and congressional reports. Items are arranged alphabetically by author under 30 subheadings in three sections: Books and Educational Materials, Resource Materials, and Trade Press. No annotations are provided for the listings so that it is difficult to judge the complexity or level of presentation. Most of the publications are, however, technical in nature.

Daniells, Lorna. *Basic Investment Sources*. Baker Library Mini-List No. 3. Boston: Harvard Business School, October 1981. 4 pp.

A listing of information sources under the following headings: corporate reports, comprehensive investment manuals, general investment services, current statistics on stock and bond prices, stock price indexes, weekly investment advisory services, charting services, dividends, security offerings, indexes to financial publications, sources of foreign investment information, and indexes for foreign companies. Very brief descriptions are given for a few of the items. Some of the publications and information services would be of interest to the more sophisticated layperson. More a guide to the resources of the Baker Library than a comprehensive bibliography.

Daniells, Lorna. *Business Information Sources*. Berkeley: University of California Press, 1976. 439 pp. $19.95.

The author is business reference librarian at the Baker Library, Harvard Business School. Her guide to business information sources is intended to aid practicing businesspeople, business students, and librarians in finding their way through the literature. Essentially, it is a selected guide to the body of information available through 1976. Daniells provides clear and descriptive annotations of a wide range of basic business and management information sources. The selection process and the reasons for the descriptive rather than evaluative nature of many of the annotations are explained in the preface. Two chapters provide a succinct guide to locating facts utilizing all types of libraries and information centers and the wide variety of basic references to be found in these institutions, such as bibliographies, indexes and abstracts, government publications, handbooks, loose-leaf services, and computerized information services. Other chapters describe sources for locating not only information on companies and individuals but also statistical data on specific industries and national and international business and economic trends. For the individual investor seeking information on companies or specific industries, these chapters provide a concise, descriptive introduction to a wide range of basic business information sources. A final chapter lists those works that the author considers essential for a beginning collection for a company library. Daniells believes that this list could be easily "adapted . . . to meet the more limited needs of a personal library." Despite the extensive changes in business practices since the book was published in 1976, this work nevertheless remains a useful introduction and guide to basic information sources.

Gordon, Marjorie. *A List of Worthwhile Life and Health Insurance Books.* Washington, DC: American Council of Life Insurance, Health Insurance Institute, 1979. 72 pp.

A selection of materials available from commercial publishers, the federal government, and private organizations, compiled to assist professionals in the insurance business, librarians, students, and consumers generally. Two of the 11 sections are of interest to the nonprofessional—Consumer Information and Student Information. Books and pamphlets are listed on such topics as family money management, uses of life and health insurance, pensions, and benefits. A useful compilation despite the fact that many of the titles are considerably dated. It does not list books critical of the insurance industry. Contains lists of periodicals, publishers, and an index.

Grant, Mary M., and Cote, Norma. *Directory of Business and Financial Services.* 7th Edition. New York: Special Libraries Association, 1976. $18.80.

This directory deals "exclusively with information services which provide continuous coverage of some facet of business activity and provide data which should assist the user determine the service's application to his needs." It is divided into two broad categories: Business and Financial Services and Selected List of Stock and Commodity Exchanges. The first section is an alphabetical listing by title of some 1,000 publications. Access to these materials is provided by the subject index through a unique number assigned to each entry. The emphasis is on information services, newsletters, trade journals, government publications, and special periodicals that provide data and statistics on special subjects. Title, publisher's name and address, a short description of the type of coverage provided, imprint date, format, frequency, and price are given for each source. The second half of the book lists the names and addresses of stock and commodity exchanges.

Johnson, H. Webster. *How to Use the Business Library: With Sources of Business Information.* 4th Edition. Cincinnati, OH: South-Western, 1972. 182 pp. $2.95 (paper).

The business orientation of the listed sources, the lack of a detailed subject index (most entries in the index are title entries), and the imprint date of 1972 severely dilute the usefulness of this compilation for the individual investor. The first of the 16 sections into which this volume is divided explains how to use the library. Subsequent sections are alphabetical listings by subject area and title of handbooks, yearbooks, pamphlets, almanacs, business directories, reports from commercial, industrial, technical, and trade associations, research foundations, government publications, and so on. An introductory paragraph notes the general characteristics of the materials in a given section, and nonevaluative comments follow each source. Outdated. Not recommended for collection development or for personal investment information.

Ladley, Barbara, and Wilford, Jane (eds.). *Money and Finance: Sources of Print and Non-Print Materials.* New York: Neal-Schumann, 1980. 208 pp. $24.95.
This is a compilation designed to assist the layperson in finding information on financial decision making. The authors identify more than 500 organizations that provide publications and information on personal finance. This is defined as "the art of budgeting, managing, and planning individual or family income and expenditures. Included are such topics as consumer credit, personal loans, consumer education, consumer protection, estate planning, investment, savings, cost of health care and education, taxes, employment, housing, insurance, and personal household budgets." The book is divided into 17 broad subject categories, covering a wide range of books, pamphlets, newsletters, periodicals, films, filmstrips, audiocassettes, and other information formats produced by the 500 organizations. Entries are arranged alphabetically by title of organization and provide name, address, and telephone number, including toll-free numbers, brief descriptions of the goals and activities of the organization; special programs or services, such as telephone hot lines; membership fees and special discounts; and scope of the organization's publishing program, with representative titles, including price, date of publication, number of pages, running time, rental price, and so on. The descriptions of the organizations and publications are provided largely by the organizations themselves. The editors make no attempt to provide an exhaustive listing of all titles available from a producer, seeking rather to impart "an indication of the organization's focus." Nor do they attempt to evaluate the quality of the material listed. Much of the material is scattered throughout the book. Despite the existence of a chapter on Banking, Money and Credit, references to credit-related information can also be found in five other sections. Teachers and those planning programs on personal money management will find the section Consumer Education Programs for the Classroom very useful. This covers a wide range of subject areas and many different formats, along with information on the type of audience addressed. This is a valuable compilation of relevant organizations rather than a standard bibliography. The coverage is extensive, but the lack of description and evaluation of the publications listed limits its usefulness for collection development purposes.

Subject Bibliography Index. Washington, DC: Superintendent of Documents, Government Printing Office.
A listing of several hundred bibliographies intended to provide subject access to more than 25,000 publications, periodicals, and subscription services for sale by the Superintendent of Documents. The subject bibliographies are updated periodically. A number of these bibliographies are of interest to money management:

Banks and Banking. SB-128. November 16, 1981. 5 pp.
Consumer Information. SB-002. September 8, 1982. 20 pp.
Financial Aid to Students. SB-085. August 25, 1982. 3 pp.
Home Economics. SB-276. December 15, 1982. 14 pp.
Insurance. SB-294. November 16, 1981. 5 pp.
Internal Revenue Service Tax Information Publications. SB-194. November 16, 1981. 5 pp.
Price, Wages and the Cost of Living. SB-226. November 16, 1981. 18 pp.
Retirement. SB-285. December 2, 1982. 6 pp.
Securities and Investments. SB-295. November 16, 1981. 5 pp.
Social Security. SB-165. November 4, 1981. 9 pp.
Taxes and Taxation. SB-195. December 6, 1982. 11 pp.
Veterans Affairs and Benefits. SB-80. September 30, 1981. 7 pp.

The Wall Street Review of Books. South Salem, NY: Redgrave. Quarterly. $21 per year, individuals; $29 per year, institutions.

A quarterly publication containing analytic and evaluative reviews of some 30 books in each issue. The scope is broader than the title implies in that the subjects covered include economic policy, the monetary system, and international trade, in addition to investments. The value judgments are particularly helpful in book selection; as an example, ". . . I can recommend these books neither to the serious investor nor the serious student of the times . . . the advice contained in them is either trivial, risky, or questionable. . . ." Most of the books reviewed are professional rather than popular books.

Wasserman, Paul, Georgi, Charlotte, and Woy, James (eds.). *Encyclopedia of Business Information Sources: A Detailed Listing of Primary Subjects of Interest to Managerial Personnel, with a Record of Sourcebooks, Periodicals, Organizations, Directories, Handbooks, Bibliographies, On-Line Data Bases and Other Sources of Information on Each Topic.* 4th Edition. Detroit: Gale, 1980. 778 pp. $115.

This publication was "prepared with the businessman primarily in mind." Approximately 1,215 subject headings, arranged in dictionary form, and further subdivided by types of materials, provide access to information sources on all aspects of business and commercial activity. Subject headings used in the body of the work serve as an extended table of contents. The cross-references are aimed at helping the user in "exploring an entirely new subject and . . . in coordinating the user's terminology with the editors." Sources are identified under types of material, such as encyclopedias and dictionaries, handbooks and manuals, bibliographies, and statistical sources. If the title of the source is not self-explanatory, a very brief description is provided. Citations give title, author, publisher's address, date of publication, frequency, and price. No beginning dates are given for serial publications. Professional and technical publications are listed together with popular materials with no differentiation. The descriptions provided for each publication are scanty with no attempt at evaluation or indication of level of complexity. Although there are no subject headings for personal finance or personal money management, there is a fair amount of lay-oriented information sources if one is prepared to hunt, sort, screen, and sift out the popular materials. More detailed descriptions of the items listed would make this task much easier.

Woy, James. *Commodity Futures Trading: A Bibliographic Guide.* New York: Bowker, 1976. 206 pp. $21.50.
An early bibliography of commodity futures trading that has become "the fastest game in town." Woy lists alphabetically various commodity trading mechanisms, methods, and procedures (with definitions) and provides references to textbooks, popular books, and magazine articles, some of which date back to 1920. More than 100 terms and concepts are included. This is an excellent reference source to find information on Elliott wave principle, hog-corn ratio, soybean meal spread, and "The Voice from the Tomb" (seasonal dates for buying and selling corn and wheat supposedly revealed from a search of the papers of a dead commodity speculator). Relevant government reports and periodicals are included together with author and subject indexes. Still of use.

Woy, James. *Investment Methods: A Bibliographic Guide.* New York: Bowker, 1973. 220 pp. $11.95. O.P.
Woy identifies and defines 150 popular investment strategies such as contrary opinion, hedging, odd-lot theory, and support and resistance levels, with relevant sources of information described immediately after each definition. This combined dictionary-bibliography is "intended primarily for use by the individual, nonprofessional investor," with the emphasis placed on investment writing that is easy to understand. The references listed provide specific page numbers within the books in which the subject is discussed. A separate section lists periodical articles by subject covering 1965 to early 1973. The articles are derived from *Barron's, Changing Times, Institutional Investor,* and others. Contains author, title, and subject indexes. A very useful guide with an innovative format. Worth updating.

Zerden, Shelden. *Best Books on the Stock Market: An Analytical Bibliography.* New York: Bowker, 1972. 168 pp. O.P.
Evaluative reviews of books on investment methods, the history of the stock market, and the psychology of investment. The main body of the work consists of reviews of approximately 150 books in six categories: technical analysis, fundamental analysis, mutual funds, options, psychology, and speculation. Other sections contain reviews of books on history, biography, books for the beginner, how to beat the stock market, general works, and textbooks and reference books. The evaluative annotations are aimed at assisting the novice seeking education about the markets, as well as the investor wishing to sharpen his or her skills. Unfortunately, this bibliography is too outdated to be of much value.

3

Money and the Consumer

GENERAL

Ackerman, Martin, and Ackerman, Diane. *Living Rich: A Manual for Would-Be Big Spenders.* New York: Playboy Press, 1978. 208 pp. $10. O.P.
Money management at the rich end of the economic spectrum—living well with couture clothes, cocktail parties in Monte Carlo, lunch at La Caravelle, St. Laurent silk shirts, skiing at Gstaad, English nannies for the children, private airplanes, and so on. But regardless of the source of money, what you do with it in terms of investment is the key to living rich. The authors review the investment practices of the wealthy. Amusing, but not very practical or informative.

Bottom Line/Personal, Experts (ed.). *The Book of Inside Information.* New York: Boardroom Books, 1982. 500 pp. $50.
A compilation by the Editors and Experts of *Bottom Line/Personal* on money, health, success, marriage, education, car collecting, fitness, home, travel, shopping, taxes, investments, and retirement. Information is arranged by specific topics—how credit bureaus work, late mortgage payments, rules for picking common stocks, when not to trust a stockbroker, how to judge a mutual fund, traps for the real estate investor, deducting a spouse's convention tab, avoiding a tax audit, how Keogh plans work, life insurance for two-income families, balancing business and personal life, saving on title insurance, taking back a second mortgage, hiring a lawyer, beating air fare increases, when to sue for medical malpractice, college budget plans, and hundreds of other topics. Information is derived from books, magazines, newsletters, and experts, such as investment counselors, accountants, attorneys,

medical specialists, and real estate brokers. An excellent source of browsing information, but not particularly useful as a quick retrieval tool. The quality of the book would be enhanced by the inclusion of supplementary *printed* sources of information in that most readers do not have access to the many experts cited as information sources. The index is somewhat abbreviated considering the wide scope of the content and the high price of the publication.

Casey, Douglas. *International Investing: The Complete Databook to the World's Last Frontiers for Smart Money Management Overseas.* New York: Everest House, 1981. 150 pp. $9.95 (paper).
A most informative compendium of data on financial opportunities around the world: international real estate investment; money, banking, and foreign exchange; comparative taxes in 40 countries; working abroad; welfare benefits, old age and survivors' insurance schemes in 41 major cities; tax havens; citizenship requirements; types of passports; how to conduct business abroad. Casey also compares many countries (including Third and Fourth World) with regard to politics, economy, visas, residency, money and banking, and taxes. An excellent although somewhat opinionated book for both expatriates and international investors. Packed with data not readily available elsewhere. Recommended.

Fodor, R. V. *Nickels, Dimes and Dollars: How Currency Works.* New York: Morrow, 1980. 96 pp. $7.75 (grades 4–6).
A simple explanation for young readers of money and money management, the stock market and investment, credit, the balance of payments, and international exchange rates. Good pictures and illustrations.

Halverson, Richard P. *Financial Freedom: Your New Guide to Economic Security and Success.* San Francisco: Harbor, 1981. 384 pp. $16.50.
Attempts to be an encyclopedic compilation of information to explain the present state of the economy (inflation, high interest rates, and scarce energy); personal financial crises of the 1980s; money management to achieve greater financial freedom; dealing successfully with the great financial traps of credit, risk, and retirement; and how to invest in stocks, bonds, real estate, commodities, and collectibles. The content falls far short of the book's lofty objective. An overambitious attempt to present a grand plan.

Harden, Linda, and Harden, Gerald. *The Money Book for People Who Live Together.* New York: Bantam, 1980. O.P.
A personal finance guide for every kind of living together relationship. Discusses precautions, ground rules, and suggestions for those living together for fun and profit, for married couples, and for those about to divorce. Covers ownership of property (buying, sharing, and splitting it up), communal living, premarital agreements, how to beat the marriage tax, predivorce strategies, alimony and child support, and a checklist of things to remember for those divorcing. A useful compilation of basic information for roommates, unmarried liaisons, de facto marriages, lovers/mistresses, consensual unions, friends, and lovers-in-residence.

Heil, Paula. *Your Personal Guide to Financial Fitness.* New York: Cornerstone Library, 1981. 126 pp. $4.95 (paper).
Heil prescribes exercises for financial fitness calculated to use money in order to make money. Exercises include setting goals, recording expenditures, choosing a bank, insurance isometrics (life insurance review), tax planning, decisions to cut spending, and selecting investments. Other exercises cover the financial "physical" (estimating your net worth) and staying in shape (continuing activity to improve one's health). A strained analogy between physical health and financial health, and slight in content, this book can be safely ignored without impairing the health of your collection.

Klein, Howard. *Fad Money: How to Make Money from Fads, Crazes, and Trends.* New York: Watts, 1979. 224 pp. $8.95. O.P.
Klein argues that cashing in on fads is the last great game of American capitalism. Insight is provided into how to spot a fad; characteristics of successful fads (the cheaper the object, the more money there is to be made in it); the fad life cycle (discovery, catch on, wildfire boom and expansion, fizzle); how to manufacture, market, sell; fad mutual funds; how to set up shop; how to get out fast before the collapse. An amusing, tongue-in-cheek view of the world of pet rocks, hula hoops, Star War merchandise, Farrah posters, and skateboards. How to have fun and make money at the same time.

Levi, Maurice. *Economics Deciphered: A Layman's Survival Guide.* New York: Basic Books, 1981. 192 pp. $13.95; 1982. $7 (paper).
A book for those bewildered by economics intended to help them make personal and professional decisions for survival and prosperity in a complex, changing environment. Offers simple explanations of concepts such as inflation, causes of unemployment, monetary versus fiscal policy, what makes the stock market go up and down, how the bond market behaves, gold prices, international exchange rates, and so on. Contains an annotated bibliography of classical works on economics together with a list of noteworthy books. Good introductory text, using a question-and-answer format; suitable for high school students and beyond.

Miller, Theodore (ed.). *Make Your Money Grow.* A Kiplinger Changing Times Book. New York: Dell, 1981. 384 pp. $3.95 (paper).
The scope, content, and style of this book draw heavily from ideas developed for *Changing Times* magazine. Provides a concise and relatively simple explanation of a wide variety of topics: using credit wisely; choosing a bank; kids and money; buying, selling, and renting a home; condominiums and cooperatives; mobile homes; life and car insurance; stocks, bonds, mutual funds, and options; real estate investing; gold and silver; tax-saving ideas; tax shelters; retirement planning; and wills. A comprehensive and basic guide.

Porter, Sylvia. *Sylvia Porter's New Money Book for the 80's.* New York: Avon, 1980. 1,328 pp. $9.95 (paper).
An encyclopedic compilation by a leading financial columnist of essential and useful information calculated not only "to show you how to survive in the U.S. economic

jungle but also how to triumph in the marketplace." As such, the book covers most aspects of consumer economics: inflation, food, homes, energy conservation, transportation, health care, education, jobs and careers, clothes, jewelry, vacation and travel, sex and money (weddings, contraception, divorce), banking, credit, retirement planning, funeral expenses, stock market, mutual funds, bond markets, jewelry, gems, collectibles, and more. The book is enhanced by suggestions for further reading, addresses and phone numbers, consumer rights and redress organizations, definitions of technical terms at the end of most sections, and cost-saving tips. An ambitious and highly successful attempt to improve the personal, financial habits of the U.S. public. Something of interest for everybody. Highly recommended.

Quinn, Jane B. *Everyone's Money Book*. New York: Delacorte, 1979. 874 pp. $14.95.
An encyclopedic compilation of essential information on ways to save money, checking accounts, borrowing money, credit, rights in the marketplace, buying a car or home, rentals, real estate, life insurance, health insurance, income taxes, investments, wills and estate planning, social security, retirement planning, divorce, and funerals. Contains a consumer complaint and information directory. Excellent and comprehensive source of information on a wide variety of topics. Highly recommended as a first place to look for answers.

Rahney, Philip. *Do-It-Yourself Family Money Kit: A Four Step Method to Building Financial Security*. Omaha, NB: Kimberly Jones, 1982. 189 pp. $14.95; $9.95 (paper).
Rahney considers that possessing a large income does not in itself ensure security from money problems, and that financial security does not necessarily mean making more money, but rather learning how to manage, save, invest, and protect the money you do make. He describes how to prepare and follow a financial plan; why, how, and where to set up a sound savings program; investment opportunities (real estate, stock, mutual funds, collectibles); and insurance to guarantee that a financial program will not be interrupted by illness, accident, or death. The chapters on insurance (health, Medicare, life, automobile, and homeowner's) are particularly valuable.

Rifenbark, Richard K. *How to Beat the Salary Trap: 8 Steps to Financial Independence*. New York: Avon, 1979. 276 pp. $2.50 (paper).
The author outlines a program for the methodical building of wealth suited to the needs of a salaried person, starting with little capital, limited free time, and no wish to jeopardize the family's future with risky schemes. A simplistic recipe for how to get off the salary treadmill.

Ritter, Lawrence S., and Silber, William J. *Money*. 4th Revised Edition. New York: Basic Books, 1981. 336 pp. $13.46; $6.95 (paper).
An excellent reference source on all aspects of monetary policy: the essentials of money and its relationship to the overall economy; the conflict between the monetarists and the Keynesians; the impact of monetary policy on the economy; national priorities and international finance. A good background to assist in understanding high interest rates and the ups and downs of the stock market.

Rosefsky, Robert S. *Money Talks: Bob Rosefsky's Complete Program for Financial Success.* New York: Wiley, 1982. 650 pp. $14.95.

What you need to know about sound money management by the host of the PBS program "Personal Finance." In down-to-earth language, Rosefsky ranges far and wide over the whole spectrum of money management topics. The 20 chapters covering budgeting, smart buying, buying and selling houses, credit and borrowing, investments, life and health insurance, financial planning, estate planning, and taxes are enhanced by the inclusion of "consumer beware" stories alerting the reader to problems and pitfalls that may not be anticipated and personal action checklists that show how to perform the calculations necessary for effective financial decision making. The book is crammed with useful information, practical suggestions, and clear explanations. Highly useful as a source of basic information on all aspects of money management. A bargain at the price. Highly recommended.

Rosenberg, Jerome R. *Managing Your Own Money.* New York: Newsweek Books, 1979. 506 pp. $12.95.

Good sensible advice and clear explanation on a wide variety of money management topics: computing your net worth, cash flow, budgeting, tax planning, estate planning, life insurance, health and casualty insurance, credit, real estate, tangible and intangible property, whether to lease or buy, and futures.

Rutberg, Sidney. *Playboy's Investment and Financial Planning Guide for Singles: Making It and Keeping It in the Eighties.* New York: Playboy Press, 1981. 214 pp. $14.50. O.P.

Singles are not only young people of marriageable age but also include hordes of divorced men and women of all ages and a growing number of unmarried people living together. Rutberg focuses on the financial needs of various types of singles (young professionals, those living together, and others) and analyzes how to budget, how to invest in most major financial areas from money markets and stocks to real estate, commodities, art and collectibles, to diamonds and gold. Specific attention is paid to tax status, cash-flow requirements, living situations, and financial plans for the future. Good advice on coping financially with cohabitation. A book more distinguished by point of view than content.

Skousen, Mark. *Mark Skousen's Guide to Financial Privacy.* New York: Simon & Schuster, 1982. 253 pp. $12.95.

How to preserve your financial privacy against snoopers, tax collectors, salespeople, and meddlers. Skousen, consulting editor of *Personal Finance* newsletter, shows how to maintain a low profile and avoid exposure of one's financial affairs. In specific terms, he details how to preserve banking privacy in view of the Bank Secrecy Act of 1970 and the use of such substitutes as credit cards, money orders, cashier's checks, and traveler's checks. Also described are the use of foreign bank accounts, requirements imposed by the IRS in reporting foreign accounts, transferring money to and from the United States, and use of tax havens. Skousen advocates nothing illegal—only the liberal use of numerous privacy techniques still available. A fascinating, thoughtful, yet somewhat paranoid look at "big brother" and financial privacy. Recommended.

28   *Money and the Consumer*

Sprinkel, Beryl W., and Genetski, Robert J. *Winning with Money: A Guide for Your Future.* Homewood, IL: Dow Jones-Irwin, 1982. 245 pp. $6.95 (paper).
An analysis of major economic trends in relation to monetary policy, inflation, investments, and the balance of payments and their impact on the individual's pocket book. For the advanced student.

Stillman, Richard. *More for Your Money: Personal Finance Techniques to Cope with Inflation and the Energy Shortage.* Englewood Cliffs, NJ: Prentice-Hall, 1980. 288 pp. $13.95; $6.95 (paper).
A systematic exposition of a sound money management program utilizing a personal finance model that incorporates a number of major components: objectives, personal finance topics, resources or educational tools, functions to be performed, and the decision-making process. A formal management approach applied to borrowing money, food, clothing and personal health, transportation, rental and purchase of a home, insurance, banking, the stock market, real estate, income tax, and retirement planning. An academic treatment of money management.

Trower-Subira, George. *Black Folks' Guide to Making Big Money in America.* Newark, NJ: Very Serious Business Enterprises, 1980. 184 pp. $11.
Starting with the premise that "racism is one hell of a consideration and handicap for black folks in making money in America," Trower-Subira tries to show how to cope with financial ignorance, what is wealth, what holds blacks in poverty, the intricacies of real estate, and similar matters. Mixes polemics with money management, and does justice to neither.

Van Caspel, Venita. *Money Dynamics for the 1980's.* Reston, VA: Reston, 1980. 718 pp. $16.
A comprehensive investment guidebook by a well-known expert on financial planning. Van Caspel provides a lucid, balanced, and readable analysis of all aspects of money management: coping with inflation, success in the stock market, investment strategy, real estate, home purchasing, gold and diamonds, collectibles, credit, life insurance, retirement planning, financing college costs, and how to choose a financial planner. A valuable resource book on how to win the money game.

Van Caspel, Venita. *The New Money Dynamics.* Reston, VA: Reston, 1978. 461 pp. $13.95.
A very readable survey at an introductory level of the essentials of inflation, stocks, mutual funds, investment techniques, real estate, life insurance, tax sheltering and deferral, planning for your children's education, and how to win the money game. Out of date on a number of topics such as retirement planning.

Van Caspel, Venita. *The Power of Money Dynamics.* Reston, VA: Reston, 1982. 662 pp. $18.
Van Caspel offers an up-to-date encyclopedic compilation of basic facts on inflation, investments, the stock market, real estate, renting and buying homes, collect-

ibles (silver, gold, coins, oriental rugs), banking, insurance, taxes, and the like. Helpful to those who wish to design their own program for financial security. Glossary of investment terms. Basically, an update of her *Money Dynamics for the 1980's* (see p. 28).

Williams, Gordon L. *Financial Survival in the Age of New Money.* New York: Simon & Schuster, 1981. 382 pp. $14.95.
A fascinating and engrossing look at the big financial picture—the Federal Reserve and the banking system, savings and loan associations, the stock market, gold, Eurodollars, petrodollars and the gnomes of Zurich, electronic money, tax havens, shelters, and dodges. For the individual, it is necessary to invest to survive in financial markets that will remain erratic. A final chapter gives pointed advice on how to plan for survival in the age of new money. A well-written, informative book by a senior editor of *Business Week* and radio commentator.

Wishard, Bill, and Wishard, Laurie. *Men's Rights: A Handbook for the 80's.* San Francisco: Cragmont, 1980. 265 pp. $12.95; $6.95 (paper).
For many men, the women's movement has left in its wake confusion, bitterness, and hostility. The authors (an attorney and his social worker daughter) examine the effects of women's liberation on the problems men experience as individuals and in their relationships with women and children. Among the topics discussed are men's rights in marriage, living together, father-child relationships, abortion, reverse sex discrimination, going to court, marital settlement agreements, alimony, child support, custody, and visitation. Provides an excellent blend of legal information and psychological insight. Lists 15 men's rights organizations. Recommended.

The World Almanac Consumer Information Kit. New York: World Almanac Publications, 1983. 64 pp. $1.50 (paper).
A source book of basic money-related information on a wide variety of consumer issues, such as income taxes, consumer price indexes, purchasing power of the dollar, mortgages, savings, investments, IRAs, social security, and life insurance. Provides numerous tables of data derived from the Bureau of Labor Statistics, the Federal Trade Commission, the Federal Reserve System, Merrill Lynch, the Social Security Administration, and others. An excellent reference source; also good for browsing. A bargain at its price. Highly recommended.

Zimmerman, Gary. *Managing Your Own Money: A Self-Teaching Guide.* New York: Wiley, 1980. 224 pp. $7.95 (paper).
Explains how the ordinary person can ensure financial security through prudent planning, sound investment, and savings. In step-by-step fashion, the handbook follows the financial cycle of the average person or family from budgeting, use of credit, insurance, investments, tax reduction to retirement planning. A text emphasizing basic principles.

MONEY-SAVING STRATEGIES AND TIPS

Appleman, John. *How to Increase Your Money-Making Power in the 80's.* 4th Revised Edition. New York: Fell, 1981. 320 pp. $12.95.
Practical advice on a wide variety of money topics: the stock market, real estate, insurance, banking and finance, selecting a profitable career, running a business, investment opportunities. The far-reaching coverage tends to dilute the content. Rather trite.

Bingham, Joan, and Riccio, Dolores. *The Smart Shopper's Guide to Food Buying and Preparation.* New York: Scribner's, 1982. 311 pp. $14.95.
Calculated to improve the average person's shopping skills: Is this week's special really a bargain? Is the jumbo size always the best deal? Does it pay to shop in food warehouses and street markets? The authors give good coverage to price comparison, interpreting labels, couponing and refunding, and alternatives to frozen food. More than half the book is devoted to nutrition, selecting and using fruits and vegetables, grains and nuts, dairy products and eggs, meat, poultry, and fish, fats and oils, and sugars and syrups. An informative book likely to lead to better quality purchases for less money.

Bohigan, Valerie. *Successful Flea Market Selling.* Summit, PA: TAB Books, 1981. 255 pp. $9.95 (paper).
For those bitten by the flea bug: "garbage will glow; money will flow; retail will offend." This is an interesting how-to-do-it manual explaining when to flea, how to flea, what to flea, pricing, and potential profits. Bohigan claims that flea marketing has become more than just a rapidly spreading craze. Inflation has increased its importance and elevated it to an economic trend of major proportion. A fascinating hobby that combines a money-saving venture and unbounded fun.

Cox, Wesley. *Kiss Ma Bell Good-bye: How to Install Your Own Telephones, Extensions and Accessories.* New York: Crown, 1983. 146 pp. $4.95 (paper).
How to save money and gain immense pleasure by installing and maintaining your own telephone and extensions. Cox predicts that with the reorganization of AT&T, installation costs by local phone companies will continue to skyrocket, while service calls of $50 are now common. In response, Cox shows how to do it yourself with reference to installation, wiring, extensions, sockets, and jacks. Of particular value is the advice on the purchase of telephone accessories, such as answering machines, automatic dialers, redialers, and amplifiers, cordless telephones, and modern couplers. By way of example: "Never, but never, buy a cordless unit without getting a guarantee that you can exchange it for another and get your money returned if your own location proves impractical for good service." Recommended for those who are gadget-minded.

Darack, Arthur, and Consumer Group Inc. *Used Cars: How to Avoid Highway Robbery.* Englewood Cliffs, NJ: Prentice-Hall, 1983. 256 pp. $18.95; $7.95 (paper).

A consumer's guide to shopping for a used car—comparisons of the used cars currently available and estimates of repairing the most common defects. Read this book before kicking the tires on a used car lot.

Davidson, James D. *The Squeeze.* New York: Simon & Schuster/Summit, 1980. 281 pp. $11.95; New York: Pocket Books, 1981. $2.95 (paper).

A brilliant exposition of the money squeeze, the tax squeeze, the energy squeeze, the bureaucratic squeeze, the legal squeeze, the health-care squeeze, the housing squeeze, the quality squeeze, and the unemployment squeeze. Davidson outlines how to avoid being bled dry by overpriced doctors, self-interested lawyers, and do-nothing bureaucrats. General discussion rather than specific advice.

The Directory of Toll-Free Phone Numbers. Suffern, NY: Celebrity Publishing, 1980. 192 pp. $6.95 (paper). O.P.

Save money by using toll-free (800) telephone numbers. The listings are arranged by category, for example, airlines, automobile manufacturers, hotels, insurance companies, and tow operators. Most categories are subdivided geographically.

Dowd, Merle. *How to Live Better and Spend 20% Less.* Englewood Cliffs, NJ: Prentice-Hall, 1972. 274 pp. $10.95; New York: Ballantine, 1980. 320 pp. $2.50 (paper).

How to save 20 percent or more on cars, life and health insurance, boats, watches, clothing, furniture, and vacations by buying out of season, taking advantage of discounts, conserving, buying less, using a spending plan. Needs a thorough updating.

Flanagan, William G. *How to Beat the Financial Squeeze: Don't Just Get Mad—Get Even.* Garden City, NY: Doubleday, 1980. 240 pp. $10.95.

The author is a columnist for the *Wall Street Journal.* His book offers an entertaining and sensible discussion of borrowing money, investment, home ownership, pitfalls of the stock market, tax sheltering, and retirement planning. A section entitled "Where to Cut Expenses—Without Bleeding" is particularly helpful, covering ways to save money on clothing, furniture, life insurance, cars, financing education, and auto repair. Provides good tips on career changes and job hunting. A useful book meant to be read rather than to serve as a reference book.

Freeman, Kerry (ed.). *Chilton's Guide to Consumer's Auto Repairs and Prices: How to Save Money on Auto Repairs and Accessories.* Radnor, PA: Chilton, 1980. 296 pp. $10.95; $9.95 (paper).

An excellent guide to the economics of car purchase and maintenance. This valuable book helps one decide which repairs can be done economically by oneself and which need professional assistance; shopping for parts and tools; buying batteries and tires; selecting a repair facility (car dealerships versus service stations and independent repair shops); dealing with your mechanic; warranties; buying new and used cars; financing and insurance. A substantial part of the book itemizes the estimated labor charges for common repairs and automotive services on domestic and imported cars based upon *Chilton's Professional Labor Guide and Parts Manual,* which is widely used to accurately quote the price of repair jobs. Highly recommended for all car owners.

Fuhrman, Noah. *Seven Keys for Doubling Your Standard of Living (Without Increasing Your Income).* New York: Macmillan/Collier Books, 1982. 160 pp. $6.95 (paper).

Seven concrete approaches that can double your standard of living involve increased consumer awareness, a consumer game plan, knowing where the bargains are, use of supershopper savvy, spotting the tricks of the trade (game dealers play), strength in numbers (joining with other consumers to save money), and consumer conservation, or making what you have go further. Contains good tips on shopping at thrift stores, seeking out discount outlets, comparing prices of gasoline, locating travel bargains, and avoiding salespeople's dirty tricks such as lowballing and highballing. Much of the content is well known and painfully obvious to most consumers.

Hatton, Hap, and Torbet, Laura. *Helpful Hints for Hard Times: How to Live It Up while Cutting Down.* New York: Facts on File, 1983. 237 pp. $7.95 (paper).

A splendid book that confronts economic reality: "Everyone, at some level, feels the economic pinch, whether it's a matter of not trading in the car this year, or eating meat less often, or moving to a smaller house and keeping the thermostat turned down. This is quite a change from the affluent-and-recent-past." To cope with adverse economic circumstances, Hatton and Torbet offer a primer on economy, conservation, and cooperation distilled from countless books and pamphlets on everything from home buying and installation to car repair and money management. Good insight into needs, skills, goals, and strategies is provided in relation to buying a home, energy conservation, home maintenance, and automobile purchase and repair. Crammed with helpful hints, clever suggestions, and money-saving tips. Lists books, pamphlets, and where to write for further information. Indispensable. Highly recommended.

Hicks, Tyler. *How to Build a Second Income Fortune in Your Spare Time.* Englewood Cliffs, NJ: Prentice Hall/Reward, 1979. 207 pp. $3.95 (paper).

How to define wealth goals and accumulate wealth through pyramiding, stock, low capital ventures, personal services, foreign exchange, mortgage ventures, hobbies, and so on. Trivial and superficial.

Horatio, Algernon. *The Penny Capitalist: How to Build a Small Fortune from Next to Nothing.* New York: Crown/Arlington House, 1979. 244 pp. $10.

An anonymous professor at a large midwestern university has written a book "aimed at the average middle American who runs out of money on the 25th of every month, has no savings account, and doesn't know where the money is coming from to get his daughter's teeth straightened." The approach recommended is to think small but save money by cutting expenses, spending other people's money, "garage saling," investing on a shoestring, and moonlighting. Light reading.

Hubbard, L. Ron, and Winfrey, Dennis W. *How to Flourish, Prosper, and Survive the 80's Despite Everything! The Working Person's Financial Crash Course.* From the Works of L. Ron Hubbard. Hollywood, CA: Survival Books, 1981. 225 pp. $15.95 (paper).

A self-study manual dealing with the basic principles of the economic system and how to move ahead. A strong dose of personal philosophy laced with much invented terminology. Not recommended.

Hyman, Henry. *The Where to Sell Anything and Everything Book.* New York: World Almanac Publications, 1981. 400 pp. $7.95 (paper); New York: Ballantine, 1981. 400 pp. $7.95 (paper).
Lists more than 500 dealers and collectors willing to buy dolls, banjos, cigar bands, rifles, autographs, oriental rugs, doorknobs, typewriters, beer cans, violins, stamps, valentines, quilts, china, and a wide variety of other items. Contains information on condition, pricing, appraisal, and shipping. Interesting suggestions on how to turn throwaways into cash.

Johnstad, Jack, and Johnstad, Lois. *The Power of Prosperous Thinking: A Practical and Inspirational Guide to Making, Managing, and Multiplying Your Money.* New York: St. Martin's Press, 1982. 256 pp. $12.95; $5.95 (paper).
Very simple advice on how to prepare a personal financial statement and balance sheet, paying bills, saving, insurance, and how to stretch bucks—through couponing, avoiding impulse buying, part-time jobs, and other sources of income. Leans heavily on achieving financial peace of mind by improving self-esteem, positive affirmations concerning financial matters, and visualization (seeing ourselves as we want to be). Superficial; by no means an essential title.

Joselow, Froma. *Get Your Money's Worth: The Book for People Who Are Tired of Paying More for Less.* New York: New American Library/Signet, 1983. 214 pp. $3.50 (paper).
The key formula used here is "price awareness." Although the Consumer Price Index is the official government yardstick, it does not mention how individuals experience it. "You determine your personal inflation rate by the way you spend your money, and you can lower your personal inflation rate by changing your spending habits." Money-saving tips are provided on a wide range of topics, such as home buying, appliances, transportation, travel, food, health, taxes, saving, investing, credit, and retirement. Due to its overambitious objective, the treatment of many subjects is superficial and of limited value.

Levinson, Jay. *555 Ways to Earn Extra Money.* New York: Holt, Rinehart & Winston, 1982. 421 pp. $9.95 (paper).
"By tapping more of your skills and talents, you can earn more money—lots and lots of it." How? By a system of "patchwork economics" that allows you to adapt your work time to your life situation. It is possible to work and earn money *without* a job. Levinson outlines the money-making opportunities in selling, teaching, building and repairing, publishing, and such pursuits as tracing lost pets, delivering meals for restaurants, and teaching people to have successful interviews. Duplicates much of the content of the author's *Earning Money without a Job* (see p. 57).

McLachlan, Christopher. *Inflation-Wise: How to Do Almost Everything for Less.* New York: Avon, 1981. 243 pp. $4.95 (paper).

McLachlan has energetically accumulated dozens of clever ways to cut costs and eliminate wasteful spending, which were once widely known and practiced but have been subsequently lost or forgotten. His objective is to find hidden costs, locate easy savings, eliminate unnecessary expenditures, and thereby live happily and well at bargain prices. Hints and tips are arranged alphabetically, ranging from automobile purchase and maintenance, borrowing, clothes, cosmetics, drugs, entertainment, laundry, refrigerators, sales, toys, to woodstoves. A great grab bag of hints, suggestions, phone numbers, addresses, worksheets, recommended books, and innovative ideas. Each entry is coded to indicate the estimated annual dollar and/or percentage savings possible if the idea is implemented by a reader. Unfortunately, the coding system is cumbersome and confusing and adds little to the text. Imaginative and clever.

McClintock, Mike. *Getting Your Money's Worth from Home Contractors.* New York: Crown/Harmony Books, 1982. 192 pp. $11.95; $5.95 (paper).

McClintock, a former general contractor, is a consumer expert on WMCA radio in New York City. His book contains fundamental guidelines on how to shop for professional services, soliciting and evaluating estimates, checking professional qualifications, evaluating informal agreements and formal contracts, and remedying grievances. Also lists consumer agencies by state, county, and city. A good guide to dealing effectively and economically with asphalt pourers, basement waterproofers, carpenters, electricians, painters, plumbers, roofers, and so on. Calculated to save money.

McConnally, Kevin (ed.). *How to Get More for Your Money.* Washington, DC: Kiplinger Washington Editors, 1981. 183 pp. $2.95 (paper). O.P.

A handbook for the careful shopper on how to select, question, and probe the quality of a large number of products and services. Covers autos (new and used), carpets, employment agencies, firewood, food (generics and unit costs), insulation, jewelry, lawyers, microwave ovens, ranges, recalls, lawn mowers, smoke detectors, snowthrowers, telephones, travel, and more. Not a guide to specific products, but rather advice on how to become a skillful consumer. Useful.

Michaels, Richard. *Moonlighter's Guide to a Sparetime Fortune.* Englewood Cliffs, NJ: Prentice-Hall/Reward, 1982. 215 pp. $4.95 (paper).

Packed with good suggestions: how to select a profitable moonlighting business, tested ideas for making a great fortune (flea markets, billing services, cookies for sale, bicycle rentals, digital watch repair, soccer shop), franchise moonlighting, turning your home into a moonlighting bonanza. Michaels gives step-by-step directions on borrowing money, record keeping, advertising, and so on. Highly readable.

Miller, Nancy. *Managing Your Money.* Syracuse, NY: New Readers Press, 1979. 64 pp. $2.25 (paper). O.P.

A very simple text explaining how to spend less for housing, food, travel, clothes, health and recreation; how families use money; and help from money managers (on banks, credit, estate planning). Useful for schoolchildren.

The 1980 Yearbook of Agriculture: Cutting Energy Costs. Washington, DC: U.S. Department of Agriculture, 1980. 397 pp.
A fact-filled compilation of energy-saving ideas for all segments of society. Topics discussed range from raising hogs for less money to money-saving tips for home appliances, cutting high heating costs, do's and don'ts of home insulation, energy-efficient homes of the future, and 50 ways to save energy dollars.

Phalon, Richard. *Your Money: How to Make It Work Harder Than You Do.* New York: St. Martin's Press, 1981. 320 pp. $5.95.
Top dollar tips by a financial writer on savings, checking, borrowing money, life insurance, financing a home, condominiums, success in the stock market, managing one's income tax, and retirement planning. Somewhat outdated.

Rosen, Lawrence R. *The Dow Jones-Irwin Guide to Interest: What You Should Know about the Time Value of Money.* Revised Edition. Homewood, IL: Dow Jones-Irwin, 1981. 262 pp. $14.95.
This book is intended to assist the public in forming an accurate picture of the financial implications of everyday money decisions. More than 200 pages of tables and graphs are provided as a guide to computing the true costs and values of mortgages, savings accounts, bonds, installment loans, annuities, and so on. Typical questions that can be answered are: "If I buy a bond for $800, which matures in 13 years, paying interest of $60 per year, what is my yield to maturity?" or "How much money do I need to invest each month in order to have a $2,000 per month income when I retire?" Unfortunately, the very small amount of explanation is buried in a morass of tables, graphs, and mathematical computations. Difficult to use in view of the lack of guidance to the tables and graphs.

Rotchstein, Janice. *The Money Diet: How to Save Up to $360 in 28 Days.* New York: Crown, 1982. 192 pp. $4.95 (paper).
What appears to be a novelty book is in reality a valuable guide to saving money. In the same way a weight-loss diet sheds pounds, so a money-saving diet can reduce expenses. In 28 days, Rotchstein's recommended regime will save $310 if you're single, $347 if you're a couple, and $360 if you're a family of four. Money-saving ideas fall into a number of categories: food, transportation, home maintenance, purchases, and entertainment. The dollar savings are computed for each money-saving suggestion: use thread instead of dental floss, buy lamb blade or round bone instead of sirloin chops; purchase disposable razors instead of refill blades; put two empty half-gallon milk cartons in the toilet tank; snip facial tissues in half; make your own window cleaner; use plastic bags instead of disposable gloves; make a baking soda and water mouthwash; screen a movie from the public library. Special seasonal diets are recommended for spring/summer, fall/winter, and for holidays, birthdays, weddings, and grand occasions. Diet worksheets are provided to help calculate the cost savings. Innovative, imaginative, and useful. Recommended.

Rothchild, John. *Stop Burning Your Money: The Intelligent Homeowner's Guide to Household Energy Savings.* New York: Random House, 1981. 258 pp. $15; New York: Penguin, 1982. $5.95 (paper).

A money-saving guide for anyone who has to buy energy to heat, cool, and maintain a home. Answers the basic questions on energy conservation dealing with oil and gas furnaces, heat pumps, conversion from oil to gas, insulation, caulking and weatherstripping, and alternatives such as solar heaters, woodstoves, fireplaces, and burning coal. An excellent handbook of the cost-benefit relationships of various energy investments. Of interest to those concerned with the escalating costs of heating and air conditioning. Recommended.

Self, Robert. *Long Distance for Less: How to Choose Between Ma Bell and Those "Other" Carriers.* New York: Telecom Library, 1982. 160 pp. $75.

A guide to the 124 different ways to call between major U.S. cities for those who want to reduce long-distance phone bills. The author explains the price structure and operation of Bell's Direct Distance Dialing, operator-assisted calls, InWats (800 Service) and OutWats Service, and the alternative OCCs (Other Common Carriers)—MCI, ITT, SPC (Southern Pacific Communications), and WU (Western Union). Self also analyzes the costs and operations of the resellers such as ALLNET and ALLTELCO. All that you will ever want to know on long-distance calling.

Simon, Samuel, and Waz, Joseph. *Reverse the Charges: How to Save $$$ on Your Phone Bill.* Washington, DC: National Citizens Committee for Broadcasting, 1982. 86 pp. $4.95 (paper).

Designed to help those who are burdened with the cost of "reaching out and touching someone." If you average $25 or more in a month in long-distance calls, it is possible to save up to 40 percent on calls. This book assembles for the concerned consumer the latest information on buying versus renting your phone, choosing your local phone service, selecting among competitive long-distance services, and your rights as a telephone consumer. The authors lucidly describe monthly service charges, rates for local phone service, custom calling (call waiting, call forwarding, speed calling, and three-way calling), deposits required by the phone company, choosing phone equipment, plugs and jacks, tips on shopping for phones, alternative companies such as Sprint, MCI, and ITT, and the telephone consumer's "bill of rights." Particularly interesting is the description of the restructuring of AT&T and its dramatic effect on how telephone companies will now do business with consumers. Appendixes list long-distance resellers, telephone companies, and where to go for help. Guaranteed to save money. Highly recommended.

Sirico, Louis J. *How to Talk Back to the Telephone Company: Playing the Telephone Game to Win.* Introduction by Ralph Nader. Washington, DC: Center for Study of Responsive Law, 1979. 201 pp. $6.

Sirico analyzes what you can and should expect from your telephone company and offers a telephone consumer's "bill of rights." This includes the right to service priced as low as reasonably possible, right to be informed of all service options, including budget rates, right to purchase telephone equipment, right to accurate, readable bills, and so on. A detailed, somewhat technical account of the economics (and politics) of the telephone monopoly. This is a very useful, authoritative reference book for consumers interested in influencing the rate-setting process of telephone service.

Stossel, John. *John Stossel's Shopping Smart: The Only Consumer's Guide You'll Ever Need.* New York: Berkley, 1982. 222 pp. $4.95 (paper).
Tips and strategies for buying cars, houses, food, drugs and cosmetics, travel hints, and principles of financial planning. Stossel is a TV consumer reporter; a superficial discussion more suited to TV caption-style journalism. Skip this title.

Sutton, Remar. *Don't Get Taken Every Time: The Insider's Guide to Buying Your Next Car.* New York: Viking, 1982. 353 pp. $12.95.
Using an imaginary salesman, "Killer Monsoon," Sutton takes a somewhat frightening look at the car business, "the great slaughterhouse of wheeling and dealing where millions of people each year willingly submit to being taken." This book is a highly useful guide to what to buy, when to buy, how to negotiate, best sources of financing, and how to evaluate a car. Must reading for those wishing to penetrate the fog hanging over the car-buying process. Highly recommended for those about to do battle in the automobile showroom.

Toll-Free Digest: A New Enlarged Directory of Over 17,000 Toll-Free Listings. New York: Warner, 1979. 473 pp. $4.95 (paper). O.P.
A comprehensive digest of 800 numbers arranged by several hundred subject classifications. An excellent way to reach manufacturers, hotels, magazine subscription agencies, trailer parks, or automobile manufacturers without paying long-distance charges.

Trubo, Richard. *The Consumer's Book of Hints and Tips.* Middle Village, NY: Jonathan David, 1978. 319 pp. $12.50.
Brief, cursory information on such diverse topics as preparing a budget, food, health care, clothing, household economics, automobiles, banking and investing, credit and loans, insurance, and taxes. At a very simple level of explanation.

Ungaro, Susan. *The H and R Block Family Financial Planning Workbook.* H and R Block Series. New York: Macmillan/Collier Books, 1980. 100 pp. $4.95 (paper).
Ungaro, senior editor of *Family Circle* magazine, attempts to show how to stretch your dollars as never before. The key is organization, and the author outlines how to keep records and budget; how to keep track of insurance policies, bankbooks, checks, diplomas, licenses; how much one should save; how to use credit wisely; when to use a credit counseling service; dollar-saving suggestions; tax tactics and tips; and retirement planning. Detailed worksheets and a list of money saving booklets, newsletters, and hot lines are provided. Simple explanations. Useful.

CONSUMER REDRESS

Dorfman, John. *Consumer Tactics Manual: How to Get Action on Your Complaints.* New York: Atheneum, 1980. 239 pp. $6.95 (paper).
What to do if something has gone wrong? Part 1 is a complaint encyclopedia covering gripes about automobiles, appliances, banks, clothing, credit, dating services, furniture, health spas, houses, insurance, mail order houses, real estate, travel

agents, unsolicited merchandise, and so on. Part 2 shows how to fight back—how to make a telephone complaint, how to use the Better Business Bureau, Federal Trade Commission, Consumer Product Safety Commission, small claims court, Consumers Union, action lines, and the media. Informative, concise, practical advice. Recommended.

Horowitz, David. *Fight Back! and Don't Get Ripped Off*. San Francisco: Harper & Row, 1979. 308 pp. $8.95.

A book supposedly for those who wish to raise their consumer consciousness: "No longer will you be easy to embarrass, easy to intimidate, easy to bluff, or easy to con when it comes to money." Horowitz offers good advice in relation to automobiles, shopping in the supermarket, restaurants, mail-order purchases, credit and finance, moving, and so on. At times the advice is trite: "Buy your new automobile from a dealer with a solid gold reputation for fairness, service and satisfaction, and be an informed but skeptical buyer." The tone of the book deteriorates when Horowitz discusses the professions: "Many professional people are living high off the hog . . . they've become hopeless addicts supporting very expensive habits: status and greed." With such writing, Horowitz throws away his credibility.

Newman, Stephen, and Kramer, Nancy. *Getting What You Deserve: A Handbook for the Assertive Consumer*. New York: Doubleday/Dolphin, 1979. 328 pp. $8.95 (paper).

A very ambitious and successful attempt to cover the whole territory of consumerism written by a professor of law and an attorney with the New York Public Interest Research Group. The authors range from how to complain effectively to pitfalls, rip-offs, frauds in cars, door-to-door sales, supermarkets, funerals, home improvement, real estate, buying by mail, vacations, credit, drugs, hearing aids, health clubs, and even legal fees. Crammed with relevant information and good advice. Excellent cartoons and illustrations. Recommended.

Suthers, John W., and Shupp, Gary L. *Fraud and Deceit: How to Stop Being Ripped Off*. New York: Arco, 1982. 144 pp. $6.95 (paper).

Two district attorneys combine efforts in exposing a wide variety of frauds, rackets, confidence games, and deceptive advertising. This is an excellent guide on how to counter, for example, commodity futures fraud, bait and switch advertising, the funeral industry, going-out-of-business sales, automobile repair frauds, self-improvement schemes, charity rackets, credit card fraud, and classic cons such as the missing heir scheme, obituary frauds, and the pigeon drop. Contains a glossary of the language of fraud and deceit and a list of consumer protection agencies by state. An excellent book likely to save money even for more sophisticated consumers. Highly recommended.

INFLATION AND FINANCIAL SURVIVAL

Abert, Geoffry F. *After the Crash: How to Survive and Prosper during the Depression of the 1980's*. New York: New American Library, 1980. 298 pp. $2.50 (paper).

Yet another countdown to Armageddon. In view of runaway inflation, impending economic collapse, and social chaos, Abert proposes stockpiling a food and water supply, reviewing physical security of one's home, purchasing coins and diamonds, opening a foreign bank account, starting a victory garden, practicing survival skills, and preparing for the ultimate crash. Alarmist nonsense mingled with economic piffle.

Appel, Gerald. *99 Ways to Make Money in a Depression.* Revised and Updated Edition. Westport, CT: Crown/Arlington House, 1981. 256 pp. $14.95.
A doomsday prediction of a forthcoming depression by an investment counselor. No one will be safe, but forewarned is forearmed. The blueprint for survival, or master plan, recommended is familiar: remain liquid, utilize money funds, stay away from real estate, invest in gold, coins, and collectibles, consider currency futures, and watch for the upturn. Appel has assembled a vast amount of assumptions, predictions, forecasts, warnings, and speculations that do not present a coherent picture.

Benge, Eugene J. *How to Lick Inflation before It Licks You.* New York: Fell, 1981. 176 pp. $9.95.
Against a backdrop of what he sees as continuing inflation fanned by the "drunken sailors of Capitol Hill," Benge warns of the consumer debt trap and suggests ways of increasing skills and earning power and how to save on food, clothing, shelter, health care, and utility bills, Superficial diagnosis and prescription for solving a complex problem.

Bladen, Ashby. *How to Cope with the Developing Financial Crisis.* New York: McGraw-Hill, 1979. 178 pp. $14.95; New York: McGraw-Hill, 1981. $4.95 (paper).
The inflationary overexpansion of debt is leading to turmoil. The author claims that we cannot expect to go on indefinitely maintaining a higher standard of living than we are earning through our own productive efforts. The real standard of living will continue to fall. While not subscribing to the apocalyptic school that predicts total financial and social disaster, Bladen recommends locating a rural hideaway and having liquid savings to cope with crisis and dislocation. Other recommendations include staying away from real estate, investing only in sound, growth stocks, avoiding retirement as long as possible, and being prepared. Sane and challenging.

Browne, Harry. *New Profits from the Monetary Crisis.* New York: Morrow, 1978. 542 pp. $12.95; New York: Warner, 1979. $2.95 (paper).
Investment philosophy, strategy, and tactics during inflationary times. Much of the material in this book has been updated and expanded in the author's *Inflation-Proofing Your Investments* (see below).

Browne, Harry, and Coxon, Terry. *Inflation-Proofing Your Investments.* New York: Morrow, 1981. 385 pp. $14.95; New York: Warner, 1982. 560 pp. $3.95 (paper).
Confronting the problem of continuing inflation, the authors examine five possibilities: that inflation will level off and stay there, will continue to rise slowly, will speed

up and culminate in runaway inflation, will ease down gently, will fall violently toward a deflationary depression. In the light of these possible developments, Browne and Coxon consider the comparative merits of investing in gold, silver, foreign currencies, real estate, stocks, collectibles. Good pointers on how to build a portfolio during inflationary times. Contains a useful glossary of economic and investment terms.

Casey, Douglas. *Crisis Investing: Opportunities and Profits in the Coming Great Depression.* New York: Simon & Schuster/Pocket Books, 1981. 290 pp. $3.50 (paper).

The author states: "I'm convinced that gale-force winds will soon hit us, followed by tidal waves of panic and collapse. Most investors will be stunned by these losses; many will be utterly destroyed; a canny few will not only survive, but prosper." Casey foresees this collapse accompanied by chaotic conditions involving runaway inflation, chaotic shortages, black markets, rationing, bankruptcy, unemployment, bank failures, collapse of the social security system, and the destruction of investments. The author is better at the dramatic depiction of the impending doomsday than at suggesting possible counterremedies, apart from the somewhat conventional advice to purchase gold and collectibles and to utilize Swiss banks. Fascinating reading, mixing philosophy with economics.

Casey, Douglas. *Strategic Investing: How to Profit from the Coming Inflationary Depression.* New York: Simon & Schuster, 1982. 445 pp. $15.95.

Repeats the essential theme of the author's earlier work, *Crisis Investing* (see above). We are witnessing the beginnings of massively reduced standards of living, titanically moving markets, huge government deficits, and much higher inflation. Casey paints three scenarios for the course the depression will take, differing only in degree of collapse. His outlook is full of gloom and doom: "All of the government's debt—the Federal Reserve's unbacked paper currency and no one really knows how many trillions of dollars of bonds, mortgages, notes, bank credit, Eurodollar deposits, consumer credit loans, just to name a few things—could vanish tomorrow under a variety of circumstances." As protection, Casey recommends: rent don't buy, purchase utilities, penny stocks, gambling stocks, gold stocks, strategic materials. "Liquidate, create, consolidate and then speculate." Intriguing.

Clark, Doug. *The Greatest Banking Scandal in History: And How It Affects You.* Eugene, OR: Harvest House, 1981. 192 pp. $9.95; $4.95 (paper).

Clark has an alarmist message: a credit collapse, a currency collapse, a real estate collapse, and an incredible depression will take place unless a stop is put to wild government spending and high interest rates. The private banking interests, wielding unbelievable power within the Federal Reserve Board, make self-serving decisions relating to the money supply. More government borrowing and spending leads to more government power, which is the royal road to socialism. In view of the impending international depression and collapse, Clark's prescription is to buy gold coins, plan an escape route, have a food storage plan, and acquire special clothing, materials, and equipment to survive the disaster. A melange of biblical prophecy, pseudo-economics, and hysterical argument. Not an essential title.

Consumer Guide, with Peter A. Dickinson. *How to Make Money during Inflation/Recession*. New York: Harper & Row, 1980. 128 pp. $8.75. O.P.

A clear, concise, and informative discussion of the impact of inflation and the need to have an investment strategy. Covers gold and silver, stocks, money market funds, government securities, real estate, collectibles, savings accounts, foreign currencies, and so on. Illustrates model portfolios—for young singles, developing families, retired couples, widows or widowers, and others. Sensible advice; a good book to study first. Recommended.

Curtis, Richard. *How to Prosper in the Coming Apocalypse*. New York: St. Martin's Press, 1981. 96 pp. $3.95 (paper).

A delightful spoof of those books that prophesy the coming apocalypse and financial collapse. Curtis details how to furnish a bunker, where to hide (silos, woodsheds, outhouses), stocking a larder (hot dogs, french fries, Ruffles), accumulating fuel, ammunition for bartering (2 Barbara Cartlands = 1 teaspoon vanilla, 1 egg yolk, pinch of nutmeg), and new careers in Armageddon (evacuation travel). Continuing in this light vein, Curtis describes how to establish a hiding agency that provides services such as group evacuations, hideaways, and evacuation luggage. Good advice is given on what to wear to doomsday. To keep warm, Curtis suggests the burning of the "doomsday" books. Great satire. Highly recommended.

Eder, G. *What's behind Inflation and How to Beat It*. Englewood Cliffs, NJ: Prentice-Hall, 1979. 266 pp. $9.95.

A sensible and academically oriented discussion of the causes of inflation and possible hedges against it, such as real estate, collectibles, and gold. Eder urges that a stop be put to government spending in order to reverse four decades of inflationism, collectivism, and Keynesian aberration. Highly polemical with some useful advice on anti-inflationary strategies.

Hefferlin, Jonathan. *Making Inflation Pay! How Limited Funds in Gold, Silver, Coins, Stamps, Real Estate at the Right Time Can Win Big*. San Francisco: Harbor, 1981. 224 pp. $10.95.

To ensure financial survival during the next decade of inflation, Hefferlin claims that it is necessary to invest in gold, silver, stamps, and rare coins. The author, owner of the largest retail dealership in gold and silver in America, shows how to predict the future supply of gold and silver, how to buy and sell for big profits, why rare coins can make the best investments, and how to diversify for maximum gain. Contains a good chapter on frauds, swindles, and deceptive advertising—"test marketing," movable dealers (fly-by-night), airport watch artists, "boiler room" swindles, and the like. Lists coin and bullion dealers and relevant newsletters, magazines, and books. An overenthusiastic presentation by a supersalesman.

How to Prosper in the 80's. Skokie, IL: Consumer Guide, 1980. 96 pp. $1.25 (paper). O.P.

Encapsulated advice on how to beat inflation through investment in stocks, money market funds, government securities, property, gold and silver, and tax shelters. Good hints on how to survive in the worst of times—inflationary recession.

Nauheim, Fred. *Move Your Assets to Beat Inflation*. Englewood Cliffs, NJ: Prentice-Hall, 1980. 288 pp. $11.95.
Tactics to cope with rising prices, taxes, and interest rates, particularly for those contemplating retirement. Covers familiar ground: ready cash, savings, stocks and securities, insurance, real estate, trusts, tax shelters. Undistinguished and pedestrian.

Paris, Alexander. *The Coming Credit Collapse: An Update for the 1980's*. New York: Crown/Arlington House, 1980. 241 pp. $12.95.
The sword of Damocles is seen to be the steadily growing government intervention in the private sector and its excessive credit creation to finance those activities. The credit process is viewed as the proximate cause of price inflation, rising interest rates, accelerating volatility, declining production, and other economic woes. Credit growth has consistently been two to three times faster than the growth in the ability to produce goods and services. To cope with the volatility and the emotional cyclical swings in the economy, Paris suggests a flexible strategy that allows the switching of investment vehicles and the weighting of a portfolio at the right phase of each cycle. Cogent and sensible statement that deserves careful reading.

Romero, George. *The Great Dollar Deception: Losing When You Think You're Winning*. New York: Books in Focus, 1980. 176 pp. $4.95 (paper).
A mixture of philosophy, politics, economics, and morality. Advocates accumulating money to invest in intangible assets that will increase in value faster than inflation and taxes. Financial advice from a microbiologist!

Ruff, Howard. *How to Prosper during the Coming Bad Years*. New York: Times Books, 1979. 248 pp. $8.95; New York: Warner, 1980. 384 pp. $3.95 (paper).
The editor/publisher of the *Ruff Times*, who claims to be more often right than wrong, believes that the United States is about to enter its greatest test period since the Civil War with "an inflationary spiral leading to a depression that will be remembered with a shudder for generations." The scenario depicted includes exploding inflation, price controls, erosion of savings, collapse of private and government pension programs such as social security, more government regulation, and an international monetary holocaust. Ruff urges a number of countermeasures: Buy gold and silver, sell all big-city or suburban real estate and invest in small-town income property; prepare for a black market (and barter) by storing consumer goods such as seeds, tools for self-sufficiency, ammunition, and durable clothing; stock enough food for one year—prepare for panic and a run on food and water. This book is the biggest best-seller on money in the history of American publishing. Recommended for those who like exciting reading.

Ruff, Howard. *Howard Ruff from A to Z: A Timeless Money Making Odyssey through the First Four Years of America's Leading Financial Advisory Service*. San Ramon, CA: Target, 1980. 769 pp. $24.95. O.P.
By the author of *How to Prosper during the Coming Bad Years* (see above). The contents of the book draw heavily from material written for the *Ruff Times*. The coverage is alphabetical and encyclopedic in scope, including, for example, banks, bonds and the bond market, coins, commodity market, diamonds, estate planning,

gold, inflation, insurance, investments, IRS, money market funds, municipal funds, poverty, real estate, retirement plans, taxes, and wage and price controls. Strictly economic topics are interspersed with moral and philosophical issues, such as abortion, laetrile as a cancer treatment, crime, homosexuality, and nutrition. The advice is familiar: Caught in an irreversible inflationary spiral, one should purchase gold, silver, and diamonds, dispose of all fixed value securities, and store food and other necessities for personal survival following the ultimate collapse. An excellent compendium for Ruff admirers.

Ruff, Howard. *Survive and Win in the Inflationary Eighties.* New York: Times Books, 1981. 280 pp. $12.50; New York: Warner, 1982. 400 pp. $3.95 (paper).
More of the world according to Howard Ruff. Once again the message is that inflation, taxes, and government regulations have brought the economy to a standstill and now threaten the liquidation of America. Ruff claims that this new book is a last-ditch effort and an "opening salvo on the ignorant and often venal clods in Washington and the State Houses and capitals of America." Personal failure avoidance strategies are outlined: Diversify by purchasing real estate, diamonds, gold, silver, collectibles; avoid loaning money to banks and savings and loans; buy gold and silver coins; watch the markets; develop self-survival techniques and barter arrangements. In view of the then prevailing high inflation, recession, collapse of the bond and mortgage markets, high interest rates, Ruff as the prophet of doom or the Jim Jones of the financial world seems remotely plausible. Provocative—deserves careful reading and contemplation. Recommended.

Schultz, Harry. *Panics and Crashes: How You Can Make Money Out of Them.* Revised Edition. Westport, CT: Crown/Arlington House, 1980. 256 pp. $12.95.
Examines the financial panics, crashes, and business cycles of the last 150 years in order to measure the panic factor in men and women and how we may cope more successfully in the future. After reviewing panics and business recessions since 1929, Schultz argues that the classic signs of monetary panic are shaping up in the United States and that the country is sliding into the gentlest (if not longest) recession in history. He recommends high liquidity, short-term, interest-bearing time deposits, avoidance of small banks and savings and loan associations, and caution in leaving cash balances with brokers. An analytical, historical look at current economic problems. Stimulating.

Shulman, Morton. *How to Invest Your Money and Profit from Inflation.* New York: Random House, 1980. 160 pp. $10.95; New York: Ballantine, 1981. $2.50 (paper).
Shulman argues that there is no longer any safety in investing in stocks and bonds, life insurance, and mortgages. Instead, the author advocates buying real estate, gold, commodities, foreign currencies, stamps, wine, art, and antiques. His message is clear and perhaps overly simple: Get rid of paper investments and buy equity. Overstated but provocative.

Smith, Adam. *Paper Money.* New York: Summit, 1981. 335 pp. $13.95; Boston: Hall, 1981. $15.95 (Large Print Book); New York: Dell, 1982. $3.95 (paper).

Smith, also known as George J. W. Goodman, is also author of *The Money Game* and *Supermoney*. In this book, Smith argues brilliantly and incisively about inflation, the energy crisis, OPEC, stability of the dollar, the possibility of an international banking crisis, deflation, depression, the future of nuclear power, and sundry topics. As always, Smith writes lucidly and with eclat. He concludes that "All investments are speculations in the age of paper money."

Smith, Jerome. *The Coming Currency Collapse: And What You Can Do about It.* New York: Books in Focus, 1980. 250 pp. $13.95; New York: Bantam, 1981. 205 pp. $3.95 (paper).

Smith points to the evils of global runaway inflation, why inflation cannot be stopped, the consequences of inflation, and its effects on conventional investments: "inflation causes massive distortions, misallocations of resources, mounting uncertainties and is bad for business." The solution? Smith offers three essential general rules for capital survival strategy: own real assets, owe money debts, and stay liquid. A suggested portfolio for runaway inflation would include silver bullion, common silver coins, gold bullion, platinum bars, gold coins, diamonds, and cash in an appreciating currency, preferably held in a Swiss bank. The most serious trap to avoid is having funds locked in fixed return instruments. Fascinating yet dubious advice considering the recent (1983) abatement in inflationary pressure.

Stein, Ben, and Stein, Herbert. *Money Power: How to Make Inflation Make You Rich.* New York: Harper & Row, 1980. $8.95; New York: Avon, 1981. $2.95 (paper).

The authors argue that the three prime inflation-beating vehicles are houses, gold, and foreign currencies. Other good buys are collectibles and short-term money market instruments such as treasury bills. Oversimplified and somewhat outdated.

Weiss, Martin. *The Great Money Panic: A Guide for Survival and Action.* Westport, CT: Crown/Arlington House, 1981. 256 pp. $15.95.

The "great money panic" is entirely different from anything yet experienced. It is "a boomerang reaction to decades of accelerated expansion; an outpouring of stockpiled goods; a sudden contraction in consumption, production and distribution; an historic shift in values and behavior patterns; and most important, an explosive demand for cash." Weiss points to the accumulation of $4.4 trillion in bonds, mortgages, and loans that threatens to sabotage every economic policy of the government. The solution lies in avoiding problem banks, sticking with 24-hour liquidity, and avoiding long maturities. Intriguing, hyperbolic writing.

White, Robert. (ed.). *The Duck Book: Investment for Survival in the 1980's.* New York: Morrow, 1982. 192 pp. $15; $6.50 (paper).

White is the editor of *Duck Book* magazine and Head Duck of the Duck Clubs and the Duck movement. In this fascinating potpourri of contributions, he blends political conservatism with libertarian philosophy: "Your freedom, and your ability to make an honest buck in a free-enterprise system, is your most valuable asset, and *that* you can take to the bank." Some 40 articles by various authors cover such topics as gold, Swiss banking, estate planning, coins, effects of interest rates on inflation, choosing a survival location, and the biggest profit earners for 1982. Challenging and provocative. Recommended.

MONEY AND THE FAMILY

Burkett, Larry. *The Financial Planning Workbook.* Burkett Financial Planning Series. Chicago: Moody Press, 1982. 76 pp. $6.95 (paper).

A very simple, illustrated workbook to show how to devise a workable plan for home money management "that brings the financial area under God's control and relieves the burdens of worry, frustration and anxiety." Clear discussion of budgets, spending analysis and guidelines, allocation and control of spending, discipline, and simple accounting procedures. Good cartoon-style illustrations.

Dayton, Howard. *Your Money: Frustration or Freedom?* Wheaton, IL: Tyndale House, 1979. 160 pp. $2.95 (paper).

A biblical guide to earning, saving, spending, investing, and giving. Dayton points out that one out of every ten Bible verses talks about money, lending, or saving, and 16 of the 38 parables are concerned with how to handle money and possessions. With liberal quotations from the Bible, Dayton applies biblical principles to problems of debt, investing, budgeting, sharing, and money management.

Felix, Joseph. *It's Easier for a Rich Man to Enter Heaven Than for a Poor Man to Remain on Earth.* Nashville, TN: Nelson, 1981. 203 pp. $4.95 (paper).

Money management from a Christian point of view—the best way to provide for tomorrow is to give generously of today's surplus to those who need it. Concern for others must be accompanied by prudent and wise conservation of limited resources. Felix offers specific suggestions on how to save money on food, clothing, housing, utilities, income tax, education, medical bills, insurance, and recreation.

J. K. Lasser Tax Institute. *J. K. Lasser's Financial Planning for Your Family.* New York: Simon & Schuster/Cornerstone Library, 1979. 160 pp. $2.95 (paper). O.P.

The basics: how to develop a financial program, how and when to save money, using credit wisely, buying a home, selecting investments, shopping for life insurance, and retirement planning. Requires updating.

Kilgore, James E. *Dollars and Sense: Making Your Money Work for You and Your Family.* Nashville, TN: Abingdon Press, 1982. 144 pp. $5.95 (paper).

An analysis of money management within the context of family growth and enrichment. Kilgore, a marriage and family therapist, shows how money is related to family life, security, happiness, personal relationships, and togetherness. Specific suggestions made to reduce money conflict include improving communication and increased participation in spending and savings decisions.

Mumford, Amy. *It Only Hurts between Paydays: A Practical, Exciting, and Fun Plan for Getting Control of Your Personal Finances.* 2nd Edition. Denver: Accent Books, 1981. 160 pp. $2.95 (paper).

The story of Mike and Lynn, two terrific young people with a shaky five-year marriage, a three-year old son, and an inability to manage their finances. Money management from the Christian point of view, including a discussion of establishing goals, controlling credit, learning to say "I can't afford it," budgeting, and tithing. Simple and hopeful.

Thomason, James. *Common Sense about Your Family Dollars*. Wheaton, IL: Victor Books, 1979. 132 pp. $3.95 (paper).
Thomason, an administrator in a Baptist church, analyzes money management problems, budgeting, debt, clothing, insurance, and wills within the family setting and shows how difficulties can be overcome. His book is part of the Family Concern Series dealing with major questions confronting Christian families today. Elementary presentation.

VanArsdale, Mary G. *A Guide to Family Financial Counseling: Credit, Debt and Money Management*. The Dorsey Professional Series. Homewood, IL: Dow Jones-Irwin, 1982. 400 pp. $29.95.
A book about money and the problems that money can cause for individuals and their families written to help family financial therapists understand the complex web of credit, debt, and money management. VanArsdale analyzes the sources and types of credit, the collection process, insurance, bankruptcy, savings, and investment to provide a context for her discussion of how financial counseling can assist clients in resolving their financial problems. An interesting analysis of how people can be helped to use and spend their money more effectively.

WOMEN AND MONEY

Ackerman, Diane. *Getting Rich: A Smart Woman's Guide to Successful Money Management*. New York: A & W, 1981. 288 pp. $11.95.
Argues convincingly that money matters can be easily comprehended by any intelligent, thinking woman to achieve financial independence. Women should overcome any emotional commitment to the belief that only men can master money management. Ackerman discusses financial planning; how family relationships have to be taken into account (single/married/divorced/cohabitating); and how to maximize one's assets through financial investments, real estate, art, and so on. A chapter entitled "Live-in Lovers, 'Palimony,' and Vanishing Husbands" offers some terse advice: ". . . act quickly. Try to find your vanishing spouse, but meanwhile start legal proceedings to protect your flanks . . . your passivity could give him time to relocate." Strongly feminist. Interesting.

Ackerman, Diane. *The Only Guide You'll Ever Need to Marry Money*. New York: Simon & Schuster/Fireside, 1982. 150 pp. $8.95 (paper).
Feigning the lofty purpose of showing women how to cope with the responsibilities of marrying into money, Ackerman focuses her attention on practical strategies calculated to attract and ensnare a wealthy mate: how to recognize money (clothing, life-style) and acquire a basic financial knowledge (read the *Wall Street Journal* and

Forbes), techniques of meeting men with money (clubs, fitness centers, jogging, first-class lounges at airports), and the use of sex—"exploiting your sexuality to attract, ensnare and marrying money is nothing to be ashamed of." Ackerman also analyzes risks and pitfalls (risk/gain ratio) with reference to alcohol, drugs, psychological problems, and extramarital sex; what you have to give up in marriage; how to use linguistic leverage to smoke out a proposal; and how to get your fair share in a marriage by protecting your interest in your husband's assets. As a bonus, Ackerman relates her own early marriage, divorce, subsequent remarriage, and financial experiences. A crass and tasteless book likely to offend many people.

Brien, Mimi. *Moneywise*. New York: Bantam, 1982. 320 pp. $3.50 (paper).
Starting with the premise "Never, never take it for granted that a man knows more about money than you do," Brien shows how to become a financially responsible woman. She shows how to get organized, set goals, obtain the best deal in banking services, secure loans, apply for credit, select the best investment opportunities, finance a home, and be a full financial partner in a marriage (or divorce). A sensible, well-written, and elementary presentation of what it takes to be a financially smart and secure woman.

Briles, Judith. *The Woman's Guide to Financial Savvy*. New York: St. Martin's Press, 1981. 192 pp. $10.95; 1982. 240 pp. $6.95 (paper).
The author, president of her own financial planning company, shares some of her expertise and knowledge accumulated in ten years as broker, financial counselor, and money manager. Briles maintains that the same skills that help women choose the best goods in a market can be applied to the stock exchange. Topics include how to assess your assets and how to invest them in the stock market, real estate, and limited partnerships; how to pay the lowest possible taxes; how to cope with inflation; and how to get and make the best use of credit. Highly informative and detailed presentation for the more independent and sophisticated woman. Recommended.

Lee, Steven J., and Hassay, Karen A. *Women's Handbook of Independent Financial Management*. New York: Van Nostrand, 1979. 182 pp. $12.95.
The authors maintain that many women have a problem with money management because they have been directed solely into household economics and have insufficient background in other forms of money management. To remedy the deficiency, Lee and Hassay provide basic information on budgets, credit, stock, options, bonds, real estate, banking, taxation, and insurance. The four chapters on investment—covering types of stock, selecting a broker, judging a company, options and bonds—are clear and informative. Glossary. Tutorial style; easy reading.

Lumb, Fred A. *What Every Woman Should Know about Finances*. Rockville Center, NY: Farnsworth, 1978. 163 pp. $8.95; New York: Berkley, 1979. $2.25 (paper).
A pedestrian discussion of the essentials of spending and saving, insurance, credit, real estate, wills, and trusts. In many matters, it is considerably outdated. Inferior to Judith Briles, *The Woman's Guide to Financial Savvy* (see above), and Carole Phillips, *The Money Workbook for Women: A Step-by-Step Guide to Managing Your Personal Finances* (see p. 48).

Mackevich, Gene. *The Woman's Money Book: How to Make Your Money Grow.* Washington, D.C.: Acropolis, 1979. $14.95; $7.95 (paper); New York: Bantam, 1981. 224 pp. $2.95 (paper).

The author believes that "women have been sheltered, underestimated, ignored, deceived, and even ripped off by a male-dominated system that has denied many of them the opportunity to learn to manage money." Mackevich, a stockbroker, covers familiar territory: stocks, bonds, gold, options, real estate, tax shelters, deferred annuities. Most of the content is better presented elsewhere.

Minkow, Rosalie. *Money Management for Women.* New York: Playboy Paperbacks, 1981. 256 pp. $2.50 (paper).

A handy primer to help women catch up with men in financial expertise. The book is intended to show women how to take a yearly inventory of net worth; how to reconcile a checking account; how to make up a budget; how to obtain credit and keep a good credit rating; how to invest; how to purchase insurance; how to be informed on taxes; how to plan for retirement; and when and how to complain. Consciousness-raising writing aimed at teaching women to be assertive and responsible in money matters.

Perkins, Gail, and Rhoades, Judith. *The Women's Financial Survival Handbook.* New York: New American Library/Plume, 1980. 285 pp. $5.95 (paper).

Practical, survival know-how for "every woman" to enable her to take charge of her own financial life. Covers careers and employment; obtaining credit cards and loans; picking a bank; buying stocks, insurance, houses, and cars; social security payments and benefits; retirement planning (IRA and Keogh plans); estate planning; how to avoid being left a widow without assets. Sensible advice.

Phillips, Carole. *The Money Workbook for Women: A Step-by-Step Guide to Managing Your Personal Finances.* New York: Arbor House, 1982. 158 pp. $13; $5.95 (paper).

A very simple and readable primer for women on financial planning covering saving, borrowing, insurance, investment, retirement planning, and estate and tax planning. Clear directions are given on how much and where to save, how to read the stock market page, how to calculate a return on a real estate investment, what kind of life insurance to buy, how to plan for retirement, and so on. Lucid and concise explanation likely to help women take better control of their finances. The author is president of a financial management and consulting firm and teaches courses on women and money. Recommended.

Rogers, Mary. *Women, Divorce and Money: Plain Talk about Money, Procedures, Settlement, Financial Survival for Women Who Are Divorced or Thinking about Divorce.* New York: McGraw-Hill, 1981. 228 pp. $10.95; 1982. $4.95 (paper).

This book is intended to remedy a situation in which women have been programmed to believe that money and its management are the privilege only of males. Women must be prepared to fight for their rights as equal partners in a marriage. Rogers argues that the transaction of divorce is probably the most important financial event that will occur in a woman's life. Her advice is to read the rules pertaining to temporary support, division of property, custody and support of children, and guidelines for settlement. She provides specific instructions on obtaining the essential information concerning the husband's finances, estimating his assets, preparing a budget, choosing an attorney, maintaining credit, obtaining support money, preparing a new will, coping with interrogatories and depositions, negotiating and dividing assets such as money, real estate, personal property, and pension benefits. An excellent, realistic book for women with an overriding message: Don't sell yourself down the river! Highly recommended.

Rogers, Mary, and Joyce, Nancy. *Women and Money.* San Francisco: San Francisco Book Company, 1978. 218 pp. $8.95; New York: Avon, 1979. 176 pp. $2.25 (paper).

This book has a basic premise: Every woman must face the fact that she is probably going to be alone at some time in her life, either because of death or divorce. Consequently, women must take responsibility for their financial future. Writing from a woman's point of view, the authors discuss in simple terms the importance of financial record keeping, life insurance, annuities, automobile insurance, investments, real estate (buying and selling a home), tax sheltering (IRA, Keogh), retirement, divorce, and death. Good basic information to ensure that the woman alone makes sound financial decisions.

Schlayer, Mary E., with Cooley, Marilyn. *How to Be a Financially Secure Woman.* New York: Ballantine, 1978. 206 pp. $2.95 (paper).

Informs women how to get money, how to keep it, and how to make it grow. Particularly helpful are the chapters on the economics of money when married or cohabitating, special tips for the widow or divorcee, the dynamics of being single, and wills. Provides most useful checklists, suggestions, instructions, computations, and guidance. One of the better books on money management for women, although it needs updating.

Simons, Gustave, and Simons, Alice. *Money and Women.* New York: Popular Library, 1979. 287 pp. $2.75 (paper).

A how-to-do-it book directed toward the financially unsophisticated woman calculated to help her escape from financial slavery and become an equal partner with men in the world of personal finance. Covers spending, investing, borrowing, insurance, retirement planning, marriage, divorce, and how to select professional advisers such as accountants, lawyers, and insurance agents.

CHILDREN AND MONEY

Davis, Ken, and Taylor, Tom. *Kids and Cash: Solving a Parent's Dilemma.* New York: Bantam, 1981, 320 pp. $2.95 (paper).

A most sensible and helpful book that offers parents clear and consistent policies in giving money to their children. Suggests a reasonable allowance system and explains why parents should bring their children into the family partnership by sharing with them a reasonable understanding of the family budget. Other chapters are directed toward the children: Where Jobs Come From, How Competition Works, Why People Pay Taxes, How Inflation Affects Us, and the Importance of Saving and Investing. Particularly helpful are the chapters that explain to children how to advertise for jobs such as pulling weeds, car washing, painting house numbers on curbs, washing windows, knife sharpening, and so on. Informative, readable, and humorous. Recommended.

Landau, Elaine. *The Smart Spending Guide for Teens.* New York: Messner, 1982. 127 pp. $9.29.
Advice for teenagers on budgeting, correct use of credit, shopping for clothing, financing an education, purchasing groceries, banking services, and consumer rights. Sensible and highly readable. The author is a librarian in the New York Public Library system. Recommended.

MacGregor, Malcolm. *Training Your Children to Handle Money.* Minneapolis, MN: Bethany House, 1980. 144 pp. $3.95.
Allowances, part-time jobs, family spending, saving, and financial responsibility for children according to the Scriptures. The author identifies "the kind of attitudes and approaches God commends toward our money and how those apply to the training of children."

MAKING MONEY AT HOME

Bierbrier, Doreen. *Living with Tenants: How to Happily Share Your House with Renters for Profit and Security.* Arlington, VA: Housing Connection (Box 5536, Arlington, VA 22205), 1983. 128 pp. $7.
Taking a tenant into your home is profitable in that the tenant pays rent and a share of the utility bills. In addition, "tenants can help you with the household chores; they can provide a measure of security if you would otherwise live alone; and they can take in the mail and feed the cat when you are on vacation." Bierbrier concisely covers the practical details: selecting a house to buy, finding responsible tenants, drawing up a rental agreement on the basis of a fair rent, complying with zoning laws, and the tax implications. A sensible approach to the many business and human relations problems that can be encountered.

Howard, Alice, and Howard, Alfred. *Turn Your Kitchen into a Gold Mine.* New York: Harper & Row/Stellar Books, 1981. 325 pp. $12.95.
How to make money at home by selling master-size chocolate chip cookies, six-foot party sandwiches, roast turkey and all the trimmings, home-made baked beans, hearty sausages, gourmet meals, and so on. Good money making ideas for the "Kitchen Ladies of America."

Income Opportunities (eds.). *Dollars on Your Doorstep: How to Run a Business from Your Own Home.* New York: Stein & Day, 1978. 208 pp. $4.95 (paper).
Ideas on how to make money from harvesting timber to paper hanging, operating a cat hotel and pet taxi service, running a horse camp for kids, making candles, assembling kits for others, and more. Imaginative.

King, Norman. *Turn Your House into a Money Factory*. New York: Quill, 1982. 225 pp. $6 (paper).

King suggests and illustrates some exciting alternatives to addressing envelopes: baking for profit, rug weaving, soap opera writer, indexer, home typist, piano teacher, accounting, running a pet cemetery, renting out rooms. Also described are how to set up a business, secure a loan, advertise, and deal with the IRS. Imaginative.

Traister, Robert, and Ingram, Rich. *Making Money with Your Microcomputer*. Summit, PA: TAB Books, 1982. 152 pp. $7.95 (paper).

The authors offer 33 practical ways to make money at home with a microcomputer, including compiling unit pricing information for local supermarkets, operating a lost pet service, record keeping for churches and synagogues, maintaining baby-sitter listings, preparing mailing lists, and so on. Good, practical ideas and software for innovative people who would like to work at home.

PSYCHOLOGY OF MONEY

Berg, Adriane. *Moneythink: Financial Planning Finally Made Easy*. New York: Pilgrim Press, 1982. 256 pp. $13.95.

Berg, an attorney and financial planner, urges you to relax about money and realize your own personal psychology. Her objective is to show how to think clearly and without emotional conflict about money, how you can earn it, how you invest it, and how you spend it. Guidance is given on estate planning, wills, probate, taxes, trusts, gifts, life insurance, investments, and retirement planning. Despite the lofty aim of imparting the confidence and motivation to cope with money, this is a very pedestrian treatment. Disappointing.

Charell, Ralph. *The Magic of Thinking Rich*. New York: Simon & Schuster, 1981. 204 pp. $12.95.

For those who never travel first class, but know that it is the only way to go, and for those who yearn for the best food and drink in a setting of fine crystal and china. Charell describes how to develop money consciousness, a catalytic agent in fortune building that can also enhance the enjoyment of wealth; how to choose ways best calculated to multiply money; and how and when to bet, call, raise, and fold. Dubious psychology, with very little magic.

Colman, Carol. *Love and Money: What Your Finances Say about Your Personal Relationships*. New York: Coward-McCann and Geoghegan, 1983. 300 pp. $15.95.

A novelty book stressing the feminist point of view—who should have charge of the checkbook and make financial decisions—and illustrating how money management influences dependence, independence, and fulfillment. A good discussion of the financial implications of divorce and live-in relationships. Unusual.

Gillies, Jerry. *MoneyLove: How to Get the Money You Deserve for Whatever You Want*. New York: Evans, 1978. 168 pp. $7.95; New York: Warner, 1979. 208 pp. $2.95 (paper).

Argues that money is an extension of one's personality and that the more loving one is, the more money one will attract. The goal is to get the most for one's money in terms of pleasure and by building a positive frame of mind to produce more money creatively. Only a brief glimpse into the psychology of money.

Goldberg, Herb, and Lewis, Robert T. *Money Madne$$: The Psychology of Saving, Spending, Loving and Having Money.* New York: Morrow, 1978. 265 pp. $8.95.
Explores the self-destructive patterns, magical notions, and unrealistic fantasies that surround and generate people's money attitudes. Readable analysis of assorted money games, gambits, ploys, pastimes and the paradoxes, hypocrisies, inconsistencies, illusions, and lies connected with money. Interesting.

Judd, Stanley H. *Think Rich.* New York: Dell, 1980. 212 pp. $2.50 (paper).
The key to making money lies in understanding the psychology of money. Judd identifies and describes six personality profiles reflecting different money attitudes: poverty attitude, clerk's attitude, middle income attitude, executive's attitude, entrepreneur's attitude, and millionaire's attitude. To raise one's attitude from a middle income to an executive's or millionaire's attitude, Judd offers lessons in the basics of successful money management (buy a pocket calculator, keep clear accurate records, etc.). Half-baked psychology leavened with simplistic financial advice.

Juroe, David. *Money: How to Spend Less and Have More.* Old Tappan, NJ: Revell/ Power Books, 1981. 192 pp. $4.95 (paper).
An analysis of overspending behavior and why people become "spendaholics." Juroe believes that living beyond our means is not the answer to meeting the crises of life. After describing the psychological types of spenders and their spending habits, he enumerates the basic warning signals for those caught in the spending trap. The conclusion is that spiritual values and deep relationships rather than an attachment to "things" make life meaningful. A psychological and spiritual prescription for overspending and poor money management.

Lindgren, Henry. *Great Expectations: The Psychology of Money.* Los Altos, CA: Kaufmann, 1980. 262 pp. $13.95.
A psychologist analyzes the part money plays in human behavior and provides a fascinating insight into borrowing, lending, spending, giving, saving, investing, and other areas of human activity involving money. Lindgren also discusses money and its relationship to self-worth and mental health. Worth spending money on.

Maital, Shlamo. *Minds, Markets, and Money: Psychological Foundations of Economic Behavior.* New York: Basic Books, 1982. 320 pp. $14.37.
Maital, an Israeli economist educated at Princeton, applies psychology to explain why productivity has slowed and why some people become wealthy while others squander and gamble. He also discusses the reasons for persistent inflation, increased tax evasion, and savings shortages. Of particular interest are the chapters on people as consumers. A fascinating account of the relationship between psychology and social and economic problems. Highly recommended for the sophisticated reader.

Segall, Mark, and Tobin, Margaret. *How to Make Love to Your Money.* New York: Delacorte, 1982. 96 pp. $6.95.

All you need to know about fondling your funds, indulging in money lust, and fiduciosexuality! A fabulous spoof on personal finance and money management featuring financial fantasies, bulls and bears do it, playdough, the mystic tome entitled "The Way of the Dow," spending orgies, secluded spots for a tryst with your trust fund. Delightful. Highly recommended.

Weinstein, Bob. *Winning the Battle with Your Money Hang-Ups.* New York: Wiley, 1982. 162 pp. $7.95 (paper).

Advice on how to develop a healthy attitude toward money. Covers money in relation to personal worth, careers, failure, gambling, miserly behavior, success, fantasies, and prosperity. Weinstein shows how to build a prosperity consciousness, develop positive thinking, set realistic goals, get out of debt, and adopt inflation-fighting tactics. Pop psychology applied to financial behavior. Not very illuminating.

CREDIT AND BORROWING MONEY

Clark, Cathy. *Credit!* Fountain Valley, CA: Eden Press, 1982. 45 pp. $7.95 (paper).

An aggressive approach to winning in the credit game. Clark describes the rules—as formulated by the lenders who set the rules—and shows how to measure up to their notions of a good credit player. Credit worthiness is calculated according to a number of factors, such as stability of income, age, expenses, and debt record. A strategy is outlined for achieving the financial reforms necessary to provide an AAA credit rating within 30 days. The method advocated involves an investment of $400 and the shifting of this sum between three bank loans obtained for demonstrating a payment record. Sensible advice on credit cards and consumer rights.

Galanoy, Terry. *Charge It: Inside the Credit Card Conspiracy.* New York: Putnam's, 1981. 264 pp. $11.95.

A carefully compiled accumulation of information about the bank card industry. Galanoy was director of Communications of National Bankamericard (later VISA). By mid-1980, 79 million U.S. residents held more than 125 million VISA and Mastercards. In 1979, card users spent $151 billion with credit cards. The author analyzes the economics of the credit card industry and has some useful suggestions as to how one can save money, mainly involving restraint in the use of credit cards.

Gibbs, Gerald. *The Complete Guide to Credit and Loans: Everything You Should Know about Successful Borrowing.* New York: Playboy Paperbacks, 1982. 224 pp. $2.95 (paper).

Americans are hooked on credit to the extent that buy-now-pay-later is the prevalent philosophy. Credit becomes of paramount importance as we move into a cashless society. In this book, Gibbs offers a very concise yet thorough review of the major types of credit (unsecured loans, single-payment loans, credit cards, secured loans), where to obtain credit (commercial banks, sales finance companies, credit unions), computing the cost of credit, credit contracts, how to apply for a loan and consumer protection. Particularly helpful is the chapter on overextended credit and bankruptcies in which Gibbs explores the causes of overextension and last-ditch measures that can be taken to avoid the ultimate disaster, bankruptcy. One long appendix reprints numerous credit forms, personal financial statements, and loan application forms, but the absence of accompanying explanation makes for a complete wastage of some 63 pages.

Graver, Fred. *Get Out of Debt Now: How to Gain Control of Your Financial Affairs Once and for All.* Boston: Little, Brown, 1982. 240 pp. $11.95.

Relief for those receiving dunning notices in the mail, frequent calls from collectors, juggling payments to creditors, or for those beleaguered by the American way of debt. Graver carefully explains how people get into debt; figuring your present financial position; coping with emergency situations (receipt of a dunning letter, harassment, legal action, wage garnishment, repossession, and deficiency judgment); developing a debt management program and sticking to it; credit bureaus and credit reports; sources of credit available from bank cards, charge cards, credit unions, finance companies, and pawnshops; collection agencies; consumer rights; bankruptcy; life after debt. Proven, practical, and useful advice on credit, debt, and good financial management. Definitely the best book on credit. Highly recommended.

Gross, Robin, and Cullen, Jean. *Help: The Basics of Borrowing Money.* New York: Times Books, 1980. 178 pp. $9.95. O.P.

How to become an informed shopper for other people's money. Describes who should borrow, valid and wrong reasons for borrowing, how to add up one's assets, the cost of borrowing, ten major sources of money (friends and relatives, life insurance loans, commercial banks, savings banks, brokers, credit unions, etc.), financing a home, borrowing for education, raising money to start a business, and consumers' rights. Sensible, practical advice.

Johnson, Bert. *Bert Johnson's Credit Loopholes: An Instant Credit Guide.* San Francisco: Harbor, 1982. 112 pp. $4.95 (paper).

A book for those caught in the credit squeeze. Johnson outlines a number of strategies for restoring and maintaining credit and claims that for the price of a stamp and 30 minutes' work, anyone can have bank cards, department store cards, and other cards within two weeks. The author is president of United Credit Consultants.

Johnson, Bert. *Credit: Get It, Use It, Stretch It, Save It.* San Francisco: Harbor, 1981. 180 pp. $9.95 (paper).

Johnson explains simply how to apply for credit, how to obtain credit cards, how to establish credit if you are a married woman, how credit reporting agencies operate, what your credit file contains, how collection agencies work, and what to do when you are unable to pay. Useful appendixes summarize consumer credit laws and enforcement, list Federal Trade Commission regional offices and consumer credit counseling services, with sample bankruptcy forms. Useful as a guide in maintaining a healthy credit rating.

Nelson, Paula. *Where to Get Money for Everything: A Complete Guide to Today's Money Sources*. New York: Morrow, 1982. 279 pp. $12.

A very concise and informative summary of the principal sources of money for personal loans, paying off creditors, financing cars and homes, home improvement loans, education, grants, and businesses. Sensible and simple advice on how to borrow money, use credit cards effectively, debt consolidation, maintaining good credit, negotiating loans. Useful overview.

Prochnow, Herbert V. (ed.). *Bank Credit: An Indepth Study of Credit or Loan Practices by 30 Outstanding Banking Authorities*. New York: Harper & Row, 1981. 448 pp. $24.95.

A collection of essays on a wide variety of topics, including types of loans, how applications are processed, sources of credit information, and risk factors. A rather academic presentation.

Walker, Glen. *Credit Where Credit Is Due: A Legal Guide to Your Credit Rights and How to Assess Them*. New York: Holt, Rinehart & Winston, 1979. 208 pp. $10.95; $4.95 (paper).

Credit is here to stay: In 1978, consumers owed $223 billion in debt to banks, retailers, credit card companies, finance companies, and credit unions. This book supplies essential information on types of credit cards, what happens if a card is lost or stolen, truth-in-lending, women and credit, how to stand up to the credit bureau, how to halt time payments on defective merchandise, how to correct billing errors, how to battle bill collectors, and how to cope with repossession, garnishment, and bankruptcy. Good advice on what to do if you are turned down for credit or a loan and how to establish a perfect credit rating. An appendix provides a partial listing of consumer credit counseling services. An excellent consumer book showing how to take advantage of the recent credit laws. Recommended.

STUDENT FINANCIAL AID

Donald, Bruce. *Cutting College Costs: The Up-to-the-Minute Manual for 1983-1984*. New York: Dutton, 1982. 128 pp. $5.25 (paper).

A high school guidance counselor focuses on the crucial question: How can parents purchase the most appropriate education for their child at the lowest price? Donald explains the mechanics of financial aid, how eligibility is determined, need-based aid programs, college comparison shopping, cooperative education, military academies, foreign study, "no-need" scholarships (academic, athletic, etc.). Particularly valuable is the chapter on "best buys" in which Donald identifies 20 institutions offering quality education at reasonable prices and 40 additional good buys. An appendix lists merit scholarships awarded without regard to financial need. Practical, useful presentation. Recommended.

Kornfeld, Leo L. et al. *How to Beat the High Cost of Learning: The Complete and Up-to-Date Guide to Student Financial Aid*. New York: Rawson Wade, 1981. 310 pp. $13.95; $7.95 (paper).

A comprehensive guide to the billions of dollars in financial aid still available. The authors claim that "there is something for everybody with few exceptions." The following are explained in detail: federal grants—the Pell Grant and Basic Educational Opportunity Grant (BEOG); Supplemental Educational Opportunity Grant (SEOG); State Student Incentive Grant (SSIG); Scholarships in Health Services; federal loans—Parents' Loan for Undergraduate Students (PLUS); Guaranteed Student Loan Program (GSL); National Direct Student Loan Program (NDSL); Health Education Assistance Loan (HEAL); Nursing Student Loan Program; the College Work Study Program (CWSP); veterans and social security benefits; state financial aid; private sources of financial aid; and support for special students such as the handicapped. Answers the essential questions: Can I qualify? If so, for which programs? How much money can I get? What must I do in order to get the money? An excellent survey of financial aid programs and eligibility. Highly recommended.

Lane, Paul. *The Dow Jones-Irwin Guide to College Financial Planning.* Homewood, IL: Dow Jones-Irwin, 1981. 285 pp. $14.95.
Presents more than most people will ever need to know about financial aid. Highly detailed and somewhat technical exposition of financial planning covering college costs (the family contribution), financial aid and taxable income, types of aid and packaging, sources of aid (federal, state, institutional, and private), loans, social security and veterans benefits, and the mechanics of the application process. Of more use to high school counselors, accountants, bank officers, and attorneys than to the average parent in that the essential facts are buried in a morass of detail.

Leider, Robert. *Don't Miss Out: The Ambitious Student's Guide to Scholarships and Loans.* 7th Edition, 1982-1984. Alexandria, VA: Octameron Associates, 1982. 60 pp. $2.50 (paper).
A wealth of helpful ideas, tips, suggestions, addresses, inflation savers, and programs calculated to help lower the costs of college. Outlines how to pick the right college and pinpoints sources of financial aid—the federal government, state, private organizations, employers, special scholarships—together with financial support available for minorities, the handicapped, women, and other special groups. Highly informative and detailed tables, charts, and diagrams indicate available aid and how best to obtain it. Answers most questions likely to be raised concerning scholarships and loans. Recommended.

Leider, Robert. *Your Own Financial Aid Factory: The Guide to Locating College Money.* Alexandria, VA: Peterson's Guides, 1982. 184 pp. $6.95 (paper).
Probably the best book on financial aid, crammed with factual information, hints, tips, sources of aid, addresses, phone numbers, worksheets, and more. Leider provides thorough and comprehensive coverage of eligibility; determination of financial needs; financial aid packages; federal, state, and private sources; money from employers and local communities; sources of money for brains, talent, and athletic prowess; money for minorities and women; merit scholarship; Pell and other federal grants; loans for medical training; cooperative education opportunities; and so on. A superb, factual, and informative treasure trove of information that focuses on the

basic issues: Am I eligible, and for how much? and How should I apply? Highly recommended.

Moore, Donald. *Money for College! How to Get It.* 2nd Edition. Woodbury, NY: Barron's Educational Series, 1982. 240 pp. $3.95 (paper).
Opportune advice for students, school counselors, and parents on how to finance a college education in view of the rising cost of such. Assesses college costs in various types of schools and describes application procedures, need analysis, major federal and state aid programs, student loan programs, veterans benefits, grants and scholarships, and aid for minority and disadvantaged students. Somewhat obsolescent.

BARTERING AND THE UNDERGROUND ECONOMY

Bawly, Dan. *The Subterranean Economy.* New York: McGraw-Hill, 1982. 187 pp. $19.95.
A rather technical explanation of the operation of the underground economy showing how the cash-and-barter economy works. Bawly reviews the many tax-avoidance schemes involving tax havens and tax shelters. In his view, inept government and inflation together feed the underground economy. The author is an Israeli and a certified public accountant.

Burkett, Larry, and Procter, William. *How to Prosper in the Underground Economy.* New York: Morrow, 1982. 288 pp. $11.50.
Like other crisis proponents, the authors believe that inflation and unchecked government spending, combined with a lack of individual financial discipline, will result in a devastating money collapse. The remedy advocated is not a rural hideout in the woods but the extensive use of the underground economy—a legal system based upon a network of channels of community support involving bartering arrangements, food cooperatives, and other sharing strategies. Burkett and Procter urge maintenance of close control over personal finances and the development of an economic self-help network to barter, share tools and other equipment, pool clothing, purchase food on a cooperative basis, develop self-employed ventures, and so on. More sensible than most of the doomsday books on the market.

Burtt, George. *The Barter Way to Beat Inflation.* New York: Everest House, 1980. 215 pp. $10.95; $6.95 (paper).
Burtt claims that virtually everything that a person needs to live can be provided by barter without payment of cash. He provides a checklist to determine one's aptitude for successful bartering. Examples of bartering are given together with various strategies. A list of active U.S. trade clubs is supplied. Useful resource for those wishing to get started in bartering activity.

Levinson, Jay. *Earning Money without a Job.* New York: Holt, Rinehart & Winston, 1979. 204 pp. $10.95; $4.95 (paper).

Making the transition from job earning to jobless earning is a tough decision to make. The economics of freedom offers no single way of earning money but is based on the concept of modular economics—devoting yourself not to just one job but to a number of pursuits. Almost anything that can be done full time can be done part time on a freelance basis. Levinson offers countless suggestions on how to position oneself, how to advertise, how to seek work with no capital, tiny capital, if you have a car. The ideas are varied: Sell waterbeds to motel owners, start a flea market, teach a class, write advertisements for houses, remove your clothes (nude modeling), feed an office (meal delivery), pan for gold, share a franchise, remove snow, renovate a house, offer bed and breakfast. Probably of more value as a means of supplementing regular income than as a method of replacement.

Long, Charles. *How to Survive without a Salary*. New York: Sterling (published by Horizon, Toronto), 1981. 232 pp. $6.95 (paper).
Long advocates a change in lifestyle from being a consumer to being a conserver that so reduces the need for cash that it can easily be met with casual income. The same techniques that allow one to live without a salary can also be used by all those desirous of bolstering an existing income. A very methodical and analytical method is outlined focusing upon defining needs, establishing objectives, and formulating money saving strategies. Good coverage is given to casual income, the secondhand market, auction buying, and tips on cheap clothing, furniture and appliances, and taxes and insurance. Good, imaginative, and sensible reading. Definitely superior to Jay Levinson, *Earning Money without a Job* (see p. 57).

Paulsen, Gary. *Beat the System: A Survival Guide*. New York: Pinnacle, 1983. 256 pp. $2.75 (paper).
How to survive outside the regular monetary system by means of barter, farming, improvising, and hunting. Deals with the basic necessities of food, clothing, and shelter. A book likely to appeal to those living in a rural setting.

Proulx, Annie. *What'll You Take for It: Back to Barter*. Charlotte, VT: Garden Way, 1980. 160 pp. $5.95 (paper).
There is much more to barter than mere profit. For many, barter gives the sense of security that goes with knowing that your own skills and products will supply many of life's necessities and pleasures. Barter is a satisfying and profitable arrangement for exchanging possessions and skills to the benefit of all. The author tells how to start bartering, how to place a value on skills to be bartered, how to join specialized barter groups, techniques for creative bartering, group barter organizations, and income tax requirements. Lists information sources, barter publications, trade clubs, and community barter organizations. Helpful hints and suggestions with amusing cartoons. Highly recommended.

Simm, Dyanne. *The Barter Book*. New York: Dutton/Sunrise, 1979. 152 pp. $4.95 (paper). O.P.
A guide to individual horse trading and swapping, collective bartering through clubs, networks, and exchanges, economics of barter, and how to set up a barter group. Lists barter organizations. Bibliography.

Simon, Carl P., and Witte, Ann D. *Beating the System: The Underground Economy.* Boston: Auburn House, 1981. 354 pp. $21.95; $12.95 (paper).
Two economists analyze the extent, mode of operation, and characteristics of the underground economy. Tax evasion accounts for approximately half of the underground economy's net income. Other sectors of the economy described are illegal immigration, the drug trade, fraud arson, illegal gambling, loan sharking, and prostitution. It is estimated that the national income of the underground economy in 1980 was $170 to $300 billion. An excellent exposition of what is a worldwide phenomenon.

Tuccille, Jerome. *Inside the Underground Economy: Over Twenty Million Americans Are Avoiding Income Taxes—And May Be Getting Away with It.* New York: New American Library, 1982. 168 pp. $2.50 (paper).
A combination of soaring inflation and high taxes has forced many otherwise law-abiding citizens to hide much of their income from the IRS. Moonlighting, bartering, and other techniques account for an estimated $700 billion in unreported income annually. Tuccille outlines the rise of the taxpayers' rebellion and shows how discounts are given for cash payments that cannot be traced and the use of cash-free barter exchanges. On a positive note, the author offers suggestions for legal profits through IRA accounts, All-Savers Certificates, and utilities dividend reinvestment.

Webster, Harriet, and Webster, Jonathan. *The Underground Marketplace: A Guide to New England and the Middle Atlantic States.* New York: Universe Books, 1981. 173 pp. $6.95 (paper).
The message conveyed is simple: "Whatever your budget and whatever your taste, there is a place for you in the underground marketplace, a buying or selling situation that actually makes you feel good about spending money." The Websters outline the opportunities available at country auctions, tax auctions, gallery sales, estate auctions, government surplus auctions, and so on. Junkyards suffer from an image problem. Readers are advised that the best way to appreciate a junkyard is to visit one. But beware of the dog!

COUPONING AND REFUNDING

Hayes, Mary Anne. *Ask the Coupon Queen: How to Buy Seventy-one Dollars and Seventy-one Cents Worth of Groceries for Seven Dollars and Nineteen Cents.* New York: Pocket Books, 1979. 192 pp. $2.25 (paper).
A centsational book, or how Mary Anne discovers cash in the trash! Hayes tells how she obtains, organizes, and uses labels, forms, exchange letters, refund offers, and coupons; how she gets refunds; and how to beat the system, legally. She explains how to comply with the qualifier requirements (purchase confirmation, quality seal, proof of purchase seal, tearoff strip, neck band, box top, UPC—Universal Product Code). Recommended for those with couponmania.

Samtur, Susan J., and Tuleja, Tad. *Cashing in at the Checkout.* New York: Warner, 1980. 152 pp. $1.95 (paper).

Samtur is the publisher of *Refundle Bundle*, a newsletter with more than 30,000 subscribers. She shows how to beat inflation and high prices by winning at the supermarket game through the liberal use of coupons, refunds, and special offers. She uses a question-and-answer format to respond to the most common questions and supplies a refunder's dictionary, lists of manufacturers' addresses, and refunding bulletins. Good supershopper savvy.

Samtur, Susan, with Tuleja, Tad. *Coupon Magic: The Beginner's Kit of Tricks for Slashing Supermarket Costs*. New York: Grosset & Dunlap/Stonesong Press, 1980. 58 pp. $4.95 (paper).
A crash course in couponing and refunding. Supershopping involves cash-off coupons, cash refunds, and free gifts. Supermarket shopping should be planned to use coupon collections arranged by shopping aisles (cereals, pet foods, canned goods, etc.). Full advantage should be taken of specially marked packages (SMPs), hang tags (HTs) on bottles and jars, and markdowns. Concise advice on how to get organized.

Sloane, Martin. *The Nineteen Eighty-One Guide to Coupons and Refunds*. New York: Bantam, 1981. 204 pp. $2.95 (paper).
Martin is the founder of the American Coupon Club. He shows how to plan supermarket shopping to take advantage of the 7,000 refund offers and more than 80 billion cash-off coupons distributed annually. He explains how to clip, file, and save coupons and thereby save at least $20 per week; how to obtain and use refund forms; proofs of purchase; sending for refunds; cashing in on cash-off coupons; "double-play discounts" (combining coupons and refund discounts); "triple play discounts" (combining a supermarket special, a cash-off coupon, and a refund offer); supermarket shopping strategies; trading refund forms by mail; and starting a coupon club. Reproduces many coupons and refund offers to illustrate the variety of savings possible. A comprehensive guide for those willing to take the necessary time and trouble in order to save money on their shopping safaris. Recommended.

SAVING ON TRAVEL

Brosnahan, Tom. *Frommer's How to Beat the High Cost of Travel*. 1982–1983 Edition. New York: Frommer/Pasmantier, 1982. 285 pp. $3.95 (paper).
Not a guide book but rather "a training course in successful travel," showing how to save money before leaving home, how to cut transportation costs, how to save money on the trip, how to shop for bargains, and more. The information is both concise and useful: sources of free information, choosing a guidebook (look for prices, phone numbers, and directions), selecting and getting value at hotels, restaurant dining (eat what and where the locals eat), exchange rates and getting money from home, cutting down on the telephone surcharges. Little attention is given to unscrambling the complexity of air fares, and consumer rights are not even mentioned, two major flaws of what is otherwise a valuable book.

Gieseking, Hal. *The Complete Handbook for Travelers*. New York: Pocket Books, 1979. 377 pp. $7.95 (paper).

How to save lots of money on airlines, hotels and resorts, tours, rental cars, and cruises. This is a splendid book that spells out the pitfalls and deceptions often found in advertising for tours and cruises (for example, differences among escorted tour, hosted tour, and package tour; the age of major cruise ships). Special problems—sending your pet by air, lost luggage, crime, customs, travel insurance—are also discussed. Sources of free travel literature are listed and rated according to the quality of information supplied. Contains a consumer's travel dictionary, answers to most common travel questions, and electric voltages of the major countries. Highly recommended.

VanMeer, Mary, and Pasquarelli, Michael. *Free Attractions, USA*. Charlotte, NC: East Woods Press, 1982. 446 pp. $8.95 (paper).

How to take advantage of the thousands of free attractions in the United States—art galleries, museums, parks, gardens, natural wonders, zoos, bird sanctuaries, historical sites, tours, exhibits, churches. Listings are alphabetical within state. A good source of money-saving information to supplement the conventional travel guides.

Weintz, Caroline, and Weintz, Walter. *The Discount Guide for Travelers over 55*. New York: Dutton, 1981. 224 pp. $5.75 (paper).

A listing of discounts available for those over 55, with proof of age, for hotels, restaurants, museums, car rental agencies, and various attractions. Listings are by state. It is not clear whether the discount coupons bound in the back of the book represent paid listings. Of limited use in relation to changing conditions of the economy.

STRIKING IT RICH

Kaplan, H. Roy. *Lottery Winners: How They Won and How Winning Changed Their Lives*. New York: Harper & Row, 1978. 173 pp. $9.95.

Case histories of winners: what happened to them, how they spent their money, how their jobs, lifestyles, relations with families, friends, and coworkers were transformed—based on interviews of more than 100 winners in five states. The more popular expenditures were on cars, new homes, and remodeling of existing homes. In many instances, the fortunes acquired were rapidly dissipated due to poor money management.

LeBlanc, Terry, and LeBlanc, Rena. *Suddenly Rich*. Englewood Cliffs, NJ: Prentice-Hall, 1978. 191 pp. $8.95. O.P.

The true stories of ordinary men and women from all walks of life, from all parts of the country, who suddenly became rich—through a lottery, inheritance, marriage—and what it did to their lives. In a series of actual case histories, the authors show that lotteries are the purest form of instant wealth offering an escape from the rat race of struggling with bills, mortgages, and car payments. Supplies interesting insight into the truism that money does not sweep away all problems, dissolve personality flaws, sweeten human relationships, or deliver every heart's desire.

Tyndall, Carolyn, and Tyndall, Roger, with Tuleja, Tad. *And the Lucky Winner Is . . . A Complete Guide to Winning Contests and Sweepstakes.* New York: St. Martin's Press, 1982. 160 pp. $3.95 (paper).
A contest is always a promotion in which you have to demonstrate some skill or talent to win (baking a cake, writing a jingle), whereas a sweepstake is determined strictly by chance. The authors explain how contests and sweepstakes work and show why many are called but few are chosen. In general, it is necessary to enter often, follow the rules, and think "win." On a very specific level, instructions are given on how to maximize one's chances of winning—use of eye appeal and "feel" appeal in envelopes, flooding (multiple entries), adherence to block letters, and so on. The Tyndalls are editors of the *Contest Newsletter*. Useful for those who like sweepstaking and the fun of contesting.

BANKS AND BANKING

Brown, Fern. *The Great Money Machine: How Your Bank Works.* New York: Messner, 1981. 96 pp. $8.29 (grades 4–6).
A simple text for schoolchildren at the elementary level on banks and the operation of the banking system. Glossary.

Cook, John A., and Wool, Robert. *All You Need to Know about Banks.* New York: Bantam, 1983. 202 pp. $13.95.
An inside view of how banks operate and how bankers view loan applicants. The authors offer some intriguing advice on how to become a preferred customer, how to apply for loans, and how to use successfully the wide range of services provided. The title is a misnomer in that the main thrust of the book is how to cope with bankers. One chapter is entitled "How to Deal with a Frightened Banker: Take Him to Lunch." Good advice on how to get the most out of your bank and banker.

Kinsman, Robert. *Your New Swiss Bank Book.* Revised Edition. Homewood, IL: Dow Jones-Irwin, 1979. 299 pp. $19.95.
Kinsman outlines how the Swiss banking system operates; reasons for using Swiss banks—secrecy, stability, security, specialized services, and the strength of the franc; how one can open a Swiss bank account; Swiss banks in the two tax havens closer to the United States—the Bahamas and Cayman Islands; and how to select a Swiss bank.

Meyer, Martin. *Don't Bank on It: How to Make Up to 22% or More on Your Savings—All Fully Insured.* Rockville Center, NY: Farnsworth, 1979. 226 pp. $9.95; New York: Pocket Books, 1980. 240 pp. $2.50 (paper).
An inside look at how the banking system works. Meyer describes how to earn interest and take advantage of the "float," the clearance time before a check is re-

turned to the bank for payment; how to make money from the use of credit cards (charge, invest the money freed up, and then pay the credit card bill on time). Good ideas to make a little money, if one is mathematically inclined.

Roethenmund, Robert. *The Swiss Banking Handbook: A Complete Manual for Practical Investors.* New York: Books in Focus, 1980. 235 pp. $19.95.

A Swiss banker describes how Swiss banks operate and how they can be used profitably. Roethenmund analyzes the structure and operation of the Swiss National Bank, the five big banks, the 28 cantonal banks, and the regional, savings, and private banks. Detailed and authoritative information is given on how to select a bank, how to open an account, how to transfer funds (and the reporting required by the U.S. government concerning the international transportation of currency or monetary instruments), banking secrecy provisions, types of accounts, the essentials of conducting business with Swiss banks, tax implications, and restrictions. Also summarizes how to obtain residency and work permits and the requirements for citizenship. The most authoritative and best book available on Swiss banks. Highly recommended.

Thypin, Marilyn, and Glasner, Lynne. *Checking and Balancing: (Banking).* Consumer Education Series: No. 2. St. Paul, MN: EMC Corporation, 1980. 60 pp. $3.50 (paper).

Bert is a stock clerk in a department store; Rosa is a file clerk in a big office. To illustrate the principles of budgeting, spending, banking, and saving, this book relates their adventures at the restaurant, supermarket, savings and loan association, and bank. A very simple explanation of banking for elementary grades.

UNEMPLOYMENT BENEFITS

Honigsberg, Peter. *The Unemployment Benefits Handbook.* Reading, MA: Addison-Wesley, 1981. 158 pp. $5.95 (paper).

How the unemployment program works and the steps needed to collect benefits. The author, an attorney, explains eligibility, weekly benefits, extended benefits, in-state and interstate claims, legal rights, and coverage. Honigsberg also provides advice on how to cope with the unemployment bureaucracy, how to complete the forms with examples of answers to typical questions, and how to behave during the interview. Detailed information is also provided on the appeal process and how to present witnesses, subpoenas, and affidavits. An appendix summarizes coverage and benefit provisions by state. Informative, clear, and helpful. Highly recommended.

DEBT AND BANKRUPTCY

David, Ann. *Get Out and Stay Out of Debt.* New York: Simon & Schuster/ Cornerstone Library, 1980. 160 pp. $5.95 (paper).

A debt counselor spells out the reasons why people get into debt: ignorance, adapting to new, costly attitudes toward education, recreation and health, and so on. The author shows how to avoid credit card temptations and cope with emotional spending. The principal technique advocated is a money-control plan that is based on a budget to pinpoint exactly how much is spent for what and a checking account to control expenditures. A typical money-control plan is outlined for each decade of life, reflecting different objectives and needs. Detailed information is presented on legal rights to stop creditors from harassing you and steps that can be taken to avoid salary garnishments, repossessions, and foreclosures. The major features of Chapters 7 and 13 of the Bankruptcy Reform Act of 1978 are described. Useful information for both those in debt and for those tempted.

Girth, Marjorie. *Bankruptcy Options for the Consumer Debtor.* New York: Practicing Law Institute, 1981. 177 pp. $30.
A technical, legal examination of the alternatives that became available for consumer debtors whose bankruptcy cases were filed after October 1, 1979, as a result of the Bankruptcy Reform Act of 1978. A consumer debtor is defined as any individual not engaged in business when the bankruptcy proceeding is filed. Two options are detailed: Chapter 13, which results in a financial reorganization if the debtor is able to pay at least part of the accumulated obligations, and Chapter 7, which requires that the debtor's nonexempt assets be liquidated and distributed to unsecured creditors, but does not anticipate any further payments. Girth gives a good explanation of the structure of the system for administering bankruptcy cases. Authoritative; requires careful reading.

Kaplan, Melvin J., and Drotning, Phillip T. *How to Get Your Creditors Off Your Back without Losing Your Shirt.* Chicago: Contemporary Books, 1979. 205 pp. $9.95.
Summarizes the Bankruptcy Reform Act of 1978 and explains voluntary, negotiated repayment plans and court-supervised repayment plans under Chapter 13. Kaplan explains the procedures under Chapter 13, how to stop harassing phone calls from creditors, how to compel creditors to accept reduced payment schedules, how to halt repossessions, garnishments, and foreclosures, and how to get out of debt without materially reducing your standard of living. An appendix contains reproductions of the official forms used in filing Chapter 13 cases under the Federal Bankruptcy Code. Clear, nonlegal explanation.

Kaufman, Daniel. *How to Get Out of Debt: Without Despair and without a Lawyer.* Los Angeles: Pinnacle, 1981. 208 pp. $7.95 (paper).
For those with more bills than they can handle. A step-by-step guide showing how to protect your assets while making your own debt arrangements. A good outline is given on how to get out of debt without declaring bankruptcy—identifying most important creditors and paying them and making your own debt arrangements or seeking a credit counselor—and how the bankruptcy law applies if all else fails. Kaufman shows that relief techniques short of bankruptcy are directly tied to relief in bankruptcy. The steps taken to avoid bankruptcy are the steps that must be taken in

expectation of bankruptcy. Not as comprehensive as Janice Kosel, *Chapter 13: The Federal Plan to Repay Your Debts* (see below).

Kosel, Janice. *Bankruptcy: Do It Yourself.* Reading, MA: Addison-Wesley, 1980. 192 pp. $11.95.
A step-by-step guide for preparing and filing personal bankruptcy in federal or state courts. Explains how bankruptcy works, its effect on property and debts, which debts will be dissolved and which will be paid, alternatives to bankruptcy, how to summarize debts and complete the necessary forms, when an attorney is needed, meeting with creditors, and how to cope with the emotional side of bankruptcy. Provides a summary of state exemption statutes, definitions, bankruptcy checklist and forms, and a listing of states and cities in which bankruptcy courts are located. A clear exposition of the essential facts. Recommended.

Kosel, Janice. *Chapter 13: The Federal Plan to Repay Your Debts.* Berkeley, CA: Nolo Press, 1982. 152 pp. $12.95 (paper).
A do-it-yourself guide to Chapter 13 of the bankruptcy law that permits an individual under court supervision and protection to develop and perform a plan to pay his or her debts, in whole or in part, over a three-year period. Kosel reveals how to end creditor harassment, wage attachments, and other collection efforts by filing a Chapter 13 repayment plan. Step-by-step, Kosel explains the different kinds of debts and how they are treated under the law, the exemption system and personal property, and alternatives to filing a Chapter 13 plan. Line-by-line instructions are provided for completing the required Chapter 13 court forms. Also provided is a summary of state exemption statutes. A sobering, practical, and clear guide to Chapter 13 that will doubtless offer hope and assistance to those burdened with crushing debt. Highly recommended.

Nicholas, Ted. *How to Get Out of Debt.* Wilmington, DE: Enterprise, 1980. 146 pp. $12.95; $4.95 (paper).
The reasons for bankruptcy are manifold: divorce, sudden medical bills, lawsuits, prolonged unemployment, misuse of credit, and so on. Only one-quarter of bankruptcies involve lack of prudent financial management. Nicholas describes how to file for a debt readjustment plan (Chapter 13), psychological and financial factors in arriving at a decision to declare bankruptcy, commonly asked questions, and the necessary forms and how to complete them. The subject matter of this book is, however, covered more informatively and clearly elsewhere.

Rogers, Harry. *The American Bankruptcy Kit.* 2nd Edition. Carmel-by-the-Sea, CA: Lawkits, 1982. 208 pp. $11.95 (paper).
A step-by-step, do-it-yourself guide to the necessary procedures involved in bankruptcy: whether, in fact, bankruptcy is the solution, estimating property that can be kept, how to figure the financial benefits of bankruptcy, how to prepare and file the necessary papers, court appearances, and dealing with trustees and creditors. Although much can be done to prepare for bankruptcy, Rogers recommends that nobody should proceed with his or her own bankruptcy without one consultation

with a lawyer to be certain that the correct procedures have been followed. Contains worksheets and tear-out forms. More technical than Janice Kosel, *Bankruptcy: Do It Yourself* (see p. 65).

Silvers, William L., and Harkness, Richard M. *I Filed Bankruptcy and I'm Glad I Did.* 2nd Revised Edition. Muncie, IN: Bryden Press, 1979. 155 pp. $6.95 (paper).
Shows how a family in financial trouble can, legally and effectively, cure their immediate financial woes and recover in both the financial and emotional sense. Covers causes of financial collapse, plans for avoiding bankruptcy, how one files for consumer bankruptcy, Chapter 13, court-supervised debt consolidation, and how to reestablish credit. Answers most of the commonly asked questions about bankruptcy.

4

Investments and the Stock Market

INVESTMENTS: GENERAL

Aliber, Robert. *Your Money and Your Life: A Lifetime Approach to Money Management.* New York: Basic Books, 1982. 239 pp. $15.95.
Aliber argues that the investor has to match changes in attractive investment opportunities from one year to the next with the accumulation and eventual decline of wealth over a personal lifetime. "There is a personal life cycle: a time to accumulate and a time to spend. . . ." Although the author provides a good perspective and context for investment, reviewing the recent history of inflation, changes in the popularity of various types of stocks, rise and fall of gold and silver and so on, little positive guidance is given. One chapter is aptly entitled "Selling Advice Beats Buying Advice as a Way to Get Rich," in which the author points to the analogy between going to the racetrack and investing in the financial markets. Aliber argues that nobody ever suggested that the winner of the Illinois State Lottery had good insights. "The key question is whether the winners among the investment advisors have more skill and insight than the winners of the Irish Sweepstakes and the Illinois and New York lotteries." An amusing, well-written book that adds nothing to the traditional advice offered by the investment advisers criticized by the author.

Bondy, Susan. *How to Make Money Using Other People's Money.* Indianapolis, IN: Bobbs-Merrill, 1982. 228 pp. $12.95.
A financial consultant and syndicated columnist shows how to borrow money and make more money through suitable and profitable investment. "Cheap" sources of money include borrowing from life insurance, profit-sharing plans, credit unions,

commercial banks, second mortgage companies, finance companies, and stockbrokers. Bondy identifies degrees of risk and reviews a wide variety of investment opportunities (stocks, bonds, options). Five basic investment strategies are identified and illustrated: cost-saving strategies, no-risk strategies, low- to medium-risk strategies, inflation hedges, and high-risk strategies. A very readable and easy-to-understand discussion of the essentials of financial planning.

Bridwell, Rodger. *The Battle for Financial Security: How to Invest in the Runaway 80's.* New York: Times Books, 1980. 288 pp. $12.95.
How you can most effectively cope with an ever-expanding government and its handmaiden, inflation. Bridwell is bullish on the stock market and believes that the 1980–1990 decade will be the "bull market decade." He believes that stocks are a good hedge against inflation and argues that any nonregulated company with a high debt-to-equity ratio and low labor costs should be in an ideal position to prosper during the inflationary 1980s. Bridwell provides a list of 23 companies that have an almost unlimited potential for growth—the IBMs and Xeroxes of the future. A book that rambles without really getting to the point of its title.

Brown, Thomas E. *Layman's Guide to Oil and Gas Investments.* Houston, TX: Gulf Publishing, 1981. 136 pp. $9.95.
Written by a geologist and investment consultant, this book is for those wishing to capitalize on the boom in oil and gas. Brown explains how oil and gas deposits are found and how return estimates are made. He examines the federal regulations affecting the industry and tax advantages as investment opportunities. Presents pointed advice for those contemplating oil and natural gas investments and gives examples of typical scams, fraud, and deception.

Buckley, Julian, and Loll, Leo. *The Over-the-Counter Securities Market.* 4th Edition. Englewood Cliffs, NJ: Prentice-Hall, 1981. 480 pp. $24.95.
Although primarily intended as a text for the NASD (National Association of Securities Dealers) Qualifying Exam for Registered Representatives, this is a highly useful, tutorial-style book for the individual investor, offering excellent coverage of common and preferred stocks, bonds, U.S. treasury and agency securities, IRAs, new issues market, options, methods of analyzing the stock market, operation of organized securities exchanges, municipal securities, stock and bond transactions, and securities analysis. Also contains a very clear explanation of the NASDAQ (National Association of Securities Dealers Quotation) system for over-the-counter stocks. Recommended.

Cerami, Charles A. *More Profit, Less Risk: Your New Financial Strategy.* New York: McGraw-Hill, 1982. 240 pp. $14.95.
Cerami, the foreign affairs and investment editor of the Kiplinger Washington Publications, envisages the following scenario: a resurgence of the housing industry, rise of the consumer industry (carpeting, furniture, appliances), resurgence of inflation and higher interest rates, and a fall in the international value of the dollar. The solution for the average investor? Diversity to ensure a safe financial future. Cerami analyzes 12 types of investment or speculation (stocks, bonds, options, commodities, gold, and so on) and shows how to construct a balanced portfolio in rela-

tion to one's income, tax bracket, career, and family situation. A very penetrating and relevant analysis of present and future trends. A brilliant strategy book. Highly recommended.

Cohen, Jerome B., Zinbarg, Edward, and Zeikel, Arthur. *Guide to Intelligent Investing.* Homewood, IL: Dow Jones-Irwin, 1978. 351 pp. $12.50.
Geared to the investor who wants to create and manage his or her own portfolio. What, when, and how to buy stock; should you choose blue chips or speculative options, income stocks, growth stocks, or performance stocks? Still useful.

Cook, Timothy, and Summers, Bruce. *Instruments of the Money Market.* 5th Edition. Richmond, VA: Federal Reserve Bank of Richmond, 1981. 148 pp. Free (paper).
Excellent, textbook-style description of the major money market instruments and the institutional arrangements in which the instruments are traded. Domestic market instruments discussed include treasury bills, federal agency securities, federal funds, repurchase agreements, certificates of deposit, commercial paper, and bankers' acceptances. There are also chapters on Eurodollars, the Federal Reserve discount window, the dealer market for U.S. government securities, and short-term investment pools (money market funds, short-term tax-exempt funds, credit unions). Authoritative.

Day, Adrian. *Investing without Borders: The Best Opportunities around the World for the 80's.* Alexandria, VA: Alexandria House Books, 1981. 294 pp. $14.95.
Day, managing editor of *Personal Finance* and *Tax Angles*, argues that when selecting international investments, it is necessary to look first for the country or area that appears to offer the greatest potential for growth. Markets move in cycles, and by following, for example, 50 stock market cycles around the world, the investor can multiply his or her opportunities. Also, one would do well to diversify internationally for insurance and safety in view of the possibility of eventual foreign exchange controls in the United States. During the decade of the 1970s, while U.S. stocks increased in nominal value by 16.3 percent, the Hong Kong market grew by 644.7 percent and Singapore stocks rose by 370.6 percent. Day reviews the operation of international stock markets, the availability of fixed-interest investments in various countries, the operation of foreign banks, and international opportunities in commodities, currencies, and real estate. On a very practical level, Day provides names and addresses of U.S. brokers specializing in international investments, foreign banks, investment companies and mutual funds, and commodity exchanges in other countries, as well as a directory of newsletters, books, and other sources of information. U.S. Reporting Requirements on International Currency Transactions are described in detail. A superb, unique book. Highly recommended.

Dorfman, John. *Family Investment Guide: A Financial Handbook for Middle-Income People.* New York: Atheneum, 1981. 268 pp. $14.95.
Sensible, informative, and readable advice from the author of the *Consumer Tactics Manual* (see p. 37). Dorfman covers the essentials involved in savings and NOW accounts, certificates of deposit, money market funds, corporate bonds, common

stocks, mutual funds, tax shelters, gold and silver, and retirement accounts. He provides 20 investment rules: Try to invest 15 percent of after-tax income; don't invest until you have enough insurance; keep at least 20 percent of investment income in those investments that involve some risk; buy stocks when they are undervalued; hold stocks for the long run; diversify; and so on. Not a get-rich quick book, but rather one calculated to help the reader earn a higher return for his or her money. Recommended.

Fabozzi, Frank J., and Zarb, Frank G. (eds.). *The Handbook of Financial Markets: Securities, Options and Futures.* Homewood, IL: Dow Jones-Irwin, 1981. 825 pp. $42.50.
An authoritative compilation, with 40 expert contributors, of information on the environment and structure of the securities markets, the instruments involved, private financial intermediaries (banks, life insurance companies, etc.), the options market, and the futures market. An excellent source of information on topics such as the money market, money market investments, U.S. government and federal agency obligations, the mortgage market, organization and operation of banks and savings and loan organizations, mechanics of options trading, futures contracts, commodity futures markets, and so on. Also explains the factors that determine interest rates in the securities market and the returns and risks associated with each type of investment instrument. Scholarly and eminently readable. Highly recommended.

The "Get Rich" Investment Guide. May 1980 Investment Guide Issue. Chicago: Consumer Digest, 1980. 354 pp. $10 (paper). O.P.
Surveys familiar territory: how to choose a broker, the stock market, bonds, mutual funds, commodities, treasury bills, Swiss banking, diamonds, real estate, and other investment choices. Expensive, containing nothing new.

Gitman, Lawrence J., and Joehnk, Michael D. *Fundamentals of Investing.* New York: Harper & Row, 1981. 736 pp. $24.50.
An investment text, aimed at the individual investor or student, in six parts: role and scope of investments; analysis, evaluation, and markets of common stock; fixed-income securities; speculation vehicles—warrants, puts and calls, commodities and financial futures markets; other popular investments such as mutual funds, real estate, gold and tangible assets; investment and portfolio management. An appendix lists general financial publications and investment advisers. A solid reference work.

Haft, Richard. *Investing in Securities. A Handbook for the '80's.* Englewood Cliffs, NJ: Prentice-Hall, 1982. 208 pp. $5.95 (paper).
A fairly comprehensive but somewhat sophisticated explanation of how the stock market works, how to buy stocks, and what to expect from stockbrokers. Haft, a New York broker, describes how to identify growth and income investments and undervalued securities. Particularly useful are the chapters on mutual funds (describing the major types and mode of operation) and reading and interpreting the financial news. The latter chapter contains a guide to the major tables and columns of the *Wall Street Journal.* A tutorial approach with questions listed at the end of each chapter.

Hardy, C. Colburn. *Dun and Bradstreet's Guide to Your Investments, 1983.* 28th Edition. New York: Harper & Row, 1983. 224 pp. $15.34; $9.57 (paper).

An authoritative guide designed to help investors understand securities and commodities, the operation of the markets, and methods proven to be successful. Comprehensive coverage includes information on growth stocks, how to read annual reports, preferred stocks, convertible stocks, fixed-asset investments, tax-exempt bonds, how to use leverage, tax savings and shelters, techniques of buying and selling, investing for retirement, and commodities and futures. Good glossary and index. A long-time proven classic. Highly recommended.

Hassan, Bernard (ed.). *The Beginning Investor.* Oradell, NJ: Medical Economics Books, 1982. 131 pp. $9.95 (paper).

This book is adapted from a popular series of articles—"The Beginning Investor" published in *Medical Economics* magazine. Although prepared for a physician audience, the articles are of generalized interest, covering stocks, bonds, mutual funds, money market instruments, real estate, options, commodity futures, and tax shelters. Simple information and basic principles with a strong conservative flavor. Recommended for the novice investor.

Holt, Thomas J. *How to Survive and Grow Richer in the Tough Times Ahead.* New York: Rawson Wade, 1981. 262 pp. $10.95; $5.95 (paper).

Investment advice strongly flavored with philosophical and historical interpretation of the past and present state of the economy. Holt writes diffusely and never seems to get to the point. Of little help to the average person confronted with investment decisions.

Huskin, J., and Monsees, William. *How to Get Rich while You Sleep.* New York: Simon & Schuster/Cornerstone Library, 1981. 158 pp. $4.95 (paper).

Investment must be tailored to individual needs, goals, resources, capabilities, and temperament. The authors point out that 95 percent of people over the age of 65 are nonwealthy. They offer a number of guidelines for evaluating an investment—risk, yield, growth, liquidity, predictability, and shelter. They use these guidelines for rating the following types of investments: savings accounts, commodities, stocks, mutual funds, bonds, art, miscellaneous investments, insurance, mortgages, and real estate. Huskin and Monsees rate insurance and savings accounts very low and consider real estate to be the best investment to get rich while you sleep. They declare real estate to be "wonderful, marvelous, fabulous, groovy, wild, swinging." A novel approach to investment.

Levitt, Arthur, Jr. (ed.). *How to Make Your Money Make Money: The Experts Explain Your Alternatives, the Risks, the Rewards.* Homewood, IL: Dow Jones-Irwin, 1981. 220 pp. $17.50.

An encyclopedic compilation edited by the chairman of the Board of Governors and chief executive officer of the American Stock Exchange. The book consists of 20 chapters by specialist contributors on such topics as savings banks, stocks, bonds, mutual funds, real estate, gold and silver, gems, coins and stamps, commodity futures, art, and investments in movies, theaters, and wines. This is a highly informative, sensible book written by a stellar cast of experts who portray risks and rewards. Highly recommended as a reference resource.

Meltzer, Bernard. *Bernard Meltzer Solves Your Money Problems: Borrowing, Buying and Investment Strategies to Profit from Inflation.* New York: Simon & Schuster, 1982. 220 pp. $14.50.
Practical information on a wide variety of topics, laced with Meltzer's homespun, personal philosophy. Covers whether, how, and where to get loans for almost anything, types of loans and interest rates, how to buy autos, houses, condos, mobile homes on credit, how to make safe, profitable investments, retirement plans, the best investments to beat inflation. A somewhat overambitious attempt to discuss major aspects of borrowing, buying, and investing together with a strategy for combating inflation.

Meltzer, Yale. *Putting Money to Work: An Investment Primer for the 80's.* Englewood Cliffs, NJ: Prentice-Hall, 1981. 294 pp. $7.95 (paper). O.P.
A very informative textbook-style treatment of the money and capital markets, the federal funds market, stock market operation, money and interest rates, the Eurodollar market. A good explanation of the relationship between money and interest rates. One chapter describes "Where You Can Get Information and Data on a Continuous Basis."

Nagan, Peter. *Fail-Safe Investing: How to Make Money with Less Than $10,000 . . . Without Losing Sleep.* New York: Putnam's, 1981. 192 pp. $10.95.
A guide not to making a quick fortune, but rather how to preserve real worth or buying power from foolish mistakes and the inroads of inflation. Good, if somewhat conservative, advice on how to design an investment plan, how and when to purchase life insurance, U.S. Treasury obligations, corporate bonds and notes, municipal bonds, common stocks, real estate, and tax shelters. Additional chapters cover "Speculating Instead of Investing"—in gold, silver, diamonds, commodities, and collectibles. An attractively written and sensible book that can serve as an effective antidote to the doomsayers advocating extreme measures in the light of the impending collapse of the economy. Recommended.

Nelson, Wayne. *How to Buy Money: Investing Wisely for Maximum Return.* New York: McGraw-Hill, 1982. 163 pp. $10.95.
Attempts to help successful and busy individuals make better decisions about managing their money. Nelson maintains that the act of saving money is the start of buying money. He reviews the investment options available: stocks, bonds, government securities, tax shelters, tax deferred annuities, and so on. Good constructive advice on how to pick stocks, how to find a brilliant broker, where to find information (read *Barron's, Wall Street Journal,* and *Value Line*).

Schmeltz, L. *Playing the Stock and Bond Markets with Your Personal Computer.* Summit, PA: TAB Books, 1981. 308 pp. $16.95; $9.95 (paper).
How to integrate a personal computer into an investment program by using it as a data source and management aid. Schmeltz shows how to select a personal computer

(for example, Apple or TRS-80), purchase and write programs, build a data base, and develop projections, simulations, and record keeping. By way of example, the author details how his Fundamental Analysis Program calculates operating profit margins, liquidating ratio, asset value per share, and so on. The general assumption underlying the book is that by developing one's own decision-making process, one is eliminating the need for a lot of high-priced investment advice. Two glossaries are provided: one of computer terms and another of investment terms. Also lists commercially available software programs and sources of further information such as computer manufacturers, periodicals, investment advisory services, and telecomputing services. A unique and innovative book. Recommended.

Scott, William L. *Investing at the Racetrack*. New York: Simon & Schuster, 1981. 287 pp. $15.50.
Scott, a pen name for an attorney, claims to have a method of investing money in racehorses that is even safer than common stocks, returns a far greater percentage on investment, and requires so little initial capital that almost anyone can engage in it. This method appears to have paid off handsomely during six successive days racing at Belmont Park in New York during June 1980. The method of play, which turns horse racing into an investment rather than gambling, involves analyzing a horse's ability times, true time in a race, and sprint distance times. Instructions are given on when and how much to bet. An essential book only for avid readers of the *Daily Racing Form* who are mathematically inclined. Esoteric.

Sharpe, William. *Investments*. 2nd Edition. Englewood Cliffs, NJ: Prentice-Hall, 1981. 654 pp. $24.95.
An encyclopedic treatment of the nature of investment, speculation, and gambling; securities markets; valuation of riskless and risky securities; portfolio analysis; inflation; fixed-income securities; bond prices, yields, and returns; valuation and earnings of common stocks; options; futures contracts; investment companies; financial analysis; and investment management. An excellent reference book.

Simons, Myron. *How to Profit from Disinflation*. Piscataway, NJ: New Century, 1982. 192 pp. $12.95.
Investment opportunities are manifold in a time of disinflation, a lessening of the pressure of inflation. Bond prices are at near record lows, and many shares of stock are below book value. Simons explains why it is smart to invest during a recession and advocates raising cash and purchasing long- or intermediate-term bonds and stocks in five broad industrial groups (defense, medical, high technology, robots, and computer-controlled tools). Despite the more recent meteoric rise of the stock market and increase in bond prices, Simons' message is still relevant.

Stigum, Marcia. *The Money Market: Myth, Realities and Practice*. Homewood, IL: Dow Jones-Irwin, 1978. 578 pp. $29.50.
A comprehensive guide to the U.S. money market. Stigum describes in detail the operations of money market banks and money market dealers and brokers and covers the individual markets that make up the total market. For each market, Stigum describes the instruments traded, risks, liquidity, and return offered and how

74 Investments and the Stock Market

the market is made. Good explanation, solid technical treatment. Useful as a reference book.

Tobias, Andrew. *The Only Investment Guide You'll Ever Need.* New York: Bantam, 1981. 200 pp. $2.75 (paper).
A very simple, somewhat outdated introduction to the stock market, investment techniques, life insurance, and mutual funds. A pretentious title.

Tuccille, Jerome. *Everything the Beginner Needs to Know to Invest Shrewdly: A Step by Step Guide to the Basics of Financial Growth.* New York: Barnes & Noble, 1979. 192 pp. $4.50 (paper).
A brief primer on stocks, bonds, money market instruments, tax shelters, options, and how to invest. Contains an investment dictionary defining the basic vocabulary of investment. Out of date in many aspects.

Tuccille, Jerome. *The Optimist's Guide to Making Money in the 1980's: A Complete Program for Investing in the American Economic Miracle of the Next Decade.* New York: Morrow, 1978. 203 pp. $7.95; $4.95 (paper).
A predictive look at the future in view of the author's thesis (in 1978) that the United States was entering a period of moderate inflation and steady economic growth beginning slowly and accelerating through the next decade. Tuccille also held that by 1982 the stock market would enter one of its stronger and best sustained bull cycles in history.

United Business Services (ed.). *Successful Investing: A Complete Guide to Your Financial Future.* New York: Simon & Schuster, 1979. 509 pp. $14.95.
This book is intended to serve as a reference book on all aspects of investing—planning and building a portfolio; investment alternatives such as growth stocks, common stocks, corporate bonds, mutual funds, options, commodities, tax shelters, real estate; how to make choices by using cyclical indicators, technical analysis, and annual reports; marketing strategies and tactics; choosing a broker; investments and financial planning. Contains an extensive glossary of investment terms. Comprehensive treatment and useful as a reference resource despite the fact that some of the content is obsolete.

Vreeland, Richard. *Become Financially Independent: An Investment Plan That Really Works.* Englewood Cliffs, NJ: Prentice-Hall, 1979. 320 pp. $11.95; $5.95 (paper).
How to develop and systematically follow a solid money management plan that leads to financial independence and a tangible net worth of $100,000. The plan suggested involves saving $2.74 for the rest of your life; investing your savings in a balanced portfolio with a reasonable probability of earning a 9 to 15 percent return over an extended period of time; and not withdrawing one cent of investments unless it is a matter of life or death. Vreeland reviews basic low-risk investments and opportunities for greatest profits. Somewhat simplistic in tone.

STOCK MARKET: GENERAL

Ansbacher, Max G. *How to Profit from the Coming Bull Market.* Englewood Cliffs, NJ: Prentice-Hall, 1981. 256 pp. $12.95.
Ansbacher argues that gold, silver, real estate, and other tangibles have all run their course. All the pieces are in place for the Dow Jones average to smash through the 2,000 barrier within the next few years. For those who have the courage to buy stocks when they are unpopular, the payoff will be large. The author lists Five Commandments of Stock Selection: Buy stocks with a low P/E ratio; consider the earnings growth of the company; look for dividends; favor stocks with high book value; and diversify. Ansbacher also presents some useful rules for trading options. Excellent advice for those who are prepared to believe that the stock market will soar to never previously attained heights in the very near future. Stimulating.

Blamer, Thomas, and Shulman, Richard. *Dow 3000: The Investment Opportunity of the 1980's.* New York: Simon & Schuster/Wyndham Books, 1982. 206 pp. $13.50.
By the end of 1989, the authors predict a Dow-Jones Industrial Average of 3,000. This prediction, based on two distinct value formulas (the asset formula and the earnings formula), is not surprising to Blamer and Shulman in that stock prices have more than tripled in a decade twice already in this century. Further predictions are that by 1989 the Dow's price/earnings ratio should be back to its historical average, and that the Dow's earnings should double from their present 122 to 244 as a result of an assumed 8 percent inflation in the 1980s. The method used to arrive at these conclusions is described in detail and then applied to each of the 30 Dow stocks individually to arrive at a forecast of its 1989 price. A decidedly bullish point of view.

Boeckh, J. Anthony, and Coghlan, Richard (eds.). *The Stock Market and Inflation.* Homewood, IL: Dow Jones-Irwin, 1982. 225 pp. $14.95.
Answers the basic questions—How can an investor make a large enough return to outpace inflation? Are common stocks the answer? Do company earnings reflect inflation? Twelve stock market experts provide insight into how the market can be expected to react during the 1980s. The editors conclude with an overview of likely economic and financial developments over the next few years.

Cobleigh, Ira U., and Dorfman, Bruce K. *The Roaring 80's on Wall Street: How to Make a Killing in the Coming Stock Market Boom.* New York: Macmillan, 1981. 192 pp. $11.95.
The authors of *The Dowbeaters* (see p. 80) continue to advance a bullish philosophy, believing that the Dow is poised for an explosive upswing to the 2,000 mark within this decade. A massive "short-squeeze" rally will create a wall of volume, trading up to 150 million shares in a day, with the result that the far-sighted investor will liquidate his or her portfolio at alpine prices. The book offers an informative, readable discussion of how to structure a portfolio, procedures for speculation among low-priced shares, factors in purchasing growth stocks for long-term capital gains, and when to sell. Provides performance records and vignettes of a number of stocks and a good glossary. Provocative.

Egan, Patricia B., and Maran, Marie Y. *This Way to Wall $treet.* Westlake, OH: Market Ed, 1980. 200 pp. $9.95 (paper); Instructor's Manual. $5.95.

Using the evolution of a fictitious company, Candle Bright Corporation, the authors show how common stock is offered and the market operates. Their textbook-style presentation provides very clear definitions of such basic terms as preferred stock, warrant, tender offer, stock split, bonds, convertible securities, and types of municipal bonds. A lucid explanation of the fundamentals of the stock market useful as a resource book or text for courses in economics, consumer education, and business.

Gargiulo, Albert F., and Carlucci, Rocco. *The "Questioned Stock" Manual: A Guide to Determining the True Worth of Old and Collectible Securities.* New York: McGraw-Hill, 1979. 193 pp. $15.95.

A helpful authority for those who have old, obsolete, and collectible securities stashed in the attic. For example, Marconi Wireless Telegraph Company of America shares issued 60 years ago are convertible into shares of RCA Corporation. This is a useful book to track down companies that have changed their names or liquidated their businesses, leaving large amounts of obsolete securities. Procedures and sources to determine the status of questionable stocks and how to detect fraudulent securities are detailed. A unique book. Recommended.

Krefetz, Gerald. *The Smart Investor's Guide: How to Make Money in the Coming Bull Market.* New York: A&W, 1982. 240 pp. $12.95.

The bears have had their day and are heading into hibernation! Krefetz rejects the arguments of the doomsayers, cynics, and pessimists and believes that it is now realistic to anticipate a robust and expansive economy, dedicated to rapid technological change, spurred by innovative and creative imagination. Five promising investment areas are suggested, dubbed by Krefetz as "Engines of Change": genetic engineering, recombinant agricultural technology (genetic plant breeding), robotics, energy, and telecommunications (the wiring of society). Fun reading; long on philosophy and speculation, but short on specific recommendations.

Lasry, George. *Valuing Common Stock: The Power of Prudence.* New York: AMACOM, 1979. 260 pp. $16.95.

Lasry provides the average shareholder with an understanding of what common stock is and how to place a dollar value on it. He argues that a share of common stock does not, as popularly assumed, represent ownership interest in the assets of a business. Instead, it is simply a claim on the income produced from those assets by management. Lasry points out the limitations of such popular concepts as the price/earnings ratio and believes that any valuation of common stock must be based not on market price but on the return-on-equity ratio, book value, and shareholder's opportunity cost.

Lee, Barbara, with Morgenson, Gretchen. *The Woman's Guide to the Stock Market: How to Make Your Own Investment Plan.* New York: Crown/Harmony, 1982. 183 pp. $11.95.

This book offers nothing new in that the content is familiar—setting investment goals, the language of the stock market, how it operates, choosing a stockbroker, understanding brokerage forms, reading the financial pages, stock market myths and truths, and so on. Lee adopts a somewhat patronizing approach toward women, despite her protestation that "making money is not a question of gender." Duplicates what has been better said elsewhere.

Little, Jeffrey B., and Rhodes, Lucien. *Understanding Wall Street.* Cockeysville, MD: Liberty, 1982. 220 pp. $7.95 (paper).
Little and Rhodes offer one of the most concise and lucid accounts of the stock market yet produced. They provide a highly readable explanation of the basics: what a share of stock is; how to read and analyze corporate financial statements and understand the financial pages of a newspaper; how to recognize growth stocks; how to calculate bond yields; principles of technical analysis; stock options; and so on. Their text is enhanced by high-quality diagrams, charts, and photographs. This is the book in which to look for definitions and explanations of margin account, bear market strategies, capital gains, municipal bonds, arbitrage, coupon, debenture, preferred stock, NASDAQ, P/E ratio, short sale, treasury bill, and the like. An excellent compendium of information not readily available in one source elsewhere. Indispensable; highly recommended.

Metz, Robert. *Future Stocks: Investing for Profit in the Growth Stocks of the 1980's.* New York: Harper & Row, 1982. 256 pp. $12.98.
A fascinating and intriguing look into the world of high technology in the form of microprocessors, minicomputers, innovative software design, computer-aided manufacture, and solar power. Metz, for 25 years author of the daily "Market Place" column in the *New York Times,* shows how to identify promising high-technology stocks and invest where the opportunities are. A good insight is provided into the operation of Genentech, Wang, Commodore, Intel, Tandy, and Computervision. Pointed advice on how to select stocks calculated to have sales and earnings ten times as large as today within just ten years. Lists 27 companies for realizing such gains over the next decade. Recommended.

Pike, William. *Why Stocks Go Up (and Down): A Guide to Sound Investing.* Homewood, IL: Dow Jones-Irwin, 1982. 298 pp. $14.95.
Although written for the novice or "advanced amateur," this book is likely to strain the comprehension of most readers. Using an 18-year case history of Polaroid stock, Pike gives a complicated explanation of common stock, bonds, and preferred stock, P/E ratios (when a stock is "low" and "high"), listing and trading on the stock exchanges, and why stocks go up. Difficult reading.

Taylor, Thomas J. *Get Rich on the Obvious: How to Turn Your Everyday Observations into Money.* New York: Harcourt Brace Jovanovich, 1982. 180 pp. $12.95.
The author, a stockbroker for more than 20 years, is currently a senior vice-president for investments of Shearson/American Express. Taylor advocates "Open-Air Analysis," which involves the sensing of public moods, changes in fashion, shifts in buying habits, and bottoms of stock markets. As an example, Taylor advises "just go to a McDonald's or a Kentucky Fried Chicken and try to get waited on." The investment opportunity, he claims, is obvious. Therefore, the technique observes trends and translates these observations in terms of stock market. Of particular value

is Taylor's discussion of how to select a stockbroker, what to expect, when to use a discount broker, how to build a good client-broker relationship, when to fire your broker. Finally, Taylor identifies some impending breakthroughs and trends. Readable, stimulating, and provocative.

Teweles, Richard J., and Bradley, Edward S. *The Stock Market*. 4th Edition. New York: Wiley, 1982. 474 pp. $23.95.

A revision of earlier editions by the late George Leffler and Loring C. Farwell, this book is written for investors, members of brokerage firms, and college students. Its emphasis is on the history and operation of the stock market from the viewpoint of its structure and mechanics rather than investment strategy and technique. The authors provide a scholarly treatment of trading floor practices, short selling, customer-broker relationships, margin trading, the Securities Exchange Act, fundamentals of stock prices, technical analysis, sources of information and security ratings, securities options, and so on. Comprehensive glossary. Recommended as an authoritative reference source.

Thorsell, Richard L. *Investing on Your Own: How to Find Winning Stocks in Your Own Backyard*. New York: McGraw-Hill, 1979. 444 pp. $13.95. O.P.

How to spot uncommon stocks (those that have not yet followed the crowd). Thorsell describes how to forecast a company's earnings, key indicators of company quality, benchmarks for appraising a stock, and how to predict future stock prices. The author provides a prospect list of 7,200 companies, arranged by zip code, that offer investment potential. Detailed instructions are given for assessing the future of the companies.

Warfield, Gerald. *The Investor's Guide to Stock Quotations and Other Financial Listings*. New York: Harper & Row, 1983. 384 pp. $25; $10.95 (paper).

At last a comprehensive guide to the numerous tables contained in the *Wall Street Journal*, the *New York Times*, and business sections of major newspapers. A good explanation is provided of stock exchange listings, options tables, mutual funds prices, over-the-counter quotations, bond tables, futures prices, and so on. Also provides a glossary of investment terms and a complete list of stock names and abbreviations with ticker symbols and exchange symbols. Recommended.

STOCK MARKET: STRATEGY

Abrams, Don. *The Profit-Taker: The Proven Rapid Money-Maker in Good and Bad Markets*. New York: Wiley, 1980. 124 pp. $9.95.

The strategy recommended, using a question-and-answer format, combines ultraconservative investment techniques with huge profit potential. It involves "hedging," which combines investments in convertible securities with the sale of common stock underlying them. For the more sophisticated.

Barry, James A., Jr. *Financial Freedom: A Positive Strategy for Putting Your Money to Work*. Reston, VA: Reston, 1981. 303 pp. $14.

A sampler of various types of investments, explaining the risk-reward potential of real estate, annuities, stock market, mutual funds, energy investments, fixed-income investments, hard assets, and exotic investments. Emphasis is placed on taking an active role in charting your own financial destiny. Undistinguished discussion of a poorly defined, pyramid investing strategy.

Beadle, Patricia. *Investing in the '80's: What to Buy and When.* New York: Harcourt Brace Jovanovich, 1981. 224 pp. $12.95.

Beadle, a former beauty queen turned investment adviser, believes in the existence of predictable economic cycles that can help forecast economic booms in stocks, real estate, commodities, and business ventures. Good investment timing is most closely associated with cycles. The author analyzes the convergence of stock cycles, the role of Wheeler's weather cycle and the theories of Nicholai Kondratieff, and predicts a "mini-crash" in stock prices for late 1981 or early 1982. This analysis suggests a strong economic recovery for the latter part of the 1980s, followed by a traditional age of prosperity during the 1990s. A popularization of the work of Kondratieff, Beveridge, Edward Dewey, and the Foundation for the Study of Cycles. Assumes that a knowledge of cycles will help increase investment profits: "To everything there is a season. . . . A time to plant, and a time to pluck up that which is planted. . . ." Intriguing.

Cappiello, Frank. *Finding the Next Super Stock.* Cockeysville, MD: Liberty, 1982. 160 pp. $6.95 (paper).

If only we had bought IBM and Xerox 20 years ago! Cappiello, an experienced money manager and regular panelist on "Wall Street Week," believes that it is possible to identify the super stocks of tomorrow. His strategy focuses on smaller yet promising companies out of the mainstream of institutional interest in a number of key areas such as technology (robots and computer software), health and medical, consumer and business services, and energy. The recommended method involves identification of nine characteristics present in previous successes: small to medium-size company, rising unit sales volume, rising pretax profit margins, above average and improving return on stockholders' equity, strong earnings per share growth relative to most stocks, low payment ratio with rising dividends, low debt ratio, low institutional holdings, and increasing price earnings multiple. The application of the method is illustrated by actual case studies—Xerox, Walt Disney Productions, 3M, and Bristol-Myers. A useful how-to book for the serious investor. Recommended.

Church, Albert M. *The Sophisticated Investor: How to Target Prime Investment Opportunities.* Englewood Cliffs, NJ: Prentice-Hall, 1981. 166 pp. $15.95; $7.95 (paper).

The key to success is understanding and applying rate of return and risk concepts. Church explains the meaning of these concepts and offers methods, techniques, and examples calculated to promote sound, well-informed investment decisions. By means of a problem-solving approach, the author shows how to analyze the factors that determine current and future value and return and risk of various types of investments. Particularly helpful is the analysis of the characteristics of conventional and nonconventional investments, fixed-income securities (certificates of deposit,

U.S. federal government bonds and notes), equities, mutual funds, commodities, and collectibles. Somewhat technical, as the title indicates.

Cobleigh, Ira U., and Dorfman, Bruce K. *The Dowbeaters: How to Buy Stocks That Go Up.* New York: Macmillan/Collier, 1979. 181 pp. $8.95. O.P.

An upbeat, if overly enthusiastic, advocacy of multilevel investment strategies that will enable investors to reap huge profits in the years ahead. Gives specific selections of "dowbeater" stocks and bonds. A classic work that needs to be updated in the light of more recent developments in the market.

Dirks, Ray. *Heads You Win, Tails You Win: The Dirks Investment Formula.* New York: Bantam, 1980. 192 pp. $3.50 (paper).

Dirks claims to take the guesswork out of investing in stocks and believes that the reader knows a great deal more about investing than the average retail stockbroker. Forget real estate, collectibles, and mutual funds as investments. Reject the growth stock, follow-the-trend, and random walk theories. The magic formula of Dirks is to buy stock when the selling averages of the Dow Jones industrials fall below their book values. A depressed market provides great opportunities for bargains in the form of stock selling far below their actual worth. Dirks tells how to maximize these opportunities.

Dreman, David. *The New Contrarian Investment Strategy: The Psychology of Stock Market Success.* New York: Random House, 1982. 322 pp. $16.95.

Dreman notes that in the decade ending in 1978, 85 percent of the 141 largest bank trust departments and insurance companies managing $140 billion underperformed the market. "The errors are so great, people would do better in most instances selecting stocks by throwing darts at the stock pages, or perhaps even having their family dogs choose them by pawing the financial pages." After analyzing and critiquing the essentials of technical analysis, fundamental analysis, and the efficient market hypothesis, Dreman advocates investment strategy involving low price/earnings (P/E) ratios. Specific directions are given on how to use low P/E strategies for maximum advantage. This updated edition includes a discussion of financial futures, options, and IRA and Keogh accounts. A sensible and challenging book. Recommended.

Engel, Louis, and Boyd, Brendan. *How to Buy Stocks.* 7th Revised Edition. Boston: Little, Brown, 1982. 370 pp. $15.50.

The latest edition and update of a classic. The authors give a concise account of the operation of the stock market, how and why new stock is sold, bonds and investment banking, government and municipal bonds, the over-the-counter market, buying on margin, options, mutual funds, the folklore of the market, and why you should invest if you can. Lists further reading. Good, solid treatment.

Engel, Louis with Wyckoff, Peter. *How to Buy Stocks.* 6th Revision. New York: Bantam, 1977. 366 pp. $3.50.

A pocketbook version of the Little, Brown 6th Revised Edition (1976). Engel argues that the average stock has paid a better return and provided a better balance of protection against risks than any other form of investment. The coverage is comprehensive: common stock, bonds, how stocks are bought and sold, how a market is made, how you do business with a broker, what it means to speculate, how to buy on margin, options, how to read the financial news, how your broker can help you, when to sell. More detailed and technical than Claude Rosenberg, *Stock Market Primer* (see p. 84).

Herzfeld, Thomas. *The Investor's Guide to Closed-End Funds: The Herzfeld Hedge.* New York: McGraw-Hill, 1980. 210 pp. $19.50.

Closed-end funds, which are not mutual funds, trade in the open market exactly like common stocks. Herzfeld shows how these funds can be used by both individual and institutional investors seeking income, capital gains, or arbitrage. The Herzfeld Hedge is an arbitrage strategy that involves establishing a long position in a closed-end fund and a short position in the listed options whose underlying stocks are in that fund's portfolio. Technical.

Herzfeld, Thomas, and Drach, Robert F. *High-Return Low-Risk Investment.* New York: Putnam's, 1981. 228 pp. $16.95.

After analyzing the principles and rules of stock selection, the authors present a commonsense, straightforward approach to seeking successfully consistent profit with low risk. Three programs are outlined—for capital gains, income, and income and capital gains. All three are derived from a combination of the Herzfeld Hedge and Drach Market Research. The Herzfeld Hedge is essentially a collection of investment strategies utilizing closed-end funds (also known as closed-end investment trusts, or CEITs). Technical, but worth the effort to read.

Kandel, Myron. *How to Cash In on the Coming Stock Market Boom: The Smart Investor's Guide to Making Money.* Indianapolis, IN: Bobbs-Merrill, 1982. 191 pp. $12.95.

A much better book than the title implies! Kandel, financial editor and economic analyst of the Cable News Network, has assembled the collective wisdom of a number of Wall Street professionals who give their expert opinion on conservatism versus speculation, golden rules on how to beat the market, cutting losses and letting profits ride, finding growth stocks, rules for picking technology stocks, and so on. Six courageous stock pickers also list half a dozen stocks that each thinks hold special promise in 1982 and beyond. In addition to advice from the pros, Kandel has some excellent chapters on seizing opportunities, switching in and out of no-load mutual funds, picking the best investment advisory service, unlocking the secrets of the annual report, and how Dow stocks influence the market. Stimulating and noteworthy. Highly recommended.

Lichello, Robert. *How to Make $1,000,000 in the Stock Market—Automatically.* Revised Edition. New York: New American Library, 1980. 201 pp. $2.75 (paper).

The author claims that with his new, dynamic investment technique called AIM (Automatic Investment Management) it is possible "to earn profits from stocks or mutual funds with a degree of dependability, regularity and *safety* never before possible with any other investment method." AIM does not require stock market expertise, time, or a large investment. "The greatest financial adventure of your life" involves a mathematical formula incorporating factors such as portfolio control, stock value, buy/sell advice, market order, portfolio value, stock adjustment factor equalizer, and so on. An arcane scheme larded with gratuitous advice and generalizations. Skip this title.

McQuown, Judith. *Playing the Takeover Market: How to Profit from Corporate Mergers, Spin-Offs, Tender Offers and Liquidations.* New York: Seaview, 1982. 256 pp. $14.95.
A guide to identifying likely candidates for "special situations"—mergers, tender offers, spin-offs, liquidations, and redemptions—that may offer spectacular profits. McQuown defines these special situations and shows how to analyze annual reports for significant clues (book value per share, profitability ratios) and the role of technical analysis. The author focuses on basic issues—once a merger is announced, what action should the stockholder take, whether to get into the game after an acquirer makes a merger offer, should you always tender, what if you don't want to sell? An appendix describes the types of information that can be obtained from the Securities and Exchange Commission's Corporate Filings required by the federal securities laws. A somewhat technical book, requiring concentrated reading, for those who wish that they had owned Conoco or Marathon stock before the mergers.

Malabre, Alfred. *Investing for Profit in the Eighties: The Business Cycle System.* Garden City, NY: Doubleday, 1982. 216 pp. $15.95.
Malabre has a message: "Be your own investment manager. Be wary of the establishment, the famous financial institutions, the giant, well advertised banks and brokerage houses who would oversee your nest egg and safely shepherd your savings in a perilous economic climate." His strategy involves learning the rhythms of the business cycle and how cyclical behavior influences major investments such as stocks and bonds. The leading indicators to be watched include length of average work week, new building permits, stock-price index and money supply, and data that can conveniently be obtained from the Commerce Department's *Business Conditions Digest*. Of interest to the more sophisticated investor.

Malkiel, Burton. *The Inflation Beater's Investment Guide: Winning Strategies for the 1980's.* New York: Norton, 1980. 190 pp. $8.95; $3.95 (paper).
The author is chairman of the economics department at Princeton, a former member of the President's Council of Economic Advisers, and the author of *A Random Walk Down Wall Street* (see below). Malkiel reviews the major investment alternatives and reveals how to purchase diversified portfolios of stocks and bonds at substantial discounts below their market value. His assumption is that stocks appear dirt cheap in an investment market where almost everything else is fully priced. Consequently, with the right strategies, stock investments could bring extraordinary returns to counter the effects of inflation.

Malkiel, Burton. *A Random Walk Down Wall Street.* 2nd Edition. New York: Norton, 1981. 285 pp. $6.95.
The classic statement of the thesis that a blindfolded chimpanzee throwing darts at the newspaper's financial pages could select a stock portfolio that would do just as well as one carefully selected by the experts. Therefore, investment advisory services,

earnings predictions, and complicated chart patterns are useless. Malkiel offers a powerful analysis and criticism of both fundamental and technical analysis and suggests some practical, useful strategies for reviewing and selecting investment options. The writing is stimulating and imaginative—a Stroll to the Bank, a Promenade through Bond Country, a Measured Step through the Mutual Fund Mine—and is delightful reading. Finally, Malkiel gives four rules for successful stock selecting. Challenging. Highly recommended.

Pring, Martin. *How to Forecast Interest Rates: A Guide to Profits for Consumers, Managers and Investors.* New York: McGraw-Hill, 1981. 196 pp. $14.95.
Interest rate fluctuations can be viewed not as an obstacle to sound financial planning but as an opportunity on which to capitalize. After describing the structure of the U.S. debt market, Pring focuses on the indicators that can be used to predict interest rate movements—manufacturing capacity utilization, help-wanted advertising, housing starts, Composite Index of Leading Indicators, and so on. Pring believes that individuals are better advised to form their own judgment based on a consensus approach of the indicators rather than a consensus view of the experts quoted in the popular press. Convincing.

Pring, Martin. *International Investing Made Easy: Proven Money Strategies with as Little as $5,000.* New Edition. New York: McGraw-Hill, 1980. 236 pp. $15.95.
An informative guide to foreign equity, debt, currency, and gold markets. Pring also lists British, Canadian, Japanese, and Eurobond dealers, gold investment funds, international mutual funds, and U.S. no-load mutual funds. Using a technical approach, he analyzes the characteristics of the market, major cyclical turning points, and how they may be utilized for making investment decisions.

Pugsley, John. *The Alpha Strategy: The Ultimate Plan of Financial Self-Defense for the Small Investor.* Beverly Hills, CA: Stratford Press, 1981. 242 pp. $13.95.
Pugsley argues that belief in tomorrow's prosperity is an unfortunate and costly illusion. Inflation, taxation, and recession rob one of wealth. Pugsley's advice is not to store wealth in paper claims; instead, invest savings in real things that can be consumed in the future. "The Alpha Strategy is a plan in which an individual completely avoids conventional investment markets, and instead invests his wealth in real tangible and intangible goods, and stock piles these goods until he is ready to consume them, or until it is convenient to trade them for goods he wants to consume." The author outlines what to stockpile in terms of expected shelflife and obsolescence, where to store the goods, and how to build a personal Alpha Portfolio. Blends economics with mysticism.

Purcell, W. R., Jr. *Understanding a Company's Finances: A Graphic Approach.* Boston: Houghton Mifflin, 1981. 160 pp. $10.95.
For investors, business students, managers, and others who wish to decipher the hieroglyphics of financial reports. By the liberal use of diagrams, Purcell shows how to picture the balance sheet of a company in terms of assets, income, return-on-equity ratio, profits, cash value, and so on. A useful technique for evaluating the financial health of a company and its potential as a source of income for investors.

Rieder, Thomas. *Sun Spots, Stars, and the Stock Market.* New York: Dutton/Pagurian Press, 1974. 126 pp. $5.95 (paper). O.P.

Presents data to support the conclusion that the stock market, or more precisely the Dow Jones Industrial Average, is sensitive within limits to certain recurring planetary systems. Rieder's essential thesis is that the vagaries of the Dow average are a reliable distillation of the level of pessimism or optimism among investors, and that a demonstrable correlation exists between planetary systems and these levels of pessimism and optimism. His book is replete with astrological assumptions and planetary diagrams. Esoteric.

Righetti, Raymond. *Stock Market Strategy for Consistent Profits.* Chicago: Nelson-Hall, 1980. 176 pp. $15.95.

Righetti believes that endeavoring to forecast stock prices with a meaningful degree of consistent accuracy is an exercise in futility. Instead, he offers a number of axioms: Buy only rising stocks, never prominent stocks that have descended to "bargain" prices; never buy a stock that is dropping, but only stock that is rising; true growth stocks are never overpriced; speculating in puts, calls, related options, and commodity futures is a treacherous path that leads to the poorhouse.

Rolo, Charles. *Gaining on the Market: Your Complete Guide to Investment Strategy: Stocks, Bonds, Options, Mutual Funds and Gold.* Boston: Little, Brown, 1982. 310 pp. $14.95.

Rolo, the Wall Street columnist for *Money* magazine, has produced one of the best of the introductory books on investments and the stock market. His approach is essentially educational: "My aim is to provide you with a step-by-step grounding in the fundamentals of investing and money management—how to judge the value of a stock; how to use tools that have proved helpful in trying to anticipate major movements in the market; how to choose and implement an overall investment strategy that suits your goals and your temperament." The result is a combat manual that teaches the principles of investment strategy, what makes stock prices move, how to get advice and information (using a broker, annual reports and investment advisory services), analytic approaches to the market (fundamental, technical, psychological and political), choosing a portfolio strategy and predicting market movements, merits of mutual funds, options, and convertible bonds and stocks, and areas of fastest growth in the 1980s. Helpful appendices include a list of 160 little-known stocks with growth potential, a guide to no-load mutual funds, and a glossary of investment terms. A superb, how-to-do-it book calculated to educate investors and sharpen their skills. Sacrifice another title, if necessary, to acquire this one. Highly recommended.

Rosenberg, Claude. *Stock Market Primer.* New York: Warner, 1981. 370 pp. $14.95; $3.95 (paper).

A very helpful, concise book that provides practical information on how the stock market functions, factors to consider in judging where the market is going, facts of life for stockholders, how to read the financial pages, stock splits, dividends, when to buy and what to buy, how to spot growth companies, utility stocks, investment trusts, and so on. Five strategies are suggested for making money in the market, while one chapter is devoted to do's and don'ts in relation to investments and the stock market. Easy to read.

Schultz, Harry. *Bear Market Investment Strategies.* Homewood, IL: Dow Jones-Irwin, 1981. 232 pp. $14.95.
A bear is defined as an investor or trader who believes that the trend of stock prices is down and trades and invests with the trend by selling his or her stock and/or selling short. Schultz does not advocate escape from bad stocks and currency by walling oneself up in a survival farm, but rather shows how to capitalize on disaster itself. The tactics and benefits of short selling are explained in detail. Provocative in view of the theory that the ability to think contrary is crucial to making money.

Smith, Thurman. *Investors Can Beat Inflation: A Practical Guide.* Revised Edition. Cockeysville, MD: Liberty, 1981. 150 pp. $4.95 (paper).
A strategy book that advocates the use of mutual funds. Smith shows how to select funds, sources of performance information, how to interpret a prospectus, and when to buy and sell.

Sokoloff, Kiril. *The Thinking Investor's Guide to the Stock Market.* New York: McGraw-Hill, 1978. 234 pp. $15.95.
A classic work on investment strategy that helps explain the method, madness, and randomness of the stock market. Sokoloff believes that the recent past has little, if any, validity for predicting the future action of stock prices. An excellent perspective of market movement and mood psychology, together with guidelines for picking market tops and bottoms. Highly recommended.

Sokoloff, Kiril, Laird, Joseph, and Mack, Thomas. *Investing in the Future: 10 New Industries and over 75 Key Growth Companies That Are Changing the Face of Corporate America.* Garden City, NY: Doubleday, 1982. 178 pp. $14.95.
The authors examine the effects of disinflation, changing technology, government deregulation, and the distribution of goods and consumer spending patterns on ten new emerging growth areas—personal automation hardware, video entertainment software, office automation hardware, information vending, factory electronics, deregulation of transportation, energy exploration, energy services, health care, and specialty retailing. An excellent, forward-looking analysis of emerging investment opportunities. Highly recommended.

Sullivan, Colleen. *High-Risk, High-Reward Investing: An Expert Guide to Twenty-five Growth Fields.* New York: St. Martin's Press, 1982. 238 pp. $12.95.
Risk is inherent in any activity where there is uncertainty. Five basic groups of investor types are identified and described: Tentative Triers, Sports, Nathan Detroits, Cautious Calvins, and High Fliers. The potential risks and profits are analyzed for a large number of investments: high-yield stocks (growth stocks, penny stocks), options, commodities markets (metals, agricultural products), commodity options, drilling, real estate, fine arts and collectibles (painting, furniture, books, coins, stamps, photographs, rugs), gems and jewelry, and horses. For each type of investment, Sullivan identifies the level of risk (Caution, Danger, Red Flag), the minimum

investment required, and the type of investor best qualified to participate. She also outlines where or how the investment is sold or traded, fundamental factors that affect the price or volatility of the investment, as well as common frauds and scams. Each chapter concludes with a list of suggested readings for further exploration. A clever, interesting book with a novel approach. Recommended.

Train, John. *The Money Masters: Nine Great Investors, Their Winning Strategies and How You Can Apply Them.* New York: Harper & Row, 1980. 296 pp. $12.95; New York: Penguin, 1981. 296 pp. $4.95 (paper).
Train, an investment counselor, analyzes and explains the ideas and strategies of nine notable portfolio investors—T. Rowe Price, John Templeton, Philip Fisher, Robert Wilson, and others. Conclusions reached include: Buy stocks when they have few friends, invest and be patient, buy only what is cheap right now, decide on a strategy and concentrate on it, avoid popular stocks, stay away from fad industries, avoid new ventures, "official" growth stocks, heavy blue chips, and gimmicks, forget about technical analysis, and so on. Interesting reading.

Tuccille, Jerome. *Dynamic Investing: The System for Dynamic Profits—No Matter Which Way the Market Goes.* New York: New American Library, 1981. 151 pp. $9.95 (paper). Revised Edition. 1982. $2.50 (paper).
More advice from Jerome Tuccille, the perpetual optimist. The author identifies a number of Automatic Trigger Signals (ATSs) that provide the timing for the purchase and selling of stocks. The signals are for situations where, for example, the Dow-Jones Industrial Average (DJIA) is 780-800, DJIA under 780, short-term rates 12 percent or more, DJIA 900 and trending up, short-term rates falling below 12 percent; monetary growth slowing down. In general, "when the worst economic news starts making the front pages of the newspapers, it is time to think about buying stocks." A thought-provoking approach worthy of consideration.

STOCK MARKET: TECHNICAL ANALYSIS

Appel, Gerald. *The Stock Option and No Load Switch Fund Scalper's Manual.* Brightwaters, NY: Windsor Books, 1979. 204 pp. $35.
Guidelines for the automatic trading of stock options, volatile stocks, and mutual funds. Appel shows how to determine buy-and-sell signals and how to let the action of the stock market itself point the way to trading profits. Reviews various types of market indicators and strategies. A good book for technicians, but not as exciting as the title may imply.

Charell, Ralph. *How to Make Big Money in Low-Priced Stocks in the Coming Bull Market.* New York: Morrow, 1981. 224 pp. $9.95.
Charell is convinced that the stock market is in a unique historic position to facilitate the building of your personal future. Enormous fortunes will be made as concentrations of massive funds move in and out of the market, creating mammoth price swings. To make money, it is necessary "to interpret the significant technical in-

dicators, and (to have) the discipline and strength of character to wait until all or most of the signs and signals are chanting the same message." Provides a very good explanation of technical analysis of stock trends, but gives little hint as to what types of stocks will be favored in the predicted bull market. Also offers an interesting insight into the crowd psychology of the stock market and the necessity to insulate oneself against rumor and stampede. Recommended.

Coslow, Samson. *Make Money on the Interest Rate Roller Coaster: A Proven Method for Profitable Investment in a Rising or Falling Market.* New York: Coward-McCann and Geoghegan, 1982. 187 pp. $12.95.

The author views the perilous roller coaster ride of inflation as fueled by the three Gs—greed, graft, and government. The nation's debt has swelled to an incredible trillion dollars. Eventually interest rates will decline only to rise again as business picks up. The strategy advocated involves selecting appropriate types of investment according to the stage the interest rate happens to be in at the time of investment. At Stage I (rising interest rates) buy only money market funds; at Stage II (top plateau of the cycle) buy treasury bills and certificates of deposit; at Stage III (declining interest rates) buy high-quality bonds; at Stage IV (bottoming out) buy longer-term bonds. A good insight into the art of chart reading that underscores the great importance of timing. (Coslow is also a well-known songwriter, author of "Cocktails for Two" and other hits.)

Diamond, William. *Bulls, Bears, and Massacres: A Proven System for Investing in the Stock Market.* Belmont, CA: Lifetime Learning Publications, 1982. 160 pp. $21.

Diamond writes for investors who have a history of little or no success in investing in the stock market and who have at least $5,000, but less than $25,000, to invest. Starting with eight premises, Diamond shows how to construct trend lines on a daily market chart in order to identify sudden fluctuations or reversals in the market. The calculation of an Index of Merit, using a calculator, permits the determination of whether a particular stock is overpriced or underpriced. Of great interest to those who wish to take an active stance in managing their own portfolio.

Granville, Joseph. *Granville's New Strategy of Daily Stock Market Timing for Maximum Profit.* Englewood Cliffs, NJ: Prentice-Hall/Parker, 1976. 375 pp. $19.95.

A classic work by the well-known market analyst in which the author argues the case for technical analysis. "Fundamental data . . . lag behind the technical data by about nine months, on the average." Granville explains the various market indicators and how these can be used to maximum advantage in the game (the Grand Strategy of Stock Trading). Readable and fascinating. Recommended.

Hardy, C. Colburn. *The Investor's Guide to Technical Analysis.* New York: McGraw-Hill, 1978. 185 pp. $15.95.

After contrasting technical versus fundamental analysis (the fundamentalist is a conservative who invests for the long term and the technician is a trader who buys and sells for short-term profit), Hardy analyzes the technical approach to the stock market and explains trend lines, chart patterns, forecasting indicators, moving averages, and timing. He writes concisely and clearly in a tutorial style.

Mamis, Justin. *How to Buy: An Insider's Guide to Making Money in the Stock Market.* New York: Farrar, Straus & Giroux, 1982. 245 pp. $11.95.
A fascinating book for the more sophisticated investor. Mamis believes in the technical view of the market—the notion that market behavior itself tells the story. "Technical analysis is based entirely on what is knowable: yesterday's price, not a hunch of tomorrow's." The author shows when to buy stock, when not to buy, market timing, how to use the indicators, basic buying strategy, what to buy, and betting in the options markets. The best concise explanation yet of how to interpret and use technical data. Highly recommended.

Prechter, Robert, and Frost, Alfred. *Elliott Wave Principle: Key to Stock Market Profits.* 2nd Edition. Gainesville, GA: New Classics Library, 1981. 189 pp. $21.
Prechter is editor of the *Elliott Wave Theorist*, an investment newsletter devoted to market timing. In this volume, the authors cover the theory of the Elliott wave principle, a system of empirically derived rules for interpreting action in the major stock market averages. Elliott held that the market unfolds according to a basic rhythm or pattern of five waves up and three waves down to form a complete cycle of eight waves. Prechter and Frost summarize Elliott's philosophy and provide a fascinating insight into wave formation, Fibonacci relationships, fixed time cycles, momentum, sentiment and supply-demand factors, and their productive capability. Will appeal to serious market students with some technical background.

Pring, Martin. *Technical Analysis Explained: An Illustrated Guide for the Investor.* New York: McGraw-Hill, 1980. 440 pp. $24.95. O.P.
Technical analysis assumes that stock prices move in trends and that it is possible to study the action of the market itself to determine subtle changes in its character that have historically preceded major market turning points. The major areas of technical analysis involve sentiment indicators, flow-of-fund indicators, and market structure indicators. Pring explains trend determination techniques, market structure, relationships between interest rates and the stock market, and other aspects of market behavior. A definitive and essential book on technical analysis and market timing. For the more sophisticated investor.

Touhey, John C. *Stock Market Forecasting for Alert Investors.* New York: AMACOM, 1980. 192 pp. $11.95.
Touhey maintains that the major bull and bear markets of the last two decades have consistently been signaled by changes in 11 leading indicators that run ahead of the business cycle, including 90-day trading bill yield, total time savings deposits, authorized housing permits, brokers' cash accounts, real earnings, gold prices, and federal deficit. The author shows how to buy and sell stocks using the predictors. The fundamental premise of the book is that individuals who take responsibility for their own investments will obtain better returns than those who entrust their money to stockbrokers, trust officers, and other professional money managers. Thought-provoking.

STOCK MARKET: PSYCHOLOGY

Bernstein, Jacob. *The Investor's Quotient: The Psychology of Successful Investing in Commodities and Stocks.* New York: Wiley, 1980. 275 pp. $16.95.
Attempts to arrive at an investor's quotient, which measures the strengths and weaknesses of an investor. Various procedures are prescribed to connect behavior and attitudes that inhibit progress and success. Discusses sexual aspects of the market and how to use psychology to maximize investment success. Not a very convincing application of psychological principles and psychoanalytic theory to investment behavior.

Blotnick, Srully. *Winning: The Psychology of Successful Investing.* New York: McGraw-Hill, 1978. 245 pp. $15.95.
What kind of investor succeeds in the stock market? What kind fails? By following 1,103 investors, small and large, over a decade, the author has some intriguing answers. The largest losses were incurred by the most knowledgeable and sophisticated investors; "hot stocks" were not the big money makers and proved the single surest way to failure; 5 percent of the group made sizable gains, yet not one of these highly successful investors was a serious student of the market. Blotnick profiles the younger investor, adult investor, and older investor, and shows differences in approaches to investing. He also shows that investors and the market go through a behavioral cycle of four stages of galloping greed: Stage I, where intent focuses on blue chip and glamor stocks, Stage II, on NYSE stocks of lesser quality and some Amex issues, Stage III, on Amex and OTC issues, Stage IV, on OTC and new issues. A fascinating and thought-provoking insight into the psychology of investment behavior.

Smith, Charles. *The Mind of the Market: A Study of Stock Market Philosophies, Their Use and Their Implications.* Totowa, NJ: Rowman and Littlefield, 1981. 218 pp. $16.95.
A sociologist looks at the stock market and finds four basic overviews, orientations, or philosophies: the fundamentalist/economic view, the insider/influence view, the cyclist/chartist, and the trader/market action view. These "ideal types" are True Believers. They are also Market Salesmen and Market Rationalizers. An intriguing and fascinating analysis of market philosophy, market style, and market behavior. An appendix supplies some practical advice utilizing the insights provided. Sociological terminology at times obscures the meaning.

Tuccille, Jerome. *Mind over Money: Why Most People Lose Money in the Stock Market and How You Can Become a Winner.* New York: Morrow, 1980. 188 pp. $8.95.
Tuccille takes the reader behind the scenes at a typical investment firm (which he calls Bull, Banks, Forbes, and Trotsky) to reveal, through witty and entertaining scenarios, some of the psychological games brokers play with clients and vice versa. An interesting psychological insight into why people lose money in the stock market and how they may win. Tuccille presents guidelines for establishing realistic investment goals with model portfolios appropriate to every income level. Among the

many suggestions: "Don't sleep with your broker." The recommendations for specific stock purchases seem somewhat off-target several years later.

OPTIONS

Dames, Ralph T. *The Winning Option.* Chicago: Nelson-Hall, 1980. 128 pp. $16.95.
The "little guy's" investment casino lies in the stock options market. The author's advice is to stay away from stocks and only risk investment capital in the options market at opportune times. The method recommended, requiring $4,000 to $5,000 in risk capital, consists of buying near-term, far-out call options in positive market environments. The underlying stocks should be actively traded, volatile issues in favorable industry groups. Dames backs his recommendations by using market indicators and timing tools. Not for the fainthearted.

Gastineau, Gary L. *The Stock Options Manual.* 2nd Edition. New York: McGraw-Hill, 1978. 389 pp. $18.95.
The author is manager of the Options Portfolio Service at Kidder, Peabody and Company. Gastineau presents a short history of options, how the over-the-counter options market works, characteristics of listed options, risk-reward characteristics of option strategies, tax-saving opportunities, evaluation of option contracts, and margin requirements. Contains a somewhat outdated bibliography and glossary. Useful for the serious student of options.

McMillan, Lawrence G. *Options as a Strategic Investment: A Comprehensive Analysis of Listed Option Strategies.* Englewood Cliffs, NJ: Prentice-Hall, 1980. 484 pp. $22.
Basic properties of stock options (right to buy or sell a particular stock at a certain price for a limited period of time), options strategies—call writing, bull and bear spreads and straddles, and put selling. Advanced-level discussion.

Tso, Lin. *Complete Investors Guide to Listed Options: Calls and Puts.* Englewood Cliffs, NJ: Prentice-Hall/Spectrum, 1981. 240 pp. $19.95; $11.95 (paper).
A comprehensive text analyzing the what, how, and why of options—a business contract that allows its holder to buy or sell stock in 100-share units at a certain price within a certain period of time. Tso covers methods of call selling and spreading, put buying and selling, put spreading, straddles, and tax considerations. Useful to those with specialized interests.

FUTURES TRADING

Angell, George. *Winning in the Commodities Market: A Money-Making Guide to Commodity Futures Trading.* Garden City, NY: Doubleday, 1979. 333 pp. $12.95.
An introduction to the excitement and risks involved in trading in copper, cattle, coffee, silver, gold, and other commodities. Also explains how the commodity ex-

changes work, contract specifications, margins, commissions, hedges, spread trading, and tax straddles. For the reader who likes to speculate.

Barnes, Robert M. *Making High Profits in Uncertain Times: Successful Investing in Inflation and Depression.* New York: Van Nostrand Reinhold, 1982. 208 pp. $35.
Most of what you need to know about buying commodity futures—cattle, coffee, gold, hogs, lumber, silver, wheat, and other commodities.

Geczi, Michael L. *Futures: The Anti-Inflation Investment.* New York: Avon/Discus, 1980. 208 pp. $2.95 (paper).
A concise, well-written explanation of how the futures market operates. Covers agricultural, metals, and financial futures (currencies and interest-bearing), debt instruments such as the three-month treasury bills and four-year T-notes. Answers most questions concerning arbitrage, brokers, commissions, contracts, ledgers, speculators, and the various exchanges (Amex, Commodities Exchange, Kansas City Board of Trade, Minneapolis Grain Exchange, New York Coffee and Sugar Exchange). Also provides sample commission rates, sources of market information, and an excellent glossary. Most informative, highly recommended.

Gould, Bruce. *The Dow Jones-Irwin Guide to Commodities Trading.* Homewood, IL: Dow Jones-Irwin, 1981. 361 pp. $27.50.
Designed to help even amateur investors understand and trade profitably. The *Guide* goes from a simple definition of commodities and futures through a complete review of trading and its mechanics, the complexities of pricing for the principal commodities, and instructions for designing one's own trading program. Gould argues that trading commodities is one of the last fields of speculative investment in the United States that is both rational and legal. An authoritative and fascinating book likely to interest novices, students, practiced traders, speculators, and brokers alike. Recommended as a reference source.

Horn, Frederick, and Farah, Vicker. *Trading in Commodity Futures.* New York: New York Institute of Finance, 1979. 373 pp. $18.95.
Analyzes the mechanics and intricacies of commodity futures trading. Technical coverage of federal legislation, opening, handling, and closing of accounts, margin requirements, placing and executing orders, hedging, technical and fundamental approaches to forecasting, and commodities strategy. Useful as a reference resource.

Huff, Charles, and Marinacci, Barbara. *Commodity Speculation for Beginners: A Guide to the Futures Market.* New York: Macmillan, 1980. 256 pp. $13.95.
A clear and methodical exposition of commodity markets and trading designed for uninformed general readers. Explains the probabilities, speculations, risks, and insurance involved in commodities trading, types of commodities traded, charting, hedging, and spreads. An excellent introductory book, the value of which is further enhanced by a list of further readings, names, and addresses of brokerage firms that handle commodity accounts, commodity pool operators, advisory services, charting services, wire services, and the commodities futures exchanges in the United States. Recommended.

Loosigan, Allan. *Foreign Exchange Futures: A Guide to International Currency Trading.* Homewood, IL: Dow Jones-Irwin, 1982. 350 pp. $27.50.

A book for those individuals and companies who do business in the international marketplace and seek to limit the exchange risk to which they are normally exposed when they spend, earn, or invest money outside their own country. Loosigan distinguishes between immediate or spot and forward rates and describes the mechanics and mathematics of future trading in foreign currencies. Also explained are balance of payments and the effects of market psychology, rumor, and conjecture on exchange rates. Particularly useful is a chapter on the hazards of speculating in foreign exchange.

Loosigan, Allan. *Interest Rate Futures.* Homewood, IL: Dow Jones-Irwin, 1980. 431 pp. $27.50.

Addresses basic issues such as what makes interest rates rise and fall, how to read and interpret bond and money market news, how to hedge against adverse interest rate news, and how to execute spreads and arbitrage. Covers the operation of the markets and the determination of prices. Technical.

Powers, Mark. *Getting Started in Commodity Futures Trading.* Cedar Falls, IA: Investor Publications, 1981. 324 pp. $9.95 (paper).

Powers introduces the reader to the world of commodity trading by explaining the basics of buying and selling of commodity futures. He points out that such transactions involve a good deal of risk in view of the high leverage and low margins. People trading commodity futures tend to be hedgers, "scalpers," or position traders. Powers covers the essentials of hedging, spreading, mortgage futures markets, treasury bill contracts, and strategies for trading options. Appendixes contain a commodity trader's score card and a set of instructions for doing some practice trading and a useful glossary. Powers provides valuable guidance on sources of information on commodities such as grains, soybeans, hogs, beef cattle, feeder cattle, pork bellies, sugar, metals, coffee, and cocoa. A clear description designed for those who wish to undertake trading in commodities.

Powers, Mark, and Vogel, David. *Inside the Financial Futures Markets.* New York: Wiley, 1981. 320 pp. $19.95.

Futures contracts include those on mortgage certificates, treasury bills, treasury bonds, commercial paper, and foreign currencies. The authors introduce, explain, and illustrate the basic concepts of trading interest rate futures contracts, the economic purpose of trading, and the development of a hedging plan. Foreign exchange futures are treated in a separate chapter. Technical discussion for advanced readers.

Reinach, Anthony. *The Fastest Game in Town/Trading Commodity Futures.* New York: Commodity Research Bureau, 1980. 175 pp. $10.

"If the name of the game is 'leverage and volatility,' " Reinach observes, "pork bellies make your fastest moving stocks resemble, by comparison, prime commercial paper." Commodity trading metes out justice with impartial speed. However, the potential rewards of competency and skill are virtually unlimited. Reinach graphically shows how the market works in pork bellies, wheat, soybean oil, gold, silver, cotton, and so on. The various types of commodity market action are explored in depth with a good explanation of the fundamental and technical approaches. A well-written, witty presentation of the spectacular profit (and loss) opportunities available in the commodity market. "Though oats, like snails, are very slow, they're faster than most stocks I know." Recommended.

Schwarz, Edward W. *How to Use Interest Rate Futures Contracts.* Homewood, IL: Dow Jones-Irwin, 1979. 217 pp. $27.
A primer of the fundamentals of commodity trading and the concepts of interest rate futures contracts. Details what you need to know before trading on a commodity exchange. Mark Powers, *Getting Started in Commodity Futures Trading* (see p. 92), covers much the same ground in language more intelligible to the layperson.

Williams, Larry. *How to Prosper in the Coming Good Years.* Chicago: Regnery-Gateway, 1982. 181 pp. $14.95.
Williams rejects the ideas of the theoreticians of the apocalypse (Ruff, Schultz, and Meyer) and believes that the gloomy, pessimistic trend has had its day. Good days are coming! He considers commodities to be the fastest game in town and the best investment opportunity, not only because the reward potential is so great but also because the data supporting the commodities market are clearer and more honest than the data underlying investing in gold, diamonds, real estate, and stocks. Specific methods are suggested for timing commodity trades. Williams also shows how to pick low-price stocks and how to take advantage of the real estate market and offers a forceful, bullish statement in support of Reaganomics.

Wolenik, Robert. *Buying and Selling Currency for Profit.* Revised Edition. Chicago: Contemporary Books, 1980. 197 pp. $5.95 (paper).
Wolenik explains the international supply and demand for money, how inflation affects currency rates, and the impact of Eurodollars and petrodollars. He also shows how to trade in currency futures. His book is more useful as a guide to the operation of the foreign currency market than as a source of investment advice. Presents a gloomy view of the future of the dollar. Obsolescent; needs updating.

Yarry, Mark. *The Fastest Game in Town: Commodities.* Englewood Cliffs, NJ: Prentice-Hall, 1981. 192 pp. $9.95.
A warning by a past president of the New Orleans Commodities Exchange that commodities trading is not a game for the faint of heart or for thin wallets. At least eight out of ten investors lose all or part of their investments. Yarry, after explaining the operation of the commodities market, exposes the various scams, stings, sales pitches, and swindles used to pickpocket millions from the innocent. He argues that the commodities industry requires a keen eye and a firm hand by the regulatory authorities. Specific suggestions for improving the odds on gaining in the market include carefully choosing a broker, starting with a minimum of $15,000 in risk capital, and making one's first play in a commodity with low volatility such as oats. A strong flavor of disillusionment is paramount: "Never again would I play the commodities market. I wasn't a compulsive gambler, but had nearly become a

commodities junkie. . . . I'm sleeping like a baby. Goodbye T-bonds, farewell pork bellies, adieu copper." Appendixes list the U.S. commodities exchanges and commodities actively traded on listed exchanges. A thought-provoking book likely to chill speculation fever. Recommended.

PENNY STOCKS

McWilliams, Bruce. *Penny Stocks: How the Small Investor Can Make Large Profits in the Penny Market.* Garden City, NY: Doubleday, 1982. 264 pp. $15.95.
The risks and the rewards of venture stocks, mostly priced under $5. McWilliams outlines the operations of the OTC (over-the-counter) market and the NASDAQ system; how venture capital is raised and traded and how to evaluate the more than 30,000 stocks traded; examples of high-technology stocks; oil and mining penny stocks; how to pick stocks and hitch your portfolio to the right market; how to select and use a broker; and the future of venture stocks. Lists penny stock brokerage houses and sources of penny stock information. Glossary. More detailed and informative than Jim Scott, *How to Make Money in Penny Stocks* (see below). Recommended.

Scott, Jim. *How to Make Money in Penny Stocks: The Ultimate Solution for the Small Investor.* Louisville, KY: Love Street Books, 1982. 96 pp. $14.95; $6.95 (paper).
Scott, a brokerage account executive, claims that the penny stock avenue is the last remaining place where the average investor can make a small fortune. In this slender volume, he describes the nature of penny stock offerings, the typical prospectus and high degree of risks involved, selecting a knowledgeable trading firm, over-the-counter stock trading, examples of speculating, basic trading rules, strategies for success, and how to open an account. Lists selected securities firms. Interesting.

BONDS

Holt, Robert. *Bonds: How to Double Your Money Quickly and Safely.* Oceanside, CA: California Health Publications/California Financial Publications, 1980. 184 pp. $10.
Bonds are interest-bearing certificates issued by a business corporation or a government agency, promising to pay the holder specific interest payments on particular dates, usually every six months. Holt covers bond yields, maturities, types and ratings of bonds, price fluctuations, and where to purchase bonds. Guidelines are given for researching and buying bonds, selection of mutual funds, money funds, tax-free bonds, and how to choose a bond expert.

Holt, Robert. *The Complete Book of Bonds: How to Buy and Sell Profitably.* New York: Harcourt Brace Jovanovich, 1981. 224 pp. $13.95.
For both beginners and experienced investors with information on how changing interest rates influence bond prices, types of bonds available, where they can be pur-

chased, how to increase income or capital by means of bonds, sources of research information, whether to purchase new-issue or listed bonds, limitations of various bond funds, when tax-free bonds are preferable to taxable bonds, how to avoid the many pitfalls that occasionally confront all investors, and more. A good guide to the bond market and finding the right bonds for one's needs. Informative but somewhat overenthusiastic exposition of the desirability of bonds relative to other types of investments.

Reilly, Jim. *Bonds as Investments in the Eighties.* New York: Van Nostrand Reinhold, 1982. 304 pp. $24.95.

Reilly argues that investing in bonds is the most profitable way to direct one's savings and provides full coverage of indexing, interest rate futures, money market funds, tax exemption for state and local bonds, and optimal timing. Reilly is bond editor of the *Market Chronicle.*

MUTUAL FUNDS

Donoghue, William, with Tilling, Thomas. *William Donoghue's Complete Money Market Guide: The Simple Low-Risk Way You Can Profit from Inflation and Fluctuating Interest Rates.* New York: Harper & Row, 1981. 224 pp. $12.95.

All you wanted to know about money funds, treasury bills, money market and small saver certificates, unit investment trusts, and other money market instruments. Donoghue advocates moving money from low-yielding passbook savings accounts into money funds. He explains how money funds work, how to evaluate a fund's portfolio, how to find a money fund, how to read the yield tables in newspapers, the ten top money funds for the past five years, how to buy T-bills, and fund switching, moving money profitably taking full advantage of the "float." Lists of funds are provided to help investors select those best suited to their needs. Donoghue is the publisher of *Moneyletter* and *Money Fund Report.* Recommended.

Donoghue, William, with Tilling, Thomas. *William E. Donoghue's No-Load Mutual Fund Guide.* New York: Harper & Row, 1983. 238 pp. $13.95.

To those who have read Donoghue's previous work, *William Donoghue's Complete Money Market Guide* (see above), the message will sound familiar: The only place to keep your money is in a money market fund, not in a bank. To use mutual funds to their full extent, Donoghue and Tilling advocate investment in no-load funds offered by the new families of funds (stock, bond, and money funds) clustered under one mutual umbrella. As conditions change, one can switch from one fund to another. The technique advocated is the SLYC 12 percent solution. This involves Safety, Liquidity, Yield, and Catastrophe Proofing, and getting the best of both the money and stock markets. Twelve percent is the key money market rate above which you want to be 100 percent in the money market and below which you want to move cautiously into stock market mutual funds. The authors explain the mechanics of investing in no-load mutual funds, IRAs and Keoghs, and mutual funds, and how to withdraw funds in the most profitable manner. Three appendixes list recommended investment newsletters, details of the 12 percent switching solution, and a directory of mutual funds showing address, year organized, assets, and rates of return. Informative and well organized. Recommended.

King, Norman. *The Money Market Book.* New York: Grosset & Dunlap/Ace Books, 1982. 128 pp. $3.95 (paper).
A guide to the attractive interest rates available from money market mutual funds. Explains the various types of short-term instruments used in money market funds: treasury bills (T-bills), treasury notes, U.S. government agency securities (FHA, Fannie Mae, and so on), commercial paper, negotiable certificates of deposit (CDs), banker's acceptances, repurchase agreements, Eurodollar CDs, and Yankee CDs. Explains how and where to purchase these instruments and lists the principal money market mutual funds, with minimum initial investment, minimum check amount, and average yields for 1979 and 1980. A good primer on how to get the maximum return on the investment dollar.

Rugg, Donald D., and Hale, Norman B. *The Dow Jones-Irwin Guide to Mutual Funds.* Revised Edition. Homewood, IL: Dow Jones-Irwin, 1982. 213 pp. $14.95.
Rugg and Hale supply guidelines that show how to place oneself within one of four risk categories (aggressive, moderate, conservative, extremely conservative) by evaluating one's financial situation. They advocate an investment program based on intermediate to long-term trading of money market funds and no-load equity funds. Guidance is given on how to pick no-load funds and how to use market indicators and timing techniques. They point out that there is "no appreciable correlation between sales fees and performance," which gives no-load funds an appreciable advantage. Good coverage of IRA and Keogh plans. A most useful book. Highly recommended.

Sarnoff, Paul. *The Smart Investor's Guide to the Money Market.* New York: New American Library, 1981. 193 pp. $3.50 (paper).
Sarnoff, a popular investment writer, shows how to get the best yield possible with the least risk on your reserve money. Money market mutual funds offer shares to the public, invest those shares at low risk in selected short-term debt securities, and allocate the interest income to each registered shareholder. Sarnoff explains how money funds work, typical yields, safety and performance compared with bank certificates of deposit, how you buy and redeem shares, check redemption privileges, and so on. Also covered are the various types of short-term money market instruments—T-bills, government bonds and notes, bank certificates of deposit, commercial paper, and corporate notes. Includes details of how to use money market funds to the best advantage and a list of all the major funds, addresses, phone numbers, deposit requirements, and the author's personal rating of each fund. Readable and concise.

GOLD AND SILVER

Beckhardt, Israel. *The Small Investor's Guide to Gold.* New York: Woodhill Press, 1979. 207 pp. $2.95 (paper).

The author believes that gold is the only insurance policy you can buy, and that while gold is money, paper is nothing but a promise. An overenthusiastic guide to the purchase of gold bullion, coins, gold mining shares, and other gold-related investments.

Breckner, Steven K. *The Hard Money Book: An Insider's Guide to Successful Investment in Currency, Gold, Silver, and Precious Stones.* New York: Capitalist Report Press, 1979. 148 pp. $19; $6.95 (paper).

An economic journalist looks at the worsening inflationary trend, the operation of the federal paper dollar mill, government bonds (certificates of guaranteed confiscation), and global hyperinflation and concludes that "hard" assets are the answer since they provide the opportunity to preserve, and even increase, one's capital. In a practicable and readable manner, Breckner shows how to invest in gold, silver, foreign currencies, and futures trading. Excellent coverage of the investment opportunities in foreign currency.

Cavelti, Peter. *How to Invest in Gold.* Piscataway, NJ: New Century, 1980. 192 pp. $5.95 (paper).

The author is senior vice-president of a bank, in charge of its international dealings in precious metals and foreign currencies. His book is an excellent compendium of useful information on gold and inflation, supply and demand for gold, how it is traded, how to select a dealer and how much to invest, advantages, disadvantages, opportunities, and pitfalls of bullion coins (Krugerrands, etc.), numismatic coins, bullion certificates, gold mining shares, penny gold stocks, gold future contracts, and jewelry. Also provides a useful glossary, lists of major gold mining operations, bullion dealers, acceptable refiners and assayers, a bibliography, and a complete listing of gold coins minted since the year A.D. 1000. Recommended.

Cobleigh, Ira U. *Double Your Dollars in 600 Days.* New York: Harmony, 1979. 196 pp. $9.95. O.P.

How and why to invest in gold, silver, diamonds, platinum, tungsten, and molybdenum. Describes what to buy, whom to buy from, and when to buy and sell. The enthusiastic recommendations need to be reconsidered with some caution.

Feinman, Jeffrey. *How You Can Profit from Today's Gold Rush.* A Dolphin Book. Garden City, NY: Doubleday, 1980. 94 pp. $4.95.

How to buy and sell gold, silver, and other precious metals in today's volatile market. Feinman provides a succinct summary of essential data: whether to buy gold, buying and selling of gold coins, bullion, stocks, futures, and jewelry, and investing in silver, diamonds, and platinum. Feinman advises the buyer to pay close attention to authenticity, market price, and overcommitment.

Green, Timothy. *The New World of Gold: The Inside Story of the Mines, the Markets, the Politics, the Investors.* New York: Walker, 1982. 260 pp. $15.95.

All you want to know about gold from the mines of South Africa to the markets in London, Zurich, New York, Hong Kong, and Singapore. An intriguing compendium of information about gold, but not very useful from the investment point of view.

Kettell, Brian. *Gold.* Cambridge, MA: Ballinger, 1981. 283 pp. $22.50.
A reference work on all aspects of gold—physical properties, history, role of gold in the international monetary system, major factors affecting supply, demand and price, the future of gold, and more. Two chapters discuss gold as an investment and the world's gold markets. The Laffer Plan and the Bareau Plan to restore a gold-related standard are also analyzed. Informative but dull reading.

Merton, Henry. *Your Gold and Silver: An Easy Guide to Appraising Household Objects, Coins, Heirlooms, and Jewelry.* New York: Macmillan/Collier, 1981. 127 pp. $5.95 (paper).
A book designed to take the mystery out of words such as solid gold, karat gold, gold-filled, vermeil, gold plate, coin silver, sterling silver, gold flash, and so on. Of particular value is the glossary of words and terms for precious metals. Merton provides an informative guide to buying and selling gold and silver in its many forms.

Sarnoff, Paul. *Trading in Gold: How to Buy, Sell, and Profit in the Gold Market.* New York: Simon & Schuster, 1982. 129 pp. $14.95.
A clear and concise treatment of the mechanics of the volatile market for gold. Sarnoff, director of research at Rudolf Wolff Commodity Brokers, describes trading in gold bullion, medals and coins, gold shares and funds, and gold futures and options. The coverage of gold trading strategies, future contracts, spreading, and hedging is particularly lucid. Helpful information on investing in gold. Recommended.

Sinclair, James, and Schultz, Harry. *How You Can Profit from Gold.* Westport, CT: Crown/Arlington House, 1980. 168 pp. $14.95.
The authors contend that a monetary system must be devised that is sound, viable, and disciplinary—with the help of gold. After reviewing the history of gold, Sinclair and Schultz advise the judicious purchase of gold bullion, coins, shares, and futures. They answer 20 frequently asked questions about gold and supply a glossary of monetary and foreign exchange terms. This book is more an analysis of the economic, political, historical, and philosophical implications of gold than an investment manual.

Smith, Jerome, and Smith, Barbara. *Silver Profits in the Eighties.* New York: Books in Focus. 1982. 218 pp. $16.95.
The authors believe that silver prices must move up strongly in the 1983-1985 period and beyond and that silver could become more valuable than gold. "Silver in 1982 is a cheap precious metal on the way to becoming a scarce and expensive strategic metal within this decade." The Smiths analyze the supply and demand for silver, existing stockpiles, and the operation of the silver market from 1960 to the present time. Silver, gold, and platinum price movements are compared and specific information is given on how, how much, where, and when to invest in precious metals. An informative compendium for those interested in investment in silver.

What's It Worth? 1983 Investors Guide: Silver Bullion and Coins. New York: Dell, 1982. $2.95 (paper).
A compact handbook on grades of silver, purity and value, bullion, coins, and pricing information for silver dimes, quarters, half dollars, and foreign coins. Contains

much practical information for the small investor such as how and where to buy silver. Assumes that investment in silver is judicious and irresistible in view of worldwide inflation.

Wolenik, Robert. *How You Can Share in the Futures Being Made in Gold*. Chicago: Contemporary Books, 1980. 136 pp. $9.95. O.P.
The author provides an introduction to gold investment and explains the supply and demand for gold, pricing of gold in world markets, and buying and selling of gold bullion. Particularly useful is the information on numismatic gold coins such as Gold Eagles, Maple Leafs, Krugerrands, Mexican 50 pesos, and Austrian ducats and a list giving gold content and other data for the major gold coins of the world.

STRATEGIC METALS

Goldberg, Philip, and Posner, Mitchell J. *The Strategic Metals Investment Handbook*. New York: Holt, Rinehart & Winston, 1983. 225 pp. $17.50.
A global analysis of the supply and demand for strategic metals with emphasis on market operation and investment possibilities. A good reference resource.

McLendon, Gordon. *Get Really Rich in the Coming Super Metals Boom*. New York: Pocket Books, 1981. 254 pp. $4.95 (paper).
How to buy and sell strategic metals such as cobalt, gallium, germanium, molybdenum, silicon, tungsten, and tantalum. Unfortunately, the practical advice is buried in a morass of political and economic commentary aimed at establishing the author's point that all paper money over time becomes valueless. Consequently, it is argued that the prudent investor must seek the safety of durable tangibles. Not an easy book to use.

Sinclair, James E., and Parker, Robert. *The Strategic Metals War: The Current Crisis and Your Investment Opportunities*. Arlington, VA: Arlington House, 1983. 310 pp. $14.95.
Politics and economics are intermingled in this review of chromium, manganese, platinum, tungsten, cobalt, and related nonfuel minerals. The authors provide helpful suggestions on how to select a broker, how to avoid fraud, how to utilize the tax advantage of investment in strategic materials, and how to benefit from future developments. The book is an enthusiastic endorsement of the investment potential of strategic metals.

Szuprowicz, Bohdan. *How to Invest in Strategic Metals*. New York: St. Martin's Press, 1982. 224 pp. $13.95.
Strategic metals—rhodium, iridium, germanium, uranium, indium, gallium, silicon, selenium, beryllium, platinum, titanium—are those that play a crucial role in military defense and high-technology industry. Szuprowicz describes the availability and supply of "the gold of the 1980's," and the accompanying investment opportunities. Also explained are where to obtain metals price information and quotations (from trade and specialized periodicals), finding a reliable strategic metal broker, what to ask the broker of your choice, when to sell strategic metals, types of mutual

funds, and specific companies as strategic metals investment opportunities. Contains a comprehensive listing of sources of useful and authoritative information on strategic metals. Fascinating and futuristic. Recommended.

Youngquist, Walter. *Investing in Natural Resources: 1980's Guide to Tomorrow's Needs.* 2nd Edition. Homewood, IL: Dow Jones-Irwin, 1980. 281 pp. $14.95.
A geologist reviews the mineral, agricultural, and forest resources of the United States. A good reference resource on the availability of precious metals and long-term investment opportunities.

DIAMONDS AND GEMS

Dohrmann, Bernhard. *Grow Rich with Diamonds: Investing in the World's Most Precious Gems.* San Francisco: Harbor, 1981. 167 pp. $12.95.
Despite the overpriced and overextended diamond market following the panic buying of 1980, Dohrmann believes that, with selective buying, diamonds remain the premier form of investment in the world. After showing how diamonds function in the marketplace and the history of diamond prices, Dohrmann describes how to invest in diamonds. For those who believe that diamonds are not only forever, but also an investor's best friend! Michael Freedman, *The Diamond Book* (see below), is more comprehensive and informative.

Freedman, Michael. *The Diamond Book: A Practical Guide for Successful Investing.* Homewood, IL: Dow Jones-Irwin, 1981. 160 pp. $14.95.
Freedman, editor of *The Gemletter*, a quarterly newsletter devoted to diamond market news and trends, reviews diamond production, and supply and demand in the modern era. Of particular value are his chapters on the four determinants of a diamond's value (color, clarity, cut, and carat weight), certification and grading by the Gemological Institute of America (GIA) and the European Geological Laboratory (EGL), when, where, and how to buy and sell diamonds, and an appendix on guidelines for buying diamonds. Excellent, practical, authoritative advice on diamonds as an investment. Highly recommended.

Hudgeons, Marc. *The Official Investors Guide to Buying and Selling Gold, Silver and Diamonds.* Orlando, FL: House of Collectibles, 1981. 197 pp. $6.95 (paper).
Become an expert in buying and selling intelligently! Hudgeons, in one small volume, provides a wealth of essential information on the origin, forms, value, and buying and selling of gold, silver, and diamonds. He explains, for example, diamond crystal shapes and terminology, grading, carat weight, color, clarity, and cleaning and how to tell real diamonds from fakes. Diamonds for investment should be at least one full carat in weight and have high clarity and color rating. Except in rare cases, they should be loose rather than mounted in jewelry. They should be accompanied by GIA (Gemological Institute of America) certification to eliminate the possibility of misgrading. A gem of a book! Highly valuable to those purchasing gold, silver, or diamonds. Recommended.

Wykoff, Gerald L. *Beyond the Glitter: Everything You Need to Know to Buy . . . Sell . . . Care for . . . and Wear Gems and Jewelry Wisely.* Washington, DC: Adamas, 1982. 216 pp. $17.95.
Much interesting information about gems and jewelry, but little on the subject of investment opportunities. Disappointing.

Zucker, Benjamin. *How to Buy and Sell Gems: Everyone's Guide to Rubies, Sapphires, Emeralds and Diamonds.* New York: Times Books, 1979. 117 pp. $12.95.
The author, a dealer in gems, believes that they are a worthwhile long-term holding and recommends that 10 to 20 percent of one's assets be in gems. Since 1900, the price of fine rubies, emeralds, sapphires, and diamonds has increased sixtyfold. Zucker describes how to evaluate a precious stone, where to shop for one, and where to sell a stone or piece of jewelry that you already own or have inherited. Recommended gem-purchasing portfolios are given for those with $10,000, $20,000, or $100,000 to invest. A good bibliography is included. High-quality photographs and diagrams enhance the text. A valuable guide to the gem market. Recommended.

COLLECTIBLES: ART, AUTOMOBILES, COINS, STAMPS

Assael, Michael. *Money Smarts.* New York: Playboy Paperbacks, 1982. 285 pp. $3.25 (paper).
Assael provides yet another game plan for beating inflation—exchange dollars for forms of wealth sustained most by inflation. These he calls magic assets or tangible investments. Most of the book consists of advice on how to invest in art, antiques, coins, gems, silver, strategic metals, and baseball cards, with information on bartering, bargaining, borrowing, inflation-beating hobbies, and inflation-proofing for retirement. Most of the advice is questionable for the average investor: "You can still pick up fine investment-quality oils for only $500"; and diamonds, stamps, and cars are excellent vehicles for an IRA account. To be read with caution.

Auerbach, Sylvia. *An Insider's Guide to Auctions.* Reading, MA: Addison-Wesley, 1981. 256 pp. $12.95; $7.95 (paper).
The action's at the auction—what goes on at auctions, how to bid, buy, and sell, and how to make money at auctions. Also what influences prices and how to sell an estate through an auction house. A good behind-the-scenes look.

Crumbley, Larry, and Crumbley, Tony. *The Financial Management of Your Coin/Stamp Estate.* New York: Arco, 1978. 234 pp. $16.50.
Analyzes the tax implications for those who collect stamps or coins. The authors differentiate among collectors, investors, and dealers showing the differences in tax laws applicable. Much of the information also applies to hobby-related investments, such as antiques, artwork, and model trains.

David, Carl. *Collecting and Care of Fine Art.* New York: Crown/Michelman Books, 1981. 160 pp. $10.

A factual manual for collecting and investing in art, written by the director of a well-known art gallery. The comprehensive coverage ranges from where to buy and sell art, what influences prices, opportunities and pitfalls of auctions, problems of forgery and restorations, to insurance, appraisals, security, and shipping. Detailed attention is given to the tax benefits and implications of long- and short-term investing in art. The tax advantages of donating works of art are also discussed, together with the Internal Revenue Service procedural guidelines governing the appraisal of contributed works of art. David provides a list of the major European and American schools of painting, with representative artists of each school, that can be considered for purchase. A good introduction to the intricacies of the art market for those contemplating the collection of paintings. Recommended.

Jenkins, Emyl. *Why You're Richer Than You Think*. New York: Rawson Wade. 1981. 249 pp. $12.95.
How to inventory and determine the value of your silver, china, furniture, antiques, collections, and treasures hidden away or packed in storage and how to find an appraiser. Lists books, price guides, magazines, and newsletters on antiques and collectibles.

Naifeh, Steven, with Smith, Gregory. *The Bargain Hunter's Guide to Art Collecting*. New York: Quill, 1982. 284 pp. $8.50 (paper).
Naifeh analyzes the pleasures and profits of collecting art. The author has accumulated a vast store of information on all aspects of art collection and investment: essential ground rules for investment, how to price an object, where to buy and sell art (dealers, auctions, flea markets, garage sales), what to collect (prints, photographs, contemporary art, American art, antiques) and what not to collect (limited editions and "schlock" art), care and preservation of art (security, conservation, and insurance). Particularly valuable are the lists of dealers and galleries, recommended readings and information sources, and the photographs. A fascinating book to browse and study. Recommended.

Pritchard, Jeffrey. *Heads You Win, Tails You Win: The Inside Secrets to Rare Coin Investing*. Reston, VA: Reston, 1983. 214 pp. $15.95.
In 1978, 242 gold pieces, purchased 30 years previously for $13,832, were sold at public auctions for $1.2 million, 87 times the original cost. Pritchard explains why rare coins are such an attractive and viable alternative to more traditional investments. Practical and sensible advice is offered on the determinants of investment quality in coins, acquiring coins from auctions and dealers, precautions to be taken in purchasing, tax advantages, storage and preservation, liquidating coins for cash (when and where to sell), recommendations for gold coin purchases, and an in-depth market analysis. Pritchard cautions that "rare coins are intended as a complement to a balanced portfolio, not as a replacement for one!" Contains glossary of numismatic terms and bibliography. Recommended.

Rush, Richard. *Automobiles as an Investment*. New York: Macmillan, 1982. 277 pp. $17.95.
Collector (or investment) cars are classified into five categories: postwar American classics (Ford Thunderbird), postwar foreign classics (Ferrari Daytona), prewar

American classics (Duesenberg), prewar foreign classics (Mercedes-Benz S Series), and antiques (Model T Ford). From 1970 to 1980 the price of collector cars, averaged for all cars in all five categories, rose almost seven times. Rush outlines the characteristics that turn an automobile into an investment—exotic quality, pioneering design, mechanically sound, large engine, original good condition, prestige—and argues that top-quality cars appreciate the most. He shows how to assess the condition of a car in order to make a judicial purchase and reviews the market and price trends for Rolls-Royce, Mercedes-Benz, Ferrari, and the major European and American classics. A highly informative exposition of the essentials involved in buying and selling exotic cars. Excellent photographs. Recommended.

Rush, Richard. *Selling Collectibles for Profit and Capital Gain.* New York: Harper & Row, 1981. 288 pp. $15.25.

How to cash in on art, antiques, and collectibles in view of the spectacular rise in prices since 1970. Rush, author of *Art as an Investment* (1961) and *Automobiles as an Investment* (see p. 102), maintains that the Rolls-Royce may very well in the future rival IBM stock as an investment. He focuses on how to sell, when to sell, and where to sell, describing the use of auction houses, dealers, collectors' clubs, newspaper advertisements, and museums. After reviewing the principal channels and methods of selling collectibles, Rush provides an appendix of selected North American auction houses, associations, and dealers, with names and telephone numbers of specialists (in clocks and watches, oriental art, rugs and carpets) at the larger auction houses. Coin and stamp dealers are also listed. Another appendix shows price trends in recent years for Old Master paintings, Impressionists, Italian Baroque, Dutch and Flemish paintings, antique furniture, classic cars, and Georgian silver. Fascinating. Highly recommended.

Shulman, Morton. *Anyone Can Make Big Money Buying Art.* New York: Macmillan, 1977. 136 pp. $7.95. O.P.

What, when, where, and how to buy and sell paintings, drawings, carvings, jade, stones, and other objets d'art. Shulman suggests a strategy for the smallest investor "to get his feet wet." Practical and readable.

Wagenheim, Kal. *Paper Gold: How to Hedge against Inflation by Investing in Postage Stamps.* New York: Peter Wyden, 1976. 202 pp. $8.95. O.P.

A classic, vintage book on the basic rules to follow in investing in stamps. Wagenheim shows how and what to choose, how to calculate a worthwhile return, how to check for steady appreciation, and the four favored areas (United States, Great Britain, most nations of Western Europe, and those with Western-style economies—Japan, Taiwan, Israel). A good guide to books, periodicals, auctions, catalogs, and sources of information on stamps.

5

Real Estate

BUYING AND SELLING A HOME

Bove, Alexander. *Joint Property: Everything You Must Know to Save Time, Trouble, and Money on Your Jointly Owned Property.* New York: Simon & Schuster/Fireside, 1982. 223 pp. $8.95 (paper).

A very readable and understandable explanation of the characteristics of and differences between joint property, tenancy by the entirety, and tenancy in common. Most of the real estate owned by husbands and wives in the United States is held in joint tenancy. To this must be added joint bank accounts, joint ownership of stocks and bonds, joint safe deposit boxes, and so on. Good coverage of rights and responsibilities of co-tenants, creditors' rights to jointly held property, joint tenancy and divorce, tax problems (and benefits) of joint property, avoiding probate, and helpful suggestions. Recommended.

Cahill, Thomas D. *How to Save Tax Dollars as a Homeowner.* Oakland, CA: Rampart, 1981. 52 pp. $9.95 (paper).

Explains the basic tax laws of buying and selling a personal residence. Itemizes and analyzes tax deductions relating to home purchase, improvements, repairs and maintenance, residential energy tax credits, casualty losses, selling costs, moving expenses, and home tax deferral. Not as comprehensive or lucid as Stephen P. Radics, Jr., and Miriam S. Geisman, *Your Home as a Tax Shelter* (see p. 110).

Drotning, Phillip. *You Can Buy a Home Now.* Chicago: Contemporary Books, 1982. 178 pp. $11.95.

105

This book's message is terse: "If you have stable employment, a reasonably good income, a decent credit rating, the willingness to spend some time and energy to inform yourself, and the motivation to search for the most attractive opportunity, buying now may afford the best chance you'll ever have to realize the American dream." To take advantage of the good buying opportunities before the predicted inflationary boom that will emerge when pent-up demand can no longer be contained, Drotning shows how to select a home, find the right broker, determine affordability, select the best housing option (old home, new home, condominium), determine a fair price, choose a new neighborhood, and financing alternatives such as graduated payment mortgages and seller financing. Useful to consumers in making intelligent decisions in home purchasing. Recommended.

Feins, Judith, and Lane, Terry S. *How Much for Housing? New Perspectives on Affordability and Risk.* Cambridge, MA: Abt Books, 1981. 189 pp. $19.

The authors offer new ways to consider what people can and should spend for housing. They suggest that the affordability issues for renters and home owners are very different and must be linked to income levels. The guidelines offered are based on the observed spending patterns of recent home buyers at a variety of income levels. To a far greater extent than the old 25 percent rule, these standards provide guidance to consumers on the range of possibilities for their budget decisions and to lenders on the range of acceptable shelter income ratios for mortgage applicants. A solid research study.

Gadow, Sandy. *All about Escrow: Or How to Buy the Brooklyn Bridge and Have the Last Laugh.* Richmond, CA: Express, 1981. 183 pp. $8.95 (paper).

Step-by-step guidance through the escrow process, explaining how property changes hands. Escrow involves an impartial third party brought into the transaction to see that the primary parties, the buyer and the seller, perform as they agreed they would. Gadow concisely answers many questions such as: What are the requirements for escrow? How does the escrow holder get paid? How does one open escrow? What is involved in a title search, financing, or title insurance? How do prorations work? A helpful glossary explains commonly used terms: abstract of title, bill of sale, certificate of title, deed, easement, fee simple estate, lien, promissory note, set back. Provides access to information not readily available to most people. Recommended.

Gilmore, Louis. *For Sale by Owner.* New York: Simon & Schuster/Fireside, 1979. 169 pp. $4.95 (paper).

How to sell your own home without a broker and save thousands of dollars. Discusses how to set the right price, how to prepare real estate ads that sell, how to market and show your property, and how a lawyer can help your sale. This book was written before the advent of a depressed real estate market and the intricacies of creative financing that can complicate a sale. Outmoded.

Hughes, Alan. *A Home of Your Own for the Least Cash: The Home Buyer's Guide for Today.* Washington, DC: Acropolis, 1982. 304 pp. $8.95 (paper).

A treasure trove of information on the more affordable types of housing currently available. Particular attention is paid to factory-built frame houses, panelized home packages, modular or sectional homes, and shell homes. Hughes discusses condominiums, cooperatives, and duplexes, suburban and country rehabilitations, mobile homes, log houses, dome houses, and earth-sheltered homes. The second part of the book covers how to get financing, loan shopping and qualifying, FHA, VA loans, and "points," the new adjustable-rate mortgages (ARMs), graduated payment mortgages (GPMs), shared appreciation mortgages (SAMs), and other inflation-oriented mortgage plans, "buy downs," land contracts, and joint ventures, settlement costs, and the closing process. Two glossaries cover house construction terminology and real estate/home financing terms. Superb explanation of a complex, volatile field. Highly recommended.

Irwin, Robert. *How to Buy a Home at a Reasonable Price.* New York: McGraw-Hill, 1979. 246 pp. $13.50.
Covers the basics: what you can really afford, how to buy at a reasonable price, condominiums, rehabilitating rundown houses, how to build your own house, alternatives such as domes, log cabins, barns, kits, and prefab. An appendix lists producers of modular homes, log cabins, barns, panelized houses, and other manufactured homes and products. Good suggestions for saving money.

Janik, Carolyn. *The House Hunt Game: A Guide to Winning.* New York: Macmillan, 1979. 182 pp. $6.95. O.P.
What to consider in buying a dream home: location, age, style, and livability, potential trouble spots (how old is the water heater?), working with a sales agent, negotiating, contracts and closing, and mortgages. Janik emphasizes the necessity of exercising rational judgment and not responding emotionally to factors such as period decorating and white picket fences. Sensible.

Janik, Carolyn. *Selling Your Home: A Guide to Getting the Best Price with or without a Broker.* New York: Macmillan, 1982. 208 pp. $8.95; $4.95 (paper).
An updated expansion of the author's *The House Hunt Game* (see above). Rational advice on when to sell, setting a price, preparing the property for sale, advertising, showing the house, closing, and selling by the owner. If a house does not sell after four or five weeks, one should use the services of a real estate agent. Janik explains how to select an agent from the various types of realtors (franchises, supergiant, local agency), negotiating strategy, and closing. The author provides a checklist of essential points to be considered before signing a real estate contract. A good explanation of the pros and cons of selling with and without an agent. Realistic and informative. Recommended.

Jensen, Ronald W. *Sell Your Home "By Owner" and Save the Commission.* New York: Warner, 1979. 184 pp. $4.95 (paper).
Jensen gives "the nuts and bolts" of selling your own home. He argues that a real estate transaction is very complicated, but the only two professionals necessary in most cases are an appraiser and attorney. The author shows how to determine fair market value, how to advertise and "show" a house, how to treat potential buyers, and how to draw up a sale agreement and write in contingencies. Finally, Jensen explains how to deal with typical real estate salespeople: Mr. Twoface, Mr. Phony, Mr.

Setup, Mr. Blockbuster, Mr. Wheel and Deal, and Mr. Threatening Violence. Opinionated but stimulating and amusing.

Kiev, Phyllis. *The Woman's Guide to Buying Houses, Co-ops, and Condominiums.* New York: Ballantine, 1981. 352 pp. $7.95 (paper).
In 1981, women were buying one-third of all the condominiums and 10 percent of all the houses sold. Kiev covers conventional topics: selecting property, financing the deal, types of mortgages, houses, co-ops, condominiums, rental properties, how to profit from the new tax laws, and so on. However, all of this has been more comprehensively and lucidly discussed elsewhere. There is very little to distinguish this book apart from its feminist point of view, which, unfortunately, is often lost in the discussion. Skip this title.

Kratovil, Robert, and Kratovil, Ruth. *Buying, Owning and Selling a Home in the 1980's.* Englewood Cliffs, NJ: Prentice-Hall, 1982. 340 pp. $19.95; $15.95 (paper).
A compendium of information in question-and-answer format on most aspects of home ownership: rent or buy, affordability, where to locate, you and your broker, appraisals, inspecting the home, contracts and titles, closing deals, mobile homes, inspecting a home, discrimination, and insurance. Also covers new types of home mortgages, including renegotiable interest rates and shared profit mortgages. An oversize book rather difficult to use as a ready guide.

Lank, Edith. *Home Buying.* Chicago: Real Estate Education Company, 1980. 48 pp. $3.95 (paper).
Factors to be considered in home buying—who, why, when, how much can you spend, relationship with a real estate broker, costs of home ownership. Badly out of date in view of new developments in creative financing.

Lee, James S. *Buyer's Handbook for the Single-Family House.* New York: Van Nostrand, 1979. 162 pp. $7.95 (paper).
This practical guide leads the potential buyer through each key step of the purchase process—the initial search, thorough inspection, negotiating with the seller, selection of a lender, and closing of the sale. Detailed instructions are given on, for example, exterior inspection of patios, decks, driveways, roof, outside surface, and so on. The liberal use of diagrams, illustrations, cartoons, and worksheets enhances the value of this book. An attractive, readable, and useful book. Recommended.

Mason, Alexander. *The Real Estate Broker's Inside Guide to Selling Your Own Home (And Keeping the Commission!)* New York: Coward-McCann and Geoghegan, 1982. 288 pp. $11.95.
How to determine the correct selling price, advertise, show a house to the best advantage, technicalities of negotiating and closing a deal, and sources of mortgages and creative financing. A balanced discussion of the advantages and difficulties of "for sale by owner."

Murphy, Michael. *How to Buy a Home while You Can Still Afford To.* New York: Sterling, 1981. 160 pp. $10.95; $5.95 (paper).

Attempts to take the mumbo-jumbo and confusion out of home buying. Murphy analyzes the housing market and addresses a fundamental question—Should I wait for interest rates to drop? Also covered are how to compute your taxes as a renter versus income taxes saved if you own a house, avoiding legal problems with contracts and mortgages, financing to your best advantage, how to pick the right neighborhood and home, how to shop for a mortgage. Includes a sample mortgage application form and tables to compute monthly mortgage payments. Pedestrian presentation.

Nessen, Robert L. *The Real Estate Book: A Complete Guide to Acquiring, Financing and Investing in a Home or Commercial Property.* Boston: Little, Brown, 1981. 229 pp. $12.95.
An experienced real estate lawyer and investment banker outlines what is involved in the purchase of a home: renting versus owning, the down payment, mortgages, condominiums and cooperatives, effects of inflation, and the expected return on the investment. Also discusses principles of investing in commercial property such as rental housing, raw land, shopping centers, and office buildings. Good explanation of "points," closing costs, equity, etc., but somewhat weak on alternative and creative financing.

Nielsen, Jens, and Nielsen, Jackie. *How to Save or Make Thousands when You Buy or Sell Your House.* Garden City, NY: Doubleday/Dolphin, 1979. 179 pp. $6.95.
The Nielsens provide a lucid explanation of the true costs in buying or selling a house. They show how to set a fair market value and sell for a profit, outlining what is involved in appraisals, banker's commissions, title insurance, points, and closing costs. Conversely, if buying, how to evaluate and select property, finance a deal, and arrange for deed and title. Also discussed are the legal and financial aspects of closing, proration, fixtures, easements, liens, and mortgages. Comprehensive and comprehensible. Recommended.

O'Neill, Richard. *The Homebuyer's Guide for the 80's: A Complete Guide to Every Step You Need to Take for the Biggest and Best Investment You'll Ever Make.* New York: Grosset & Dunlap, 1980. 256 pp. $7.95 (paper).
Useful as a checklist to determine whether you can afford to buy a house, how to choose the right house, sources of financing, and the legal and financial procedures for purchasing property. A good general survey of the subject. Glossary of basic terminology.

Petersen, Kristelle. *The Single Person's Home-Buying Handbook.* New York: Dutton/Hawthorn, 1980. 320 pp. $7.95 (paper).
The basics of real estate from the point of view of the single investor: housing alternatives, how to evaluate the quality of a prospective home, mortgages and financing, negotiating and settlement costs. Although much of the content is covered elsewhere, this book contains several valuable chapters: "Special Tips for Single Persons Buying Together," "Advice for the Single—Again," and "Suggestions for the Single Parent."

Phipps, Antony A., and Moseley, Norma F. *The Homebuying Guide.* Cambridge, MA: Abt Books, 1978. 137 pp. $12.50; $7.95 (paper).

Highly unusual presentation of basic factors involved in home purchase employing imaginative and clever graphics in the form of tables, charts, diagrams, cartoons, and worksheets. On a very elementary level, the essential topics are covered: to buy or not to buy, choosing the right house, negotiating the sales price and financing, purchase contracts and closing costs, obtaining a mortgage, home maintenance. Highly recommended for the lucid illustrations that successfully clarify the complex decisions and problems involved in buying and owning a home.

Pomeroy, Ruth. *Redbook's Guide to Buying Your First Home.* New York: Simon & Schuster/Fireside, 1980. 215 pp. $4.95 (paper).

Easy-to-understand discussion of the factors involved in home purchase: how much you can afford, locating the right neighborhood, how to judge a house, appraisals, building inspectors, and lawyers, financing and types of mortgages, closing, planning the move, and settling in. Excellent photography of various types and styles of houses. Contains home buyer's dictionary and list of booklets worth sending for.

Price, Irving. *How to Get Top Dollar for Your Home in Good Times or Bad.* New York: Times Books, 1980. 187 pp. $9.95.

Most valuable in this book are the 100 low-cost improvements most likely to sell a house, such as wash all windows inside and out, fix the front door bell, repair the gargage door so that it opens and closes, replace defective gutters, and so on. Price also provides helpful information on finding a broker/realtor, reducing legal fees and closing costs, and minimizing tax liability. Other chapters describe how to survive a company transfer, what to do in the event of attempted foreclosure, and 101 reasons why your sale may not go through. Practical advice. Recommended.

Radics, Stephen P., Jr., and Geisman, Miriam S. *Your Home as a Tax Shelter: How to Save Taxes When You Buy, Hold, or Sell Your Home.* Rockville Centre, NY: Farnsworth, 1982. 112 pp. $8.95 (paper).

A comprehensive and lucid guide to the many tax regulations and advantages governing home ownership. Tax benefits are derived from moving expenses when buying, closing and selling costs, improvements and maintenance (additions, air conditioning, kitchen equipment, lawns, and landscaping), energy tax credits, mortgage interest and property tax deductions, selling costs and golden benefits (capital gain up to $125,000 may be forgiven). Sample forms and worksheets are provided with file pockets for inserting slips, receipts, invoices, and cancelled checks. Straightforward, thorough, and methodical. Recommended.

Rejnis, Ruth. *Her Home: A Woman's Guide to Buying Real Estate.* Garden City, NY: Doubleday/Anchor, 1980. 183 pp. $8.95.

Forthright, concise advice for women on whether to buy a house, financing, house hunting, condominiums, mobile homes, housing choices for special times in your life (after divorce, as you approach retirement), living together and property rights, investing in other forms of real estate (syndicates and REITs). Each chapter contains a section recommending future readings. Highly recommended.

Rejnis, Ruth. *How to Buy Real Estate without Getting Burned.* New York: Playboy Paperbacks, 1981. 288 pp. $3.50 (paper).

A slick, somewhat superficial treatment of the basics of real estate: why buy, finding a house, how to buy a condominium, vacation homes, ownership of land, and avoiding home improvement rip-offs. Very weak on creative financing and the variety of innovative mortgages now available.

Speraw, Linda. *How to Buy Your First Home.* New York: Facts on File. 1983. 139 pp. $14.95.

Advice on the creative strategies now available to those with limited means who wish to buy a home, whether for pride of ownership, sense of security, or as investment. Speraw contrasts the conventional approach to home financing (banks, savings and loan associations, FHA) with the newer creative methods such as assumption, second and third mortgages, wraparounds, land contracts, buy-downs. This is a very practical and helpful book, well written in a very readable style, that also offers some interesting observations on the pros and cons of real estate agents and the mechanics of purchasing a home (contracts, escrow, etc.). Contains a good glossary. Recommended.

Sumichrast, Michael, and Shafer, Ronald. *The Complete Book of Home Buying: A Consumer's Guide to Housing in the 80's.* Homewood, IL: Dow Jones-Irwin, 1980. 366 pp. $14.95.

Sumichrast is chief economist, National Association of Home Builders; Shafer is on the staff of the *Wall Street Journal.* They review housing as an investment, types of homes, condominiums and town houses, rehabilitation, financing and mortgages, tax considerations, home improvement, and how to sell a house. Dull textbook style; out of date.

MORTGAGES AND CREATIVE FINANCING

Coffee, Frank. *Everything You Need to Know about Creative Home Financing.* New York: Simon & Schuster, 1983. 256 pp. $15.50; $5.95 (paper).

Coffee analyzes the mathematics of the new forms of mortgages available on today's market, such as graduated payment, variable rate, shared appreciation, and new techniques such as land contract and wraparounds. A good authoritative source, but not as readable as Robert Irwin, *The New Mortgage Game* (see p. 112).

Consumers Guide to Mortgage Payments. Aurora, IL: Caroline House, 1981. 254 pp. $5.95 (paper). O.P.

Answers the most commonly asked questions about mortgage financing. Describes very briefly how mortgages work, sources of mortgage money (conventional mortgages, FHA loans, FHA graduated-payment mortgages, VA loans, renegotiable-rate mortgages), and prepaying a mortgage. Most of the book consists of mortgage payment tables, ranging from 9 percent to 18¼ percent, showing monthly payments necessary to amortize a loan. Also contains points discount tables showing the annual percentage rate on a mortgage when from one to five points discount are taken, and loan progress charts. Useful for consumers planning purchase of real estate.

Crittenden, Alan. *How to Adjust to Adjustable Home Mortgages.* Sacramento, CA: Cougar Books, 1981. 46 pp. $4 (paper).

Simple answers to key questions: Which is better for you—a fixed or adjustable rate? How often will the rate move? Is there a maximum limit on each rate change? How much can the rate change over the term of the loan? What index will be used? Will the payment be fixed, and for how long? What is the interest rate? What are the loan fees and costs? Mortgages are not simple any more. This book can help explain the intricacies of adjustable mortgages. Good glossary. Recommended.

Gabriel, Richard. *How to Buy Your Own House When You Don't Have Enough Money.* Englewood Cliffs, NJ: Prentice-Hall, 1982. 136 pp. $11.95; $5.95 (paper).

The days of easy cash, easy mortgages, and low-priced houses have disappeared. The most important consideration now is the ability to raise cash and structure the financing of the purchase. Gabriel shows how to build bank credit, how and where to borrow money (life insurance, personal loans, and so on), how to use collateralized loans, other loan sources ("Executive Loans by Mail" organizations), and more. Extensive coverage is also given to creative financing techniques such as assumable mortgages, land contracts, wraparound mortgages, purchase money mortgages, and land lease. Good advice on how to handle a broker and how to use effective negotiating techniques. Complements Robert Irwin, *The New Mortgage Game* (see below), which covers much the same ground. Recommended.

Haskell, Richard. *Sell Your House through Creative Financing—Without a Broker.* New York: Simon & Schuster, 1982. 230 pp. $17.95; $7.95 (paper).

How to sell a house and save the 6 or 7 percent in brokers' commissions. Since the ability and willingness of the seller to provide financing are critical in making a sale, Haskell reviews the types of owner financing and examples of contracts. A useful book to be used in conjunction with professional legal counsel. Most people will doubtless prefer to use a broker in view of the thicket of legal complications that may arise.

Irwin, Robert. *The New Mortgage Game.* New York: McGraw-Hill, 1982. 228 pp. $16.95.

The most understandable and readable explanation of the intricacies of creative financing—adjustable-rate mortgages (ARMs and VRMs), shared-appreciation mortgages (SAMs), graduated-payment mortgages (GPMs), land leases, municipal mortgages, reverse annuities. Irwin demonstrates the existence of a two-tier market for homes based upon the paper price (the seller taking no part in the financing) and the cash price (the seller carries all or part of the financing). The more financing the seller carries, the greater the difference between the paper and the cash price. In addition, Irwin shows how to get 5 percent down without creative financing (using private mortgage insurance), requirements of FHA and VA mortgages, advantages and disadvantages of fixed-rate mortgages, how to use Fannie Mae (FNMA) rollovers, and how to get a mortgage from a lender. Of great value to buyers and sellers alike at a time when the right type of financing can mean thousands of dollars in savings. Takes the mystery out of creative financing. Highly recommended.

Jacobe, Dennis, and Kendall, James N. *How to Get the Money to Buy Your New Home.* Homewood, IL: Dow Jones-Irwin, 1981. 224 pp. $14.95.
What you need to know about fixed-rate, variable-rate, graduated-payment, adjustable-rate, shared-appreciation, split-rate, and adjustable mortgages. Good, usable advice on how much you can afford to spend, how big a down payment you should make, when to get a mortgage loan, the essentials of creative financing, and how to cope with the necessary loan paperwork. Somewhat difficult reading in view of the complexity of the subject, but worth the effort considering the amount of money involved in purchasing a home.

Malcolm, Maurice. *How to Survive (And Make Money) in the Coming Real Estate Crunch.* New York: Ace Books/Charter Books, 1982. 232 pp. $2.95 (paper).
The great American dream has turned into a nightmare: Net home building is on the decline, people who want to sell cannot, and people who have to buy are finding mortgage loans almost impossible to obtain. High interest rates have led to the collapse of the real estate market. Malcolm shows how to buy and sell in a depressed market: Utilize creative financing (adjustable rate, balloon mortgage, convertible mortgage, escalated mortgage, flexible mortgage, floating mortgage, graduated-payment mortgage, renegotiable-rate mortgage, rollover mortgage, variable-rate mortgage), sell your own house, select a real estate agent, if you must, carefully, and save on taxes. Good advice on how to buy and sell a house in a depressed economy. Easy to read and understand. Recommended.

Morris, Hal, and Irwin, Robert. *How to Stop Foreclosure: What to Do When Your "Balloon Is Due and You're Laid Off or Facing Other Financial Crises."* San Francisco: Harbor, 1982. 224 pp. $9.95.
Of timely interest considering the popularity of creative financing and adverse economic conditions. In California, $6.5 billion worth of balloon payments will be due in the next three years. The authors discuss what to do if faced with foreclosure by explaining how the foreclosure process works and how the law can protect you, steps you can take to delay or prevent foreclosure, when to seek professional legal counsel, and how to negotiate with your lender. Readable and relevant.

Stloukal, Robert. *The Greatest Real Estate Book in the World: The One Way You Can Make a Fortune in the 80's.* New York: Times Books, 1980. $12.95.
The essentials of purchasing real estate, covering types of financing such as FHA loans, land contracts, graduated-payment loans, variable-rate mortgages, taxes, appraisals, buying and selling a home, property management, condominium conversion, and income property. Difficult to read; highly misleading title.

Temple, Douglas. *Creative Home Financing: You Can Buy a House, Condominium or Co-Op in Today's Market.* New York: Coward-McCann and Geoghegan, 1982. 287 pp. $13.95.

114 Real Estate

The key to home purchasing lies in creative financing in which the seller of the real estate helps to finance the buyer's mortgage, often at a lower rate than that offered by banks. Temple explains the intricacies involved in balloon mortgages, wrap-around mortgages, buy-downs, shared equity, and adjustable mortgages. Each chapter lists key terminology and refers the reader to the glossary at the back of the book.

CONDOMINIUMS

Bullock, Paul. *How to Profit from Condominium Conversions.* Wilmington, DE: Enterprise, 1981. 231 pp. $17.95.
Conversions are a natural consequence of the expanding demand for condominium-type housing. Bullock analyzes the magnificent investment opportunities for prospective buyers and covers the selection of property, acquisition and financing, the legal process of conversion, financing, marketing, and selling the units, tax angles, and profit tips. A bullish point of view reflecting a HUD projection that 4 percent of all rental stock will be converted by 1985.

Butcher, Lee. *The Condominium Book: Getting the Most for Your Money Revised for the 1980's.* Homewood, IL: Dow Jones-Irwin, 1980. 150 pp. $11.95 (paper).
A readable outline, with photographs, of the essentials involved in selecting and purchasing condominiums. A good analysis of the promise and the problems.

Cassiday, Bruce. *The Complete Condominium Guide.* New York: Dodd, Mead, 1979. 185 pp. $8.95. O.P.
An interesting look at the condominium lifestyle and its increasing popularity. Cassiday explains what a condominium is and the basic types: residential, urban, suburban, garden apartment, cluster housing unit, town house, duplex, fourplex, mansion unit, country estate. Other topics discussed are comparison shopping for the right condominium, checklist for buyers, 24 typical condo traps, how to finance a mortgage, legal documents required for closing a purchase, and the homeowners association. The author's message: Condominiums are conducive to happiness. Good bibliography. Valuable.

Heatter, Justin. *Buying a Condominium.* Third Edition. New York: Scribner's, 1982. 166 pp. $12.95.
Explains what condominiums and co-ops are, the roles of the lender and developer, homework a buyer must do, how to judge a property and find one suitable to one's lifestyle, pitfalls to avoid, when to sell, and how to approach the legal, financial, and insurance aspects of a purchase. Practical and detailed, but not very readable.

Ludy, Andrew. *Condominium Ownership: A Buyer's Guide.* Landing, NJ: Landing Press, 1982, 128 pp. $7.95 (paper).
A concise treatment of the mechanics of purchasing condominiums and cooperatives. Covers conversions, financing, types of condominiums, and time sharing. Ludy provides a very useful comparison between the relative merits and drawbacks of a con-

dominium, cooperative, and single-family house, each possessing the same number and size of rooms, workmanship, and extras. Extensive glossary. Recommended.

Natelson, Robert G. *How to Buy and Sell a Condominium.* New York: Simon & Schuster/Cornerstone Library, 1981. 160 pp. $4.95 (paper).
A book for those who own a condominium or plan to do so in the near future. Natelson, a real estate lawyer, discusses the differences between condominiums and cooperatives, advantages and disadvantages of condominiums, things to look for in buying (maintenance fees, interest rates, location, amenities, construction), the role of the attorney, methods of financing, title insurance, and the contract. For those who already own a unit, the author covers rights and duties as a condominium owner, how to deal with problems, renting your unit, and selling. A comprehensive and readable book of interest to many persons in view of the frenetic spread of condominiums in recent years. Recommended.

MOBILE HOMES

Fenwick, Daman. *Mobile Home Living: The Money-Saving Guide.* Blue Ridge Summit, PA: TAB Books, 1981. 224 pp. $14.95; $8.95 (paper).
Fenwick distinguishes between a trailer and a mobile home. A trailer is something you hitch to the back of your car for a weekend at the lake; a mobile home is not mobile—"some of them are harder to move than the pyramids of Giza." With a delightful sense of humor, the author describes the basic types of mobile homes (expandos, tipouts, tag-alongs, doubles, single wides), how to purchase and finance a mobile home, choosing a mobile home park and the right lot, saving on heating, cooling, and common repairs, driveway and roof problems, setup and maintenance, lawns and landscaping, and how to cope with the details of water hookups, laundry facilities, and common emergencies. Excellent pictures and diagrams. Indispensable reading for those contemplating mobile home living. Highly recommended.

Kramer, J. J. *The Mobile Home Guide: Your Affordable Manufactured House.* Indianapolis, IN: Bobbs-Merrill, 1982. 203 pp. $10.95 (paper).
Mobile homes offer 1,000 square feet or 3,000 square feet of living space from $15,000 to $35,000 compared with $75,000 to $200,000 for standard construction, excluding the land. Kramer discusses selection, financing, installation, and landscaping. Rather skimpy coverage of costs and financing.

Raskhodoff, Nicholas. *The Complete Mobile Home Book: The Guide to Manufactured Homes.* New York: Stein & Day, 1982. 240 pp. $21.95; $14.95 (paper).
A well-illustrated, informative guide to mobile home construction, accessories, problems, improvements, and maintenance, and other topics of importance to buyers and owners. Raskhodoff provides useful checklists for buying a mobile home, selecting a mobile home park, and estimating costs. Recommended.

RESORT TIME SHARING

Coltman, Michael M. *Resort Condos and Timesharing: Buyer Beware!* Seattle: Self-Counsel Press, 1981. 119 pp. $4.50 (paper).

This book covers both hotel condominiums and time sharing or "condominium ownership by the slice." A hotel condominium is one in which rooms (or units) are individually owned and which can be used by or rented to guests. With time sharing, which is less expensive, the buyer does not have title of ownership and is usually only allowed to use the room or suite for a limited period each year. The major emphasis is on time sharing, and Coltman explains the concept, basic types, and management contracts. The book's major value lies in its presentation of the consumer's point of view—is time sharing for you, how to shop for time-share units, how to cope with "grind sessions" (high-pressure sales presentations), key questions to ask before purchase, and financing considerations. Don't sign a contract until you read Coltman's book! Highly recommended.

Spencer, Phyllis. *Vacation Timesharing: Upper Income Holidays on Middle Income Budgets.* Toronto: Personal Library, 1982. 109 pp. $7.95 (paper); $8.95 Canada.

A guide to time sharing from the consumer's point of view. Spencer explains what is involved in time sharing, a curious hybrid of the hotel, tourism, and real estate industries. Time sharing is for those who want the luxury of a vacation home but cannot afford it in either time or dollars. The author shows what you are buying (membership, fee simple, lease rights, etc.), types of accommodations available, costs, how the exchange system works, and the legalities. Contains a time-share buyer's checklist, answers to typical questions, and addresses of the major exchange networks and industry organizations. Excellent pictures. Of great value to those considering time sharing as an alternative to hotels and vacation cottages.

Trowbridge, Keith W. *Resort Timesharing: How You Can Invest in Inflation-Proof Vacations for Life.* New York: Simon & Schuster, 1982. 192 pp. $11.50.

Resort time sharing is the purchase of a luxurious vacation home in increments of a week or more by a number of buyers, each of whom buys only the time they will use each year. Offers a detailed explanation of the essentials involved: how it works, various forms of time sharing, how to purchase resort time shares, what to expect in management and maintenance costs, worldwide exchange networks, buying in a foreign country, and legal guidelines and protection. Reflects somewhat an overenthusiastic evaluation of time sharing: "the hottest innovation in real estate to reach the consumer in this decade." Contains a short bibliography.

INVESTING IN REAL ESTATE

Allen, Robert G. *Creating Wealth: How to Make It—And Keep It!* New York: Simon & Schuster, 1983. 320 pp. $14.95.

Another enthusiastic, and inflated, statement of the riches available from real estate investment. Careful selection of property in the right neighborhood, renovation, property management, and eventual resale will doubtless, according to Allen, result in a fortune.

Allen, Robert G. *Nothing Down: How to Buy Real Estate with Little or No Money Down.* New York: Simon & Schuster, 1980. 255 pp. $13.95.

The author's message is simple, if not simplistic: "Don't wait to buy real estate; buy real estate and wait!" Allen believes that the cost of real estate will continue to grow, and the sooner one invests, the faster one's investment will grow. Instructions are given on how to identify, select, negotiate, finance, and sell income property. Similar in vein to Albert Lowry, *How You Can Become Financially Independent by Investing in Real Estate* (see p. 122). Needs updating in the light of subsequent developments in the real estate market.

Baker, Ruth. *Getting Rich in Real Estate Partnerships.* New York: Warner, 1981. 275 pp. $12.95.

Baker assumes that real estate values will go up faster than inflation. Group investment is the key to the whole field of real estate in that the group invests in property and shares the cost, income, profits, and risk. The author offers a workbook that explains the role of the general partner (who puts the deal together and manages the partnership and property), what to look for in a general partner, which kind of group you should choose (apartments, retail stores, shopping centers), how to tell a good property from a lemon, and how and where to obtain expert advice. Contains a useful glossary. Clear explanation; easy to read.

Bruss, Robert. *The Smart Investor's Guide to Real Estate: Big Profits from Small Investments.* New York: Crown, 1981. 270 pp. $12.95.

Comprehensive, authoritative guide to real estate by a well-known syndicated columnist. Explains why real estate is an excellent investment, how to find bargain properties, how to maximize tax benefits, how to finance purchases, how to price and sell houses, and how to obtain a lifetime income from property. A good explanation of the intricacies of wrap-around mortgages, lease options, and the principal residence replacement rule. Particularly helpful is the information on creative financing. Recommended.

Cabot, Val. *Goldmining in Foreclosure Properties.* Revised 2nd Edition. Pleasant Hills, CA: Impact, 1982. 207 pp. $13.50 (paper). O.P.

Cabot argues that now is a good time for knowledgeable investors to step in and enrich themselves while at the same time helping troubled owners resolve their problems. Mortgage payments generally consume a larger part of family income than before, creating difficulties for home owners. Cabot outlines the creative financing and negotiating techniques that can spell profits for investors. A number of specific case histories are presented in order to illustrate how to spot foreclosure property, analyze the investment potential, obtain financing, negotiate with troubled owners, inspect the property, and close a deal. Financial opportunism clothed in altruism.

Cardiff, Gray E., and English, John. *The Coming Real Estate Crash.* New Rochelle, NY: Crown/Arlington House, 1979. 192 pp. $12.95.

The authors analyze the anatomy of past real estate booms—Chicago in the 1830s, California in the 1980s, Florida in the 1920s—and relate the findings to the modern boom in real estate. They warn that concentrations of money in one investment outlet is a sign of vulnerability and suggest other investment alternatives to real estate such as stocks, bonds, and annuities. In view of a possible, precipitous collapse of real estate values, they advocate a transfer of assets out of real estate investments.

Cummings, Jack. *Cashless Investing in Real Estate*. New York: Playboy Press, 1982. 310 pp. $14.95.
Another how-to-get-rich-in real-estate book that assumes escalating inflation and an increase in real estate values. Cummings outlines in detail 40 ingenious techniques for acquiring real property with other people's money. These techniques range from shifting mortgages around to create more equity to the use of scrip to make real estate purchases and the private punt (private mortgages with "kickers" or benefits and incentives offered to private lenders). Ingenious game plans for the *highly* sophisticated individual investor.

Cummings, Jack. *Successful Real Estate Investing for the Single Person*. New York: Playboy Press, 1982. 368 pp. $3.95 (paper).
The basics of real estate investment oriented toward the needs of single persons: reasons why singles need to own real estate, who should buy and how much cash it should take, how to establish goals, investment strategies, buying versus renting, small apartment buildings, condominiums, recreational property, financing. Useful.

Davis, Jerry. *Rehabbing for Profit*. New York: McGraw-Hill, 1981. 182 pp. $17.50.
How to select, finance, rehabilitate, and sell inexpensive buildings for maximum return. Davis explains how to choose property and accurately estimate the building's value, how to finance, and how to reconstruct. Dull reading with poor photographs. Decidedly inferior to Mary Weir, *House Recycling* (see p. 124).

Dooner, William, and Proctor, William. *How to Go from Rags to Riches in Real Estate: A Guide to Turning Depressed, Neglected, or Little-Known Property Investments into Millions in the 1980's*. New York: Morrow, 1982. 224 pp. $13.50.
Advocates the "purple tree in the forest" concept involving a striking, sometimes negative initial reaction. This concept is applied to identifying out-of-place, "purple tree in the forest" real estate that may eventually prove to be immensely popular. The authors discuss selection and financing of property with illustrative examples.

Glubetich, Dave. *Double Your Money in Real Estate Every Two Years*. Pleasant Hill, CA: Impact, 1980. 232 pp. $13.95.
The author considers that the purchase of real estate is the only really effective way to combat inflation and avoid the great American slide to the poorhouse. Tough times mean exciting opportunities, and Glubetich advises the immediate purchase of as much real estate as possible with the smallest down payment. Slick, if not dubious advice that is highly incongruent considering the subsequent souring of the real estate market.

Glubetich, Dave. *How to Grow a Money Tree: Earn 20 to 30 Percent and More with Safe Second Mortgages and Trust Deeds*. 2nd Edition. Pleasant Hill, CA: Impact, 1981. 137 pp. $8.95 (paper).

An analysis of the lucrative returns available from secondary financing of real estate—loans secured by a second mortgage or deed of trust on real property. Glubetich shows how to invest in second mortgages, differences between deeds of trusts and mortgages, how to purchase money notes yourself, and when to use the services of a licensed loan broker. A good insight into the intricacies of promissory notes, acceleration clauses, title insurance, computation of monthly interest, default, and foreclosure. Of interest at a time when creative financing alternatives are so widely utilized.

Glubetich, Dave. *The Monopoly Game: The "How To" Book of Making Big Money with Rental Homes.* Pleasant Hill, CA: Impact, 1979. 147 pp. $9.95 (paper).

Another upbeat, optimistic tract outlining the fortunes to be made in buying and selling real estate—how to get started, select property, use leverage, shop for mortgages, maintain one's property, sell at a profit, and more. Needs updating in the light of the current market.

GNMA Mortgage-Backed Securities Dealers Association. *The Ginnie Mae Manual.* Homewood, IL: Dow Jones-Irwin, 1978. 101 pp. $7.95. O.P.

In 1968, GNMA (Government National Mortgage Association) developed a new type of mortgage-backed security—the pass-through Ginnie Mae, which represents a pool or package of mortgages insured by either the FHA (Federal Housing Administration) or the FMHA (Farmers Home Administration) or guaranteed by the VA (Veterans Administration). GNMA guarantees the timely payment of principal and interest on these securities. This book analyzes the investment appeal of Ginnie Mae certificates and reviews advantages, markets, types of investors, and administrative clearance procedures for Ginnie Maes. Useful glossary.

Greene, Bill. *Think Like a Tycoon: Inflation Can Make You Rich.* San Francisco: Harbor, 1980. 253 pp. $10.95.

More of Greene's practical, profit-motivated, maverick philosophy, with humorous cartoons illustrating the text. Greene considers that the stock market is a game for fools—"it requires over fourteen times as much money invested in the stock market to produce the same return available from real estate." Topics include buying property without money, finding super deals, how to manage property and problem tenants, how to make tax-free real estate exchanges, and how to minimize taxes. Unconventional and stimulating.

Hall, Craig. *Craig Hall's Book of Real Estate Investing.* New York: Holt, Rinehart & Winston, 1982. 320 pp. $14.95.

This book is not a get-rich manual but rather a detailed, technical exploration of real estate limited partnership investing. Limited partnerships usually invest in large properties through the pooling of funds from a number of investors. Hall explains how to evaluate and select general partners, how to analyze and explore investment opportunities, tax and legal ramifications, and how to plan for a 15 to 20 percent return after taxes. For the affluent and sophisticated investor.

Harney, Kenneth. *Beating Inflation with Real Estate.* New York: Random House, 1979. 288 pp. $10. O.P.

This book is based on a series of articles that ran in the *Washington Post.* Harney believes that real estate is the most practical, attractive investment available, outstripping inflation. He offers a plain-language guide to the fundamentals of investing in rental houses, second trusts and mortgages, vacation homes, condominiums and cooperatives, apartment buildings, real estate securities, and special investment opportunities. Somewhat out of date in view of the more recent changes in the housing market and related interest rates.

Hatfield, Weston. *The Weekend Real Estate Investor: The New, Low-Risk Team Approach That Transforms Everyday Opportunities into Big Profits.* New York: McGraw-Hill, 1982. 228 pp. $5.95 (paper).

Describes how a small investment group of three or four persons can purchase raw land, business property, or office buildings, maximize tax advantages, and turn a profit. Provides a prescription likely to frighten the more conservative investor.

Hicks, Tyler G. *How to Borrow Your Way to Real Estate Riches Using Government Money.* Englewood Cliffs, N.J.: Prentice-Hall, 1981. 150 pp. $15 (paper).

Zero-cash ways to start building your real estate wealth. Slick directions for using other people's money to earn millions in real estate, where to find repossessions, how to get into rehabs, how to get financing, how "mortgaging-out" works, and so on. Be adventurous and watch the money accumulate! The author is president of International Wealth Success, Inc. Imaginative.

Irwin, Robert. *How to Buy and Sell Real Estate for Financial Security.* New York: McGraw-Hill, 1979. 238 pp. $4.95 (paper).

An overoptimistic view of the real estate market as the great American road to wealth: "Real estate is the one field of investment where it is possible for the total beginner to win the first time and every time; where the working man can make his future secure." Irwin explains how to buy a first home for investment, types of loans, how to invest in groups, the "repo" market, real estate tax shelters, and investment opportunities. A paperback edition of a 1975 hardback book. Out of date.

Irwin, Robert. *Riches in Real Estate: A Beginner's Guide to Group Investing.* New York: McGraw-Hill, 1980. 209 pp. $12.95.

Addresses a basic question: "How can a small investor with just $5,000 or $10,000 in his or her pocket get into a $500,000 piece of property?" Irwin considers that recessions are probably the best time to pick up property. His method consists of syndication or limited partnerships. The pitfalls and benefits of syndication are explained, together with how to organize a syndicate of your own. A success story is narrated in which the investors make a killing by means of a syndicate.

Irwin, Robert. *Smart Money Real Estate for the 80's: New Profits in Big Properties.* San Francisco: Harbor, 1982. 185 pp. $12.95.

Although residential real estate appreciation has virtually stopped, commercial real estate such as office buildings and condominiums has continued to appreciate. Irwin predicts that commercial real estate will be as attractive to investors as single-family housing was in the 1970s. Moreover, money is available for investment real estate from pension funds, insurance companies, venture capital, and banks. He describes how to evaluate income property, tax benefits, opportunities in condominium conversion and investing in apartment buildings, mobile parks, shopping centers, office buildings, and industrial property. An excellent, timely book that opens up new vistas of investment opportunities.

Kessler, A. D. *A Fortune at Your Feet: How You Can Get Rich, Stay Rich and Enjoy Being Rich with Creative Real Estate.* New York: Harcourt Brace Jovanovich, 1981. 282 pp. $10.95.

Creative Real Estate is a registered trademark of the author and is also the title of a real estate magazine that he publishes. Kessler shows how to develop a "win/win" attitude, how to select property, negotiate, finance with little or no cash, and how to exchange and prosper. The major emphasis is on the development of a winning psychology.

Kimmel, Kenneth. *Real Estate: How to Double Your Money Every Two to Three Years with Income-Producing Properties.* New York: Simon & Schuster/Cornerstone Library, 1980. 219 pp. $9.95.

Kimmel argues that income-producing property is the only reliable investment vehicle with a strong enough performance record for novice and expert alike to double their initial investment every two to three years. He covers the fundamentals of investment, how to get started, land, commercial, industrial, and recreational properties, how to assess the value of property, buying income-producing property at the best price, conventional and creative methods of financing, tenant selection, rental property maintenance, and how to sell or exchange property. Contains a useful glossary. Pedestrian presentation.

Koch, James. *Profits from Country Property: How to Select, Buy, Maintain, and Improve Your Country Property.* New York: McGraw-Hill, 1981. 346 pp. $12.95.

A guide to the selection, financing, and improvement of country property in the form of lots, small farms, and existing houses in rural villages, rural second homes bought for weekend and vacation living, raw land bought as an investment and not to live on, and farmland bought to work or use as an investment. Covers where to locate for greatest profit, buying with professional help, and what you can afford to buy and hold. An informative book by the publisher of *Country Property News*.

Lapin, Lawrence L. *The Home Owner's Guide to Making a Fortune.* Alamo, CA: Alamo Press, 1981. 161 pp. $12.95.

How to profit from inflation by buying homes. The basic investment strategy recommended is to use the equity in one's home to purchase an income-producing property, the income from which can be employed to purchase further property. Lapin outlines how to select property, finance investments, time real estate transactions, manage property, and decide when to sell. The method described allows a continuing inflation rate of 10 percent, the ability to refinance homes at reasonable cost (taking into account points, nonpayment penalties, and so on), and the availability of second mortgages. Somewhat theoretical and glib.

Lowry, Albert. *How You Can Become Financially Independent by Investing in Real Estate*. New York: Simon & Schuster, 1982. 351 pp. $16.95.

Lowry claims to have a foolproof formula for making money in real estate: Buy sound income-producing property, arrange for a small down payment and affordable monthly payments, improve the property in your spare time, make sure that it is managed economically and profitably, sell or exchange the property, and reinvest some or all of the gains to repeat the process with other properties. A new, revised edition of a best-seller. Enthusiastic and sensible analysis of the opportunities in real estate investment. Recommended.

McLean, Andrew J. *Foreclosures: How to Profitably Invest in Distressed Real Estate*. Santa Monica, CA: Delphi Information Sciences, 1980. 111 pp. $5.95 (paper).

How to take advantage of the boundless opportunities declared to exist by the author in view of the skyrocketing interest rates, more government regulations, and the shortage of housing. McLean identifies three phases of foreclosure: default, the actual foreclosure sale, and when the auction is unsuccessful at attaining a buyer at the minimum bid price or higher. A clear discussion offering step-by-step guidance in acquiring distressed property.

Marino, John. *How to Make Big Money in Real Estate*. Bonita, CA: Master Key Publications, 1979. 170 pp. $8 (paper).

An overenthusiastic statement of the potential fortunes available in real estate—"For everyone who has lost money in the stock market, in commodities, in oil wells, in cattle feeding, and in a business—be happy!" The solution offered is investment in real estate. Marino shows how to select property, obtain financing, and make a fortune. Simplistic generalization. Skip this title.

Morris, Hal. *Crisis Real Estate Investing: Increase and Protect Your Assets from Potential Disaster*. San Francisco: Harbor, 1982. 270 pp. $12.95.

Morris analyzes the disaster in the real estate market with prices plunging, high interest rates, foreclosures, bankruptcy of real estate brokerage firms, and financial chaos. His prescription for success in a time of real estate crisis lies in lease options, equity sharing, profiting from distressed properties, and investment in geographical areas of high potential (ten top cities are identified in terms of predicted growth). Gloomy.

Nickerson, William. *How I Turned $1,000 into Five Million in Real Estate—In My Spare Time*. New York: Simon & Schuster, 1980. 577 pp. $12.95.

Despite the inflated claim made in the book's title, this is a highly useful and valuable compendium of information relating to the purchase and improvement of rental property. Detailed guidance is provided on choosing property, negotiation and purchase, financing, improvement to the interior and exterior, how to show and rent apartments, drawing up apartment leases, how to collect rents, eviction procedures, how to hire and supervise an apartment manager, ways to borrow money, how to save on income taxes, what to do about rent controls, how to pyramid for more property, and more. Calculated to save money by avoiding costly mistakes. Highly recommended.

Pivar, William. *Get Rich on Other People's Money: Real Estate Investment Secrets.* New York: Arco, 1981. 208 pp. $11.95; $6.95 (paper).

A formal exposition of the essentials of real estate investment that Pivar considers to be one of the safest possible. After reviewing taxation, financing, partnerships and syndicates, property management, and buying and selling, he compares the investment opportunities available: single-family homes, building homes for resale, vacation homes, "fixer-uppers," apartment rentals, and commercial and industrial properties. Dull reading.

Ramsey, Dan. *How to Make Your First Quarter Million in Real Estate in Five Years.* Englewood Cliffs, N.J.: Prentice-Hall, 1979. 228 pp. $10.95; 1982. $4.95 (paper).

Another real estate millionaire's game plan outlining five magical steps or wealth stages leading to a real estate fortune. The message appears to be—"Property with potential multiplied by imaginative financing plus creative purchasing multiplied by accelerated equity plus productive marketing equals substantial profits."

Seldin, Maury. *Real Estate Investment for Profit through Appreciation.* Reston, VA: Reston, 1980. 211 pp. $18.95; same as *You Can Profit from Real Estate Appreciation.* Reston, VA: Reston, 1980. 211 pp. $10.95 (paper).

Reviews the traditional risks and rewards of real estate and how current conditions present special profit opportunities. Seldin analyzes the factors involved in price appreciation, such as the land component of real estate. Compares investment in rental houses, multifamily housing, and nonresidential income property.

Seldin, Maury, and Swesnick, Richard. *Real Estate Investment Strategies.* Second Edition. New York: Wiley, 1979. 345 pp. $21.95.

The authors explain the risks and benefits of investing, financing arrangements, choosing between land, houses, garden apartments, stores and shopping centers, methods of taking title, and considerations of liquidity and diversification. Marred by typographical errors and an out-of-date bibliography.

Snyder, Earl. *Before You Invest: Questions and Answers on Real Estate.* Reston, VA: Reston, 1981. 211 pp. $12.95.

A syndicated real estate columnist answers hundreds of questions relating to investments, syndicates, land, tax liability, appraisal, condominiums, financing, income property, and so on. Informative answers to basic questions. Useful to browse, but difficult to locate information on specific topics.

Tanzer, Milt. *Real Estate Investments and How to Make Them: The Only Guide You'll Ever Need.* Englewood Cliffs, N.J.: Institute for Business Planning, 1980. 356 pp. $29.95; $6.95 (paper).

Should you invest in real estate, where to find sources of investment capital, guidelines for choosing real estate investments, how to locate investment property, how to prepare a financial analysis of your property, when to sell, and why. Also covers purchase and management of investment property.

Tappan, William. *The Real Estate Acquisition Handbook: Money-Making Techniques for the Serious Investor.* Englewood Cliffs, NJ: Prentice-Hall, 1980. 165 pp. $16.95; $7.95 (paper).

A somewhat technical exposition of techniques of acquiring real estate. Tappan analyzes 32 techniques for acquiring real estate when you don't have cash, private financing techniques, methods of using leases, and how to use options to acquire real estate. An appendix contains guidelines for evaluating real estate investments.

Temple, Douglas. *Investing in Residential Income Property.* Chicago: Contemporary Books, 1981. 320 pp. $7.95 (paper).

So long as interest rates remain above the 10 to 12 percent range, it will be very difficult to find a property that will give a cash income in excess of cash expenses if one is making loan payments. Temple defines two basic investment objectives: to maximize current income and to maximize long-term capital appreciation, especially for retirement. With this in mind, he shows how to analyze investment opportunities and calculate before- and after-income tax yield, how to arrange for financing, negotiate the purchase, and close the deal, how to manage property to obtain the greatest return, how to find and keep the best possible tenants, and how to maximize benefits under current income tax regulations. Useful.

Temple, Douglas. *Real Estate Investment for the 80's: How to Build Financial Security in the Face of Inflation.* Chicago: Contemporary Books, 1981. 378 pp. $14.95; 1982. 336 pp. $8.95 (paper).

A step-by-step guide to investing in all types of property—single-family homes, condominium apartments, residential and business income property, and vacant land. Explains the essentials of leverage and borrowing money, negotiating deals, selling and investing, liquidation and refinancing, and tax-deferred property exchanges. Informative but difficult reading.

Weir, Mary. *House Recycling: The Best Real Estate Opportunity for the 80's.* Chicago: Contemporary Books, 1982. 156 pp. $11.95.

Recycling involves finding a house, bidding low, buying with an advantageous mortgage, making improvements to raise its market value, and selling out at the highest possible price. Weir explains how to select the right house in an "up neighborhood" and how to recycle house systems (plumbing, heating), exteriors, interiors, and landscaping. Detailed guidance is provided on insulation, plumbing, heating, electrical work in order to maximize recycle profit. Particular attention is paid to mortgages, financing, and selling. Weir maintains that recycling houses yields a better return than investments in stocks, money market funds, certificates of deposit, and conventional home owning. An imaginative and creative way to beat inflation. Recommended.

6

Taxes

GENERAL

Anderson, B. Ray. *How to Save 50% or More on Your Income Tax—Legally*. New York: Macmillan, 1982. 256 pp. $13.50.
Up-to-date coverage of tax deferral, IRAs, annuities, trusts, tax-exempt bonds, and tax shelters. Also covers deductions and credits. A good strategy book with many helpful suggestions for minimizing the tax bite.

Anderson, B. Ray. *How You Can Use Inflation to Beat the IRS*. New York: Harper & Row, 1981. 448 pp. $14.95; New York: Warner, 1982. 432 pp. $6.95 (paper).
Informative and readable handbook of information on the tax implications of life insurance, estate planning, probate, trusts, wills, gifts, tax shelters, charitable giving, and tax-deferral techniques. A useful compendium of information calculated to minimize taxes in a time of escalating inflation. Unfortunately, the book does not cover the provisions of the Economic Recovery Act of 1981.

Bernstein, Allen. *Tax Guide for College Teachers and Other College Personnel (For Filing 1982 Tax Returns)*. Washington, DC: Academic Information Service, 1983. 360 pp. $13.95 (paper).
A detailed and useful compilation updated annually for academic personnel and teachers. This book is an excellent review of general tax law concerning basic rules, medical expenses, charitable contributions, tax deductions for home owners, avoiding an audit, withholding, and so on. In addition, Bernstein supplies relevant and authoritative information on topics such as teachers' retirement plans, tax-sheltered

125

126   Taxes

plans, tax deferral, deferred compensation, foreign income, travel to professional meetings, sabbaticals, deductions for educational expenses, tax-free grants (scholarships and fellowships), prizes and awards, research expenses and research tax credit, deductions for books, supplies and equipment, and more. Well worth the cost; recommended.

Block, Julian. *Tax Saving: A Year Round Guide.* Radnor, PA: Chilton, 1981. 224 pp. $12.95; $8.95 (paper).

A clear and comprehensive explanation of the essentials of tax saving, including middle-income tax shelters, deductible expenses, dependency exemptions, tax angles for home owners, married and unmarried couples, travel expenses, child- and dependent-care expenses, charitable contributions, medical expenses, and so on. Answers most of the questions frequently asked. Needs minor updating to reflect 1981 legislation.

Bradford, W. Murray, and Reed, Ronald. *Business Tax Deduction Master Guide: Strategies for Business and Professional People.* Englewood Cliffs, NJ: Prentice-Hall, 1982. 268 pp. $19.95; $10.95 (paper).

For outside sales personnel, professionals, consultants, owner-employees of small corporations, and those conducting a second business. The authors provide a very practical guide to tax deductions, problems with entertainment expenses, automobile tax deductions, home office deductions, tax subsidies for educational expenses, income averaging, self-employed retirement plans, how to hire your dependent child tax free, and more. Clear discussion and good tables, illustrations, diagrams, and cartoons.

Buechner, Robert. *Prosper through Tax Planning.* New York: Coward-McCann and Geoghegan, 1983. 288 pp. $17.95.

Not a very exciting or readable account of the essentials of tax planning, including maximum use of deductions, tax deferral, retirement and pension plans, estate planning (trusts, etc.).

Crestol, Jack, and Schneider, Herman M. *Tax Planning for Investors: The Eighties Guide to Securities Investments and Tax Shelters.* Third Edition. Homewood, IL: Dow Jones-Irwin, 1983. 192 pp. $14.95.

Getting the most profit from a year's security transactions, according to the authors, is not a simple matter of buying low and selling high, because the tax laws determine how much of the profit can be kept. Their book is intended to aid investors in understanding how security transactions and other types of investments are taxed, taking into account the tax legislation of 1978 and 1981. Excellent coverage is given to the tax implications of short-term and long-term capital gains, "wash sales," trading in options, commodities futures, and bonds. Separate chapters summarize the tax effects for nonresident alien investors, corporations, trusts, estates, and other types of investors. Authoritative with index of citations to tax code and court decisions. Recommended.

Ferri, Robert, and Silverberg, Barry. *The Tax Organizer.* Revised Edition. New York: McGraw-Hill, 1980. 161 pp. $3.95 (paper).

An aid to record keeping, consisting of dozens of worksheets with explanation, covering medical expenses, tax and interest expenses, contributions, security transactions, moving expenses, casualty or theft losses, and so on. Emphasizes that organization is as much a way of thinking as it is a means of preparation.

Garber, Robert. *The Only Tax Book You'll Ever Need.* New York: Crown/Harmony, 1983. 305 pp. $14.95.
A pretentious title that endeavors to present "a clear translation of the Internal Revenue Tax Code into English." The reader is overwhelmed with detail on the history, philosophy, assumptions, and working of the tax laws. The chapters on topics such as interest expenses, illness, taxes, casualties and thefts, and credits, estimates, and withholding are sketchy and not very useful to the average individual. Not worth the price.

Greene, Bill. *Win Your Personal Tax Revolt.* San Francisco: Harbor, 1981. 443 pp. $14.
More of the gospel according to Bill (Tycoon) Greene, whose boyhood hero was Scrooge McDuck, Donald Duck's tight-fisted uncle. Greene offers a highly readable and amusing explanation of tax avoidance (not evasion) ploys, foreign bank accounts, tax havens and offshore corporations, tax shelters, forming your own church, barter clubs and taxation, tax-deferred real estate exchanges, and so on. Buried in the eminently readable and extravagant prose are highly valuable nuggets of information not readily available elsewhere. Brilliant cartoons. Recommended.

Hansen, George, and Anderson, Larry. *How the IRS Seizes Your Dollars and How to Fight Back.* New York: Simon & Schuster/Fireside, 1981. 222 pp. $5.95 (paper).
Hansen is on the House Banking and Domestic Monetary committees in the U.S. Congress; Anderson is a congressional staff member. They maintain that "the story of the Internal Revenue Service is a history of a tax collection agency drunk with power, ruthlessly smashing dissent among its own personnel, and brazenly roughing up taxpayers at will." Pursuing what appears to be a vendetta against the IRS, the authors cite the runaway power of the agency: Only the IRS can attach 100 percent of a tax debtor's wages and/or property; only the IRS can invade the privacy of a citizen without court process of any kind; only the IRS can seize property without a court order. Suggestions are made as to how to protect one's rights against the IRS. Although reading like a muckraking diatribe, the book is well documented and researched. Sobering reading, well worthy of serious reflection.

Holzman, Robert. *A Survival Kit for Taxpayers: Staying on Good Terms with the I.R.S.* New York: Macmillan/Collier, 1981. 178 pp. $5.95 (paper).
What a taxpayer must do to learn his or her obligations; where to get help and the extent to which he or she can rely on it; what records must be kept and for how long; what a revenue agent can and cannot request; what the alternatives are when there is a tax disagreement; fines, penalties and interest; tax traps and pitfalls. Shows how the tax system works and what to do if audited. A useful description of the essential ground rules calculated to improve one's relationship with the Internal Revenue Service. Recommended.

Jacobs, Vernon K. *The New Taxpayer's Counterattack*. Revised Edition. Alexandria, VA: Alexandria House Books, 1980. 172 pp. $14.95.

Good, sensible advice directed toward the cultivation of aggressive tax avoidance. Jacobs tells readers "to stop being a patsy . . . who thinks loopholes are just for the rich, that whatever the IRS says is gospel for all taxpayers, or that trying to reduce one's taxes isn't worth the time and expense." Starting from this premise, he presents tax-savings ideas, gimmicks to avoid, tax breaks, how to defend one's deductions, and tips on how to avoid an audit. Needs updating in view of subsequent tax legislation.

J. K. Lasser's Your Income Tax. 1983 Edition. New York: Simon & Schuster/Fireside, 1983. 328 pp. $5.95 (paper).

An update of a yearly publication explaining the essential provisions of the tax laws with respect to reporting of income, legal deductions, and computing amount of tax owed. Makes liberal use of worksheets, completed forms, and examples.

Kamensky, Dennis. *Winning on Your Income Taxes*. 1982 Edition. San Francisco: Cragmont, 1982. 192 pp. $12.95; New York: Grosset & Dunlap, 1982. 192 pp. $9.95.

A professional tax preparer provides explicit instructions on filing status, exemptions, determining gross income, capital gains and losses, sale or exchange of real estate, determining taxable income, itemizing deductions, computing tax liability, tax credits, self-employment tax, refunds, and so on. Comprehensive and clear.

Larson, Martin. *The I.R.S. versus the Middle Class: Or How the Average Citizen Can Protect Himself from the Federal Tax Collector*. Old Greenwich, CT: Devin-Adair, 1980. 209 pp. $12.95; $5.95 (paper).

The author believes that the primary purpose of the federal income tax is not so much to collect revenue as it is to control and regiment people. Much of the money paid in taxes would never be paid if taxpayers knew how to protect themselves, since much of it is obtained by false interpretation of the law or by sheer bluff. Accordingly, Larson suggests how to deal with an IRS audit, how to appeal, how to utilize tax shelters and loopholes, how to avoid pitfalls in the IRS code, how to use the Privacy Act, how to protect one's interests. An old-fashioned declaration of the freedom of the individual.

Lesko, Matthew. *How to Get Free Tax Help*. New York: Bantam, 1983. 205 pp. $2.95 (paper).

This is somewhat different from the usual run of tax books. Lesko focuses on authoritative sources of tax information and points out that many of the commercial publications are nothing more than a compilation and repackaging of government documents with some editorial comments. He reviews the free tax information available from toll-free telephone assistance (800 numbers), walk-in services, recorded tax messages (Tele-Tax) available nationally on 140 federal tax-related topics, written assistance, IRS Self-Help Service, IRS training courses, free films, teletype hot line for the hearing impaired, IRS assistance for Americans living or traveling abroad (provided in 16 foreign cities), audiocassette tapes available at many libraries, sources of free legal assistance for taxpayers involved in disputes with the IRS, and so on. Listings of in-house books and IRS publications and training manuals and 99 of the more popular tax forms are also supplied. This is a splendid guide to governmental sources of authoritative tax information. Unique, highly recommended.

Mendlowitz, Edward. *Successful Tax Planning.* Revised Edition. New York: Boardroom Books, 1982. 200 pp. $50.
Claims to give the inside track on tax avoidance through maximum use of deductions, tax postponement, and the aggressive interpretation of the new tax rules. How to fight the IRS: when to stand firm, yield, negotiate, compromise, go to court, etc. It would be prudent to consult your accountant or tax adviser before applying some of this advice!

1983 H and R Block Income Tax Workbook. New York: Macmillan, 1983. 265 pp. $5.95 (paper).
An authoritative, step-by-step workbook filled with examples of completed 1040, 1040A, and 1040EZ forms, helpful hints, detailed information, and instructions. Good coverage of tax planning for those separated or divorced. Intended to help individuals prepare their own tax return or to review their tax status prior to seeking professional consultation. Glossary of terms.

Pay Less Tax. Skokie, IL: Consumer Guide, 1981. 128 pp. $1.95 (paper). O.P.
Concise summary of basic tax information: types of income, adjustments, itemized deductions, tax credits, tax shelters, refunds, etc. Helpful with good cartoons highlighting the text.

Porter, Sylvia. *Sylvia Porter's 1983 Income Tax Book.* New York: Avon, 1983. 186 pp. $3.95 (paper).
A step-by-step, line-by-line guide to preparing your 1982 income tax forms while paying the least possible tax. Covers major tax breaks of the 1981 tax law, including IRA and Keogh plans, estate and gift taxes, two-earner married couple deduction, etc. A concise, clear explanation is given for the 1040A "short" form and the 1040EZ and 1040 forms. Detailed information is supplied on adjustments to income, tax computation, credits, and on Schedule C income and deductions. Blank forms are printed for income averaging, computation of investment credit, supplemental schedule of gains and losses, moving expense adjustment, employee business expenses, sale or exchange of principal residence, and maximum tax on personal service income. Concise and highly useful guide. Recommended.

Prentice-Hall Federal Tax Handbook, 1983. Englewood Cliffs, NJ: Prentice-Hall, 1983. 744 pp. $11 (paper).
Authoritative, clear, concise, and comprehensive tax information for businesspeople and individual taxpayers with answers to most questions on income, credits, deductions, exclusions, exemptions, refunds, and so on. Citations are given to relevant sections of the IRS code. The introduction provides a round-up of the 1982–1983 tax rules. Recommended.

Savage, Michael. *Everything You Always Wanted to Know about Taxes but Didn't Know How to Ask*. New York: Dial Press, 1982. 275 pp. $7.95 (paper). O.P.
A most informative and readable elucidation of the complexities of the U.S. income tax system. Savage, a tax attorney, defines with illustrations gross income, exclusions such as fringe benefits and scholarships, and how to arrive at adjusted gross income. Examples are given of legitimate expenses relating to transportation, travel, entertainment, education, and moving. Other deductions illustrated include medical expenses, casualty losses, charitable contributions, and interest paid. Tax credits, such as child-care expenses and home insulation, are also covered. Detailed information is supplied on capital gains and tax shelters. A lucid, readable, and humorous treatment of a complex subject of vital interest to most people. Recommended.

Schandel, Terry, and Schandel, Susan. *Tax Tactics for Teachers*. New York: Atheneum, 1982. 126 pp. $4.95 (paper).
Tax-savings ideas for teachers and professors with special emphasis on fellowships, home office deductions, sabbaticals, travel as an educational expense, professional dues, and supplies. Most of this information is covered better in the more comprehensive books on taxes, such as Allen Bernstein, *Tax Guide for College Teachers and Other College Personnel* (see p. 125).

Schandel, Terry, and Schandel, Susan. *Tax Tactics for the Retired*. New York: Atheneum, 1982. 122 pp. $4.95 (paper).
Covers income restrictions for those receiving social security benefits, tax advantages of ten-year averaging in receiving distributions from pension plans and annuities, "double dipping" (receiving disbursements from two retirement income plans), how to sell your house and defer tax on the gain, Medicare, Medicaid insurance premiums and other medical deductions, income tax credits. Not worth purchasing since the information provided is available in most general tax publications.

Schandel, Terry, and Schandel, Susan. *Tax Tactics for the Single or Divorced*. New York: Atheneum, 1982. 126 pp. $4.95 (paper).
Attempts to gather information likely to interest divorcing or divorced persons, such as child support versus alimony, baby-sitting expenses, and the like. Much of the information is general and not specifically related to the tax situation of either divorced or single persons. Disappointing.

Schiff, Irwin A., with Murzim, Howy. *How Anyone Can Stop Paying Income Taxes*. Hamden, CT: Freedom Books, 1982. 179 pp. $11.50.
Schiff's message is simple: Nearly 100 million Americans are annually tricked into filing and paying federal income taxes, and no American is legally required to file a tax return, submit to an audit, have income taxes withheld, or pay quarterly tax estimates. Justifying his claims, Schiff argues that the tax system is based on *voluntary* assessment and payment and that since the information on tax returns can be used against you, it is in violation of the Fifth Amendment. "Must" file a tax return really means "may" file a tax return. Schiff suggests that the IRS largely ignores nonfilers of tax returns and that millions of documents relating to dividends are routinely shredded and burned. Employers should not be permitted to withhold taxes from your pay, nobody needs to submit to an IRS audit, and the tax fraud is

perpetuated by a billion-dollar tax industry. The author has been tried and convicted and has served a prison term for his ingenuity.

Storrer, Philip, and Williams, Brian. *The Tax Fighter's Guide, 1983*. San Francisco: Harbor, 1983. $7.95 (paper).
For those middle-of-the-road Americans who don't have time to become scholars of tax shelters and other tax diversionary schemes. Outlines five tax-saving strategies: pay for deductions using other people's money, use marriage and divorce and other family arrangements to qualify for special filing status, make your expenses deductible wherever possible, don't postpone receiving nontaxable income and don't be in a hurry to pay nondeductible expenses, postpone receiving taxable income until another year, and increase deductible expenses in the current year. Also explains how to prepare tax returns to minimize the chances of getting audited and how to defend yourself in an audit ("don't be a blabbermouth"). Useful checklists of deductible and nondeductible items and audit source codes (indicating why you are being audited). Clear-cut, informative guidance. Recommended.

Strassels, Paul N., and Wool, Robert. *All You Need to Know about the IRS: A Taxpayer's Guide*. 1981 Edition. New York: Random House, 1981. 278 pp. $11.95.
The authors claim that the IRS has become a revenue-bringing government agency pitting itself against inflation-conscious taxpayers. They describe how the IRS manipulates the press to confuse and intimidate the public. Strassels and Wool provide a fascinating insight into the auditing process—the chances of getting audited and the operation of the computer-based Taxpayer Compliance Measurement Program. All you wanted to know about how the IRS works and what to do if audited. Indispensable reading for all taxpayers. Highly recommended.

Wade, Jack Warren. *When You Owe the IRS*. New York: Macmillan, 1983. 246 pp. $12.95.
Be prepared for the fact that the IRS is expanding its force of revenue officers by 50 percent to combat the skyrocketing number of tax delinquencies. Wade, formerly an IRS officer, explains how to protect oneself and offers dozens of survival rules. Also covers situations where you cannot pay, how to fight interest and penalty bills, prevent the seizure of your assets, face an audit, and negotiate the payment of taxes in installments. Good self-protective strategies; practical and well written. Recommended.

Your Federal Income Tax: For Individuals—For Use in Preparing 1982 Returns. IRS Publication No. 17. Revised November 1982. Washington, DC: Internal Revenue Service, Department of the Treasury. 168 pp.
Official, authoritative information explaining the tax laws that cover salaries and wages, interest and dividends, itemized deductions, rental income, gains and losses, and adjustments to income, including alimony, moving expenses, and employee business expenses. Examples are provided by means of filled-in forms and schedules with numbers keyed into the appropriate page of the text where the topic is discussed. Highly informative and useful, but not very readable.

THE 1981 TAX LAW

Arenson, Karen. *The New York Times Guide to Making the New Tax Law Work for You.* New York: Times Books, 1981. 147 pp. $4.95 (paper).
The author is a financial writer for the *New York Times*, and the content is based on a series of articles for that newspaper. Arenson explains the philosophy of the 1981 tax law designed to stimulate productivity and saving. A fairly simple description is given of a wide variety of topics: "All-Savers" certificates, IRAs, Keogh accounts, the new marriage penalty deduction, child-care credits, estate and gift taxes, capital gains, income earned outside the United States, and tax shelters. A useful summary of the essential provisions of the Economic Recovery Tax Act of 1981. Recommended.

Greene, Bill. *Bill Greene's 101 New Loopholes. The Reagan Tax Package 1983–85.* San Francisco: Harbor, 1982. 112 pp. $4.95 (paper).
Greene has a succinct message: "Don't pay those IRS vampires any more than you have to!" He lists the major provisions and shows the old rules, new rules, and pitfalls underlying each new provision. Greene argues that the 1981 tax act still leaves taxes too high and reaffirms his basic philosophy: Use leveraged real estate investment, have your own side business, and become an independent contractor. His judgment is somewhat bizarre: "The All Saver Certificate is the biggest ripoff to be foisted on the American public since the Christmas Club and the U.S. Savings Bond." This book sheds more light on Greene's maverick philosophy than it does on the Economic Recovery Tax Act of 1981.

Greisman, Bernard (ed.). *J. K. Lasser's How You Can Profit from the New Tax Laws.* New York: Simon & Schuster/Fireside, 1983. 158 pp. $4.95 (paper).
Summarizes in some detail the specifics of the new tax legislation relating to personal tax rate reductions and tax savings, saving for retirement, investment and business tax savings, and estate and gift planning. Answers most questions relating to child-care costs, charitable deductions for nonitemizers, IRA accounts, tax shelters, tax-saving deductions for working couples, new depreciation rules, and more. Authoritative and concise.

Kast, Sheilah. *Cut Your Own Taxes and Save: The Everything-You-Need-to-Know Guide for Your 1981 Tax Return.* New York: Enterprise, 1981. 96 pp. $1.95 (paper). O.P.
Step-by-step instructions, money-saving tips, and full tax tables for filing forms 1040 and 1040A and supplementary schedules. Covers changes made by Congress in 1981. Good summary of adjustments to income, deductions, tax credits, and retirement plans.

Post, William G., Jr. *How to Benefit from the New Tax Laws: Immediate Gains and Long-Term Strategies.* Boston: Little, Brown, 1981. 141 pp. $4.95 (paper).
A detailed survey of the essentials of the Economic Recovery Act of 1981. Post points out that the act has very little to do with revenue raising but is aimed almost exclusively at stimulating one segment of the economy or another through the reduction of the marriage penalty, liberalization of depletion and exploration allowances, All-Savers certificates designed to stimulate the banking industry, and so on.

Smith, Stuart, and Sprogen, Janet. *How You Can Get the Most from the New Tax Law*. New York: Bantam, 1981. 177 pp. $2.95 (paper).
Details the highlights of the Economic Recovery Act of 1981: rate reductions, indexing, relief from the marriage tax penalty, child- and dependent-care credit, All-Savers certificates, child adoption expenses, once-in-a-lifetime capital gains exclusion raised to $125,000, new tax benefits for U.S. citizens living abroad, broadened eligibility for IRA plans, increase in maximum allowable deduction for Keogh plans, changes in estate and gift taxes, business expenses, and expanded benefits for investment in business assets. A useful, concise summary of the major provisions of the 1981 tax act. Recommended.

Strassels, Paul N. *Money in Your Pocket: Using the New Reagan Tax Laws*. Minneapolis, MN: Control Data Publishing, 1981. 176 pp. $9.95.
How to save money using the provisions of the Economic Recovery Tax Act of 1981. Strassels gives plenty of examples illustrating the impact of the various tax cuts. Contains much information and helpful hints, but the organization leaves much to be desired in that it is somewhat difficult to find what you are seeking.

Tuccille, Jerome. *The New Tax Law and You*. New York: New American Library, 1981. 180 pp. $2.50 (paper). O.P.
A foreword by Congressman Jack Kemp sets the tone for this book, which is more than a simple recitation of the essentials of the Economic Recovery Tax Act of 1981. The emphasis is on showing supply side economics at work through tax cuts, investment incentives, and spending restraints. Tuccille details the benefits and incentives of the 1981 act—reduction in marginal tax rates, marriage penalty relief, dividend reinvestment, All-Savers certificates, retirement savings, gift exclusions—and how to profit from the new tax law. An enthusiastic statement of the philosophy and aspirations of those who embrace supply side economics. The author is vice president/investments with the brokerage house of Shearson/American Express.

Wiltsee, Joseph L., and Sammons, Donna. *You Can Profit from the New Tax Law*. New York: McGraw-Hill, 1982. 164 pp. $5.95 (paper).
The authors are associate editor and financial writer, respectively, of *McGraw-Hill World News*. They present an easy-to-read, narrative account of the major features of the Economic Recovery Tax Act of 1981. A supplement describes what the new law does for small business. More understandable than most books on taxation. Recommended.

TAX DEDUCTIONS

Holzman, Robert S. *Take It Off! Close to 2,363 Deductions Most People Overlook*. New York: Harper & Row, 1982. 344 pp. $16.30; New York: Barnes & Noble, 1983. 400 pp. $8.61 (paper).
Contains many more deductions than were included in the 1981 edition. Apart from well-known deductions such as child-care expenses, educational expenses, and medical expenses, little known deductions are described: hearing-ear cats for deaf persons, gambling losses, convention expenses, and travel. Deductions are arranged

134   Taxes

alphabetically. Despite the use of cross-references, it is often difficult to locate needed information.

Minkow, Rosalie, and Minkow, Howard. *The Complete List of IRS Tax Deductions, 1983.* New York: Playboy Paperbacks, 1982. 272 pp. $3.95 (paper).
Covers tax deductions, exemptions, and credits. Topics discussed include deductions for dependents, home and medical expenses, travel, charity, entertainment, retirement and pensions, divorce, alimony, and child support. The four basic rules advocated are if it isn't a deduction, don't spend it; take advantage of all deferrals of income; keep impeccable tax records with documentation; and do tax planning every day. Does not adequately reflect the provisions of the Economic Recovery Tax Act of 1981. Not the best of its kind.

Schnepper, Jeff. *How to Pay Zero Taxes: Over 100 Ways to Reduce Your Taxes—To Nothing.* Reading, MA: Addison-Wesley, 1982. 337 pp. $6.95 (paper).
An extensive and detailed handbook of the tax-savings efficiency of each form of tax reduction, exclusions (tax-free money)—educational expenses, prizes and awards, long-term capital gains, etc., tax credits (dollar-for-dollar tax reduction)—child-care credits, political contributions, energy conservation credits, etc., "above the line" (gross income adjustments) and "below the line" (itemized) deductions, such as medical expenses, taxes, and charitable contributions. Also provided is information on tax shelters and the provisions of "The Attorneys' and Accountants' Relief Act of 1981"—the Economic Recovery Tax Act of 1981! Schnepper shows clearly how to eliminate or reduce the payment of taxes in connection with insurance claims, medical expenses, alimony and support payments, charitable contributions, travel and vacation, earned income credit, and so on. Most useful. Highly recommended.

Steiner, Barry, and Kennedy, David. *Perfectly Legal: 275 Foolproof Methods for Paying Less Tax.* New York: Wiley, 1981. 201 pp. $14.95; New York: Warner, 1982. 256 pp. $5.95 (paper).
A question-and-answer format organized around 26 specific problem areas, such as income averaging, credits, divorce, alimony and child support, travel, entertainment and gifts, home office deductions, and tax shelters. Also contains extracts from the Audit Technique Handbook used by IRS agents and obtained under the Freedom of Information Act.

TAX SHELTERS

Dickson, David. *Tax Shelters for the Not-So-Rich.* Chicago: Contemporary Books, 1980. 192 pp. $9.95; 1981. $5.95 (paper).
A personal financial planner discusses the four primary ways in which tax loopholes can produce a substantial increase in a person's assets: tax shelters, tax deferral, tax exemption, and tax transformation (capital gains). Dickson analyzes tax-sheltered annuities, Keogh retirement plans, IRAs, Series EE U.S. Government Savings Bonds, deferred annuities, stock dividend tax exclusion, tax-free municipal bonds, and REITs (real estate investment trusts). Sources of funds for retirement investment

programs are suggested. Three appendixes summarize flexible, premium-deferred fixed annuities, tax qualified retirement plans, and the essential features of a number of single premium-deferred annuities. A good explanation of a difficult subject.

Drollinger, William C., and Drollinger, William C., Jr. *Tax Shelters and Tax Free Income for Everyone.* Orchard Lake, MI: Epic, 1981. 1232 pp. $24.95.
A comprehensive, detailed reference book on all aspects of tax shelters—advantages, benefits, how they work, depreciation, deferral, special tax considerations, depletion. Covers real estate, energy, equipment leasing, cable television, agriculture, entertainment (movies, records), commodities, collectibles, investment banking, and so on.

Fierro, Robert D. *Tax Shelters in Plain English: New Strategies for the 1980's.* Rockville Centre, NY: Farnsworth, 1981. 226 pp. $11.95; New York: Penguin, 1982. $4.95 (paper).
Adopting the theme "The Hell with Death and Taxes . . . Gimme Shelter," Fierro offers a buyer's guide to tax shelters. He warns that "any promoter can make it very attractive for a taxpayer in the 34% to 43% tax brackets to start dreaming thoughts of reduced tax bills, or no tax bill at all, by pulling out a calculator and pressing a few buttons." The solution: Seek out competent financial advisers—a tax attorney, a certified public accountant, or a personal financial planner. This book is a well-written, often amusing review of the advantages and disadvantages of tax shelters in real estate, energy, farming, equipment leasing, and exotica. Recommended.

McQuown, Judith. *Tax Shelters That Work for Everyone: A Common Sense Guide to Keeping More of the Money You Earn.* New York: McGraw-Hill, 1979. 296 pp. $12.95. O.P.
Tax-sheltered investments provide tax deductions that reduce taxable income and thus taxes. McQuown explains the basic concepts involved, such as depreciation, recapture, leverage, general partners versus limited partners, and so on, and shows how tax shelters work for people in various tax brackets and with differing investment objectives. Both conservative tax shelters (Clifford Trusts, charitable gifts, tax-exempt securities) and high-risk tax shelters (oil, gas and mineral, movies, equipment leasing) are described. Somewhat out of date, but still useful.

Mosburg, Lewis. *The Tax Shelter Coloring Book.* Oklahoma City, OK: Institutes for Energy Development, 1977. 153 pp. $10.95.
A review of the types of tax shelters, how they work, benefits and risks, shelters in oil and gas wells, cattle, exotics such as motion pictures, Broadway plays, and oyster farming, together with tips on selecting the best investment. An interesting attempt to bring some humor to a humorless subject.

Seidler, Lee J. *Everything You Wanted to Know about Tax Shelters, but Were Afraid to Ask.* New York: Bear Stearns, 1981. 56 pp. $60.
Seidler is a general partner of Bear Stearns and professor of accounting at New York University. In simple and concise language, he explains the steps that should be taken to evaluate and select a tax-favored investment, minimize tax risks, and com-

pare a tax shelter with any other investment. In addition to showing how tax shelters work and reviewing the opportunities in oil and gas, equipment leasing, and real estate, Seidler points out how one's family can be used as a tax shelter by the transfer of investible funds or income to children. Lucid and authoritative presentation of the essentials of a complex topic.

Skousen, Mark. *Tax Free.* New York: Simon & Schuster, 1983. 192 pp. $12.50.
What you need to know to avoid taxes at all levels of government. Skousen covers familiar territory in reviewing the use of Keogh and IRA plans, tax shelters, annuities, municipal bonds, and so on. He also identifies lesser known opportunities, such as tax havens, living abroad tax-free, state tax havens (five states have no sales tax and seven have no income tax), tax-free barter, and tax-free fringe benefits.

Swanson, Robert E., and Swanson, Barbara M. *Tax Shelters: A Guide for Investors and Their Advisors.* Homewood, IL: Dow Jones-Irwin, 1982. 311 pp. $32.50.
Crammed with information and sensible advice, this book provides a lucid and readable explanation of the benefits and pitfalls of each tax shelter, how you can invest successfully, and what can be expected from the Internal Revenue Service. Although a tax shelter is a business that exploits the tax incentives for business investment, the Swansons point out that shelters should not be a *bad* investment but rather a *good* one that will eventually make large profits for their investors. Their advice is to avoid flimflam and "aggressively structured" tax shelters. The authors provide a superb explanation of how tax shelters work, risks, leverage, capital gains, liquidity, depreciation, and the pros and cons of various types of tax shelters, such as real estate, oil and gas, movies, and Broadway shows. Highly recommended.

Tannenhauser, Robert, and Tannenhauser, Carol. *Tax Shelters: A Complete Guide.* New York: Crown, 1978. 246 pp. $10.95; New York: New American Library/ Signet, 1982. $3.50 (paper).
A somewhat technical exposition of the advantages of tax shelters and how to make the most of your investment. Covers depreciation, depletion and investment credit, real estate shelters, and shelters in oil, gas, coal, movies, books, records, and art. Designed for the investment-oriented layperson.

Tanner, Beverly, Pheffer, Marvin, and Laurins, Alex. *Shelter What You Make, Minimize the Take: Tax Shelters for Financial Planning.* San Francisco: Harbor, 1982. 265 pp. $14.95.
Lowering your taxes may be the key to economic survival. Consequently, good financial planning for highest income taxpayers must take into account tax sheltering. The authors analyze and compare various types of tax shelters: retirement plans (such as IRA and Keogh), real estate investments, deep shelters, equity builders, income shelters, and limited partnerships. Also considered are investments in oil and gas, real estate, HUD programs, leasing, agriculture, cable television, offshore trusts, gold and silver, rare coins, and currency. Risks, benefits, and mechanics of tax shelters are discussed, together with how a financial plan can be created to take maximum advantage of the numerous types of shelters available.

TAX HAVENS

Kinsman, Robert. *The Robert Kinsman Guide to Tax Havens*. Homewood, IL: Dow Jones-Irwin, 1978. 256 pp. $19.95.

Explains the advantages and disadvantages of investing your money in countries where the tax laws appear to be more favorable than those of the United States. Tax loopholes are vehicles that provide opportunity for tax-advantaged investments, while tax havens are countries having tax laws that exact little or no tax and thereby permit accumulation of capital until it is returned to a high-tax nation. The author presents detailed information on the tax laws of the Bahamas, Cayman Islands, Channel Islands, Liechtenstein, Bermuda, Hong Kong, Netherlands Antilles, New Hebrides, Panama, Turks and Caicos, and Monaco. Three chapters detail how to open a Swiss bank account and how to take advantage of Swiss financial privacy. Intriguing.

Starchild, Adam. *Everyman's Guide to Tax Havens*. Boulder, CO: Paladin Press, 1980. 112 pp. $6 (paper).

How to avoid taxation through various forms of tax havenry. Legal avoidance, not illegal evasion, uses existing measures within a nation's tax regulations to reduce or eliminate liability. Under existing U.S. legislation, it is not possible to carry on a legal, covert tax haven operation. Starchild distinguishes between no-tax, low-tax, and special-purpose tax havens, giving examples of each and describing their structure and operation. After a whirlwind (global) tour of tax havens, he discusses where to retire and avoid taxes, with special reference to Costa Rica (with *pensionado* status), Ireland, Jordan, Puerto Rico, and Holland. The tax advantages of these countries are discussed in detail.

TAX AUDITS

Jacobs, Vernon, and Schoeneman, Charles. *The Taxpayer's Audit Survival Manual*. Alexandria, VA: Alexandria House Books, 1980. 240 pp. $35; $12.95 (paper); Aurora, IL: Caroline House, 1981. $35.

Each year the Internal Revenue Service (IRS) runs a reverse lottery—the minority whose tickets are selected become the losers, while the winners are the majority whose entries are ignored. The lottery's odds are almost 45:1 in favor of winning against having your ticket (tax return) picked at all. Jacobs and Schoeneman show how tax returns are chosen for audit, the organization of the IRS, different levels of audit, how to cope with an audit, and measures to take to minimize the risk of being audited. Thorough, but not as lucid and comprehensive as the same authors' *The Taxpayer's Internal Revenue Service Audit Survival Manual* (see below) and Mary L. Sprouse, *How to Survive a Tax Audit* (see p. 138).

Jacobs, Vernon, and Schoeneman, Charles. *The Taxpayer's Internal Revenue Service Audit Survival Manual*. Wilmington, DE: Enterprise, 1982. 144 pp. $35.10; $6.95 (paper).

A very practical and comprehensive presentation of the audit process, how returns are selected in the audit lottery (in 1977 only 2.10 percent were audited), the DIF (Discriminant Function) selection system and the TCMP (Taxpayers Compliance Measurement Program), IRS organization and operation, limited contact audits, how audits are conducted, criminal audits, collecting the money, appeals, and suggestions on how to avoid an audit. Of particular value is an appendix containing the IRS Guidelines for Auditing Professionals—physicians, dentists, attorneys, engineers, architects, funeral directors, and real estate brokers. Explicit and revealing. Excellent, both strategically and tactically. Recommended.

Price, J. R., with Putney, Valerie. *In This Corner—The IRS*. New York: Dell, 1981. 317 pp. $2.95 (paper).

Price, a former IRS special agent, answers many of the common questions taxpayers ask about audits, penalties, appeal procedures, methods of proof, and criminal investigations. The book does not explain how to fill out tax returns or reduce tax liability but rather focuses on how returns get audited (the Discriminant Function system, etc.), how to behave if audited, what records to keep, how to use the Freedom of Information Act to obtain your IRS files, how the IRS proves the existence and taxability of unreported income (net worth, bank deposits, etc.), and what happens if a person comes to the attention of the Criminal Investigation Division. A highly informative and sobering account of the inner workings of the IRS. Recommended.

Sprouse, Mary L. *How to Survive a Tax Audit: What to Do before and after You Hear from the IRS*. Garden City, NY: Doubleday, 1981. 288 pp. $11.95; New York: Penguin, 1982. 272 pp. $4.95 (paper).

The author, formerly audit group manager of the IRS in Los Angeles, tells all: the odds on getting audited, how one is selected, the audit letter, audit etiquette, what happens during an audit, what records are required, representation and power of attorney, your rights, petitioning the tax court, and penalties. Examples are given of negligence and fraud. In 1979, office auditors and revenue agents assessed $7.2 billion in additional tax and penalties as a result of audits. An inside, often humorous look at how to play by the rules and survive. Highly recommended.

REAL ESTATE TAXES

Barash, Samuel. *How to Reduce Your Real Estate Taxes*. New York: Arco, 1979. 166 pp. $7.95. O.P.

What you can do to stand up for a fair assessment on your property. Most property assessment appeals result in reduction, yet very few home owners appeal for reduced assessments. Barash shows how property is assessed and how the assessment may be wrong, how to research an appeal, how to check for errors in assessors' records, where to find true market value for one's property, when to file timely appeals, how to present one's case, when to hire a lawyer and go to court. The author supplies completed model complaint forms, construction inspection checklists, and appraisal guides. The lucid text is well illustrated by clever cartoons. Highly recommended.

Jeddeloh, James, and Perkins, Cheryl. *Real Estate Taxation: A Practical Guide.* Reston, VA: Reston, 1982. 286 pp. $16.95.

A comprehensive and detailed guide to the tax regulations applying to every type of real estate transaction involving home ownership, vacation homes, and condominiums. Topics covered include tax concepts common to all types of real estate ownership, income tax aspects of home ownership, tax implications of vacation homes, and other real estate investments. All changes made by the Economic Recovery Tax Act of 1981 are included as supplementary information at the end of each chapter where it is relevant. Good coverage of the new accelerated depreciation system, new investment tax credits, estate and gift tax relief, rehabilitation and energy conservation credits, liberalized rollover provisions and residential property, and the increase in the 55 years or older exclusion for the sale of a personal residence. Guaranteed to answer most questions on real estate taxation. Highly recommended.

Reed, John T. *Aggressive Tax Avoidance for Real Estate Investors: How to Make Sure You Aren't Paying One More Cent in Taxes Than the Law Requires.* Moraga, CA: Real Estate Investor Information Center, 1981. 282 pp. $15 (paper).

A guide to depreciation and tax credits, maximizing expenses, installment sales and options, why you should exchange rather than sell property, and related topics. According to Reed, the bigger tax-saving technique is to "devote your day to building net worth rather than earning ordinary income." His message is pointed: "conservatism is a self-imposed audit, which is far more thorough and severe than any audit the IRS ever did. It costs you dearly. Knock it off." Provocative reading.

7

Financial Planning

PERSONAL FINANCE

Albin, Francis. *Consumer Economics and Personal Money Management.* Englewood Cliffs, NJ: Prentice-Hall, 1982. 496 pp. $18.95.
This is a textbook for consumer finance courses. The author sets himself the following objective: "I want a textbook that will help me to become a better money manager, yet . . . not so bookish or so encyclopedic that I am constantly awash in technical detail." Comprehensive yet simple information is provided on such consumer topics as food, shelter, transportation, insurance, budgeting, banking, saving, investing, taxes, retirement, wills, and estate planning. Contains excellent tables, diagrams, cartoons, and glossaries. An attractively presented, informative, and useful book by an author who has successfully refined his material as a result of more than 20 years of teaching experience.

Amling, Frederick, and Droms, William G. *The Dow Jones-Irwin Guide to Personal Financial Planning.* Homewood, IL: Dow Jones-Irwin, 1982. 514 pp. $19.95.
Clearly one of the best books available on all aspects of financial planning: careers and financial success, budgeting, saving, taxation, buying a home, credit and consumer loans, life, health, property, and liability insurance, risks and rewards of investment in stocks, mutual funds, real estate, and precious metals, financial planning for retirement, and estate planning. Highly informative and practical advice on the federal tax system, filing regulations and requirements, mortgages, controlling credit, types and costs of insurance policies, social security benefits, and so on. The authors reproduce typical tables from the *Wall Street Journal* of treasury bill yields,

government, agency, and miscellaneous securities, money rates, tax-exempt bonds, New York Stock Exchange composite transactions, and so on, and in each instance explain how to read and interpret the tables. Also explained is how to use Standard and Poor's *Stock Reports* and other sources of information. An indispensable book for all who wish to make intelligent and prudent decisions on savings, housing, credit, investment, retirement, and other matters of financial concern. Highly recommended.

Brownstone, David M., and Sartisky, Jacques. *Personal Financial Survival: A Guide for the 1980's and Beyond.* New York: Wiley, 1981. 364 pp. $19.95.
A stellar presentation of the essentials of lifelong personal planning and the organization of the financial side of your life. Brownstone and Sartisky detail the techniques and instruments of financial planning, covering stocks, bonds, mutual funds, hedges, and speculations: gold, silver, commodities, stock options, and collectibles; and real estate. Other chapters deal with insurance planning (life, health, property, and liability) and methods of accumulating wealth to meet the needs of later years. To illustrate the principles outlined, the authors present 20 financial planning examples, including people in their early, middle, and later financial planning years, whose incomes, assets, pension expectations, and personal situations vary widely. The book is enhanced further by an 80-page glossary of the jargon of financial planning and by an annotated bibliography of sources of information. A splendid book calculated to be of great assistance and comfort to the layperson. Highly recommended.

Burton, Robert H., and Petrello, George J. *Personal Finance.* New York: Macmillan, 1978. 501 pp. $21.95.
A broad textbook treatment of personal finance—getting income and spending it. Covers financial planning and control, budget planning, consumer spending, banking, investing, shelter, travel, health and life insurance, taxation. Readable yet rather outdated.

Cohen, Jerome. *Personal Finance.* 6th Edition. Homewood, IL: Irwin, 1979. 600 pp. $20.95.
A classic text for personal finance courses relating to the real-life necessity of facing and solving personal financial problems. Good use of charts, tables, and illustrations.

Goldsmith, W. B. *BASIC Programs for Home Financial Management.* Englewood Cliffs, NJ: Prentice-Hall, 1981. 314 pp. $18.95; $12.95 (paper).
Comprehensive source book offers 33 financial management programs for home computers covering money management, credit control, major asset management, and investment factors. Typical programs include checkbook reconciliation, checkwriter routine, cash flow analysis program, income tax estimator program, credit card organizer, net worth statement, auto loan analysis, real estate loan analysis, auto expense records, savings account analysis, stock plotter, and retirement fund program. Descriptions, sample runs, and program listings are easily adaptable for use with TRS-80, Apple II, and other basic home computers. A unique book likely to become increasingly popular as more people acquire home computers.

Hallman, G. Victor, and Rosenbloom, Jerry. *Personal Financial Planning*. 3rd Edition. New York: McGraw-Hill, 1982. 432 pp. $24.95.
Emphasis is placed on personal financial planning as a process of determining an individual's or a family's total financial objectives, considering alternative plans and methods for meeting the objectives, selecting the plans and methods that are best suited for the person's circumstances, implementing those plans, and then periodically reviewing the plans and making necessary adjustments. The authors offer a step-by-step guide through the setting of objectives, using insurance effectively, accumulating capital and income tax planning, investment principles (common stock, mutual funds, fixed-income securities), retirement planning, and estate and tax planning. Substantially the same content as the second edition, with some updating reflecting changes introduced by the Economic Recovery Act of 1981.

Herrick, Tracy G. *Timing: How to Profitably Manage Money at Different Stages of Your Life*. Allen, TX: Argus Communications, 1981. 255 pp. $13.95.
Money management and financial decision making are linked by the author to successive life cycle periods. Herrick identifies five adult stages of development: adolescence (14 to 22 years), adulthood (22 to 35), midlife (36 to 50), maturity (51 to 65), and age and simplicity (66 years onward). The author analyzes the financial needs, goals, and strategies of each stage and shows similarities and differences. The key to successful money management is seen to be the ability to direct wants and needs to personal development. Insightful and interesting.

Hurley, Gale E. *Personal Money Management*. 2nd Edition. Englewood Cliffs, NJ: Prentice-Hall, 1981. 528 pp. $19.95.
A textbook treatment of the basic concepts involved in consuming, saving, insuring, investing, and housing. Topics discussed include credit, banking, insurance, investments (real estate, buying and selling stock, mutual funds), retirement planning, estate planning, and taxation. Frederick Amling and William G. Droms, *The Dow Jones-Irwin Guide to Personal Financial Planning* (see p. 141) provides a superior and clearer explanation.

Moffitt, Donald. *Your Money Matters: A Guide to Personal Finance from the Pages of the Wall Street Journal*. Princeton, NJ: Dow Jones Books, 1979. 219 pp. $4.95 (paper). O.P.
A cumulation of the Monday back-page feature in the *Wall Street Journal*, "Your Money Matters." The selection of reprinted articles covers financial planning, making the most of your job, household spending and saving, insurance and protection, retirement planning, and investment. Moffitt has assembled timely and relevant information focusing on financial planning—the establishment of financial goals, analysis of means of achieving the goals, and design and implementation of a plan for attaining one's objectives. The author contributes a useful introduction. A readable and informative text reflecting the high quality of the *Journal*. Recommended.

Penson, John B., Jr., Levi, Donald, and Nixon, Clair. *Personal Finance*. Englewood Cliffs, NJ: Prentice-Hall, 1982. 480 pp. $19.95.
An introduction to the key concepts of personal finance, including how to evaluate your personal expenditures in the light of current savings objectives. Type of (and

how much) insurance you need, factors to consider when evaluating investment opportunities, how to plan for retirement income, and disposal of your estate are discussed. Excellent coverage of insurance, credit, stocks and bonds, and other forms of investment opportunities. A thorough textbook treatment of personal finance for first- or second-year students at colleges and universities. Unfortunately, the book lacks a bibliography.

Roll, Richard, and Young, G. Douglas. *Getting Yours: Financial Success Strategies for Young Professionals in a Tougher Era.* New York: Putnam's, 1982. 204 pp. $12.95.

Familiar content—principles of investment, selecting a stockbroker, money market funds, purchasing a home, new types of mortgages, minimizing the tax bite, term versus whole life insurance, and so on. The distinctive character of this book is the authors' tailoring of the discussion to the needs of young professionals who wish to make the correct decisions concerning lifestyle, financial resources, and money management. The authors outline strategies for maximizing income and enjoyment: Invest where you have a knowledge edge and where you will earn both a pleasurable and a financial return; take control of your financial life; reach forward in your "financial life cycle" to acquire real goods and assets needed in the future but likely to soar out of reach if deferred. Readable and sensible advice for those seeking to build a firm financial base. Recommended.

Rosefsky, Robert. *Financial Planning for the Young Family.* Chicago: Follett, 1978. 310 pp. $10.70. O.P.

Focuses on the special concerns of the young family from the single person entering into a stage of self-sufficiency and proceeding through the early development of a career, marriage, and the beginning of a family. Rosefsky provides financial planning worksheets to analyze assets, expenses, cash flow, and net worth. Good coverage also of housing, insurance, investment alternatives, credit, and so on. Useful but outdated.

Smith, Milton. *Money Today, More Tomorrow.* Boston: Little, Brown, 1981. 307 pp. $14.95; $9.95 (paper).

A relatively simple and clear exposition of the essentials of financial planning by an investment adviser. Smith describes goals, defines and explains annuities, bonds, unit investment trusts, stock options, futures, term insurance, stock rating services, ERISA, IRAs, Keogh, commercial paper, and so on. Useful advice is also given on how to define investment goals and to plan for financial security.

Stillman, Richard. *Money-Wise: The Prentice-Hall Book of Personal Money Management.* Englewood Cliffs, NJ: Prentice-Hall, 1978. 581 pp. $14.95. O.P.

A popular adaptation of the author's earlier *Guide to Personal Finance* (1972), a college textbook. Stillman focuses attention on both investments and savings opportunities in relation to the purchase of goods and services. The tips on strategies for saving money on food, clothing, transportation, and appliances are relevant today, but the chapters on investment opportunities and taxes need considerable reworking in the light of more recent developments.

Ward, David, and Niendorf, Robert. *Consumer Finance: The Consumer Experience.* Homewood, IL: Irwin, 1978. 492 pp. $20.95.
A text that focuses on key areas of decision making—budgeting, food, clothing, automobiles, appliances, housing, insurance, investment—with three chapters on financial planning. A good introductory text, but somewhat out of date.

Wolf, Harold A. *Personal Finance.* 6th Edition. Boston: Allyn & Bacon, 1981. 560 pp. $21.95.
Aims at explaining the principles of personal finance to consumers who are "constantly engaged in borrowing money, using credit cards, investing savings, paying taxes, buying houses and life, home and auto insurance, and many other activities that may involve some financial pitfalls." This text is eminently clear and understandable with excellent tables, diagrams, cartoons, and illustrations. More readable than most books of its kind. Recommended.

RETIREMENT PLANNING

Barnes, John. *More Money for Your Retirement.* New York: Harper & Row, 1978. 307 pp. $11.95; New York: Barnes & Noble, 1980. 320 pp. $4.95 (paper).
An overview of the essentials of retirement. Good, practical information on life insurance, annuities, social security, Medicare, pensions, Keogh and IRA plans, and how to avoid probate. Offers terse advice: Retired people should not pay premiums on individual permanent life insurance policies; don't hang on for dear life to all of your assets, refusing to spend anything but the income from them; everyone should have a will drawn by a competent attorney. Needs updating to take into account changes in IRA, Keogh, and social security regulations.

Consumer Guide, and Dickinson, Peter (eds.). *Your Retirement: A Complete Planning Guide.* New York: A&W, 1981. 128 pp. $12.95; $4.95 (paper).
How to set goals in terms of when to retire, where to retire, and how to ensure an adequate retirement income. Specific advice and guidance are given on finding an ideal location, choosing a retirement home, planning for financial security, getting the most from social security and company pensions, investing for retirement income, taxes after 65, estate planning, insurance, and health care. Checklists, sample letters, tables, charts, cartoons, and lists of information sources for further study enhance the value of the text. An excellent, elementary guide. Recommended.

Dissinger, Katherine. *Old, Poor, Alone and Happy: How to Live Nicely on Nearly Nothing.* Chicago: Nelson-Hall, 1980. 201 pp. $17.95; $8.95 (paper).
Dissinger, a bright and cheerful 70-year-old living happily in retirement, tells how to develop coping techniques and skills. The basic question is: What are you going to do with the little money you have? Accordingly, Dissinger tackles the fundamentals of money management and budgeting on a small fixed income, choosing a place to live, furnishing and decorating a small apartment, eating healthfully and cheaply, dressing and grooming on a shoestring, traveling economically, and finding free or inexpensive hobbies and amusements. Good, practical, upbeat advice. Recommended.

146 Financial Planning

Downs, Hugh, and Roll, Richard J. *Hugh Downs' the Best Years Book: How to Plan for Fulfillment, Security and Happiness in the Retirement Years.* New York: Delacorte, 1981. 401 pp. $14.95.

Downs is host of the Emmy Award-winning talk show "Over Easy" on PBS. The authors offer a sensible discussion on aging, retirement lifestyles, keeping healthy, nutrition, exercise, working and volunteering, leisure planning, and where to live in retirement. Of particular value is the coverage of financial needs and resources, sources of income, budgeting, social security benefits, pension plans, tax aspects of retirement, investment strategies, wills and estate planning, and health insurance. Readable.

Dunetz, Martin. *How to Finance Your Retirement.* Reston, VA: Reston, 1979. 227 pp. $18.95.

An examination of investment alternatives and opportunities that are particularly applicable for retirement programs. In this unique book, the author analyzes the objectives and mode of operation of public and private pension plans, pension plan investing, self-employed pension programs (Keogh), IRAs, corporate retirement plans, annuities and insurance companies, public teachers retirement systems, TIAA (Teachers Insurance Annuity Association) and CREF (College Retirement Equities Fund), and other investment alternatives. An important book for those who take an interest in their own retirement fund in view of the fact that the performance trend in managed retirement plans has not provided a rate of return on invested capital consistent with the rise in the cost of living. Recommended.

Gollin, James. *The Star Spangled Retirement Dream.* New York: Scribner's, 1981. 224 pp. $12.95.

A very readable, informative, and nontechnical discussion of the organization, operation, and benefits of private pension plans, the safeguards now provided by ERISA (Employee Retirement Income Security Act of 1974), public employee pension plans, social security retirement benefits, and how the pension industry invests its money. Also provides valuable advice on how to develop a retirement strategy and project one's estimated income. Highly recommended reading in view of the startling fact that 84 percent of those in private pension plans and 58 percent of private-plan members over 50 do not know what their retirement benefits will be.

Hardy, C. Colburn. *ABC's of Investing Your Retirement Funds.* 2nd Edition. Oradell, NJ: Medical Economics Books, 1982. 241 pp. $22.50.

Although designed primarily to help physicians invest their retirement funds more wisely and more effectively, the content is generalizable in nature. The main point is conservative: "With fiduciary funds, all investments should be prudent, should preserve capital, and should earn above-average total returns to assure ample assets for your retirement years." Hardy covers how to choose a plan (Keogh, corporate retirement accounts), types of investments for retirement plans (fixed income, stock, life insurance), and rules for investing. Solid, sensible and sound. Must reading for all, not just physicians.

Hardy, C. Colburn. *Your Guide to a Financially Secure Retirement.* New York: Harper & Row, 1983. 223 pp. $16.50.

Hardy is the author of *Dun and Bradstreet's Guide to Your Investments, 1983* (see p. 71) and *Your Money and Your Life* (see below). In this book, he starts with the basic assumption that "the majority of future retirees will (or can) look forward to comfortable, financially secure after-work years if they plan wisely, save consistently and invest profitably." Hardy reviews the necessary strategy and discipline required to achieve financial security. In concise and lucid writing, he discusses how much money you will need and have in relation to future inflation; sources of income such as social security, private pension plans and independent retirement accounts (IRAs); investing for the greatest returns in stocks and annuities; and factors to consider in life and health insurance coverage. Comprehensive, authoritative, and easily understandable. Highly recommended.

Hardy, C. Colburn. *Your Money and Your Life: Planning Your Financial Future.* 2nd Edition. New York: AMACOM, 1982. 352 pp. $19.95.

A comprehensive and thorough guide to financial planning for individuals to take charge of their own financial futures. "If you have the knowledge and skill necessary to become a successful executive or professional, you can learn to do your own financial planning." Topics include lifestyle and financial planning, coping with college costs, real estate, life insurance, use of trusts, tax shelters, retirement planning, and financial advisers. The book is aimed at the sophisticated and affluent reader—with details on corporate executive perquisites (perks) in the form of stock options, bonuses, company-provided car and planes, club memberships, and so on. Interesting and authoritative.

Irwin, Robert. *The $100,000 Decision: The Older American's Guide to Selling a Home and Choosing Retirement Housing.* New York: McGraw-Hill, 1981. 208 pp. $14.95.

A book that will help the increasing numbers of people contemplating retirement make sensible and economical decisions about choosing appropriate housing. Irwin clearly explains the once-in-a-lifetime exclusion allowance of federal income taxes on capital gain from the sale of one's home and how to calculate the exclusion in specific cases, taking into account qualifying factors such as death of one spouse, remarriage, or divorce. Irwin also outlines the steps involved in considering the advantages and disadvantages of retirement communities, condominiums, mobile homes, rental apartments, smaller homes, and various types of health-care facilities. An excellent guide to getting the best retirement housing at a reasonable cost.

Irwin, Robert. *The $125,000 Decision: The Older American's Guide to Selling a Home and Choosing Retirement Housing.* Revised Edition. New York: McGraw-Hill, 1982. 208 pp. $15.95.

This is an updated and revised edition of the author's *The $100,000 Decision* (see above). The revised text reflects the changes in the 1981 tax legislation that increased the once-in-a-lifetime exclusion allowance of federal income taxes on capital gain from the sale of one's home from $100,000 to $125,000. In this edition, Irwin lucidly shows that housing decisions are at the core of financial planning and retirement. His book explains requirements and eligibility for the exclusion and the major considerations involved in selecting retirement housing such as condominiums, mobile homes, retirement communities, and care facilities. Another alternative described is keeping one's home and obtaining an income through refinancing, annuity (reverse) mortgage, or life estate. Must reading for those concerned with retirement income, housing, and inflation. Highly recommended.

Jessup, L. F. *Law of Retirement*. 2nd Edition. Dobbs Ferry, NY: Oceana, 1979. 120 pp. $5.95 (paper).
How to fulfill the dream of a trip to Europe, a house in the sun belt, and comfortable living in the retirement years. Reviews how to accumulate assets through savings devices—bank account, pension and profit-sharing plans, insurance, securities and investments, social security. Good basic presentation calculated to assist people conceptualize and plan for retirement.

Jorgensen, James. *Your Retirement Income*. New York: Scribner's, 1982. 256 pp. $14.95.
How do you know you will have enough to live on when the paychecks stop? This is the crucial question addressed by Jorgensen, author of *The Graying of America*, who believes that retirement planning should take into account continuing inflation from 7 percent on the low side to about 20 to 23 percent on the high side. The author shows what can be expected from social security, private pension plans, and personal savings and offers good advice on how to develop a retirement strategy and accumulate the necessary funds for retirement. A readable discussion of what benefits you can reasonably expect when you retire and how to invest for long-term retirement security. Necessary reading for most Americans. Recommended.

LeClair, Robert, Leimberg, Stephan, and Chasman, Herbert. *Money and Retirement: How to Plan for Lifetime Financial Security*. Reading, MA: Addison-Wesley, 1982. 245 pp. $12.95; 1981. 256 pp. $7.95 (paper).
A very practical, step-by-step guide to taking personal responsibility for one's financial security after retirement. The essentials are well covered: how much money you will need, how long the money will last, how to project future income, the role social security benefits will play, the impact of inflation, investment alternatives (stock, mutual funds, real estate, tax shelters), life insurance, personal retirement funds, estate planning. Particularly helpful is the very concise discussion of the social security system (how to estimate retirement benefits, rights of women workers, and so on) and the questions and answers provided on IRA and Keogh plans. An excellent book that provides the necessary techniques for accumulating the resources required for secure and comfortable retirement. Highly recommended.

Ledford, Lowell, and Brock, Jeanne. *Ready or Not: Planning Your Successful Retirement*. New York: Walker, 1977. 140 pp. $3.95 (paper). O.P.
Quizzes, worksheets, organizations, and information sources on financial planning, investments, insurance, employment, leisure, and health. Still useful in its simplicity.

Michaels, Joseph. *Prime of Your Life*. New York: Facts on File, 1981. 288 pp. $14.95; Boston: Little, Brown, 1982. $8.95 (paper).
Michaels is co-host of the weekly TV show "The Prime of Your Life." In this book, he gathers practical points on subjects as diverse as security, leisure, living, and

health. Coverage is given to retirement planning, investments, pension funds, living economically, renting versus owning, energy conservation, and so on. A pedestrian presentation.

Nauheim, Fred. *The Retirement Money Book: New Ways to Have More Income When You Retire.* Washington, DC: Acropolis, 1982. 250 pp. $11.95.

Explores your choices and opportunities to shape the retirement years to your liking. Nauheim reviews retirement needs, sources of income, assets, annuities, pension plans, social security, continued employment, and investment opportunities. Also covered are methods of cutting taxes and increasing capital, IRA and Keogh plans, payout options and income averaging, tax shelters, common stock investments, mutual funds, tax-free municipal bonds, and so on. An excellent, readable book for preretirees and retirees, calculated to promote more effective decision making. Highly recommended.

Raphaelson, Elliot. *Planning Your Financial Future: Tax Shelters, Annuities, IRAs, Keoghs, Stocks and Other Investment or Retirement Opportunities.* New York: Ronald Press, 1982. 239 pp. $19.95.

A textbook-style presentation of the major factors involved in retirement planning. Academic review of sources of income, social security, life insurance, annuities, private pension plans, IRAs, traditional and nontraditional investments. Several glossaries cover mutual funds, bonds, and real estate. Dull reading.

Rubinstein, David. *Invest for Retirement: A Conservative Investor's Guide.* New York: Free Press, 1981. 320 pp. $12.95.

A conservative book for the investor past the age of 48. Recent statistics reveal that only 5 out of 100 men reaching 65 years of age can support themselves financially. Rubinstein provides some excellent, sensible advice on how to plan for future retirement: establishing financial goals, annual investment of a percentage of after-tax earnings, reinvestment of dividends, borrowing money for investment, purchase of undervalued stocks in bear markets and sale of fully valued stocks in bull markets, concern with long investment, and unconcern with interim market fluctuations. The author argues that inflation can be beaten by judicious purchase of stocks and not through fixed investments such as savings accounts, certificates of deposit and treasury bonds. Readable and informative. Does not, however, cover the changes resulting from the 1981 tax law. Recommended.

Sloan, Irving J. *Income and Estate Tax Planning.* Dobbs Ferry, NY: Oceana, 1980. 118 pp. $5.95 (paper).

Sloan reviews the essential elements of financial planning for families, advocating the Rule of Three—protection, savings, investment. With concise and specific explanation, he covers social security benefits and coverage, the role of life insurance, factors to consider in savings and investment programs, estate planning, wills, and trusts. Informative discussion at a very basic level.

Sumichrast, Michael, Shafer, Ronald, and Sumichrast, Marika. *Where Will You Live Tomorrow? The Complete Guide to Planning for Your Retirement Housing.* Homewood, IL: Dow Jones-Irwin, 1981. 313 pp. $14.95.

Hovering ominously over retirement is high inflation, which devours retirement incomes while pushing up housing costs. Early planning is essential, and the authors review the essential elements covering estimated income, social security benefits, pension plans, savings, and investments. Within this context, a detailed overview of housing options is presented. Basic topics covered include best geographical location, housing costs, cashing in housing assets, turning equity into income, owning versus renting, vacation homes, retirement communities, and so on. A valuable handbook of essential information. Recommended.

Worley, H. Wilson. *Retirement Living Alternatives USA: The Inside Story.* Clemson, SC: Columbia House, 1982. 151 pp. $9.95 (paper).

At present there are approximately 25 million people aged 65 or older. Starting with the assumption that retirement is not an end but an opening of new vistas of growth and enjoyment, the author outlines the choices available in housing, the most significant and costly expense after medical care. The advantages, disadvantages, special features, and costs are analyzed for the major alternatives—subsidized housing, shared housing, residential hotels, life-care retirement centers, market rental, and ownership housing communities. Particularly useful are a cost comparison of a retirement community apartment versus an individual home in typical suburbia and the pros and cons of a typical home versus a retirement apartment. Provides retirement community selection criteria. An excellent treatment of a wide variety of options.

IRA AND KEOGH RETIREMENT ACCOUNTS

Corrigan, Arnold. *How Your IRA Can Make You a Millionaire.* New York: Harmony, 1983. 114 pp. $3.95 (paper).

Despite the extravagance of its title, this is a most valuable book. Corrigan points out that "the most critical question for the success of your IRA is where to put your IRA dollars—how to *invest* your IRA contributions." He therefore places fundamental emphasis on analyzing and comparing the investment opportunities provided by banks, money market funds, common stocks, mutual funds, and insurance companies. Corrigan believes that investments in stocks and mutual funds will outperform other investment vehicles. Particularly helpful is his discussion of mutual funds showing types of funds, best performing funds, and addresses and phone numbers of selected no-load mutual fund groups. Most helpful in IRA decision making. Highly recommended.

Egan, Jack. *Your Complete Guide to IRA's and Keoghs: The Simple, Safe Tax-Deferred Way to Financial Security.* New York: Harper & Row, 1982. 224 pp. $13.95.

Must reading for all those who wish to take advantage of what is probably the best way to set aside money for the future without having one's savings and investments gutted by inflation and taxes. IRAs and Keoghs offer a double tax break: a deduction from taxable income for the amount contributed annually and deferred taxes on the money that accumulates in an account until withdrawals. Egan, formerly business and economic correspondent of the *Washington Post*, skillfully guides the reader through the hard-sell barrage of advertising on the part of banks, savings and loan associations, stockbrokers, and so on. Clear explanation is provided of eligibility, maximum contributions, advantages of pretax contributions, penalties for excess contributions and early withdrawal, age limits, opening an account, fees, role of the trustee-custodian, rollovers, and so on. Particularly helpful is the author's delineation of the flexibility and choices available through company plans, savings accounts, mutual funds, brokerage accounts, and insurance companies. Egan particularly favors no-load mutual funds that permit switching between funds (money market, growth, capital appreciation, etc.) and provides a list of funds ranked by performance. The book contains suggested readings and a list of newsletters that monitor mutual and money market funds such as the *Switch Fund Advisory*. Readable, concise, informative, and most valuable. Highly recommended.

Grace, William J., Jr. *The ABC's of IRA's: The Complete Guide to Individual Retirement Accounts: The #1 Investment Strategy of the Eighties*. New York: Dell, 1982. 191 pp. $3.95 (paper).
One of the best books to date on IRAs for those considering spending $2,000 a year on a retirement plan for the rest of their lives. This book is relevant reading for all those bombarded by the marketing blitz of the savings and loan associations and other organizations seeking retirement savings. Apart from explaining how IRAs work (requirements, regulations), Grace provides an excellent comparison among those offered by depository plans (banks, savings and loans, credit unions), brokerage firms, mutual fund companies, and insurance companies. The comparative discussion takes into account other retirement coverage, investment objectives, risk factors, age, investment experience, and desire for active involvement. One section answers 100 of the most common questions asked about IRAs. Highly recommended.

Greisman, Bernard (ed.). *J. K. Lasser's All You Should Know about IRA, Keogh, and Other Retirement Plans*. New York: Simon & Schuster/Fireside, 1983. 157 pp. $5.95 (paper).
Highlights the provisions of the 1982 Tax Equity and Fiscal Responsibility Act with regard to IRA, Keogh, and SEP plans, corporate retirement plans, deciding when and how to take distribution from your plan for maximum benefits, avoiding IRA and Keogh tax penalties, and estate planning for retirement benefits. Also contains a good explanation of tax-free rollovers. Concise and clear text.

IRA's: Your Complete New Money Guide: How to Open Your IRA, Manage It, Switch It, Withdraw It and Get the Best, Safest Yields. New York: Money Magazine, 1982. 104 pp. $2.95 (paper).
Confused by the complexity of regulations concerning IRAs and the variety of choices available? The editors of *Money*, the monthly magazine of personal finance, offer an in-depth guide to the essential rules and the comparative advantages and disadvantages of plans offered by banks, stockbrokers, insurance companies, and mutual funds. The guide also describes the operation of switch funds, alternatives to IRAs (company savings plans, nonprofit group annuities, salary reduction plans, and others) and answers 50 typical questions. Vital statistics in the form of addresses,

152 Financial Planning

phone numbers, minimum investment, switch fund privileges, and effective 12-month yields are given for 66 money funds and 355 stock and bond funds. In view of the high-pressure advertising and promotion of IRAs, this inexpensive publication is an excellent one-stop source of information for individuals to decide whether to start an IRA and where to invest. Highly recommended.

Pancheri, Michael, and Flynn, David H. *The IRA Handbook: A Complete Guide.* Piscataway, NJ: New Century, 1983. 192 pp. $9.95.
A comprehensive treatment of most aspects of IRAs: rules and regulations, tax deferral advantages, eligibility, opening an account, rollover contributions, penalties for premature withdrawal, distribution options, simplified employee pension (SEP) plans. Inadequate attention is, however, paid to the variety of investment opportunities confronting the average person. Not recommended.

Ullman, James M., and Bercoon, Norman. *How to Build a Fortune with an IRA.* New York: Macmillan, 1982. 144 pp. $4.95 (paper).
An outline of strategy to be used in using IRAs as a means of accumulating retirement income. A good explanation of the mechanics of IRA accounts covering regulations governing amount invested annually, penalties for early withdrawal, transfer, rollovers, and so on. Tables show what the value of IRAs would be at various rates of interest. Inflation can, however, make beggars of hopeful IRA millionaires.

ESTATE PLANNING

Brosterman, Robert. *The Complete Estate Planning Guide: Updated to Include 1981 and 1982 Tax Changes.* New York: New American Library/Mentor Books, 1982. 359 pp. $3.95 (paper).
How to accumulate capital, amass an estate, increase it, and pass it on. Conscious and continuous planning can result in very real and sizable gains. Brosterman separates planning into two distinct parts, creation and transfer, and gives equal stress to both. Special attention is paid to the provisions of the Economic Recovery Tax Act of 1981. Much more understandable than most books on estate planning. Good checklist of family objectives and needs. Recommended.

Callahan, P. J. *How to Make a Will, How to Use Trusts.* 4th Edition. Legal Almanac Series. Dobbs Ferry, NY: Oceana, 1978. 119 pp. $4.95.
Although rather old, the content is still highly relevant: what a will is, do you need a will, forms of wills, execution of wills, administration of estates, how to use trusts. Concise and clearly written.

Cantor, Gilbert. *How to Avoid Estate Taxes.* Wilmington, DE: Enterprise, 1981. 282 pp. $19.95.
Death may be inevitable, but death taxes are not. Cantor reviews the various options and techniques available to minimize one's taxable estate. Clear coverage is given to the marital deduction, orphans' and charitable deductions, lifetime gift programs, trusts, annuities, and other tax-avoidance techniques. One chapter lists 100 helpful estate planning and tax-saving tips. Cantor contends that estate planning is not a

"do-it-yourself" job and that it is necessary to seek professional assistance from a lawyer. A 40-page insert supplement updates the text in relation to the estate and gift tax changes introduced by the Economic Recovery Tax Act of 1981.

Clay, William. *The Dow Jones-Irwin Guide to Estate Planning.* New York: Bantam, 1982. 176 pp. $2.95 (paper).

Clay addresses three basic questions: Why should you create an estate plan? What kind of estate plan should you choose? When should you review and revise it? He relates how to choose an estate planning lawyer, executor, guardian or trustee, how to cut federal and state estate taxes, and how to word your will to avoid contest. Not a do-it-yourself guide but rather what a layperson needs to know and how to save money when talking to a lawyer. Provides an example of a typical short will and power of attorney.

Dacey, Norman F. *How to Avoid Probate—Updated!* New York: Crown, 1980. 608 pp. $19.95; $14.95 (paper).

Dacey criticizes the antiquated and cumbersome procedures inherent in the probate of decedents' estates and documents extensively the numerous abuses of probate— "a political toll-booth exacting tribute from widows and orphans." Essentially, Dacey recommends that property be placed in trust before the death of the owner in order to avoid having a will probated and paying heavy legal fees. In this classic work, the author explains the complexities of the system and provides a series of concise and detachable will forms to fit various situations and needs. A magnificent compilation for those who wish to take the time and the trouble to wend their way through the legal thicket. Highly recommended.

Flaherty, Patrick F., and Ziegler, Richard. *Estate Planning for Everyone: The Whole Truth—From Planning to Probate.* Revised Edition. New York: Harper & Row, 1981. 160 pp. $12.95.

A good basic explanation, but needs updating since it does not reflect the changes brought about by the Economic Recovery Act of 1981 with respect to transference of estate both during life and after death. For more up-to-date information, see Robert Brosterman, *The Complete Estate Planning Guide* (see p. 152).

Gargon, John. *The Complete Guide to Estate Planning.* Spectrum Reference Shelf Series. Englewood Cliffs, NJ: Prentice-Hall/Spectrum, 1980. 198 pp. $10.95.

Gargon goes through the basic steps of successful estate planning—the accumulation, conservation, and eventual distribution of property and wealth according to your wishes. Solid, sensible information on goal setting, building of estates through tax shelters such as mutual funds, corporate fringe benefits, and real estate investments, selecting estate planning advisers, and minimizing taxes and costs. Definitely for the more sophisticated and affluent layperson.

Ginsberg, Linda. *Family Financial Survival.* Millbrae, CA: Celestial Arts, 1981. 192 pp. $9.95 (paper).

A moving, personal narrative by the widow of a young dental specialist recently left to cope with the financial complexities of her husband's practice and business ventures. Ginsberg attempts to shock readers into making ironclad provisions for financial survival. She focuses attention on major topics such as calculating your net worth, inheritance taxes on your estate, gift taxes, wills, getting your estate in order, insurance and social security benefits, and estate planning for your future. Particularly valuable is a chapter entitled "Reality Planning," containing guidance on what to do when death occurs—how to cope with funerals, records and important papers, and estate settlement. Ginsberg provides sample letters to be sent to employers, insurance companies, and the Veterans Administration. Useful glossary, checklists, charts, and work forms. Take a firm grip on your personal finances before it is too late! Sensible and helpful. Highly recommended.

Hemphill, Charles. *Wills and Trusts: A Legal and Financial Handbook for Everyone.* Englewood Cliffs, NJ: Prentice-Hall, 1980. 244 pp. $12.95. O.P.

A fairly detailed explanation of wills, what they accomplish, how to write your own will, probate and duties of the executor or executrix, federal estate and gift taxes, charitable bequests, trusts as tools in estate planning, trusts and tax avoidance. One of a number of appendixes lists what to do immediately after the death of a loved one or friend. Informative and authoritative.

J. K. Lasser Tax Institute. *J. K. Lasser's Your Estate and Gift Taxes.* Larchmont, NY: Business Reports, 1980. 265 pp. $14.95.

Fundamentals of the estate and gift tax. Reviews wills and their role in estate planning, tax-saving gifts, pros and cons of joint property, split gifts, types of trusts, charitable bequests, and so on. Needs updating.

Kahn, Arnold D. *Family Security through Estate Planning.* 2nd Edition. New York: McGraw-Hill, 1983. 224 pp. $19.95.

Analyzes the basic legal and tax concepts of estate planning. Kahn covers tax saving, wills, trusts, life insurance, how to develop a basic estate plan, specific techniques of estate planning, and how to build a strong, working relationship with your attorney. Several basic estate plans are described for consideration and discussion. Appendixes contain preplanning worksheets, federal estate and gift tax rates, and a glossary of legal and tax terms. Useful.

Kinevan, Marcos. *Personal Estate Planning: Financial and Legal Aspects of Accumulating, Protecting, and Disposing of Your Personal Estate.* Englewood Cliffs, NJ: Prentice-Hall, 1980. 258 pp. $14.95; $6.95 (paper).

A somewhat technical textbook coverage of estate accumulation, conservation, and distribution, savings and credit, casualty insurance, survivors' benefits, estate programming, life insurance and various types of investments, nature and uses of trusts, various property arrangements among family members, and wills. An authoritative source book.

Kirsch, Charlotte. *A Survivor's Manual To: Contingency Planning, Wills, Trusts, Guidelines for Guardians, Getting through Probate, Taxes, Life Insurance, Emotional Stability, Protection from Reckless Spending, Living on a Fixed Income, Reconciling Family Differences, Avoiding Con Artists.* New York: Doubleday/Anchor Press, 1981. 240 pp. $13.95.

In a death-denying culture, Kirsch, the director of the National Study of the Bereaved, offers a book that explains the connection between death and money and the effect it has on family relationships. In particular, she focuses on the behavior and attitudes of survivors with regard to money they receive as beneficiaries of life insurance policies, pensions, trust funds, and other forms of inheritance. Contingency planning is defined as consideration of the possibility of our own death and the effect it would have on those whose living and existing connect with our own. Kirsch presents an abundance of detailed coping information on the essentials of such contingency planning—estate planning, life insurance, investments, wills, and beneficiaries. Most valuable are those chapters on survivorship—death certificates, burial, applying for insurance, pensions and social security benefits, how to get help, paying bills, investing the proceeds of insurance policies and benefits, filing for probate, avoiding con artists, and so on. Practical, valuable advice desperately needed in a time of crisis blended with insight into the psychological and emotional problems involved. Indispensable. Highly recommended.

Larsen, David C. *Who Gets It When You Go? A Guide for Planning Your Will, Protecting Your Family's Future, Minimizing Inheritance Taxes, and Avoiding Probate.* New York: Random House, 1982. 141 pp. $10; $4.95 (paper).

Explains in uncomplicated language what can happen to your property when you die. Discusses wills, if you die without a will, probate and how to avoid it, living trusts, federal estate tax and how to reduce it, and the state inheritance tax. The chapter on the essentials of making a will is particularly helpful. Simple and lucid explanation of a complex topic. Highly recommended.

Levin, Martin, et al. *You May Be Losing Your Inheritance: A Guide to Psychological, Financial, and Legal Hazards and What You Can Do about Them Now.* New York: Times Books, 1979. 150 pp. $9.95. O.P.

Five experts (three attorneys, a psychologist, and a journalist) combine to explain the problems, financial and judicial, that can enter into wills and settlement of estates. Of particular interest is the chapter on parent-child relationships that affect the will, discussing the role of guilt, fear, shame, and their effects on the family.

Lippett, Peter. *Estate Planning: After the Reagan Tax Cut.* Reston, VA: Reston, 1982. 342 pp. $17.95.

A tutorial attempt to convey the basics of property ownership, wills, probate, trusts, gift taxes, and estate planning techniques and the impact of the Economic Recovery Tax Act of 1981 on transfer taxes. Although the author supplies a glossary for each chapter and carefully reviews the essential points, it is still difficult reading. A laudable attempt to demystify estate planning and wean the average consumer from excessive dependence on lawyers. A useful book for both laypeople and for nonlawyer professionals such as bankers, stockbrokers, investment advisers, and accountants.

Lippett, Peter. *Estate Planning: What Anyone Who Owns Anything Must Know.* Reston, VA: Reston, 1979. 376 pp. $16.95.

Lippett provides comprehensive coverage of forms of property ownership, intestacy, probate, trusts, estate and gift taxes, and estate planning techniques, such as life insurance and annuities. Provides a good glossary. Written from a lay/consumer point of view, the book requires concentrated reading. For the sophisticated reader.

Moody, William J. *How to Probate an Estate: A Handbook for Executors and Administrators.* New Revised Edition. New York: Cornerstone Library, 1981. 95 pp. $3.95 (paper).
Not a very comprehensive or comprehensible explanation of the mechanics of acting as executor or administrator of an estate. Superficial, with little discussion or elucidation.

Pinto, Robert J. *How to Save Taxes through Estate Planning.* Princeton, NJ: Dow Jones, 1980. 167 pp. $8.95. O.P.
How to formulate estate planning objectives and better understand the tax and legal advice needed. Covers lifetime gifts, trusts, tax consequences of various types of assets, last wills and testaments, how to select financial planning advisers, living estate plans, and IRA, Keogh, and corporate retirement plans. Useful, although somewhat technical.

Plotnick, Charles, and Leimberg, Stephan. *Die Rich: Making It, Keeping It, and Passing It Along under the New Tax Laws.* New York: Coward-McCann and Geoghegan, 1983. 352 pp. $17.95.
A rather technical exposition of the essentials of estate planning, written by two attorneys. Difficult reading.

Whitman, Robert. *Simplified Guide to Estate Planning and Administration.* New York: Monarch Press, 1981. 192 pp. $6.95 (paper).
A logical, sequential discussion proceeding from basic questions—why plan an estate, should you hire an attorney—to specific details on tax principles, probate, lifetime planning, estate administration, wills, and trusts. Readable but not simple.

Whitney, Victor. *How to Beat the Money Grabbers: The Essentials of Estate Planning.* New York: Crown/Arlington House, 1979. 256 pp. $14.95.
A bank officer in charge of estate planning shows how to avoid the Internal Revenue agent, who can confiscate up to 70 percent of an estate and how to cope with vulturelike financial scavengers. Whitney outlines the basic elements of estate planning, settling of an estate, taxation of transfers at death, and the essentials of trusts and life insurance. Case studies illustrate estate planning for the elderly retired, the professional person, the business owner, the corporate executive, farmers, single persons, and the handicapped. A good attempt to simplify a complex subject.

TRUSTS

Hancock, William. *Saving Money through 10-Year Trusts.* New York: McGraw-Hill, 1979. 177 pp. $15.95.
A ten-year trust is a legal device by which a taxpayer may transfer income from him- or herself to another person. The chief advantage, if done properly and appropri-

ately, is that income is transferred from a high tax bracket to a low tax bracket, resulting in tax savings. Hancock shows where the ten-year trust (Clifford trust, short-term trust) may be useful, basic alternatives, pitfalls, computing tax advantages, record keeping, estate and gift taxes, and tax audits. He also suggests how to find and work with a good lawyer and what the fees should be. A good book to read before consulting a lawyer on this subject. For the more sophisticated reader.

Starchild, Adam. *Building Wealth: A Layman's Guide to Trust Planning.* New York: AMACOM, 1981. 192 pp. $15.95.
An introduction to modern trust agreements outlining the basics of the major categories of trusts, differences between charitable and insurance trusts, use of trusts in estate planning, tax aspects, probate, costs of establishing and administering a trust, and rights and duties of trustees and beneficiaries. A readable and clear outline of the principles underlying the trustor-trustee-beneficiary relationship. Recommended.

INSURANCE

Consumer Reports, Eds. *The Consumers Union Report on Life Insurance: A Guide to Planning and Buying the Protection You Need.* 4th Edition. New York: Holt, Rinehart & Winston, 1981. 384 pp. $14.95; $7.95 (paper).
What you should know about life insurance: who needs it, how much you need, basic policy types, term versus cash value, deciphering the price, switching policies, and more. Attempts to demystify the life insurance marketplace and help consumers buy the life insurance protection they require. Points out the need for better cost disclosure information. Presents Consumers Union's ratings for 199 term policies and 279 cash value insurance policies showing cost and rate of return. Also provides a useful glossary. Recommended.

Kaye, Barry. *How to Save a Fortune on Your Life Insurance.* New Edition. Los Angeles: Forman, 1981. 304 pp. $12.95.
Attempts to explain the myths, misconceptions, and sacred cows of the life insurance business, such as never drop an old policy, life insurance is a good investment, you don't need insurance when you are older, all insurance companies are the same, when you borrow on your policy, you are borrowing your own money. Kaye, who heads a life insurance agency, shows how communication may be improved between agents and consumers and how to save money when buying life insurance. Tables and endless statistics tend to clutter the text.

Kenton, Walter. *How Life Insurance Companies Rob You and What You Can Do about It.* New York: Random House, 1983. 193 pp. $12.95.
An exposé, by a graduate of the American College of Life Underwriters, a chartered life underwriter and a member of the Million-Dollar Round Table, of the ravenous wolves who push life insurance on an unsuspecting public. Kenton believes that "there's no product or commodity about which people who buy it know less." He argues that "you need life insurance, but the only way you can get it is from a ruthless industry that brainwashes its agents and sends them out to get you." Using

the experience gleaned from 17 years in the insurance business, Kenton shows how to determine the amount of insurance really needed, the basic types of life insurance (permanent, cash value, whole life, term, universal) and how to counter the high-pressure tactics of ruthless salespeople. Despite its somewhat sensationalist tone, this book offers some helpful suggestions and advice.

Majka, Paul. *You Can Save a Bundle on Your Car Insurance.* New York: St. Martin's Press, 1982. 96 pp. $3.95 (paper).
An insurance consultant probes the mysteries of auto insurance and shows how to save money by getting a nonprincipal operator classification, multicar discounts, maintaining a clean driving record, and finding rock-bottom rates. Majka outlines the factors determining rate classification—age, sex, marital status, accident and violation record, annual mileage, where the vehicle is garaged, number of vehicles, and so on. He suggests numerous premium-slashing adjustments and maneuvers, including use of multicar, driver training, and good student discounts. Sample letters are provided requesting refunds, adjustments, reductions, and so on. Valuable, informative, and calculated to save money. Highly recommended.

Mehr, Robert. *Fundamentals of Insurance.* Homewood, IL: Irwin, 1983. 640 pp. $23.95.
A basic text covering risk and insurance, how to read a policy, analysis of the principal features of home, life, auto, health, and other types of insurance. A final chapter summarizes the content by showing how to buy insurance. Brief presentation for classroom use of much of the content of Mehr and Cammack's, *Principles of Insurance* (see below).

Mehr, Robert, and Cammack, Emerson. *Principles of Insurance.* 7th Edition. Homewood, IL: Irwin, 1980. 790 pp. $22.95.
Study of the major features of various types of insurance written for the prospective insurance buyer. Comprehensive.

Milton, Arthur. *How Your Life Insurance Policies Rob You.* Secaucus, NJ: Citadel Press, 1981. 178 pp. $8.95.
An angry yet level-headed book by an insurance agent and broker on the "predatory, autocratic and sometimes criminal activities of the life insurance establishment." In particular, Milton points to the abuse of whole life, cash-value insurance policies and stresses the advantages of term insurance that gives better value. Other examples of insurance huckstering are to be found in the sale of cancer insurance and credit life insurance that carry inflated commissions. The author documents the manifest evils of what he calls a "smug industry" and suggests criteria for selecting an insurance agent. Good sensible advice on how to get the best value from one's life insurance dollar. Recommended.

Spielman, Peter, and Zelman, Aaron. *The Life Insurance Conspiracy Made Elementary by Sherlock Holmes.* New York: Simon & Schuster/Fireside, 1979. 171 pp. $4.95 (paper).

An exposé of the high pressure and misleading sales practices of the life insurance industry utilizing Holmesian logic. The authors forcefully argue that cash-value (permanent) life insurance is a "racket" that fleeces the public. They advocate that consumers should switch to term insurance. A list of highly rated companies selling term insurance is supplied. Spielman and Zelman present 20 questions to ask of your agent when he tries to persuade you not to switch to a term policy. An excellent consumer-minded book. Highly recommended.

Tobias, Andrew. *The Invisible Bankers: Everything the Insurance Industry Never Wanted You to Know.* New York: Simon & Schuster/Linden Press, 1982. 336 pp. $15.95.

A brilliant analysis of the size, operation, and profits of the U.S. insurance industry that collects $200 billion in annual premiums managed by more than 4,800 insurance companies employing 1.9 million people; $700 billion in assets are invested (hence, "invisible bankers") to yield vast profits from buildings, hotels, shopping centers, and so on. Nearly seven cents of the average American's dollar is spent directly on health, life, auto, and property insurance. Only cents of the premium dollar goes, on the average, to pay claims; the remainder is used to cover expenses, overhead, and profit. Tobias provides a great deal of valuable advice on how best to shop for life, auto, health, disability, home owners, credit, and other types of insurance. The discussion on term versus whole life insurance is particularly useful. Indispensable reading for all who purchase insurance. Highly recommended.

SOCIAL SECURITY AND MEDICARE

Dickinson, Peter, and the Editors of Consumer Guide. *Get More Money From... Social Security, Govt. Benefits, Medicare, Plus.* 1982 Edition. New York: Grosset & Dunlap, 1982. 96 pp. $4.95 (paper).

How the social security system works—provisions, eligibility, benefits, appeal procedures; disability and Medicare; how other programs such as SSI, Railroad Retirement, and Medicaid tie into social security, tax advantages after 65, and more. Clear, comprehensive, and highly useful guide. Must reading for all citizens. Highly recommended.

Harrington, Geri. *The Medicare Answer Book: The Up-to-Date, Practical and Authoritative Guide to Medicare.* New York: Harper & Row/Colophon, 1982. 352 pp. $17.25; $5.95 (paper).

At last, a comprehensive and concise explanation of what so many people need to know about Medicare: eligibility, how one enrolls, costs paid while in the hospital, nursing home and skilled nursing facility coverage, home health care, costs paid under Part A and Part B, physician services and assignment, purchase of medical equipment, second opinions, how to file Medicare claims, how to read the Explanation of Medical Benefits (EOMB) form, appealing claims, reasonable charges, Medigap insurance, HMOs (health maintenance organizations), and more. Answers

100 most asked questions and includes a glossary of Medicare terms, list of addresses of where to send Medicare claims, and toll-free telephone numbers to call for assistance. Worth every penny of the price. Indispensable.

Robertson, A. Haeworth. *The Coming Revolution in Social Security.* McLean, VA: Security Press, 1981. 400 pp. $19.75.
The author was chief actuary of the U.S. Social Security Administration from 1975 to 1978. In this book, he provides an insightful analysis of the social security system together with comprehensive information on funding, benefits, eligibility, integration of private benefit plans, inflation and automatic benefit increases, opting into and out of social security, taking the best advantage of the system, and the future outlook. An authoritative reference book.

Rubin, Richard L. *Your 1983/84 Tax Guide to Social Security Benefits.* New York: Facts on File, 1983. 188 pp. $13.95; $5.95 (paper).
A guide to the social security programs that involve nearly 40 million people collecting almost $200 billion in benefits every year. Eligibility and other provisions are explained for retirement benefits, disability benefits, survivors' benefits, Supplemental Security Income, and Medicare. Each chapter is accompanied by relevant questions and answers, such as "what do I do if my check is stolen?" or "how much income can I have and still qualify for Supplemental Security payments?" An excellent, comprehensive outline of the social security system that can be used in conjunction with the more detailed information on Medicare contained in Geri Harrington, *The Medicare Answer Book* (p. 159). Of interest to large numbers of people. Highly recommended.

Steif, Bill. *What You've Got Coming in Social Security and Medicare.* New York: Enterprise, 1979. 101 pp. $2.95 (paper). O.P.
Answers the most frequently asked questions concerning eligibility, contributions, benefits, disability, outside earnings, Medicare, impact of inflation. Needs updating.

Steskal, T. J. *Understanding Medicare.* Redondo Beach, CA: Information Products, 1980. 93 pp. $9.95 (paper).
A fairly simple explanation of the requirements, benefits, and operation of Medicare discussing hospital coverage (Part A) and medical coverage (Part B), how to submit insurance claims, the right to request a review of Medicare decisions, major services covered in the hospital (benefit period, reserve days, etc.), medical insurance coverage for outpatient hospital services, home health care provisions, and so on. Particularly useful is the chapter entitled "Guide to Purchasing Insurance to Supplement Medicare," containing a summary of what to look for with a checklist of questions to ask when considering supplemental coverage. A clear discussion of essential facts.

Waller, Kal. *How to Recover Your Medical Expenses: A Comprehensive Guide to Understanding and Unscrambling Medicare.* New York: Macmillan/Collier, 1981. 96 pp. $5.95 (paper).

Explains the major features of the Medicare program: how to obtain Medicare benefits, why and how to purchase a Medicare supplemental insurance policy as a necessary backup, how to take income tax deductions for health-care expenses not covered by Medicare or supplemental insurance. Step-by-step instructions on completing health insurance claim forms, how payment is made, and how to appeal. Contains worksheets and sample filled-in forms. Helpful—but too many charts, tables, forms, and not enough explanatory text.

8

Consumer Magazines, Business Periodicals, and Newspapers

Popular magazines, business periodicals, and newspapers offer large amounts of financial information that is of interest to the layperson. Even a casual perusal of these publications reveals a wide range of data, advice, news, commentary, warnings, exhortations, and forecasts on most aspects of money management. The subject content runs the gamut from how to stretch shrinking food dollars to investments, taxation, selling and buying homes, growth stocks, planning for retirement, municipal bonds, tax sheltering, best buys in vacation travel, and more. Recurring topics are the new tax provisions, creative home financing, IRA and Keogh plans, tax shelters, retirement income and pension plans, inflation, and coping with unemployment.

Consumer magazines and business periodicals serve the needs of various audiences and their individual coverage of money management and financial planning, although very similar in content, varies considerably in terms of complexity. This variation reflects differences in sophistication and amount of discretionary income on the part of respective readerships. Financial planning information is processed and packaged according to the specific audiences served, such as homemakers, career women, middle-income families, business executives, professional money managers, amateur investors, and persons of retirement age.

The quality of information to be found in these periodicals is quite high. Most of them make a concerted and successful effort to present relevant, practical, and succinct information on significant economic and financial topics. The magazine literature offers the information seeker a rich source of accurate, up-to-date information in understandable language. For those who want simple explanations, a magazine article may be preferable to a book. Due to the time lag in book publication, it may be necessary to rely on magazines and newspapers for data on new tax legislation and investment opportunities. In this connection it is difficult to exaggerate the importance of this literature in providing answers to topics of current consumer concern.

Since most libraries already subscribe to the more popular magazines and newspapers and have ready subject access by means of *Reader's Guide to Periodical Literature* and *Magazine Index*, more extensive use should be made of these publications. The purpose here is to review the typical content of the major consumer magazines, business periodicals, and newspapers to demonstrate their value and utility as a source of money management information. The content, level of presentation, and emphases of these publications can best be illustrated in terms of the various audiences served.

POPULAR WOMEN'S MAGAZINES

Money management information can be found in most women's magazines. The level of presentation varies from descriptions of "penny-pinching" ideas and budget-stretching techniques to analyses of the performance of mutual funds and the purchase of real estate. The differences are apparent in three categories of publications—those focusing on home and family, fashion and beauty, and working/career women.

Home and Family

Better Homes and Gardens. Meredith Corp., 1716 Locust St., Des Moines, IA 50336. Monthly; $10/year.

Family Circle. Family Circle, Inc., 488 Madison Ave., New York, NY 10022. $17/year; $.79/issue (no subscription).

Good Housekeeping. Hearst Magazines, 959 Eighth Ave., New York, NY 10019. Monthly; $12.97/year.

Ladies' Home Journal. Charter Publishing, 641 Lexington Ave., New York, NY 10022. Monthly; $9.97/year.

McCall's. McCall Publishing Co., 230 Park Ave., New York, NY 10169. Monthly; $7.95/year (subscription: McCall St., Dayton, OH 45410).

Parents. Parent's Magazine Enterprises, 685 Third Ave., New York, NY 10017. Monthly; $12/year.

Redbook. Redbook Publishing Co., 230 Park Ave., New York, NY 10169. Monthly; $7.95/year.

Woman's Day. CBS Publications, 1515 Broadway, New York, NY 10036. 15/year; $.55/issue (no subscription).

All of these magazines devote space in most issues to some aspect of prudent money management. Many have a regular money column and feature longer articles from time to time. Since the readers are primarily women homemakers, the magazines devote considerable attention to food and diet, physical fitness, beauty care, interpersonal relationships, and common consumer problems, including personal finance.

Two magazines are especially noteworthy for the number of articles offering ideas and advice for families on a limited budget: *Family Circle* and *Parents* both provide practical suggestions for stretching the family budget. *Family Circle*'s "Cashing In" is a one-page compilation of money-saving strategies for savvy consumers. Thomas Trilling's "Money Lines" in *Parents* provides information on goods and services and tips for fighting inflation in short article form.

Economic trends and financial news and developments are discussed in Barbara Gilder Quint's "Moneynews" in *Family Circle* and by Matthew Lesko in his "Money Gram" in *Good Housekeeping*. The impact of the new banking regulations, movements in interest rates, changes in the tax law, and similar topics are well covered by Katherine Barrett and Richard Greene's "Money News" in *Ladies' Home Journal*, by Grace Weinstein's "Your Money" in *Woman's Day*, by Richard Blodgett's "Money Talks" in *McCall's*, and by Ann Arnot's "Mostly Money" in *Redbook*. These financial experts, in some instances the authors of money management books, present one- or two-page compilations of concise information aimed at keeping readers abreast of developments that affect personal income. Their columns provide authoritative, current, and useful information on medical, home, and auto insurance, investment opportunities, changes in banking, movement of interest rates, tax requirements, mutual funds, and so on.

Better Homes and Gardens has longer feature articles on, for example, financing college, whether to remodel one's present home or purchase a larger home, choosing a contractor, and investments. Helpful information in the form of names, addresses, and telephone numbers of resource organizations is also included together with reading lists.

Fashion and Beauty

Glamour. Condé Nast Publications, 350 Madison Ave., New York, NY 10017. Monthly; $12/year.

Mademoiselle. Condé Nast Publications, 350 Madison Ave., New York, NY 10017. Monthly; $12/year.

Self. Condé Nast Publications, 350 Madison Ave., New York, NY 10017 (Subscribe to: Box 5267, Boulder, CO 80321). Monthly; $12/year.

Vogue. Condé Nast Publications, 350 Madison Ave., New York, NY 10017. Monthly; $24/year.

Although the principal emphasis of this type of magazine is on clothes and fashion, the financial well-being of readers is also considered. For example, *Vogue*, for women who have the leisure and the income to consider fashion a way of life, carries personal finance information on a regular basis under a variety of headings: "Money," "Talking About . . . Money," "Taxes." Longer articles may be carried from time to time.

A regular feature in *Mademoiselle* is Carol Eisner Rinzler's column "Dollars and Sense." Women age 18 to 34 can find succinct, practical advice on such subjects as the need for life insurance, how to fill out a tax return, or criteria for choosing a checking account. The accent in *Glamour* is on "how-to" for fashion and beauty conscious college and career women, a philosophy that is reflected by Barbara Gilder Quint's column "How to Get More for Your Money." *Self* emphasizes financial well-being in addition to self-improvement in the areas of health, beauty, diet, and nutrition for the active woman of the 1980s. "Money and Work," a feature carried each month, offers useful facts on taxes, consumer skills, credit, and related topics.

Working/Career Women

Cosmopolitan. Hearst Magazines, 224 W. 57 St., New York, NY 10019. Monthly; $24/year.

Essence. Essence Communications, 1500 Broadway, New York, NY 10036. Monthly; $9/year.

Ms. The New Magazine for Women. Ms. Magazine Corp., 119 W. 40 St., New York, NY 10018. Monthly; $10/year.

New Woman. New Woman, Box 9810, Fort Worth, TX 76107. Monthly; $6.97/year.

Savvy: The Magazine for Executive Women. Savvy Co., 111 Eighth Ave., New York, NY 10011 (Subscribe to: Top Box 2945, Boulder, CO 80322). Monthly; $18/year.

Working Mother. McCall Publishing Co., 230 Park Ave., New York, NY 10169. Monthly; $9.95/year.

Working Woman. Hal Publications, 342 Madison Ave., New York, NY 10173 (Subscribe to: Box 10132, Des Moines, IA 50450). Monthly; $12/year.

These magazines are designed mainly for the upwardly mobile career- or job-oriented woman who has some discretionary income for investment or saving. *New Woman* has a regular column on money matters. "Financial Matters," like much of the material in this magazine, is a digest of information that has appeared elsewhere, consisting of excerpts from articles or books. *Cosmopolitan, Ms, Savvy,* and *Essence* also foster the financial health of their readers. All publish well-written articles full of commonsense advice and ideas aimed at helping women achieve financial success. Recent topics included investment ideas, individual retirement accounts, mutual funds, sources for borrowing money, the hazards of penny stocks, taxes, money market funds, and choosing an investment adviser.

Savvy (The Magazine for Executive Women) carries features on personal finance and on investments, together with in-depth articles on financial concerns.

Working Woman, reflecting the intent of its title, supplies information and advice on communicating with a broker, money management techniques, using a financial adviser, money markets, shopping in the new financial supermarkets, as well as tips on careers, health, fashion, and travel.

A small amount of money management information can be found in *Working Mother,* but the principal focus of this publication is on needs, problems, and challenges of combining children, husband, home, and job.

OTHER AUDIENCES MAGAZINES

Black Enterprise. Earl G. Graves Publishing Co., 295 Madison Ave., New York, NY 10017. Monthly; $10/year.

Esquire. Esquire Publishing, 2 Park Ave., New York, NY 10016. Monthly; $15/year.

House and Garden. Condé Nast Publications, 350 Madison Ave., New York, NY 10017. Monthly; $12/year.

These magazines are somewhat distinct both in content and focus from the women's magazines. *Esquire* features well-written articles on aspects of collecting (art, automobiles, guns, records), advice on travel, and other topics under the heading "Smart Money." "Money" by Paul Gross, featured in *House and Garden* dispenses authoritative advice on tax shelters, investment strategy, and selecting a financial advisor.

Black Enterprise focuses on successful black professionals and black businesspeople. In addition to articles on black business ventures, the publication carries articles on many aspects of personal finance, such as mortgages, IRAs, taxes, and how to maintain a good credit rating.

PRERETIREMENT AND RETIREMENT MAGAZINES

Dynamic Years. Action for Independent Maturity, 215 Long Beach Blvd., Long Beach, CA 90801. Bimonthly; $3.25/year.

50 Plus. Whitney Communications Corp., Magazine Div., 850 Third Ave., New York, NY 10022 (Subscribe to: 99 Garden St., Marion, OH 43302). Monthly; $8.95/year.

Modern Maturity. American Association of Retired Persons (Long Beach), 215 Long Beach Blvd., Long Beach, CA 90801. Bimonthly; membership only.

Retirement Life. National Association of Retired Federal Employees, 1533 New Hampshire Ave., N.W., Washington, DC 20036. Monthly; $9 to nonmembers.

These magazines address the unique concerns and interests of those considering retirement or who have already retired. *Modern Maturity*, *Dynamic Years*, and *50 Plus* supply pragmatic, unbiased, easy-to-understand information on financial strategy and management, housing alternatives, and taxes, along with articles on health, food and nutrition, travel, and current events. The focus is on retirement planning with information on vesting of pension rights, purchase of annuities, estimating retirement income, and estate planning.

A regular feature in *Dynamic Years*, "Questions You've Asked," answers readers' queries on money management, financial strategy, retirement planning, and health. *50 Plus* features "Tight Budget Tips" by David Klein on topics such as assessing your insurance needs and how much you should keep in a passbook savings accounts, and "Personal Finance," offering tips on financial goal setting and handling a windfall. Michael Briley's column in *Modern Maturity*, "For Pre-retirees Only," is a concise one-page summation of many money topics of interest to anyone planning retirement. *Retirement Life*, published by the National Association of Federal Employees, examines and comments on new government rules and regulations as they affect retired federal employees. Approximately half of each issue is devoted to the effects of new rules and regulations on benefits and discussion of eligibility rules.

CONSUMER CONCERNS MAGAZINES

Consumer Reports. Consumers Union of U.S., 256 Washington St., Mount Vernon, NY 10550. Monthly; $14/year.

Consumers Digest. Consumers Digest, 5705 N. Lincoln, Chicago, IL 60659. Bimonthly; $8/year.

Consumers' Research. Consumers' Research, Box 168, Washington, NJ 07882. Monthly; $15/year.

Everybody's Money. Credit Union National Association, Box 431-B, Madison, WI 53701. Quarterly; $2/year.

The consumer magazines, especially *Consumer Reports* and *Consumers' Research*, should be consulted for objective examination of many aspects of money management, such as comparisons of the many types of home, auto, and life insurance, ratings of insurance companies, buying versus renting a home, and deciding whether to purchase your own telephones. *Consumer Reports* and *Consumers' Research* supply consumers with the factual, unbiased information necessary to formulate decisions in relation to family or personal expenditures.

Consumers Digest features a regular column, "Your Money and Life," with short items on how to be a smart shopper, hints on saving energy, and other consumer advice. Practical help on how to get value for your money and be a better money manager is to be found in *Everybody's Money*, with emphasis on solving consumer problems.

WEEKLY NEWSMAGAZINES

Newsweek. Newsweek, 444 Madison Ave., New York, NY 10022 (Subscribe to: Newsweek Bldg., Livingston, NJ 07039). Weekly; $39/year.

*Time.*Time & Life Bldg., New York, NY 10020 (Subscribe to: Time, Inc., 3435 Wilshire Blvd., Los Angeles, CA 90010). Weekly; $45/year.

U.S. News & World Report. U.S. News & World Report, 2300 N St., N.W., Washington, DC 20037. Weekly; $36/year.

Primarily devoted to informing their readers about trends, developments, and issues in national and international news, these magazines are most useful for tracking new business trends, implications of recent legislation, and the effects of economic policy. Their analysis of the business climate, movement of the various markets and interest rates, and the state of the economy provides a useful framework for personal financial planning. Good examples of such analyses are *Time*'s "Economy and Business" and *Newsweek*'s "Economy" sections. Jane Bryant Quinn writes in *Newsweek* about personal finance and money management, focusing on, for example, personal bankruptcy, changes in the tax rules, how to buy retail purchase agreements ("repos") with small risk, money market accounts, choosing an IRA, social security, and personal financial health.

U.S. News & World Report offers a blend of business trends, political currents and issues, and economic developments. The coverage includes financial topics of prime interest to individuals—social security, inflation, banking, taxes, real estate (mortgages and buying a condominium), and so on.

PERSONAL MONEY MANAGEMENT MAGAZINES

Better Investing. National Association of Investment Clubs, 1515 E. Eleven Mile Rd., Royal Oak, MI 48067. Monthly: $7/year.

Changing Times. Kiplinger Washington Editors, 1729 H St., N.W., Washington, DC 20006. Monthly; $12/year.

Fact: The Money Management Magazine. Fact Magazine, 711 Third Ave., New York, NY 10017. Monthly; $18/year.

Money. Time, Time & Life Bldg., New York, NY 10020 (Subscribe to: Time, 591 N. Fairbanks Court, Chicago, IL 60611). Monthly; $21.95/year.

The emphasis of these magazines is on personal money management with some accommodation made for differences in their respective readerships. *Changing Times* has the widest popular appeal and discusses the problems and concerns faced by very large numbers of consumers. Short, well-written articles offer the average American good advice on automobiles, investments, insurance, education, home ownership, career planning, health, recreation, taxes, and social security. Particularly valuable are the listings of information sources included with many articles and the regular feature "Things to Write For," which highlights booklets, pamphlets, leaflets, and other useful publications. *Changing Times* is concise, readable, and practical.

Other magazines traverse much the same territory, but with a different focus. *Money* and *Fact* appeal to a more affluent and sophisticated audience, offering guidance on investments, new types of bank accounts, credit and borrowing, housing, savings, health-care costs, financing a college education, and mutual fund performance. Topics are covered in greater depth and are calculated to appeal to individuals and families with sufficient discretionary income at their disposal to be concerned with how to invest their money for the maximum gain.

Money has regular columns such as "Investment Scorecard" (a comparison of the appreciation of stocks, fixed-income securities, commodities, etc.), "Fund Watch" (best performing mutual funds), and "Money Profiles" (strategies and investment recommendations by various individuals). Likewise, *Fact* has excellent departments on taxes, real estate, stocks, bonds, cash management, insurance, and collectibles. An interesting feature is the listing in chart form of the "25 Best" and "25 Worst Performing Stocks" of the previous month. *Fact* makes very effective use of colorful and imaginative graphics in the form of tables, graphs, and diagrams for the presentation of data.

Better Investing is a valuable source of information for the investor enthusiast or for those with special interest in various aspects of stock strategy and portfolio analysis. Regular features and articles cover the effects of legislative and government policies on the economy, analysis of the performance of individual companies, suggestions for stock selection, and projections of future market trends.

BUSINESS AND INVESTMENT MAGAZINES

Barron's. Dow Jones & Co., 22 Cortlandt St., New York, NY 10007 (Subscribe to: 200 Burnett Rd., Chicopee, MA 01021). Weekly; $43/year.

Business Week. McGraw-Hill Publications, 1221 Ave. of the Americas, New York, NY 10020. Weekly; $34.95/year.

Commodities: The Magazine of Futures Trading. Commodities Magazine, 219 Parkade, Cedar Falls, IA 50613. Monthly; $34/year.

Dun's Business Month. Technical Publishing Co. (New York), 666 Fifth Ave., New York, NY 10103. Monthly; $24/year.

Financial World. Marco Communications, 150 W. 58 St., New York, NY 10022. Semimonthly; $36/year.

Forbes. Forbes, 60 Fifth Ave., New York, NY 10011. Fortnightly; $24/year.

Fortune. Time, Time & Life Bldg., New York, NY 10021 (Subscribe to: Time, 591 N. Fairbanks Court, Chicago, IL 60611). Biweekly; $33/year.

Kiplinger Washington Letter. Kiplinger Washington Editors, 1729 H St., N.W., Washington, DC 20006. Weekly; $42/year.

Nation's Business. Chamber of Commerce of the U.S., 1615 H St., N.W., Washington, DC 20062. Monthly; $49.75/year.

These periodicals are aimed primarily at professionals in the areas of business, banking, commerce, international trade, and investment. Consequently, their emphasis is on profiles of industries and companies, interviews of personalities, analysis of the various markets, impact of legislation, labor relations, management, corporate earnings, taxation, banking, takeovers and mergers, international trade and balance of payments, market forecasts, and so on.

Forbes gives good coverage to investment alternatives and opportunities, in addition to its analysis of business and government. Regular columns report on capital markets, stocks, commodities, mutual funds, financial strategy, market trends, and contrarian investing. Consequently, *Forbes* has much to offer the individual investor. A regular column entitled "Personal Affairs" explores such topics as "Who

Holds the (Stock) Certificates?" "The Real Cost of a New Car," and "How Safe Is Your Pension?" Each January, *Forbes* presents an "Annual Report on American Industry" that measures management performance in terms of return on stockholders' equity and total capital. Growth is measured in earnings per share and in sales, with performance being tracked for the latest 12 months and the past five years. The May issue of *Forbes* features "The Forbes 500"—a ranking of the nation's largest companies according to sales, profits, assets, and market value. In early fall, *Forbes* publishes an annual survey of the performance of all the major mutual funds. This permits comparisons between categories of funds such as stock, bond and money market, and between load, no-load, and closed-end funds. Each issue contains the Forbes/Wilshire 500 Review, a graphical presentation showing percentage changes in equity markets.

Fortune, probably best known for its list of the Fortune 500 (a directory of the 500 largest corporations by volume of sales), ranks the performance of companies showing earnings per share, growth rate, and total return to investors. *Fortune*'s second 500 ranks companies 501 to 1,000 in sales. Although *Fortune*'s prime focus is on economic issues, business developments, and political climate, it also provides informative coverage of investment trends, new technologies, takeovers, mergers, taxation, and business developments that can be highly useful to the individual investor. Regular features include "Personal Investing" and "Fortune Forecast," showing projections based on analysis of economic trends.

The individual investor will also find a large amount of relevant and useful information in *Financial World*. This semimonthly publication places a heavy emphasis on investment and the stock market. It has good analyses of trends in selected industries, appraisal and comments on the markets, specific stock evaluations, investment strategy and advice, alternative vehicles such as market index futures and stripped T-bonds, impact of new tax laws, reports on corporate earnings, and declared dividends. A monthly feature, "Independent Appraisals," is a statistical review of 1,600 exchange-listed and over-the-counter (OTC) stocks, which provides a rapid summary of a company's financial position, capital structure, liquidity, earnings power, dividends, and stock price. *Financial World* also carries features such as "Wall Street Watch," "Market Comments," "Tax Topics," "Companies in the News," and "Selected Issues" (a sampling of the better quality stocks and bonds currently available for aggressive and conservative investors).

Coverage of news of national and international business, trends in industrial and corporate finance, and employment outlook, together with comment and analysis of executive and legislative action, can be found in *Business Week*, *Nation's Business*, and *Dun's Business Month*. These periodicals contain information of current developments that impinge on the financial well-being of individuals.

Business Week's main focus is on news, trends, and ideas that have an impact on the economy in general and on specific industries. Good coverage is provided of companies, finance, Wall Street, markets and investments, international business management, taxes, labor, and economic policy. A Personal Business Supplement offers guidance on such topics as IRA regulations and investment opportunities. The Business Month Update reports on the current status of a number of investments showing performance in the previous month and past year.

Dun's Business Month offers analysis of current developments in corporate finance, business, and government. A Personal Finance column features short items on subjects such as playing high-risk stocks, making an inventory of personal valuables, and calculating one's insurance needs. *Nation's Business* also contains information on personal financial planning in addition to its news of economic trends and international development.

Economic trends, industrywide studies, and company analysis are covered by *Barron's*. Edited to meet the needs of professional money managers, brokers, and corporate executives, this weekly publication analyzes and reports on the nation's economic health. It is a valuable and convenient source of statistics on the market (AMEX composite stocks, NASDAQ O-T-C stocks, options trading, etc.), the indicators (advances/declines, bond rating changes, money supply, odd-lot trading), and the stock indexes (NYSE Index, AMEX Index, Standard and Poor's Indexes, and Value Line Index). *Barron's* carries a Quarterly Survey of Mutual Fund Performance (*Barron's* Lipper Gauge) and regular columns "Up and Down Wall Street," "International Trader," "Commodities Corner," "Current Yield" (credit market), and book reviews.

Kiplinger Washington Letter is of interest for its insight into proposed and pending legislation, rules and regulations on taxation, and other issues. This is of some value to the individual investor. Individuals interested in speculating in commodity futures trading and commodity options will find *Commodities: The Magazine of Futures Trading* a valuable resource. The monthly publication is intended to appeal to both novices and sophisticated investors. Those less sophisticated will appreciate tutorial-type articles on trading techniques, listings of available educational materials, book reviews, and definitions of terms. An Annual Reference Guide to Futures Markets includes a listing of commodity exchanges, brokerage firms, key executives, and addresses of the major consulting, charting, and advisory services.

NEWSPAPERS

Financial Times. 75 Rockefeller Plaza, New York, NY 10019. Monday–Friday; $420/year.

New York Times. New York Times, 229 W. 43 St., New York, NY 10036. Daily; $211/year (mail subscription).

Wall Street Journal. 200 Burnett Rd., Chicopee, MA 01021. Monday–Friday; $94/year.

Wall Street Transcript. Wall Street Transcript Corp., 120 Wall St., New York, NY 10005. Weekly; $785/year.

Newspapers constitute an indispensable source of current information on economic and financial matters. Apart from reporting stock market statistics, newspapers also offer coverage of economic issues and related political activity, news of specific companies, unemployment, credit, banking, and international trade. Although the coverage in local newspapers is minimal, the larger metropolitan dailies—*New York Times, Washington Post, Chicago Tribune, Los Angeles Times*—devote considerable space to economic affairs.

The most popular resource for financial news is undoubtedly the *Wall Street Journal*. This widely read daily newspaper gives objective coverage to business and financial news, new products and services, and investment trends, along with digests of earnings, commodity prices, stock market statistics, transactions on the New York and American Stock Exchanges, and the other-the-counter market, Dow Jones and other averages, foreign exchange rates, and other indicators of the state of the nation's economic health. This is an indispensable resource for both personal and professional investors alike. As often noted on the Public Broadcasting System's "Nightly Business Report," articles in the *Wall Street Journal* can greatly influence the price of a particular company's stock.

In recent years, the *New York Times* has achieved a greater prominence in its coverage of economic and financial affairs. Business Day on weekdays and the Business Section on Sundays contain business news, analytical articles on trends in various industries such as video games and computer software, performance and condition of specific companies, tax legislation, banking, and international trade. Regular features include Market Place, Credit Markets, Commodities, Currency Markets, and Technology. Of particular interest to personal investors are Leonard Sloane's column "Your Money," Leonard Silk's feature "The Economic Scene," and the Personal Finance and Investing columns in the Sunday Business section.

The *Financial Times*, self-designated as Europe's business newspaper, is published in London, but its international edition is available on the day of publication in New York, Toronto, and Washington and on the following day in Boston, Chicago, Los Angeles, and Miami. The international edition is split into two or three sections: Section I is specifically concerned with the news affecting business and provides political, economic, social, and diplomatic coverage; Section II is a comprehensive review of the world's stock markets, including a global report, New York closing prices, full London Stock Exchange prices, and the leading prices on all other major exchanges; Section III, carried on most days, surveys a particular industry, market, or country. *Financial Times* has undoubtedly the best coverage of international trade and finance.

The *Wall Street Transcript* provides extensive coverage of corporate reports, company news, speeches of executive officers of corporations, round-table discussions, mergers and acquisitions, market trends, extracts from market newsletters, profiles of business leaders, and stock recommendations of industry analysts. Regular columns include "Broker Reports," "Wall Street Roundup," "Corporate Reports on File," "Technical Corner," "Options Corner," "Wall to Wall Street," and "Connoisseur's Corner" (e.g., antique oriental rugs). Primarily of interest to corporate executives, money managers, stockbrokers, and security analysts, the *Wall Street Transcript* is very helpful to sophisticated personal investors who can afford the price.

SPECIAL TOPIC NEWSPAPERS

A number of newspapers cater to the more specialized interests of both personal and professional investors. These newspapers cover such special topics as commodities, penny stocks, over-the-counter stocks, and investment in gold, strategic metals, etc. A representative selection of these newspapers follows.

Bull and Bear. The Bull and Bear, Box 4207, Winter Park, FL 32783. 10/year; 12 issues/$10.

Bull and Bear publishes security reports and news and comments on individuals and organizations. The "Investment Advisory Digest" in each issue extracts the recommendations of the more prominent stock market and hard-money advisory newsletters. Advice is provided on gold, stock market, commodities, tax shelters, real estate, currencies, coins, and monetary survival. Also features good book reviews and in-depth articles.

Consensus: National Commodity Futures Weekly. Consensus, Inc., 30 W. Pershing Rd., Kansas City, MO 64108. Weekly; $365/year.

This publication provides up-to-date commodity futures market information. Grouped by commodity, current market letters and special reports of more than 50 major commodity exchange members and commodity services are summarized. Readers can easily compare buy and sell recommendations and review current trends. Also included are tabular breakdowns of month-end open interest of large and small traders in major commodities; graphic illustrations of collective bullish opinions; daily quotations, including volume and open interest of all major commodities; comprehensive price charting of all actively traded commodities; and a market sentiment index.

National Investor News. The Official Publication of the Stockbrokers Association, 404 N. Wabash Ave., Suite 1314, Chicago, IL 60611. Monthly; $15/year.

"Dedicated to the Individual Investor," this newspaper provides information of general interest. A typical issue contains articles on individual companies, taxes, impact of economic policies, stock market strategies, options, and so on. Articles and columns provide an outlook on the financial scene. Regular features include "The Central Corporate Reports Service (CCRS) Directory of Corporate Digests"—a very useful informative service to small private investors by making corporate reports available free on request to those interested.

The National OTC Stock Exchange. 1650 S. Colorado Blvd., Suite 2, Denver, CO 80222. Weekly; $52/year.

This is edited for a broad spectrum of readers from first-time investors to experienced investors and brokers. The publication profiles stockbrokerage firms and individuals and provides information on companies. Regular features include a column designed to explain the various procedures of the over-the-counter market to new investors, a column for women investors, information on the National OTC Stock Exchange, charts of the market in seven broad areas—solar, general, high technology, medical, mining, oil and gas, and financial, a digest of the previous week's activity, Notice of Proposed Sale of Securities, New Issue Summary and New Issue Profile, the Rukeyser Report by Louis Rukeyser, and Susan Bondy's "Bondy on Money" feature.

The Penny Stock Journal. Dalton Communications, 1123 Broadway, New York, NY 10010. Monthly; $25/year.

The objective is to provide over 5,000 price quotes on stocks selling for under $10 a share. The publication carries news and articles about low-priced stocks on every exchange as well as new and little known companies. Regular features include "Going Public"—a list of selected companies now raising capital by selling stock to the public, "Bankruptcy Exchange"—a random listing of companies in bankruptcy, "50 Stocks Up the Most," "50 Stocks Down the Most," and "50 Most Active Stocks." Also contains interesting articles on emerging industries, collectibles, gold mining in South Africa, the personal computer race, and profits in bankrupt stocks.

Penny Stock News. Penny Stock News, Box 86, Columbia, MD 21045. Biweekly; $30/year.

Subtitled "A Service for the Professional Trader and Investor," this newspaper is of interest to the private investor in that it includes technical analysis, new issue ratings, profiles of selected companies, and an extensive listing of stocks trading under $5. Staff members rate new issues on a ten-point scale and state a final opinion on each issue rated. Profiles of the selected companies give the pros and cons on the overall worth of investing. Penny stocks and overall market trends are plotted on charts and graphs.

9

Investment Newsletters

In addition to the more general information on money management available in popular magazines, a large specialized literature exists on the subject of investments. Much of this is in the form of investment newsletters that offer a blend of statistics, commentary, market analysis, advice, and specific recommendations ranging over the many areas of investment opportunities. Although a few of the newsletters are general in nature, most focus upon relatively specific topics, such as investment strategy, market conditions and trends, market indicators and timing, analysis of company strengths, stock selections, growth companies, high-technology opportunities, foreign investments, international currency, options, mutual funds, inside trading, penny stocks, OTC stocks, takeovers and mergers, commodity futures, and gold. The newsletters are heavily laced with statistical compilations, computer-generated tables and charts, commentary, prognostications and forecasts, and pure speculation. Several attempt to monitor and digest the investment advice offered by other newsletters. Other publications track the performance of the newsletters in relation to their prior recommendations over a period of time.

A good review and discussion of investment and financial newsletters is provided by Charles Rolo,[1] who points out the enormous variation in quality and the tendency to puffery and self-congratulation with respect to their performance in forecasting market trends and performance. Rolo reviews 18 services and concludes that those most useful for the small investor focus mainly on fundamentals in the form of statistics on earnings projections, dividends, industry and company analyses, stock recommendations, and model portfolios. Lisa Gubernick,[2] in an article entitled "Evaluating Financial Newsletters," discusses the value and use of nine favorite services.

A recent article in *Changing Times*[3] offers a sampling of 15 investment letters and stresses that "it may take some time and experimentation to find an advisory service with which you can feel comfortable." The service selected should fit one's investment objectives and temperament.

A listing of more than 1,000 investment newsletters is available in the *National Directory of Investment Newsletters*.[4] Listings are arranged in broad subject areas—stocks (advisory and reporting services), options, commodities, mutual funds, etc. Each entry includes title, address, phone number, frequency, subscription rates, and a short, nonevaluative description of the editorial content.

George Wien, president of the Select Information Exchange, a subscription agency specializing in investment publications, estimates that some 450,000 subscribers pay from $35 to $350 per year to receive any of the more than 1,000 newsletters currently published. The Select Information Exchange (SIE) publishes a *Directory of Investment and Money-Making Publications*[5] and offers short trial subscriptions to groups of the newsletters in select categories, such as popular investment services, commodities, options, and growth stocks. For a small sum ranging from $12 to $18, subscribers receive a package of sample publications over a short trial period. SIE also offers an "All We Have" special for $65 that results in a mountain of sample newsletters and solicitations calculated to drive the subscriber's mail deliverer to despair. These trial offers are most valuable in that they allow an individual to determine the publications that best serve his or her investment objectives.

How useful are these investment services? This can only be determined ultimately by the subscribers. Probably those services that focus mainly on long-term strategies of investment by providing fundamental data on the strengths of industries, companies, performance of mutual funds, and analysis of trends in interest rates are of the most value to the personal investor. Those publications that focus on technical analysis, market timing and forecasts, short-term trading, options, and futures contracts are of more use to the professional trader and speculator than to the individual investor.

In most instances, the newsletters reflect a recognizable point of view, technique of market analysis, or timing, investment strategy, or recommended investment vehicle such as gold and silver, strategic metals, real estate, high technology stocks, options, futures contracts, and so on. Many of the newsletters have a well-defined philosophical and/or political stance. Financial gurus such as Granville, Weinstein, Zweig, Wysong, and Ruff have built up a large following through their newsletters.

The following listing of some 56 newsletters—far from complete—is intended to illustrate the basic types of newsletters with an indication of their focus and content. No attempt is made to rate these publications in terms of accuracy in forecasting or prior prediction record. In this connection, a study by the *Hulbert Financial Digest* of the first quarter performance of 83 investment portfolios maintained by 50 of the leading market newsletters reveals that 49 of the portfolios, or 59 percent, underperformed the general market.[6]

GENERAL ADVISORY AND REPORTING SERVICES

Bruce McDowell's Investment Newsletter. Bruce McDowell, Box 657, Metuchen, NJ 08840. Monthly; $95/year.

Specializes in investment recommendations, estate planning, and tax-saving instruments that are best suited for most investment portfolios. Covers investment in gold, stocks and bonds, commodities, real estate, tax legislation, and inflation-fighting strategies. Advocates less government, more individual freedom, and a return to the gold standard.

The Cabot Market Letter. Box 1013, Salem, MA 01970. 24 issues; $125/year.
Combines good market timing with careful stock selection. Each issue reviews four market timing indicators that show the direction of the market. Reviews the performance and outlook of individual stocks and tracks a model portfolio of a small number of highly promising stocks.

Consensus of Insiders. Box 10247, Fort Lauderdale, FL 33334. Weekly; $180/year.
Tracks stock issues that have been most widely bought and sold by corporate officers in inside trading. According to Perry Wysong, the editor, it is not the volume of shares traded by insiders that matters but the number of insiders who trade. This stock-picking method usually outperforms the Dow-Jones Industrials by almost 20 to 1. On the first Friday of each month, the 20 shares most favored by company officials are identified. An Insider's Model Portfolio is monitored and reported.

The Conservative Investor. Portfolio Advisory Service, 205 E. Joppa Rd., Towson, MD 21204. 11 issues; $36/year.
"Dedicated to the preservation and appreciation of capital," this newsletter is intended to assist investors in following a long-term approach to investing in common stocks. Follows a model portfolio of 20 stocks.

Dessauer's Journal of Financial Markets. Box 4224, Boston, MA 02110. 24 issues; $150/year.
Investment recommendations with respect to the American market, the world market, gold opportunities, and current selections of U.S. and foreign securities.

Dow Theory Letters. Box 1759, La Jolla, CA 92038. Semimonthly; $125/year.
Applies orthodox Dow theory to analyzing market trends and momentum. Mainly commentary with some analysis of specific stocks.

The Financial War Room. Target Publishers, Inc., Box 2000, 2411 Old Crow Canyon Rd., San Ramon, CA 94583. Weekly; $69/year.
Offered as a cure for financial survival and edited by Howard Ruff, this publication supplies comment, discussion, and advice on interest rates, investments, gold, real estate, taxation, and banking. Billed as a "window on the world" for the middle classes, access to the War Room is provided by a 24-hour hot line. Oriented toward preventing financial calamity.

Ford Value Report. Ford Investor Services, 11722 Sorrento Valley Rd., San Diego, CA 92121. Monthly; $78/year.
Contains an extensive tabulation of financial data for 1,400 leading stocks. Information for each stock includes the results of two key fundamental analyses: intrinsic value analysis and earnings trend analysis. Basic financial data presented for each

stock include earnings, dividend, estimated growth rate, and quality rating. Subscription includes the monthly *Investment Review* and Special Study Reports.

The Granville Market Letter. Drawer O, Holly Hill, FL 32017. 46/year; $250/year.
Joseph Granville is perhaps the best known of the stock market technical analysts, famous for his dramatic buy or sell announcements and warnings of market trends. His method of calling market trends is based on the tracking of indicators that detect shifts in momentum and direction. Each issue contains an analysis of trends and specific recommendations.

Income Investor. Indicator Research Group, Palisades Park, NJ 07650. Monthly; $95/year.
Surveys a wide range of investments focusing on a recommended distribution of assets in relation to common stocks, bonds and bond funds, gold stocks, money market securities, and so on. Also summarizes market trends, interest rates, and performance of specific stocks and bonds and offers recommendations taking into account fundamental, economic, technical, and cyclical factors.

Insider Indicator. J. M. Reid Co., 2230 N.E. Brazee, Portland, OR 97212. Biweekly; $125/year.
Provides investors with buy or sell signals for the American Stock Exchange, New York Stock Exchange, and over-the-counter stocks based on analysis of insider trading. Aims at improving timing results by using corporate inside signals. It is claimed that company insiders are generally two to three months early in forecasting interim buy signals (usually signifying a 6- to 12-month period of rising stock prices).

The Insiders. Institute of Econometric Research, 3471 N. Federal Highway, Fort Lauderdale, FL 33306. 24/year; $135/year.
Reports and analyzes insider buy favorites and insider sell favorites. Also gives the number of insiders who have bought or sold their company's stock in the open market within the past year for all companies on the NYSE and AMEX, plus several hundred OTC issues. Weights are assigned to each insider's trade (for example, recency of transaction and position of insider within company) to arrive at a composite insider rating for each company listed.

International Investment Letter. Box 9666, Arlington, VA 22204. Monthly; $97/year.
Reviews supergrowth stock opportunities in Japan, Australia, and Mexico; this newsletter also analyzes currency trends and such topics as Swiss mutual funds, Far East mutual funds, the Eurobond market, and international investment opportunities. Contains contributions by Douglas Casey, Mark Skousen, and Harry Browne.

Investment Quality Trends. Value Trend Analysis, 7440 Girard Ave., La Jolla, CA 92037. Semimonthly; $175/year.
Reviews 350 "Select Blue Chips" (stocks that meet six qualifications with respect to dividend raised at least five times in last 12 years, carries a Standard and Poor's

Rating in the "A" category, 25 years of uninterrupted dividends, etc.). The blue chip status given for each stock identifies the number of qualifications met. The complete statistical accounting for stocks also shows those that are undervalued, overvalued, and those with rising or declining trends. The service believes that "the ability to make money in the stock market is the ability to recognize value, the courage to purchase a stock that is undervalued, the intelligence to sell a stock when it is overvalued."

The Investment Reporter. Canadian Business Service, 133 Richmond Rd. W., Toronto, Canada. Weekly; $165/year.
Latest market and business conditions in Canada are summarized with advice on "What to Buy," "When to Buy," "When to Switch," and "When to Sell" with regard to more than 300 Canadian stocks.

The Johnson Survey. John S. Herold, Inc., 35 Mason St., Greenwich, CT 06830. Monthly; $78/year.
Each issue, consisting of 40 to 50 pages, contains highly useful information on approximately 180 carefully selected companies that showed substantial gains during the past 12 consecutive years. The relative attractiveness of these growth stocks, together with oil and gold stocks, are displayed graphically. Pertinent data included for each company cover cash earnings, capital expenditures, cash dividends, P/E ratio, and so on. Also treated are other investment opportunities such as new stock issues, high-technology stocks, utility stocks, and top-performing mutual funds.

Market Logic. Institute of Econometric Research, 3471 N. Federal Highway, Fort Lauderdale, FL 33306. 24 issues; $135/year.
Each issue provides an indicator review (key technical and monetary indicators), a master portfolio of 36 stocks, trend scan highlights, insider insights, market trends, an options portfolio, mutual fund selector, and a digest of the recommendations of other major newsletters.

Mergers and Acquisitions Journal. Robertson, James, Jon and Co., Box 2511, Boca Raton, FL 33432. Biweekly; $195/year.
Featured stocks in each issue identify merger or acquisition candidates in the near to intermediate term at substantial premiums above their current market prices. Interesting situations also described in each issue consist of an enumeration of companies that have a substantial likelihood of being acquired in the near future. Also contains Merger Monitor, detailing closely watched companies currently involved in various stages of merger and acquisition activity.

Merrill-Lynch Market Letter. Box 60, Clark St. Sta., New York, NY 10008. Semimonthly; $44/year.
Reviews major market trends, state of the economy, investment ideas, market scoreboard, and favored stock recommendations and tracks performance of categories of stocks. Conservative; follows rather than forecasts the market. Predictably bullish.

The Nicholson Report. 5901 Mariposa St., Coral Gables, FL 33146. 24/year; $119/year.

This service describes itself as devoted to stock market timing, strategy, and discipline. It provides insight into market trends by means of a Market Mood Indicator, which signals shifts in investor attitude that can ultimately determine the near to intermediate term direction of the market. Recommendations include stocks for the long-term investor and those for the aggressive trader and signals for options action.

The Outlook. Standard and Poor's Corp., 25 Broadway, New York, NY 10004. Weekly; $160/year.
Investment policy and comment on the merits and opportunities of a wide range of securities. Also contains a master list of supervised stocks recommended for capital gain and income with recommendations of individual stocks for high yield and income. Good advice on special topics such as growth stocks, municipal bonds, mutual funds, and portfolios for retirement. Authoritative and conservative.

Personal Finance—The Inflation Survival Letter. Kephart Communications, Box 9665, Alexandria, VA. 24 issues; $78/year.
Heavy emphasis is placed on strategic metals, gold, stamps, and collectibles; also covers stocks, commodities, and mutual funds. Well-written, interpretive articles with a minimum of statistical tabulation on topics such as mutual funds, trends in the insurance industry, and tax shelters.

The Peter Dag Investment Letter. 65 Lake Front Dr., Akron, OH 44319. 17 issues; $115/year.
Examines changes in stock prices, short-term interest rates, bond prices, inflation, precious metals, and overall business conditions. Recommends investment strategy and follows the performance of a model portfolio.

The Predictor. Suite 307, 304 Broad St., Windsor, CT 06095. Weekly; $195/year.
Each issue contains Wall Street Perspective, market comment, specific stock recommendations, follow-up of previous recommendations, and an in-depth analysis of select companies. Informative and well written.

The Primary Trend. Arnold Investment Counsel, 700 N. Water St., Milwaukee, WI 53202. 24/year; $110/year.
This newsletter's investment philosophy reflects a long-term view of quality companies unrecognized by the majority of investors as real bargains. Tends to discourage short-term, in-and-out trading. Recommendations are grouped according to conservative, growth, aggressive/speculative, and income stock categories.

The Professional Tape Reader. Radcap, Inc., Box 2407, Hollywood, FL 33022. Semimonthly; $250/year.
Published and edited by Stan Weinstein, one of the country's leading stock market technicians. In addition to the market letter, which utilizes Weinstein's unique "Weight of the Evidence" approach (based on a battery of 47 technical indicators), the publication also contains "Buy? Hold? Sell?" reports that rate all stocks on the NYSE, ASE, and leading OTC issues using a proprietary method four-stage

analysis. Eight booklets ("Everything You Always Wanted to Know about Charting," etc.) are available as a bonus when subscribing.

The Sindlinger Digest. Sindlinger and Co., 600 N. Jackson St., Media, PA 19063. Weekly; $300/year.
Intended to serve as "A Moving Picture of U.S. Economy Banking and Consumer Confidence," this newsletter offers a weekly monetary scoreboard of the U.S. economy providing intelligence data on key indicators such as currency in circulation, M1 money supply, money market funds, business loans, and federal bank credit. Sindlinger attempts to interpret basic data relating to consumer confidence, investor confidence, and expected employment. *The Sindlinger Alert* is distributed each week as a bonus to annual subscribers of the *Digest* and provides capsule comments under headings such as Interest Rate Alert, Stock Market Alert, Leading Indicators Alert, and M1 Alert.

Systems and Forecasts. Signalert Corp., 185 Great Neck Rd., Great Neck, NY 10021. Biweekly (24 issues); $120/year.
Provides a rundown of key stock indicators, charts, stock recommendations, hedge suggestions, convertibles, bonds, and general market commentary. Tracks market indicators and movement and trading signals.

The Wag Letter. Box 490128, Atlanta, GA 30349. 24/year; $80/year.
Each issue recommends three new stock selections, one from each exchange (NYSE, AMEX, and OTC), that are likely to outperform the overall market. Recommendations are based on earnings per share, return on equity, price/earnings ratio, long-term debt, and insiders' trading. Also offers market timing advice.

Wall Street Prophets. Suite 506, 251 Main St., Stanford, CT 06901. Biweekly; $72/year.
A biweekly stock advisory service based on stock selection and timing. The three major indexes used to analyze each stock are the fundamental buy-sell index and technical indexes for momentum and volume. For each individual stock, attention is paid to return on stockholders' equity, debt to capitalization, current profit margin, and growth of sales and earnings in order to pinpoint profit potential.

The Zweig Forecast. 747 Third Ave., New York, NY 10017. Every 3 weeks; $195/year.
Analysis of the performance of nearly 2,000 stocks with timing recommendations. A technical approach to timing. Authoritative.

GROWTH STOCKS

Equity Research Associates. 540 Madison Ave., New York, NY 10022. Twice monthly; $360/year.
Concentrates on the so-called junior growth stocks—smaller companies that sport returns on equity of 20 to 40 percent on a sustained basis. The recommended invest-

ment time frame is three to five years. Monitors about 100 junior growth companies indicating performance and price changes. Plenty of recommendations with substantiation.

Growth Stock Outlook. Box 9911, Chevy Chase, MD 20815. Semimonthly; $95/year.

Focuses attention on those companies with compounded yearly increases in earnings of 20 percent or more for at least the past four years. Very detailed, well-researched stock guide. The $50,000 Supervised Portfolio, started in June 1973, reported a gain of 307 percent as of October 1982. For brokers, institutions, and sophisticated investors who share the objective of doubling each company's listing price in five years.

High Technology Growth Stocks. 402 Border Rd., Concord, MA 01742. Monthly; $115/year.

Identifies and monitors emerging, fast-growing high-technology companies that are well positioned to achieve further substantive increases in sales and earnings over the next three- to five-year period. Examples of high-technology stocks are in the areas of minicomputers, data communications, electronic components, communication satellites, and electronic games. In addition to specific recommendations, a $50,000 model portfolio is supervised, with performance and activity reported each month.

High Technology Investments. Gianturco and Michaels, Inc., 5009 Caroline, Houston, TX 77004. Monthly; $36/year.

Using a computer scan of the universe of smaller high-technology stocks, this newsletter ranks their financial performance, evaluates their current prices, and lists the top 20 potential buys.

Junior Growth Stocks. Box 9911, Chevy Chase, MD 20815. Semimonthly; $115/year.

Covers many fledgling companies that have yet to become "senior citizens" on the NYSE. Each issue contains a stock study guide that shows pertinent data on companies including price/earnings ratio, shares outstanding, book value, and so on. Also provides a New Issue Digest. After 18 months, assuming that their outlook is favorable, companies are graduated from the New Issue Digest to full junior growth stock status.

OTC Growth Stock Watch. Box 305, Brookline, MA 02146. Monthly; $90/year.

Synopses and recommendations of little known companies in the 5 to 50 million dollar sales range and growing at considerably higher rates than most larger companies. Criteria for selection include minimal or no long-term debt, innovative management, and being relatively recession-proof.

LOW-PRICED STOCKS

The Bowser Report. Box 6278, Newport News, VA 23606. Monthly; $36/year.

Recommends purchase of mini-priced stocks likely to appreciate rapidly. Strategy advocated depends heavily on diversification through the outright purchase of 12 to 18 different issues. The Bowser Plan involves 10 Golden Rules for Investing. Each issue lists mini-priced stocks (less than $3 per share) with Bowser value ratings, together with best buy recommendations.

The Cheap Investor. Matthews and Associates, 36 King Arthur Ct., Northlake, IL 60164. Monthly; $68/year.
Specializes in stocks under $10, new issues, and penny stocks. Features the Blue Cheap Index composed of 27 stocks under $10 that are listed on the NYSE. The claim is made that since September 1981 the Blue Cheap Index has outperformed the Dow Jones Index. Researches investments that offer profit opportunities rather than "prophesying what the market is going to do."

Low Priced Stock Digest. Idea Publishing Co., 55 E. Afton Ave., Yardley, PA 19067. Monthly; $68/year.
Scans and reviews the 100 or so low-priced stock newsletters and the penny stock journals (such as the *Bowser Report*, *Cheap Investor*, and *Speculator*) and summarizes their more interesting recommendations. The focus is on stock $20 or under on the NYSE, AMEX, and Over-the-Counter Exchange. Each issue has a market consensus, Stock Alert (best buys), and reports on over 40 low-priced stocks.

Penny Stock Preview. Idea Publishing Co., 55 E. Afton Ave., Yardley, PA 19067. Monthly; $35/year.
Reports on the more risky and speculative penny stocks—those stocks $5 or under. Each monthly issue features a Sneak Preview (upcoming new stocks), top 25 percent Gainers, Penny Chatter, and Brokers List (showing stockbrokers registered to trade penny stocks in subscribers' home states). Stresses that "investing in Penny Stocks should be viewed as a game."

NEWSLETTER DIGESTS AND PERFORMANCE RATINGS

The Hulbert Financial Digest. 201 Massachusetts Ave. N.E., Washington, DC 20002. Monthly; $135/year.
A review, rating, and comparison of the investment advice presented by more than 20 of the leading investment newsletters (including *Dow Theory Letters* and *Zweig Forecast*). Extracts their consensus with respect to interest rates, state of the economy, stocks, precious metals, and other areas of investment concern. Also lists the top newsletter performers for each month and for the year, and provides a chart showing the comparative performance ratings of newsletters if $10,000 had been invested on January 1, 1982. Summarizes stocks recommended by two, three, or more of the newsletters monitored.

Investor's Intelligence. 2 E Ave., Larchmont, NY 10538. Semimonthly; $60/year.
Biweekly advisory service that features the Bearish Sentiment Index, a contrary opinion index, together with charts and indicators for both the market in general and individual stocks in particular. Also provides a cross section of the recommendations

of other investment services and summarizes the stock picks of the 95 investment services monitored. Whenever the newsletters followed reach a consensus, *Investor's Intelligence*, in view of its contrarian philosophy, recommends movement in the opposite direction.

Newsletter Digest. 2335 Pansy St., Huntsville, AL 35801. 24/year; $75/year.
Distills the opinions, economic thinking, and advice of some 200 investment advisory publications on such topics as interest rates, commodities, stocks, collectibles, tax actions, and inflation. Contains abstracts, together with comments, graphs, and articles. Covers a variety of newsletters, such as *Harry Browne's Special Reports*, *The Elliott Wave Theorist*, and *Tony Henfrey's Gold Letter*.

Rating the Stock Selectors. 4050 Cuny Ave., Sacramento, CA 95823. Monthly; $90/year.
Listing and ranking of investment advisory services and financial publications in relation to their performance. Summarizes current thinking on major investment topics.

SIE Performance Review. Select Information Exchange, 2095 Broadway, New York, NY 10023. Quarterly; $38/year.
Publication began August 1983. Promotional literature claims that it rates and numerically ranks the best performing investment publications using a computer program that takes into account short- and long-term performance, dividends, and so on. Lists the stocks most owned by investment newsletters, rates the most mentioned sale recommendations of the best performing newsletters, and offers market timing consensus. Attempts to provide objective performance comparisons of over 200 leading investment advisory services.

MUTUAL FUNDS

Donoghue's Money Letter. P and S Publications, Box 540, Holliston, MA 01741. Semimonthly; $87/year.
Authoritative statistics and data on the yields and general performance of the various types of money funds with analysis and commentary.

Growth Fund Guide. Growth Fund Research, Yreka, CA 96097. Monthly; $76/year.
In-depth, broadly based, advisory service covering a supervised list of no-load (no broker-fee) funds. The funds are selected on the basis of their dynamic characteristics and are listed so long as their good performance merits it. Tabular presentations of data permit comparisons between funds through the display of full performance data of various types of funds (aggressive growth, growth, etc.) over a period of five years. Each issue contains a ranking of the highest and lowest performing funds and the most desirable. Special Information Reports analyze high interest topics in depth—"Load vs. No-Load Funds," "Picking Mutual Funds for Maximum Growth," and so on.

Money Market Safety Ratings. Institute of Econometric Research, 3471 N. Federal Highway, Fort Lauderdale, FL 33306. Monthly; $100/year.
Safety ratings for most of the major funds computed by means of a classification scheme ranging from BBB to AAA+, taking into account a variety of variables. Each issue also contains "Best Buy" and "Buy" recommendations, "Highest Yield Forecasts," and "Highest Current Yields."

The Mutual Fund Specialist. Box 3125, Mt. Royal Station, Duluth, MN 55803. Monthly; $48/year.
Facts, statistics, performance ratings, and commentary on over 325 different funds. Also contains a broad review of leading no-load funds, international and gold funds, telephone switch funds, and high-yielding money market funds. Among the performance ratings listed is a ranking of Primary Switch Funds that have repeatedly demonstrated the best performance record in recent years. Compilations of data rather than extensive commentary.

Switch Fund Advisory. Schabacker Investor Management, 8943 Shady Grove Court, Gaithersburg, MD 20877.
No-load mutual fund rankings by category and performance. Categories used reflect investment objectives: maximum capital gains, income through high-yield common stocks and/or bonds, balanced portfolio, long-term growth of capital, income through tax-exempt municipal bonds.

United Mutual Fund Selector. Computer Directions Advisors, 11501 Georgia Ave., Silver Spring, MD 20902. Monthly; $65/year.
Performance comparisons of 434 mutual funds offering continuing guidance in the selection and holding of mutual funds. Supplies advice on best performing funds, gold funds, money market funds, go-go funds, municipal bond funds, natural resources funds, and so on. Also contains full-page digests of individual funds and articles on new developments and trends.

COMMODITIES

Bruce Gould on Commodities. Box 16, Seattle, WA 98111. Semimonthly; $285/year.
Tracks the market for commodities with the liberal use of charts to plot major trends. Gould also publishes the companion *Bruce Gould Daily*, a detailed analysis of market movements with recommendations for trading opportunities in commodities.

Harry Browne's Special Reports. Box 5586, Austin, TX 78763. 10/year; $225/year.
Conveys Harry Browne's latest thinking on gold, silver, currencies, stock, options, warrants, T-bills and bonds, commodities, and so on. Recommends a wide range of investment opportunities with special emphasis on gold, silver, and other commodities.

International Investor's Viewpoint. Box 447, Wilsonville, OR 97070. Monthly; $175/year.
A gold mining, analytical advisory service covering North American and South African gold mining companies. Digests trends in international markets, and lists stockbrokers familiar with South African and American gold stocks and foreign currencies.

The Reaper. Box 39026, Phoenix, AZ 85069. Weekly (44/year); $235/year.
Detailed information on the commodities market. Tracks short-term, intermediate, and long-term trends in gold, cotton, soybeans, cattle, T-bills, and currency trading.

NOTES

1. Charles Rolo, *Gaining on the Market: Your Complete Guide to Investment Strategy* (Boston: Little, Brown, 1982), pp. 80-95.
2. Lisa Gubernick, "Evaluating Financial Newsletters," *Diversion* (February 1982), pp. 18-22.
3. "Investment Advice You Get in Your Mailbox," *Changing Times* (December 1982), pp. 38-41.
4. *National Directory of Investment Newsletters* (Yardley, PA: Ideal Publishing, 1982). 44 pp. $12.
5. *1982 Directory of Investment and Money-Making Publications* (New York: Select Information Exchange). 32 pp.
6. Dan Dorfman, "Newsletters, with Few Exceptions, Miss the Money Boat" (column, *Chicago Tribune*), Cleveland *Plain Dealer*, April 17, 1983, p. 3E.

10

Pamphlet Resources

An extensive pamphlet literature exists on many aspects of money management and personal finance. Ladley and Wilford (see p. 19) estimate some 2,500 potential producers and distributors of pamphlets, booklets, brochures, and other types of ephemeral material. Many of these publications are valuable for their practical and accurate information offered in a very concise and inexpensive format. In most instances, the publications are part of educational, promotion, marketing, public relations, or lobbying activity on the part of organizations who wish to create an informed public on topics relevant to their mission. Publishers of these materials include federal and state agencies, trade associations, banks, insurance companies, consumer advocacy groups, stock and commodity exchanges, stockbrokers, senior citizen associations, consumer credit organizations, economic research groups, professional associations, and the Federal Reserve Bank.

In this chapter are listed some 600 titles derived from more than 120 organizations. The alphabetical arrangement by subject is designed to provide access to some 56 popular topics, such as college financing, credit, IRAs, investment, pensions, and wills. Most of the publications are popular, but a few are more technical in nature for those persons who require more specialized information. The subject content of the titles listed ranges from practical "Tips on Car Repair" (Council of Better Business Bureaus, Inc.) to "How to Make Livestock Futures Work for You" (Chicago Mercantile Exchange). See Directory of Pamphlet Resource Organizations preceding the indexes for names and addresses of organizations represented.

The criteria used in selecting titles for inclusion are based on utility, low cost, and availability. Each candidate publication was examined to ensure that it possessed the following characteristics:

189

190 Pamphlet Resources

    Of help to the individual in financial decision making, whether for long-range planning, weekly or monthly budgeting, or short-term assistance in relation to credit, investment, or bankruptcy.

    Of use to the individual in furthering or protecting his or her financial interests and well-being.

    Of assistance to individuals in developing improved consumer skills.

    Reliable in content and published by reputable, authoritative organizations.

    Appropriate to the lay reader in both language and style of writing. Technical terms appearing in the text should be defined or otherwise explained.

    Available free or at reasonable cost (less than $3). The actual cost of each publication is not shown as this information is subject to constant change.

The titles span a wide variety of major topics of current consumer concern, such as banking, credit, debt and bankruptcy, investment, stock market, buying and selling homes, taxes, insurance, estate planning, and many other aspects of money management. These pamphlets and booklets provide a most valuable and inexpensive supplement to the book literature.

Annuities

American Council of Life Insurance
What You Should Know about Annuities. The Consumer Advice Series. 11 pp.

American Institute for Economic Research
Annuities from the Buyer's Point of View. Richard P. Sparks. *Economic Education Bulletin* 22, no. 6 (June 1982). 28 pp.

Appraisals

American Institute of Real Estate Appraisers
What to Look for in an Appraisal. 1979. 9 pp.

American Society of Appraisers
Information on the Appraisal Profession. February 1981.

Society of Real Estate Appraisers
Selling Real Property, Raw Land. 14 pp.
What Is an Appraisal? Buying a House

Bankruptcy

American Bar Association
Bankruptcy and Alternatives. 1982.

Associated Credit Bureaus, Inc.
Bankruptcy . . . Some Things to Consider.

Credit Union National Association
Chapter 13: An Alternative to Bankruptcy. Consumer Facts: Everybody's Money. Revised June 1980.

Banks and Banking

American Bankers Association
 Bank Fact Book. 1978. 40 pp.
 Glossary of Banking Terms.
 The Story of American Banking. 1963. 76 pp.
 Ways to Save Your Money.
Board of Governors of the Federal Reserve System
 Federal Reserve Glossary. 1981. 29 pp.
 A Guide to Federal Reserve Regulations. 1981. 20 pp.
 A Series on the Structure of the Federal Reserve System
  No. 1. *The Board of Governors of the Federal Reserve System.* 1981.
  No. 2. *The Federal Open Market Committee.* 1981.
  No. 3. *Federal Reserve Banks.* 1981.
  No. 4. *Federal Reserve Bank Board of Directors.* 1981.
  No. 5. *The Monetary Control Act.* 1981.
  No. 6. *Organization and Advisory Committees.* 1982.
 U.S. Currency. 1980. 11 pp.
 Welcome to the Federal Reserve. 1980. 20 pp.
Credit Union National Association
 Save with High Yield Accounts. Consumer Facts: Everybody's Money. Revised August 1981.
Federal Deposit Insurance Corporation
 Consumer Information: Información al Consumidor/For Your Protection.
 FDIC: Symbol of Confidence. 26 pp.
 Your Insured Deposit.
Federal Reserve Bank of New York
 The Basis of Foreign Trade and Exchange. 1980.
 A Day at the . . . Fed. C. J. Parnow. 1980. 32 pp.
 Fedpoints 25: European Monetary System. 1979.
 I Bet You Thought . . . 3rd Edition. 1982. 33 pp.
 Keeping Our Money Healthy. 1981. 15 pp.
 Money: Master or Servant? 1980. 34 pp.
 The Story of Banks. 1979.
 The Story of Money. 3rd Edition. 1981. 21 pp.
Federal Reserve Bank of Richmond
 You and Your Money. 1974.
Federal Reserve Bank of San Francisco
 The Federal Reserve System in Brief. 1980
 Money in the Economy. 1981. 23 pp.

Bonds

U.S. Department of the Treasury, U.S. Savings Bonds Division
 Legal Aspects. 12 pp.
 Save Today: Buy U.S. Savings Bonds.
 Series EE Savings Bonds (Issued on or after May 1, 1981).
 Series HH Savings Bonds (Issued on or after May 1, 1981).

Budgeting

American Council of Life Insurance
El Assistente Financiero.
Let's Talk about Money. 24 pp. July 1980.
The Money Manager.

American Institute for Economic Research
Sensible Budgeting with the Rubber Budget Account Book. Economic Education Bulletin 20, no. 11 (November 1981).

Consumer Credit Education Foundation
Basic Principles in Family Money and Credit Management. Carl F. Hawver. 1979. 14 pp.
Money and Your Marriage. Carl F. Hawver. 1979. 56 pp.

Credit Union National Association
Money Management for Young Couples. Consumer Facts: Everybody's Money. Revised February 1980.

Checking Accounts

American Bankers Association
Your Checking Account. 1980. 21 pp.

Bank of America
A Guide to Checks and Checking.

Federal Reserve Bank of Boston
Checkpoints: How to Write and Use Checks.

Federal Reserve Bank of New York
The Story of Checks. 7th Edition. 1979. 20 pp.

Children and Money

Credit Union National Association
Consumer Education for Children. Consumer Facts: Everybody's Money. Revised January 1981.
Credit Tips for Teenagers. Consumer Facts: A Service of Your Credit Union. March 1978.

Money Management Institute
Children and Money Management. 1981. 28 pp.

Public Affairs Committee
Teaching Children about Money. Grace W. Weinstein. Public Affairs Pamphlet no. 593. 1981. 28 pp.

College Financing

Business and Professional Women's Foundation
Financial Aid: Where to Get It; How to Use It.

Credit Union National Association
Financing Higher Education. Consumer Facts: Everybody's Money. Revised August 1979.

Investment Company Institute
How Will You Ever Scrape Up the Money When Your Child's Ready for College? Read This Booklet. 1982.

New York Life Insurance Company
College Costs: 1982–83. 64 pp.

U.S. Department of Education
Federal Financial Aid for Men and Women Resuming Their Education or Training. Publication no. E–82–15003.
The Student Guide: Five Federal Financial Aid Programs 1982–83. Publication no. E–81–15001. 16 pp.

Condominiums

Institute of Real Estate Management
Consumer's Guide to Buying a Residential Condominium.

Lawyers Title Insurance Corporation
Should You Buy a Condominium?

National Association of Home Builders
Condominium Buyers Guide. 1980. 31 pp.

U.S. Department of Housing and Urban Development
Financing Condominium Housing. HUD–77–H(6). November 1978.
Questions about Condominiums: What to Ask before You Buy. 52 pp. HUD–365–H(7). March 1980.

Consumer Information

American Rental Association
Your Guide to a Safe Move.

Credit Union National Association
Everybody's Money Complaint Directory for Consumers. 1982 Edition. 88 pp.
Solving Consumer Problems. Consumer Facts: Everybody's Money. Revised September 1980.
Warranties . . . Know before You Buy. Consumer Facts: Everybody's Money. Revised May 1980.

Direct Mail Marketing Association
Bess Meyerson's Consumer Guidelines to Shopping by Mail.

Direct Selling Education Foundation
Extra Protection.
Promises: Check Them Out! Business Opportunity Fraud. 1980.
Questions Every Buyer Should Ask.

Federal Trade Commission
Door to Door Sales.
Shopping by Mail.

Credit

American Bankers Association
How to Get (and Keep) the Credit You Deserve. 1979.

American Bar Association
Your Guide to Consumer Credit and Bankruptcy. 1980. 36 pp.

194 Pamphlet Resources

American Express
Establishing Credit 101. 12 pp.

Bank of America
Managing Your Credit. The Circular: Consumer Information Report 18. 1980.

Board of Governors of the Federal Reserve System
Fair Credit Billing. 1976.
How to File a Consumer Credit Complaint. 1981.
If You Borrow to Buy Stock. 1980.
Lo Que "Truth in Lending" Significa Para Usted.
What Truth in Lending Means to You. 1981.

Credit Union National Association
Co-signing. Consumer Facts: Everybody's Money. Revised October 1981.
Managing Your Family's Credit. Consumer Facts: Everybody's Money. Revised April 1981.
Your Credit Rights: Truth in Lending; Garnishment; Fair Credit Reporting; Fair Credit Billing. Consumer Facts: Everybody's Money. Revised June 1980.

Federal Reserve Bank of Boston
Credit Points. 1980. 23 pp.

Federal Reserve Bank of Chicago
ABC's of Figuring Interest. Readings in Economics and Finance from the Federal Reserve Bank of Chicago. 1981. 9 pp.
Credit Guide. 1982.

Federal Reserve Bank of New York
The Arithmetic of Interest Rates. Richard R. Trainer. 1981. 33 pp.
Consumer Credit Terminology. 1979. 20 pp.
Credit-Ability. Consumer Credit Information no. 9.
On Using Credit. Consumer Credit Information no. 7.
The Story of Consumer Credit. 1980. 22 pp.
Truth in Lending Simplified. Consumer Credit Information no. 17.
Usted y Su Crédito. Consumer Credit Information no. 3.
Your Credit Rating.

Federal Reserve Bank of Philadelphia
How to Establish and Use Credit.

Federal Trade Commission
Cosigning a Loan. 1979.
Do You Speak "Credit"? When You Sign a Loan Contract You May Be Agreeing to Some Strange Things.
Fair Credit Billing. 1979. Publication no. L-02-L.
Fair Credit Reporting.
The Recession Decision. Facts for Consumers from the Federal Trade Commission. 1981. 4 pp.
The Rule of 78's or What May Happen When You Pay Off a Loan Early. Revised August 1981.
Utility Credit. Facts for Consumers. 1979.
Your Credit Rating. Revised 8-81.

Federal Trade Commission, Office of Consumer Education
Credit Billing Blues. Facts from the Federal Trade Commission. 1982.

Money Management Institute
Managing Your Credit. 1982. 44 pp.

National Consumer Finance Association
Using Tomorrow's Money. 28 pp.

National Foundation for Consumer Credit, Inc.
The Consumer and Truth in Lending.
Consumer Credit.
Credit and the Consumer.
Crédito y el Consumidor.
Establishing Good Credit.
The Forms of Credit We Use.
Getting a Hold on Credit.
How Much Are You Really Worth?
How Much Credit Can You Afford?
Measuring & Using Our Credit Capacity.

North Carolina Bar Association
This Is the Law: Buying on Time (Goods and Services).

Credit Bureaus

Associated Credit Bureaus, Inc.
Consumers, Credit Bureaus and the Fair Credit Reporting Act . . . An Exploration of Consumer Rights in Credit Reporting.
What Is a Credit Bureau. 1981.

Credit Union National Association
Credit Bureaus . . . Take a Close Look at Your Credit Report. Consumer Facts: Everybody's Money. Revised August 1979.

Credit Cards

American Bankers Association
Bank Card: Fact Book. 1979. 34 pp.

Board of Governors of the Federal Reserve System
If You Use a Credit Card. 1979.

Federal Trade Commission
Credit Cards: Auto Repair Protection.

Credit Counseling

Credit Union National Association
Credit Counseling. Consumer Facts: Everybody's Money. Revised April 1981.

National Foundation for Consumer Credit, Inc.
Consumer Credit Counseling.

Credit, Equal Credit Opportunity

Board of Governors of the Federal Reserve System
Consumer Handbook of Credit Protection Laws. 5th Printing. 1982. 44 pp.
The Equal Credit Opportunity Act . . . and Age. 1977.
The Equal Credit Opportunity Act and Credit Rights in Housing. 1980.
The Equal Credit Opportunity Act and . . . Doctors, Lawyers, Small Retailers and Others Who May Provide Incidental Credit. 1977.

Credit Union National Association
Equal Credit Opportunity Act. Consumer Facts: A Service of Your Credit Union.

Federal Deposit Insurance Corporation
Equal Credit Opportunity and Age: Your Rights.
Facturación Justa de Crédito.
Fair Credit Billing: Your Rights. June 1978.
Fair Credit Reporting Act/Lay Sobre Justa Información de Crédito. March 1980.
Truth in Lending. June 1977.

Federal Reserve Bank of Philadelphia
How the New Equal Credit Opportunity Act Affects You. January 1978.

Federal Reserve Bank of San Francisco
Give Yourself Credit! A Consumer's Guide to Credit Protection Laws. Revised 1981. 30 pp.

Federal Trade Commission
Equal Credit Opportunity. 1982.
Equal Credit Opportunity Act. 1977.

New York State Banking Department
Credit on an Equal Basis.

Credit Unions

Credit Union National Association
Credit Unions Are People Places. Consumer Facts: A Service of Your Credit Union. July 1976.
Credit Unions: What They Are; How to Join; How to Start One.
New Services for Credit Union Members. Consumer Facts: A Service of Your Credit Union. March 1978.
Your Credit Union: Complete and Up-to-Date. Consumer Facts. Revised March 1982.

Debt and Bankruptcy

AFL-CIO Department of Community Service
Debt Counseling. Publication no. 140. 1981.

Associated Credit Bureaus, Inc.
Consumers, Collectors and the Fair Debt Collection Practices Act. 1981.
What Is a Debt Collector? 1977.

Bank of America
What to Do When the Debts Pile Up. The Circular: Consumer Information Report 27. 1981. 4 pp.

Federal Reserve Bank of Chicago
Two Faces of Debt. Readings in Economics and Finance. 4th Revision. 1978. 23 pp.

Federal Reserve Bank of New York
Fair Debt Collection Practices. Consumer Credit Information no. 1.

Federal Reserve Bank of Philadelphia
The Fair Debt Collection Practices Act. August 1978.

Federal Trade Commission
Fair Debt Collection.

Electronic Fund Transfer

Board of Governors of the Federal Reserve System
Alice in Debitland: Consumer Protection and the Electronic Fund Transfer Act. 1980. 16 pp.

Federal Reserve Bank of New York
The Story of Checks and Electronic Transfers. 1981. 22 pp.

Federal Reserve Bank of Philadelphia
Electronic Fund Transfer (Regulation E). June 1980.

Federal Trade Commission
Electronic Banking. 1980. 4 pp.

Estate Planning

Action for Independent Maturity
Estate Planning.

American Bar Association
Planning for Life and Death. 1981. 20 pp.

American Council of Life Insurance
Planning with Your Beneficiaries. 19 pp. July 1980.

Credit Union National Association
Legacy for Survivors. Consumer Facts: Everybody's Money. October 1978.
What Every Spouse Should Know. Consumer Facts: Everybody's Money. Revised March 1980.

Deloitte, Haskins, and Sells
Estate Planning. 1982. 42 pp.

Main Hurdman
Estate Planning.

Phoenix Mutual Insurance Company
Your Estate: The Cultivation of a Good Harvest. 1982. 31 pp.

Futures

American Board of Trade
The ABT Vital Difference! Markets Based on "Here and Now" Not Fantasy. The American Board of Trade Is Proud to Present: The Nation's Only Commodity Ownership Guaranty Program for Gold and Silver Bullion, Silver Coins, Platinum, Copper and Plywood.

Commercial Paper Issued by ABT Operating Affiliates.
Exchange Traded Forward Contracts in U.S. Treasury Bills. 7 pp.
Short Term U.S. Treasury Bills.
Spot and Forward Foreign Currency Market.

Chicago Board of Trade
Commercial Paper Futures: 90-Day, 30-Day.
Financial Futures: Active Contracts.
GNMA Futures: Collateralized Depository Receipt and Certificate Delivery Contracts.
An Introduction to Financial Futures. 60 pp.
Ten-Year Treasury Futures.
U.S. Treasury Bond Futures.

Chicago Mercantile Exchange
Commodity Trader's Scorecard. 1981.
How to Make Livestock Futures Work for You. 1981. 31 pp.
Introduction to Livestock and Meat Fundamentals. 1982. 48 pp.
Risk Management Guide for AG Lenders: Forward Pricing Through Futures. 1982. 40 pp.
Trading in Tomorrows: Your Guide to Futures. 1981. 43 pp.

Chicago Mercantile Exchange, Index and Option Market
Inside S&P Stock Index Futures. 24 pp.
Opportunities in Stock Futures: Standard and Poor's 500 Stock Index Futures Contracts. 20 pp.

Chicago Mercantile Exchange, International Monetary Market
Bibliography and Information Source List: Financial Futures. 1981. 38 pp.
CD Futures Yield Calculator. 31 pp.
Inside CD Futures. 14 pp.
Inside Eurodollar Futures. 20 pp. January 1982.
Opportunities in Interest Rates: Treasury Bill Futures. 1977. 32 pp.
Understanding Futures in Foreign Exchange. 1977. 40 pp.
Understanding Trading in Gold Futures: An Introduction to the Factors That Affect the Price of Gold. 1978. 32 pp.

Commodity Exchange, Inc.
COMEX Copper Futures. 11 pp.
COMEX Gold Futures. 11 pp.
COMEX Silver Futures. 11 pp.
Glossary of Commodity Terminology.
Gold Futures. February 1982. 11 pp.
Heavy Metals: To the Untrained Eye, the Activities at COMEX, the Commodity Exchange, Resembles Nothing so Much as a Street Brawl—A Street Brawl in Which Is Traded . . . John Love. Reprinted from *TWA Ambassador* magazine. 1981.
Options on COMEX Gold Futures: A New Way to Trade Gold with Limited Risk. 44 pp.

Commodity Futures Trading Commission
Before Trading Commodities—Get the Facts. 8 pp.
Commodity Futures Trading Commission. 6 pp. Revised June 1982.

Glossary of Some Terms Commonly Used in the Futures Trading Industry. 30 pp. Reprinted November 1980.
How to Read Commodity Futures Prices Tables. 14 pp. Revised June 1982.
A Spotter's Guide to Commodity Fraud. 9 pp. September 1982.

Futures Industry Association, Inc.
Trading Techniques for the Futures Speculator. 1981. 15 pp.

Kansas City Board of Trade
The Future Is Here: Futures Trading and the Value Line Stock Index. 1982. 21 pp.
The Future Is Here: Value Line Average; Stock Index Futures. 1982.

Minneapolis Grain Exchange
The Minneapolis Grain Exchange.
Spring Wheat Futures at the Minneapolis Grain Exchange.
Sunflower Seed Futures at the Minneapolis Grain Exchange.
Understanding Commodity Futures Trading. 1981. 27 pp.

New Orleans Commodity Exchange
Cotton Futures.
Introduction to the New Orleans Commodity Exchange.
Milled Rice and Rough Rice Futures.
Soybean Futures.

New York Cotton Exchange
Citrus Futures.
Cotton Futures.
Propane Futures. June 1982.

New York Futures Exchange
"The Market Will Fluctuate . . ." Introducing New York Stock Exchange Futures Index. 15 pp.

New York Mercantile Exchange
The ABCs of Commodities. 1980. 28 pp.
A Futures Trading Account: Background Information and Member Firms Servicing Customer Accounts. 1980.
Hedging Energy Futures: Risk Management Through Commodity Futures. 1981. 19 pp.
New York Mercantile Exchange. 1981. 20 pp.
Platinum: Metal in Motion. Allen E. Agrams. 1978. 44 pp.

Gold and Diamonds

American Institute for Economic Research
Why Gold? Ernest P. Walker. *Economic Education Bulletin.* 21, no. 9 (September 1981). 37 pp.

Commodity Exchange, Inc.
The Golding of America. Henry Jarecki. Reprinted from *Euromoney.*

Federal Trade Commission
Buying Diamonds. 1978.
Gold Jewelry. Facts for Consumers. 1980.

Inflation

American Institute for Economic Research
  Money, Banking and Inflating: A Useful Description. Lawrence S. Pratt and George H. Machen. *Economic Education Bulletin* 21, no. 4 (April 1981). 24 pp.
  What Would More Inflating Mean to You? Lawrence S. Pratt. *Economic Education Bulletin* 21, no. 6 (June 1981). 32 pp.

Credit Union National Association
  What's Your Inflation IQ?

Federal Reserve Bank of New York
  A Primer on Inflation. June 1982.
  The Story of Inflation. 1981. 23 pp.

Insurance

Alliance of American Insurers
  How to Save with Insurance Discounts.

Insurance Information Institute
  A Family Guide to Auto and Home Insurance. 1978. 24 pp.
  Tenant's Insurance Basics: Renting an Apartment or a House. 1980.

Kemper Insurance Companies
  The Guide to Insurance: A Common Sense Introduction to Insurance. 1974. 32 pp.
  How to File a Claim. November 1978. 15 pp.
  We're Glad You Asked: A Consumer Question and Answer Guide to Insurance. 1976. 24 pp.

National Insurance Consumer Organization
  Buyer's Guide to Insurance: What the Companies Won't Tell You.

Insurance, Auto

Alliance of American Insurers
  A New Way to Lower Your Auto Insurance Bill. Reprinted from *Journal of American Insurance* 55, no. 3. 3 pp.

Credit Union National Association
  A Look at Auto Insurance. Consumer Facts: Everybody's Money. Revised April 1981.

Insurance Information Institute
  Auto Insurance Basics: Understanding a Few Basics about Auto Insurance Can Help You Be a More Knowledgeable Insurance Consumer. 1980.

The Travelers Insurance Companies
  Plain Talk about Auto Insurance. 12 pp.

Insurance, Disability

American Council of Life Insurance
  What You Should Know about Disability Insurance. The Consumer Series. 12 pp.

Insurance, Health

American Council of Life Insurance
What You Should Know about Health Insurance When You Retire.

Credit Union National Association
A Look at Health Insurances. Consumer Facts: Everybody's Money. Revised October 1978.
Take the Hassle Out of Health Claims. Consumer Facts: Everybody's Money.

Health Insurance Association of America
What You Should Know about Health Insurance. 21 pp.

Insurance, Household Contents and Property

Alliance of American Insurers
Growing Old Gracefully: Until the Advent of New Homeowner's Policies the Aging House Faced an Uncertain Future. Reprinted from *Journal of American Insurance* 54, no. 2. 6 pp.
Inflation Raises the Roof.
Understanding Your Insurance: A Homeowner's Gospel. Reprinted from *Journal of American Insurance* 55, no. 3. 5 pp.

Bankers Life
Insurance for the Home.

Credit Union National Association
A Look at Your Property Insurance Needs. Consumer Facts: A Service of Your Credit Union. August 1973.

Insurance, Life

American Council of Life Insurance
The Booklet You Have in Your Hand Is Not Designed to Sell You Life Insurance. 1974.
A Consumer's Guide to Life Insurance.
Plain Talk about Your Life Insurance Policy. March 1980.
RISK: Why It Affects the Cost of Life Insurance.
Understanding Your Life Insurance.

American Institute for Economic Research
Life Insurance from the Buyer's Point of View. Ernest P. Welker. *Economic Education Bulletin* 22, no. 7 (July 1982). 32 pp.

Bankers Life
A Consumer's Guide to Buying Life Insurance . . . Information That Will Help You Make Good Decisions and Save Money. 8 pp.
How Much Life Insurance Do I Need? How Much Life Insurance Can I Afford? An Objective Guide for Buyers of Life Insurance.
How to Choose a Life Insurance Plan . . . Best for You. Objective Guide #4 for Buyers of Life Insurance.
How to Select the Right Life Insurance Company. 1980. 31 pp.
Life Insurance Handbook: 50 Questions and Answers to Help You Understand the Basics. 30 pp.

Credit Union National Association
A Look at Life Insurance. Consumer Facts: Everybody's Money. Revised January 1981.

Life Insurance Marketing and Research Association, Inc.
You and Your Life Insurance Agent. 1975. 22 pp.

National Insurance Consumer Organization
How to Save Money on Life Insurance. 1982. 44 pp.
Universal Life: How Good Is It? 1982. 20 pp.

Veterans Administration
Facts about Beneficiary and Option Designation. Do You Know How the Naming of a Beneficiary or Beneficiaries and Selection of Optional Settlements Affect the Payment of Your Government Life Insurance? The Following Pages Tell You. VA Pamphlet 29-77-3. 1980.
Information Pamphlet for Converting Your Servicemen's Life Insurance to Veteran's. Group Life Insurance Supervised by the Veterans Administration. VA Pamphlet 29-74-3. 1981. 7 pp.
Questions and Answers on Servicemen's Group Life Insurance Supervised by the Veterans Administration. VA Pamphlet 29-78-1. 1981. 8 pp.
Term Insurance: Can You Afford to Continue Your NSLI under the Term Plan? Look How Your Monthly Premiums for $10,000 Insurance Will Increase as You Grow Older. VA Pamphlet 29-76-1. 1976. 8 pp.

Insurance, Title and Mortgage

Lawyers Title Insurance Corporation
Questions and Answers about Title Insurance for Prospective Homeowners. 11 pp.

U.S. Department of Housing and Urban Development
Home Mortgage Insurance HUD-43-F(8). 1979. 12 pp.

IRAs (Individual Retirement Accounts)

American Council of Life Insurance
What You Should Know about IRAs. The Consumer Series. 17 pp.

E. F. Hutton and Company
IRA '82: IRAs for All. 11 pp.

Federal Reserve Bank of Philadelphia
IRA and KEOGH: New Opportunities for Retirement Income. January 1982.

Fidelity Group
IRA: What's in It for You? 20 pp.

Information USA
13 Reasons Not to Invest in IRAs: What the Ads for Individual Retirement Accounts Don't Tell You. Special Report no. 16.

Investment Company Institute
Plan Tomorrow Today with Your Own IRA. 1982. 28 pp.

Merrill Lynch Service Center
IRA: How to Save Taxes on up to $2,000 in Income with the Merrill Lynch Individual Retirement Account. 1981. 11 pp.

U.S. Department of the Treasury, Internal Revenue Service
Tax Information on Individual Retirement Arrangements. Publication no. 590.

Investment

E. F. Hutton and Company
Investment Objectives

Money Management Institute
Your Savings and Investment Dollar. 1981. 40 pp.

National Association of Investment Clubs
Benefits and Advantages of Belonging to the National Association of Investment Clubs.
An Educational and Investment Opportunity for You: Here's the Way.
Here Is a New Low Cost Investment Plan.
Investment Education for All Investors: Learn Better Investing with NAIC Stock Study Aids.
Investors Manual: The Handbook for Learn-by-Doing Investing: For Individual Investors and Investment Clubs. 1981. 64 pp.

New York Stock Exchange
Individual Investors Directory. June 1982. 12 pp.
The Language of Investing: Glossary. 1981. 37 pp.
Understanding Convertible Securities. 1982. 28 pp.
Understanding Financial Statements. 1981. 28 pp.

Standard & Poor's Corporation
Standard & Poor's 500 Stock Price Index.

U.S. Securities & Exchange Commission
What Every Investor Should Know: A Handbook from the U.S. Securities & Exchange Commission. 1982. 44 pp.

Medicare

American Association of Retired Persons
Medicare and Health Insurance for Older Persons.

American Society of Internal Medicine
Medicare: What It Will and Will Not Pay For.

The Attorney General of Ohio
Closing the Gaps in Medicare.

Credit Union National Association
Avoid the Medigap Trap. Consumer Facts: Everybody's Money.
Medicare for the Aged. Consumer Facts: Everybody's Money. Revised May 1980.

Health Insurance Association of America
How to Use Private Health Insurance with Medicare. 13 pp.

U.S. Department of Health and Human Services, Health Care Financing Administration
Guide to Health Insurance for People with Medicare. HCFA-0211. January 1981. 7 pp.

U.S. Department of Health and Human Services, Social Security Administration
A Brief Explanation of Medicare. July 1982 Edition. SSA Publication no. 05-10043. July 1982.
Medicare Coverage in a Skilled Nursing Facility. HEW Publication no. (SSA) 77-10041. January 1977.
Your Medicare Handbook. SSA Publication no. 05-10050. April 1982. 61 pp.
Your Right to Question the Decision on Your Hospital Insurance Claim. HEW Publication no. (SSA)79-10085. June 1979. 7 pp.

Money Management

American Bankers Association
How to Manage Your Money. 1981. 76 pp.

American Institute for Economic Research
Understanding the Money Muddle and How It Affects You. Ernest P. Welker. Economic Education Bulletin 20, no. 9 (September 1980). 20 pp.

Associated Credit Bureaus, Inc.
How to Manage Your Money Cleverly.

Bank of America
What Are You Really Earning?

Institute for Information Studies
Financial Resources for Disabled Individuals. 1980. 75 pp.

Merrill Lynch, Pierce, Fenner and Smith, Inc.
Double Income Couples: What They Need to Know about Personal Finance and Investing. 1982. 31 pp.

Money Management Institute
Money Management: Your Financial Plan. 1981. 32 pp.

National Consumer Finance Association
Consumer Budget Planner.

Money-Saving Strategies

Council of Better Business Bureaus, Inc.
Facts on Shopping for Food. 1978. 15 pp.
Tips on Buying a Swimming Pool. 1978. 8 pp.
Tips on Buying Encyclopedias. 1974.
Tips on Car Repair. 1981. 14 pp.
Tips on Carpets and Rugs. 1978. 11 pp.
Tips on Saving Energy. 1980. 9 pp.

Credit Union National Association
Energy Savers. Consumer Facts: Everybody's Money. October 1980.

Funerals: No Need to Overspend. Consumer Facts: Everybody's Money. Revised January 1980.
How to Save on Beef Purchases. Consumer Facts: Everybody's Money. Revised September 1980.

Di$count America Guide
Di$count America Guide.

Energy Advisor, Inc.
Ways to Beat the Energy Crisis in the Home.

Federal Trade Commission
Auto Service Contracts. Facts for Consumers. Updated March 1982.
"Bargain" Jewelry. Facts for Consumers. 1982.
Discounts for Cash. Facts for Consumers. Updated March 1982.
Gift Giver's Guide. Facts for Consumers. 1980.
Job Hunting; Should You Pay? Facts for Consumers. 1981.
Should You Join a Buying Club? Facts for Consumers. Updated April 1982.
What Is "As Is"?

Food Marketing Institute
How to Survive High Prices and Beat the C.P.I.
Make Your Food Dollars Count. A Shopping Plan for Older Consumers.
Your Food Stamps Are Worth More When You: Buy Food High in Nutritive Value; Buy the Less Costly Brands and Sizes; Buy Foods on Sale; Mix and Prepare Your Own Foods. 1981.

Money Management Institute
Your Automobile Dollar. Revised 1979. 40 pp.
Your Clothing Dollar. Revised 1981. 40 pp.
Your Equipment Dollar. Revised 1980. 40 pp.
Your Food Dollar. Revised 1981. 32 pp.
Your Home Furnishing Dollar. Revised 1979. 40 pp.
Your Recreation Dollar. Revised 1981. 40 pp.
Your Shopping Dollar. 1980. 32 pp.

National Association of Mature People
17 Tips to Help You Save Money on Clothes You Wear. 6 pp.
29 Ways to Save Money on the Food You Eat.

National Consumer Finance Association
The Consumer's Almanac. 1977. 32 pp.

National Foundation for Consumer Credit, Inc.
Here's How to Get More Value Out of Every Dollar You Earn.

National Independent Automobile Dealers Association
Some Straight Talk on How to Buy a Used Car. 1980.

Springhill Press
How to Buy a New Car (And Not Lose Your Shirt). Peter G. Miller. 1981. 19 pp.

U.S. Department of Agriculture
Where You Shop Is as Important as What You Buy. YS-74-5. Alan Cleveland. 1974. 6 pp.

Money-Saving Strategies, Vacations

At Home Abroad, Inc.
At Home Abroad, Inc. Invites You to Select Your Villa or Castle Abroad for the Coming Season.

Holiday Exchanges
Holiday Exchanges.

InterService Home Exchange
Go Places!
Guidelines for Going Places! 12 pp.

Travel Enterprises
Money Sense Overseas.

Vacation Exchange Club
1982 Exchange Book. 224 pp.
Rent-Free Vacations and Much More. 1978

Mutual Funds

Association of Publicly Traded Investment Funds
Publicly Traded Investment Funds—Investor's Guide.
Publicly Traded Investment Funds: Membership Directory.

Investment Company Institute
The Age-Old Question: How Can I Have More Money in the Future Than I Have Today. 1982. 21 pp.
Invest Today . . . For a Child's Tomorrow. 1982.

No-Load Mutual Fund Association
1982 Directory. 24 pp.

NOW Accounts

American Association of Retired Persons
An Introduction to NOW Accounts.

Options

American Stock Exchange
Buying Options for Profit Opportunities. 1978. 16 pp.
Increasing Your Income with Options. 1978. 8 pp.
Protecting Your Investments with Options. 1978. 12 pp.

Chicago Board Options Exchange
Are Call Options for You? 1977. 32 pp.
Are Put Options for You? 1977. 44 pp.
Buying Puts, Straddles and Combinations. 1977. 32 pp.
Call Option Spreading. 1978. 32 pp.
Call Option Writing Strategies. 1975. 29 pp.
Inside the Options Exchange. 1977. 15 pp.
Market Statistics—1982. 63 pp.
Stocks Underlying All Listed Options.

Tax Considerations in Using CBOE Options. 1976. 30 pp.
Understanding GNMA Options. 1981. 37 pp.
Understanding Options: A Guide to Puts and Calls. 1977. 44 pp.
Writing Puts, Straddles and Combinations. 1978. 24 pp.

Merrill Lynch, Pierce, Fenner and Smith, Inc.
The Merrill Lynch Guide to Interest Rate Options. 1982. 32 pp.
The Merrill Lynch Guide to Writing Stock Options. 1982. 20 pp.

Pensions

Pension Benefit Guaranty Corporation
PBGC Facts.
Your Guaranteed Pension. 1982.

Pension Rights Center
A Guide to Understanding Your Pension Plan. 32 pp.
Pension Rights 1: Myths and Facts.
Retirement Income: A Report from the Pension Rights Center. 22 pp.

U.S. Department of Labor, Labor-Management Services Administration
Know Your Pension Plan Checklist. 1979.

U.S. Railroad Retirement Board
Railroad Retirement and Survivors Benefits for Railroad Workers and Their Families. 1982. 52 pp.
U.S. Railroad Retirement Board. Fact Sheet. 9 pp.

Real Estate

American Institute for Economic Research
Homeowner or Tenant? How to Make a Wise Choice. Lawrence S. Pratt. *Economic Education Bulletin* 22, no. 3 (March 1982). 32 pp.

Credit Union National Association
Housing . . . A Major Family Expense. Consumer Facts: Everybody's Money. Revised April 1981.

Manufactured Housing Institute
Housing for the 1980s.
Manufactured Housing Quarterly: Land Use, Financing and Trends in Affordable Housing. 4 issues/year.
Quick Facts about the Manufactured Housing Industry. 1982. 10 pp.

Money Management Institute
Your Housing Dollar. 1982. 42 pp.

National Association of Housing Cooperatives
Cooperative Housing: A Consumer Guide.

Reymont Associates
A Consumer's Guide to Mobile Home Ownership. Jim Buchanan. 1982. 20 pp.

U.S. Department of Housing and Urban Development
Having Trouble Paying Your Mortgage? HUD-426-H(4). 1980.
Let's Consider Cooperatives. HUD-17-H(8). 1978.

Mobile Home Financing through HUD. HUD-265-H(6). 1980.
Should You Rent or Buy a Home? HUD-328-H(4). 1979.

Real Estate, Improvement

Council of Better Business Bureaus, Inc.
Tips on Home Improvement. Consumer Information Series.

National Association of Home Builders
How to Choose a Remodeler Who's on the Level.

U.S. Department of Agriculture
Remodeling a House—Will It Be Worthwhile? Gerald E. Sherwood. YS-78-3. 1978. 18 pp.

U.S. Department of Housing and Urban Development
Fixing Up Your Home and How to Finance It. HUD-52-H(9). 1980.

Real Estate, Investment

Credit Union National Association
Income Property for Small Investors. Consumer Facts: Everybody's Money. Revised June 1980.

Inform, Inc.
Land Buyers Beware: If You Are Thinking of Investing in a Subdivision Lot to Beat Inflation.

Real Estate, Purchasing

American Bankers Association
A Home Buyer's Guide. 1975. 31 pp.

American Bar Association
Buying or Selling Your Home. 1980. 31 pp.

Council of Better Business Bureaus, Inc.
Tips on Buying a Home. Consumer Information Series.

The Family Housing Bureau
The House Hunter's Guide. 1977. 22 pp.

Federal Trade Commission
Mortgage Money Guide. 16 pp.

House Master of America
What Every Home Buyer Should Know. 1979.

Inform, Inc.
The Insider's Guide to Owning Land in Subdivisions. Patricia A. Simko. 1980. 38 pp.

Lawyers Title Insurance Company
A Look before You Leap Checklist for Homebuyers.
Why Buying a Home Now Makes Dollars and Sense.

Mortgage Bankers Association of America
Buying a House. 1980. 25 pp.

National Association of Home Builders
Home Buyer's Guide. 1974. 32 pp.

Real Estate Education Company
Home Buying. Edith Lank. 1980. 44 pp.

U.S. Department of Agriculture
Selecting and Financing a Home. 1977. 24 pp.

U.S. Department of Housing and Urban Development
Before Buying Land . . . Get the Facts. HUD-183-1(9). 1980.
"Buying a Home?" Don't Forget the Settlement Costs! HUD-342-H(9). 1980.
Buying Lots from Developers. HUD-357-1(6). 1982. 20 pp.
HUD's Homeownership Subsidy Program. U.S. Department of Housing and Urban Development: Fact Sheet. HUD-419-HPMC(2). 1976.
Move In . . . With a Graduated Payment Mortgage. HUD-H-317(4). 1980.
Wise Home Buying. HUD-267-H(10). 1980. 32 pp.

U.S. Department of the Interior
Can I Really Get Free or Cheap Land? IS No. 5. 1980.

Veterans Administration
Guaranteed, Home and Condominium Loans for Veterans: Questions and Answers. VA Pamphlet 26-4. 1981. 25 pp.
Pointers for the Veteran Homeowner: A Guide for Veterans Whose Home Mortgage Is Guaranteed or Insured under the GI Bill. VA Pamphlet 26-5. Revised 1975. 28 pp.
To the Home Buying Veteran: A Guide for Veterans Planning to Buy or Build Homes with a GI Loan. VA Pamphlet 26-6. 1981. 36 pp.

Real Estate, Renting

American Bar Association
Landlords and Tenants: Your Guide to the Law. 1982. 48 pp.

U.S. Department of Housing and Urban Development
Why Tenant Organizations? A Role for Residents of Rental Housing. HUD-339-HM(2). 1976.
Wise Rental Practices. HUD-470-NVACP(3). 1980. 39 pp.

Real Estate, Selling

Lawyers Title Insurance Corp.
The Realtor Selling Your House Needs Your Help.

Real Estate Education Co.
How to Save Tax Dollars When You Sell Your House. 4th Edition. Richard Robinson. 1980. 47 pp.

Springhill Press
How to Save Money When You Hire a Real Estate Broker (A Guide for Home Sellers). Peter G. Miller. 1981. 26 pp.

U.S. Department of Agriculture
Selling Property: Brokers, Title, Closing and Taxes. YS-78-10. 7 pp.

Retirement Planning

Action for Independent Maturity
  Financial Security.
  Looking Ahead: How to Plan Your Successful Retirement. 92 pp.
  Planning Your Retirement.

American Association of Retired Persons
  Your Retirement Money Guide. 1979. 38 pp.

American Council of Life Insurance
  Planning for Retirement: Have You Thought about What You Are Going to Do and How You Are Going to Live after You Retire? 1978.

Life Care Society of America
  Consumers' Guide to Independent Living for Older Americans. The Life Care Alternative. 1980. 24 pp.

Manpower Education Institute
  Ready or Not: A News Service Focusing on Retirement Planning.
  Ready or Not: Retirement Planning Review. A Handbook for Retirement. 9th Edition. 1982. 72 pp.

Social Security

Credit Union National Association
  Supplementing Your Social Security. Consumer Facts: Everybody's Money. April 1977.
  Your Social Security. Consumer Facts: Everybody's Money. Revised June 1980.

National Association of Mature People
  Your New Social Security and Medicare Fact Sheet. Updated every 6 months. 4 pp.

U.S. Department of Health and Human Services, Social Security Administration
  The Advantages of Social Security: A Message for State and Local Government Employee Groups. SSA Publication no. 05-10065. April 1982 Edition. 10 pp.
  Applying for a Social Security Number. SSA Publication no. 05-10064. August 1981. 6 pp.
  Estimating Your Social Security Check—For Workers Who Reached 62 in 1979-83. June 1982 Edition. SSA Publication no. 05-10088. 11 pp.
  Estimating Your Social Security Retirement Check—For Workers Who Reached 62 before 1979. SSA Publication no. 05-10047. August 1981. 9 pp.
  For the Young Worker . . . Social Security. SSA Publication no. 05-10063. July 1982.
  A Guide to Supplemental Security Income. July 1982 Edition. SSA Publication no. 05-11015. 29 pp.
  How Work Affects Your Social Security Checks. SSA Publication no. 05-10069. January 1982.
  If You Become Disabled. May 1982 Edition. SSA Publication no. 05-10029. 23 pp.
  If You're Self-Employed . . . Reporting Your Income for Social Security. SSA Publication no. 05-10022. January 1982. 8 pp.

Social Security Checks for Students 18 to 22. SSA Publication no. 05-10048. March 1982. 7 pp.
SSI for Aged, Disabled and Blind People. June 1982 Edition. SSA Publication no. 05-11000. 10 pp.
Thinking about Retiring? July 1982 Edition. SSA Publication no. 05-10055. 11 pp.
What You Should Know about SSI. SSA Publication no. 05-11011. June 1981. 19 pp.
A Woman's Guide to Social Security. May 1982 Edition. SSA Publication no. 05-10127. 15 pp.
Your Social Security. SSA Publication no. 05-10035. September 1981. 31 pp.
Your Social Security Earnings Record. SSA Publication no. 05-10044. August 1981. 13 pp.
Your Social Security Rights and Responsibilities: Retirement and Survivors Benefits. SSA Publication no. 05-10077. January 1982. 19 pp.

Stock Market

American Association of Individual Investors
A Lifetime Strategy for Investing in Common Stocks.

American Institute for Economic Research
Investment Guide.

American Stock Exchange
Journey through a Stock Exchange. 1970. 24 pp.

Banyan Books
$even Letter$: The Securities Market and You. Just What Is a Stock or a Bond? Clarence Wolf, Jr. 1980. 64 pp.

International Paper Co.
How to Read a Financial Report. Jane Bryant Quinn.

Merrill Lynch, Pierce, Fenner and Smith, Inc.
How to Read a Financial Report. 4th Edition. 1979. 31 pp.

New York Stock Exchange
Income Leaders on the Big Board. 1981. 20 pp.
Ten Questions to Ask before You Buy Stocks.
Understanding Bonds and Preferred Stocks. 1982. 23 pp.
Understanding the New York Stock Exchange.

Tax Shelters

E. F. Hutton and Company
Understanding Tax Shelters.

Taxes

Credit Union National Association
IRS: Tax Returns—Who Can Help. Consumer Facts. April 1977.

Federal Trade Commission
Should You Choose a Tax Preparer. 1982.

212 Pamphlet Resources

Merrill Lynch, Pierce, Fenner and Smith, Inc.
44 Tax-Saving Ideas for Investors. Updated to Reflect the 1981 and 1982 Tax Acts. 1983. 15 pp.

National Association of Home Builders
Tax Savings for Home Buyers . . . Home and Condominium Buyers Can Take Advantage of Tax Savings Not Available to Renters.

National Association of Mature People
Tax Saving Tips. 11 pp.

National Society of Public Accountants
Choosing Your Professional Tax Accountant and Tax Practitioner. December 1981.
Preparing to Meet Your Preparer at Tax Time. December 1981.
Tax Return Preparation—Facts and Fictions. December 1981.
Taxes and the Professional Accountant.

The President's Committee on Employment of the Handicapped
Special Report: Taxes and Disability. 8 pp.

Reymont Associates
How the Small Taxpayer Can Take the IRS to Court. 1977. 15 pp.

State of California–State and Consumer Services
Having Your Tax Return Prepared by a Tax Preparer?

U.S. Department of the Treasury, Internal Revenue Service
Charitable Contributions. Publication no. 526.
Child and Disabled Dependent Care. Publication no. 503.
Credit for the Elderly. Publication no. 524.
Disability Payments. Publication no. 522.
Energy Credits for Individuals. Publication no. 903.
Examination of Returns, Appeal Rights, and Claims for Refunds. Publication no. 556.
Exemptions. Publication no. 501.
Federal Estate and Gift Taxes. Publication no. 448.
Highlights of 1982 Tax Changes. Publication no. 553.
Income Averaging. Publication no. 506.
Index to Tax Publications. Publication no. 900.
Interest Expense. Publication no. 545.
Investment Income and Expenses. Publication no. 550.
Medical and Dental Expenses. Publication no. 502.
Miscellaneous Deductions. Publication no. 529.
Moving Expenses. Publication no. 521.
Mutual Fund Distributions. Publication no. 564.
Pension and Annuity Income. Publication no. 575.
Recordkeeping Requirements and a List of Tax Publications. Publication no. 552.
Rental Property. Publication no. 527.
Tax Guide for U.S. Citizens Abroad. Publication no. 54.
Tax Information for Divorced or Separated Individuals. Publication no. 504.
Tax Information for Handicapped and Disabled Individuals. Publication no. 907.

Tax Information for Homeowners. Publication no. 530.
Tax Information for Older Americans. Publication no. 554.
Tax Information for Survivors, Executors, and Administrators. Publication no. 559.
Tax Information on Disasters, Casualties and Thefts. Publication no. 547.
Tax Information on Individual Retirement Arrangements. Publication no. 590.
Tax Information on Self-Employed Retirement Plans. Publication no. 560.
Tax Information on Selling Your Home. Publication no. 523.
Tax Information on Unemployment Compensation. Publication no. 905.
Tax Withholding and Estimated Tax. Publication no. 505.
Taxable and Nontaxable Income. Publication no. 525.
Taxpayers Guide to IRS Information and Assistance. Publication no. 910.
Travel, Entertainment, and Gift Expenses. Publication no. 463.
U.S. Tax Guides for Aliens. Publication no. 519.
Your Federal Income Tax. Publication no. 17.

Time Sharing

American Land Development Association
Resort Timesharing: A Consumer's Guide. 1981. 15 pp.

The CHB Company
The Buyer's Guide to Resort Timesharing. Special Edition. 1981. 50 pp.

Federal Trade Commission/Bureau of Consumer Protection/Office of Consumer Education
Ten Time Share Tips. Facts for Consumers.

Vacation Horizons International
Vacation Ownership. An Exciting Idea in Vacationing.

Treasury Bills, Bonds, and Securities

Federal Reserve Bank of New York
Basic Information on Treasury Bills.
Basic Information on Treasury Notes and Bonds.
Fedpoints 7: How to Read U.S. Government Securities Quotes.
Fedpoints 24: Special Government Securities. 1981.
Fedpoints 28: How to Compute Returns on Treasury Issues.

Federal Reserve Bank of Philadelphia
Options for Savers. September 1980.
P.S. to Options for Savers. April 1982.

Federal Reserve Bank of Richmond
Buying Treasury Securities at Federal Reserve Banks. James E. Tucker. 1982. 37 pp.
Instruments of the Money Market.

Veterans Administration Benefits

Veterans Administration
Federal Benefits for Veterans and Dependents. IS-1. Fact Sheet. January 1982. 73 pp.
Former POW Benefits Act of 1981. VA Pamphlet 27-82-1. January 1982.

A Summary of Veterans Administration Benefits. VA Pamphlet 27-82-2. April 1982. 26 pp.

Wills

American Bar Association
Wills: Why You Should Have One and the Lawyer's Role in Its Preparation. 1981.

American Institute for Economic Research
How to Avoid Financial Tangles. Section A: Elementary Property Problems and Important Financial Relationships. Bruce H. French. *Economic Education Bulletin* 21, no. 10 (October 1981). 40 pp.
How to Avoid Financial Tangles. Section B: Taxes, Gifts and Help for the Widow. Bruce H. French. *Economic Education Bulletin* 21, no. 12 (December 1981). 28 pp.
How to Avoid Financial Tangles. Section C: Trusts May Be More Useful Than Many Realize. Ernest P. Welker. *Economic Education Bulletin* 21, no. 11 (November 1981). 28 pp.

Credit Union National Association
What if You Are Named Executor? Consumer Facts: Everybody's Money.
Your Will: A Plan for the Future. Consumer Facts: Everybody's Money. Revised September 1980.

U.S. Department of Agriculture
Providing for Your Heirs—Non-Sale Property Transfers. YS-78-11. Donald R. Levi. 1978. 7 pp.

Women and Money

American Council of Life Insurance
Fact Sheet on Women: Women and Social Security. 1981.
A Guide to Life Insurance for Women Only. 1978.

Board of Governors of the Federal Reserve System
The Equal Credit Opportunity Act and . . . Women. 1977.

Consumer Credit Project, Inc.
New Credit Rights for Women. 1978. 73 pp.

Federal Deposit Insurance Corporation
Equal Credit Opportunity and Women: Your Rights.

Federal Trade Commission
Women and Credit Histories.

General Motors Acceptance Corporation
Women Can Get the Credit They Deserve: Financing Factbook. 1980.

League of Women Voters of the U.S.A.
Finding the Facts: A Woman's Housing Primer.
It's Up to You: A Woman's Housing Primer. 7 pp.

Merrill Lynch, Pierce, Fenner and Smith, Inc.
You and Your Money: A Financial Handbook for Women. 1982. 40 pp.

Pension Rights Center
Pension Rights 2: Women and the Facts. 4 pp.
Women and Pensions.

State of California-State and Consumer Services
Credit for Women. 1981. 11 pp.

The Travelers Insurance Companies
Making Your Money Work: About Life Insurance for Women. 16 pp.
What Every Woman Should Know about Life Insurance. 20 pp.

11

Investments and Securities Reference Sources

To ensure the latest and most accurate information on investments, it is necessary to access the wide range of specialized reference sources that contain data relating to the financial well-being of industries and specific companies, stock prices and trends, and securities ratings and price quotations. Although these statistical sources are priced beyond the reach of most individuals, many of them are available for consultation in libraries and stockbrokers' offices.

Some of these publications focus on major industries from the viewpoint of performance, trends, outlook, and forecasts. Other publications provide data on specific companies indicating sales and earnings, profitability, financial condition, dividends record, book value, and so on. Others, utilizing technical analysis, offer charts of market data showing chart formations (patterns of behavior), channels and trading ranges, support and resistance levels, sentiment indicators, and moving averages.

These reference sources are useful for the personal investor who wishes to "pick" stocks using the fundamental approach (judging what a stock is worth) or to calculate market "timing" (when to buy and sell) using the results of technical analysis. A select list and descriptions of major publications of interest to the lay investor for these purposes are contained here. (Specific pricing information should be obtained from the publishers.)

FUNDAMENTAL INDUSTRY AND COMPANY INFORMATION

Standard & Poor's Corporation
25 Broadway, New York, NY 10004

Daily Stock Price Record (quarterly): Consists of three sets of quarterly published volumes, each set devoted to one market—NYSE, ASE, or OTC. Together, they

218   Investments and Securities Reference Sources

give a comprehensive, day-by-day account of price histories on well over 6,400 issues. The NYSE volumes contain data on more than 2,200 issues. A minimum of 1,000 issues are covered in the ASE books. Information in the OTC volumes covers 3,200 issues, made up of 500 mutual funds and 2,700 NASDAQ banks, insurance, and industrial companies. Price histories are given on up to five different stocks on each page of *Daily Stock Price Record*, carrying a full three months of day-by-day prices. The high, low, and closing prices of stocks traded are listed, plus bid and asked prices for nontraded securities (where the information is available).

Dividend Record (daily, weekly, and quarterly): Complete, detailed information on the dividend disbursements of more than 10,000 companies, with frequency of service tailored to specific individual or institutional needs. Subscribers may choose to receive *Dividend Record* daily, weekly, or quarterly. The service is arranged cumulatively, so that all subscribers eventually are in full possession of the previously published data. Ultimately, all dividend information for the entire year finds its way into Standard & Poor's *Annual Dividend Record*, which is automatically included with all subscriptions or may also be purchased separately.

Industry Surveys: Continuous economic and investment analyses of 65 leading U.S. industries and approximately 1,500 of their constituent companies, published in 33 surveys. Includes Basic Surveys (annual), Current Surveys (three times annually), and Trends and Projections Bulletins (monthly).

Stock Guide (monthly): A pocket-size, 256-page statistical summary of investment data on more than 5,100 common and preferred stocks, listed and over-the-counter, published monthly. It provides an at-a-glance review of practically every stock traded, including all issues on the New York and American Stock exchanges, and most NASDAQ issues, with 44 items of essential information on each. A special section contains vital data on more than 380 leading mutual funds. For each of the 5,100 common and preferred stocks, lists principal business, exclusive S&P earnings, and dividend rankings for common stocks, ratings for preferred stocks, institutional holdings, price range data, trading volume, dividend record (indicated dividend rates and yields), price/earnings ratios, financial position (including shares outstanding), annual earnings and earnings estimates, and interim earnings.

Stock Market Encyclopedia of the S&P "500" (annual): A comprehensive 500-page reference volume containing a wealth of important facts and figures on 500 major corporations—the same corporations comprising the S&P 500 Index. Each report provides a succinct profile of the company's activities and discusses events that have already affected or may influence its prospects for the year. There are detailed statistical tables of income and balance sheet data, generally covering the past ten years. Also included are S&P's earnings/dividend common stock rankings, per share and earnings data, a summary of business operations with sales and profit breakouts, main office addresses, phone numbers, officers and directors, and, in most cases S&P's analysis of short-term prospects and long-term outlook, including earnings and dividend forecasts.

Stock Reports: This consists of three four-volume sets on the New York Stock Exchange, American Stock Exchange, and Over-the-Counter and Regional Exchanges. Contains periodically revised two-page reports on some 3,500 companies. The reports are issued on all companies listed on the New York Stock Exchange, the American Stock Exchange, and on nearly 1,100 of the most active and widely held companies whose securities are traded over-the-counter and on regional exchanges, including Canadian. For the more than 750 companies in which most investor interest is centered, *Stock Reports* includes a special Current Outlook section that gives the Standard & Poor opinion of the prospects for each, with earnings estimates and dividend forecasts.

Stock Summary (monthly): Primarily for the individual investor, in the form of a reference guide to approximately 1,920 stocks most widely traded on the New York Stock Exchange (1,541 companies), American Stock Exchange (153 companies), NASDAQ (220 companies), and regional exchanges (8 companies). For each stock listed, *Stock Summary* provides 40 items of information. The price/earnings information includes 16-year and current-year price ranges, recent closing price, price/earnings ratio, percentage price change over past six months, indicator signaling significant earnings changes from previous month, S&P earnings and dividend rankings for common stocks, interim earnings and per-share earnings for the past three or four years, with Standard & Poor's estimates for current year. Dividend information includes new dividend announcements, yield and indicated dividend, years of uninterrupted cash dividend payments, latest dividend paid with ex-date and indicated rate, and rate paid for past two years.

Moody's Investors Service
99 Church St., New York, NY 10007

Dividend Records (twice weekly): Key dates and amounts of stock dividends on more than 11,000 issues. Includes common and preferred stocks, bond funds, income bonds, mutual funds, and foreign securities.

Industrial Manual and News Reports (twice a week): Covers every industrial firm listed on the New York, American, and regional stock exchanges. Gives company listing, subsidiaries, complete financial and operating profile, products, sales, balance sheets, and securities description.

Value Line, Arnold Bernhard and Company
711 Third Ave., New York, NY 10017

Value Line (weekly): In addition to weekly rankings on 1,700 stocks covering 92 industries, *Value Line* publishes a full-page report on each stock every three months—at a rate of about 130 a week—including 22 series of vital financial and operating statistics going back 15 years and as estimated three to five years into the future. For each of the 1,700 stocks, *Value Line* gives Rank for Probable Relative Price Performance in the Next 12 Months—ranging from 1 (highest) to 5 (lowest); Rank for Investment Safety (from 1 down to 5); Estimated Yield in the Next 12 Months; Estimated Appreciation Potentiality in the Next 3 to 5 Years—showing the future "target" price range and the percentage price change indicated; current price and estimated P/E based on past six months' earnings plus future six months' earnings; yield based on estimated dividends in the next 12 months, and the stock's Beta.

FIXED-INCOME SECURITIES

Standard & Poor's Corporation
25 Broadway, New York, NY 10004

Bond Guide: A comprehensive 192-page pocket guide presenting 41 items of descriptive and statistical data on approximately 4,800 corporate bonds and their issuing companies, arranged in a format designed for easy scanning and convenient evaluation and comparison of specific issues. *Bond Guide* also includes statistics on more than 600 convertible bonds with 26 data items for each, as well as a special section listing approximately 200 foreign bonds. Standard & Poor's Quality Ratings are given for corporate bonds and all important state and municipal general obligation and revenue bonds.

Credit Week (weekly): Comments on general trends and outlook for fixed-income securities, including money market instruments and corporate and government bonds. Also includes Credit Watch, which highlights potential changes in ratings of bonds and other fixed-income securities. This focuses on events and trends that place companies and government units under special surveillance by Standard & Poor's analytical staff. Credit analyses are supplied on select issues.

Moody's Investor Service
99 Church St., New York, NY 10007

Bond Record (monthly): Moody's ratings on 32,000 corporate issues. Included are convertibles, government and municipal issues, commercial paper, and preferred stock ratings.

Bond Survey (weekly): Designed to keep investors in touch with the value of bonds, commercial paper, and other debt instruments. Includes Moody's ratings and rationale on new financing. All segments of the fixed-income market are studied. Includes a calendar of recent and prospective corporate bonds, including their prices, yields, and Moody's ratings.

CHART SERVICES

Standard & Poor's Corporation
25 Broadway, New York, NY 10004

Trendline (includes *Daily Action Stock Charts, Current Market Perspectives, OTC Chart Manual*).
 Daily Action Stock Charts—A weekly bound presentation of 716 stock charts showing daily-plotted price action of the most popular NYSE and AMEX stocks,

brought up to date after the market closes every Friday and mailed the same night. Each chart shows a 12-month picture of stock movement with daily high, low closing prices and volume through the day of publication. Each chart also traces a 30 Week Moving Average for the stock and includes a separate chart showing yearly price ranges for the past 12 years, when available, as well as a table of comparative annual earnings and dividends for the past two years with latest quarterly earnings.

Current Market Perspectives—A monthly bound presentation of price/volume charts on 972 most widely traded listed stocks, published on the Tuesday closest to the 15th of each month. Each chart shows price and volume action of the stock on a weekly basis for up to three and a half years. Important features of these charts are the high and low price/earnings ratio lines indicating the previously established patterns of fluctuation for each stock, enabling users to ascertain at a glance whether a stock is trading high or low in relation to its historic pattern.

OTC Chart Manual—Each bimonthly issue provides charts of 840 key OTC stocks, including leading industrial, insurance, public utilities and foreign securities, plus special sections featuring low-priced issues and stock exchange newcomers. Each chart presents the weekly bid price range, closing bid, and volume (NASDAQ) for a period of up to 30 months. Annual price ranges for 11 years, capitalization, and up to six years of earnings and dividend data are also included.

DIRECTORIES

Abrecht, Stephen, and Locker, Michael (eds.). *CDE Stock Ownership Directory: Volume 5. Fortune 500.* New York: Corporate Data Exchange, 1981. 215 pp. $95.
Identifies who owns the Fortune 500 industrials. Ownership profiles identify and rank the largest stockholders in each company. The profiles rank any publicly identifiable shareholder who exercised investment power over two-tenths of 1 percent or more of a company's common stock. This reference source is of some importance considering the fact that the Fortune 500 currently represent between two-thirds and three-quarters of the total assets and sales of all U.S. manufacturing and mining companies.

Directory of American Savings and Loan Associations. 1982. 28th Annual Edition.
Baltimore: T. K. Sanderson, 1982. 460 pp. $50.
This alphabetical listing of all the savings and/or building and loan associations and cooperative banks in the United States is arranged by state and city. Information includes the complete name of the association, whether it is a stock or mutual association, address, code for the Federal Home Loan Bank in whose district it falls, key executives, branch offices, assets, and participation in the Federal Saving and Loan Insurance Corporation (FSLIC) and/or the Federal Home Loan Bank (FHLB). Notes whether accounts may be opened by mail.

Directory of Obsolete Securities: Financial Stock Guidance Service. 1982 Edition.
Jersey City, NJ: Financial Information, 1982. 1015 pp. $100.
Contains brief profiles of banks and companies whose identities have been lost as a result of one or more of the following actions: change in name, merger, acquisition,

dissolution, reorganization, bankruptcy, or charter cancellation. The listing for each company indicates the manner in which the company's identity was lost, the new name of the company (if any), and the year in which the action occurred. Wherever possible, the compilers indicate whether stock in a company has any remaining value or if a stockholder's equity still exists.

Dorfman, John. *The Stock Market Directory*. Garden City, NY: Doubleday, 1982. 512 pp. $29.95.
A comprehensive compendium of basic information on some 1,500 stocks, including every stock listed on the New York Exchange as of January 1, 1982. Spotlight profiles highlight 500 stocks of high investor interest, including the 300 largest U.S. industrial companies, the 50 most active stocks on the New York Exchange, and a number of fast growing companies. These profiles include name, ticker symbol, year founded, description of what the company does, number of employees, recent sales trends, earnings, and what would have happened if you had invested $10,000 in the company at the beginning of 1972 or 1976 in terms of dividends, capital gains or losses, and rate of return on investment. Of great decision-making value in selecting stocks.

Security Dealers of North America. New York: Standard and Poor's Corp. Twice a year. $235/year.
A national directory that lists nearly 9,000 brokerage and investment banking houses in the United States and Canada, including branch offices and their executive rosters of over 30,000 individuals. Gives firm name and address, exchange memberships, nature of business, branch offices, partners or officers, departments and managers, teletype and digital telephone numbers, and NASDAQ symbols.

ENCYCLOPEDIAS, HANDBOOKS, AND GUIDES

Blume, Marshall E., and Friedman, Jack F. *Encyclopedia of Investments*. Boston: Warren, Gorham & Lamont, 1982. 1,040 pp. $47.50.
An analytical description of more than 60 different kinds of investments, prepared by bankers, investment advisers, dealers, and financial specialists. Each section follows a standardized format covering a description of the investment vehicle, attractive features and attendant risks, primary factors that determine the monetary value of the asset, suitability for specific types of investors, where to obtain professional advice, how to buy and sell, tax implications, and unusual custodial problems. Investments analyzed include art nouveau and art deco, books, coins, commercial paper, money market funds, mutual funds, porcelain, real estate, stamps and U.S. Treasury bills. The inclusion of a glossary and suggested readings at the end of each section enhances the value of this publication.

Darst, David M. *The Handbook of the Bond and Money Markets*. New York: McGraw-Hill, 1981. 461 pp. $29.95.
An authoritative and scholarly treatment of the organization of the bond market and the forces affecting it; the effect of inflation and deflation on yield levels and rates of

real return; the investment practices and portfolio holdings of 24 different investor groups, both domestic and international, in the bond and money markets; and specialized tools and techniques for investing. The final chapter identifies and describes sources of statistical and analytical information on the functions, investors, and methods of the bond markets. This literature review is highly valuable for those who wish to explore further the subject matter of this book. A comprehensive reference source.

Moody's Handbook of Common Stocks. New York: Dun & Bradstreet. $125. Quarterly.

Provides quick and easy access to basic financial and business information on over 900 stocks with high investor interest. For each company describes background, recent developments, prospects, and statistics such as gross revenues, net income, shares, price range, and P/E ratio. Statistics and analyses are revised quarterly. Also contains a classification of companies by industry and an analysis of stock price movements by company.

Pierce, Phyllis (ed.). *The Dow-Jones Investor's Handbook.* 1983 Edition. Homewood, IL: Dow Jones-Irwin, 1983. 136 pp. $11.95.

A convenient reference source of stock and bond market indicators. Contains complete day-by-day Dow Jones averages for 1982, with earnings, dividend yield, and price/earnings ratios; individual 1982 records of stocks and bonds listed on the New York Stock Exchange and American Stock Exchange, showing the year's high and low prices, net changes, volume and dividend, and the most active stocks; and more than 2,000 over-the-counter securities quotations. A large quantity of charts, graphs, and tables designed for quick reference.

Sokoloff, Kiril (ed.). *The Paine Webber Handbook of Stock and Bond Analysis.* New Edition. New York: McGraw-Hill, 1979. $29.50.

An excellent reference book for analyzing stocks and bonds. Information is arranged by 31 industries such as the airline industry and drug industry. Each industrial category is broken down into sections: Key to Analyzing the Industry, Most Common Investor Mistakes, When to Buy/Sell Stocks, Unique Aspects of the Industry, Some Investment Considerations, and Questions to Ask Yourself before You Make an Investment. The contributors are top analysts in their specialty. Provides investors with the key questions to ask about an investment. Indispensable for effective and rational decision making.

Standard and Poor's Research Dept. *Standard and Poor's Ratings Guide: Including Corporate Bonds, Commercial Paper, Municipal Bonds, International Securities.* New York: McGraw-Hill, 1979. 417 pp. $19.95.

A thorough, comprehensive, and informative description of how Standard and Poor's, a wholly owned subsidiary of McGraw-Hill, evaluates and rates debt securities of corporations, municipalities, retail companies, insurance companies, banks and holding companies, savings and loan associations, finance companies, public utilities, project financings, and international corporations and municipalities. An excellent explanation of the fundamental factors and items of information considered in arriving at ratings that represent, in effect, the likelihood of timely repayment of principal and interest.

Wiesenberger Investment Companies Service. Investment Companies, 1982. 42nd Annual Edition. Boston: Warren, Gorham & Lamont, 1982. 709 pp. $195. Also updated monthly.

A reference source of information on some 2,710 investment companies of all types, sizes, policies, and portfolios. Part One—General Information about Investment Companies—describes types of companies, services available, investment objectives and portfolio policies, and the selection of mutual funds and other investment company securities. Part Two—Investment Companies in Use—covers common stocks and the new investor, the advantages of systematic investment, and retirement and estate planning. Part Three—Mutual Funds and Other Types of Investment Companies—lists and describes mutual funds, money market funds, variable annuity separate accounts, and tax-exempt municipal bond funds. A final section, Part Four—Closed End Investment Companies, and Mutual Fund Management Companies—includes a statistical survey, together with management results of all known publicly available companies.

ALMANACS

Hirsch, Yale. *Mutual Funds Almanac.* 1979 Edition. Old Tappan, NJ: Hirsch Organization, 1979. 160 pp. $20 (paper).
Tabulates performance of mutual funds and reviews the advantages, mode of operation, objectives, risks, and rewards of the major funds. Although the performance data are not current, the discussion of how mutual funds can be used for retirement, college education, and other purposes is still of some interest.

Levine, Sumner (ed.). *The Dow Jones-Irwin Business and Investment Almanac.* Homewood, IL: Dow Jones-Irwin, 1983. 720 pp. $19.95.
A comprehensive compendium of information, including major stock market averages, group stock averages, price/earnings ratios, review of the major futures markets, charts for futures trade commodities, tables showing options premium movements, performance of mutual funds, price performance of collectibles, and comparative returns of different types of investments. Offers very clear explanations of stock market futures, stock options, credit ratings (Moody's and Standard & Poor's), and more. Lists sources of business and economic statistics, corporate information, federal information centers, and addresses of mutual funds and money funds categorized by investment objectives.

DICTIONARIES AND GLOSSARIES

Beer, Edith L. *Monarch's Dictionary of Investment Terms.* New York: Monarch Press, 1983. 192 pp. $6.95 (paper).
A splendid dictionary providing concise definitions of more than 1,000 investment-related terms. Ten chapters cover various financial topics—Bonds, Stock Market Trading Terms, Commodities, Money Instruments, Diamonds and Precious Metals, Real Estate, Loans and Mortgages, Insurance, Financial Statements, and Investing

in a Small Business. Terms are arranged alphabetically within chapters with an ample index at the back of the book. Select titles are listed for further reading. An excellent place to look up such terms as arbitrage, balloon mortgage, and Ginnie Mae.

Brownstone, David M., and Franck, Irene M. *The VNR Investor's Dictionary.* New York: Van Nostrand, 1981. 320 pp. $16.95.

Intended to serve the needs of investors, investment and banking professionals, students, teachers, librarians, and library users, this dictionary defines words and phrases in the areas of securities, finance, banking, business, accounting, law, real estate, statistics, and government. Despite its ambitious intent, there are a number of omissions in terms commonly used in real estate and banking (e.g., land contract and NOW account).

Davids, Lewis E. *Dictionary of Insurance.* 5th Edition. Totowa, NJ: Littlefield, Adams, 1977. 276 pp. $5.95 (paper).

Brief and succinct definitions of basic terms used in insurance and related areas of accounting, taxation, and real estate.

Green, Thomas E., Osler, Robert W., and Bickley, John S. *Glossary of Insurance Terms.* Santa Monica, CA: Merritt Co., 1980. 234 pp. $11.95 (paper).

The compilers, all experts in the insurance field, define for laypeople, students, and professionals some 2,000 terms, abbreviations, and acronyms derived from all segments of the insurance industry. Especially helpful is the assignment of each term to one of 14 categories: general, automobile, aviation, home, health, inland marine, legal, liability, life, ocean marine, property, reinsurance, surety, workers compensation. Brief definitions, often accompanied by examples of usage, are most instructive for anyone unfamiliar with the language of insurance. "See," "See also," and "Compare With" cross-references guide the user to terms with similar meanings, and "Contrast With" points to terms having opposite meanings. A special section at the end includes some 35 pension terminology terms as defined by the Inter-Professional Pension Actuarial Advisory Group (January 20, 1978).

Rosenberg, Jerry M. *Dictionary of Business and Management.* New York: Wiley, 1978. 564 pp. $29.95; $9.95 (paper).

More than 800 words and terms covering such areas as accounting, banking, commodities, finance, insurance, real estate, securities, and the stock market. Fairly simple and precise definitions. Multiple definitions are supplied where the term is utilized in several fields of activity, such as "Options" in Real Estate, Securities, and Insurance.

Glossary

Adjustable Rate Mortgage (ARM) A method used by home mortgage lenders to calculate interest payments in which the interest rate is adjusted periodically with reference to a specific benchmark index. Also known as floating rate mortgage.

All-Savers Certificates Tax-exempt certificates that were available from October 1981 through December 1982. Up to $1,000 tax-exempt interest was allowed to those filing a single tax return and up to $2,000 for those filing a joint tax return. Maturity was for one year and the interest rate was 70 percent of the 52-week Treasury bill rate at the time of issue.

Alpha Strategy An investment plan in which an individual completely avoids conventional investments and instead concentrates his or her wealth in real and tangible goods, stockpiling them until ready either to consume them or trade them for other desired goods.

AMEX The American Stock Exchange, the second largest stock exchange in the United States.

Amortization Repayment of loan principal.

Annual Report Formal financial report issued yearly by a corporation showing assets, liabilities, revenues, expenses, and earnings—information of interest to shareowners.

Annuity A contract, issued most often by a life insurance company, promising the purchaser a steady stream of income in the future, usually on retirement. Annuities can be deferred, fixed, or variable in nature.

Appraisal Analytical and informed assessment of the value of property.

Note: See p. 238 for sources consulted.

Arbitrage A technique employed to take advantage of differences in price. Gold may be purchased in London at one price and sold by an arbitrageur in New York at a higher price, the difference representing profit (after deduction of expenses).

Assets Everything a corporation owns or has due to it. This includes cash, investments, money due, materials and inventories (current assets), buildings and machinery (fixed assets), and goodwill (intangible assets).

Assumable Mortgage A mortgage that can be passed on to a new owner at the previous owner's rate of interest.

Averages Produced by measuring the trend of securities prices. The most popular is the Dow Jones average of 30 industrial stocks listed on the New York Stock Exchange. The prices of the 30 stocks are totaled and then divided by a divisor that is intended to compensate for past stock splits and stock dividends. The divisor is changed from time to time.

Balloon Mortgage These have a series of equal monthly payments that do not fully amortize the loan. The payments are often for interest only. The unpaid balance, frequently the principal or original amount borrowed, comes due in a lump sum in a short period such as three to five years.

Bankers' Acceptances Closely resemble commercial paper in form. They are short-term (270 days or less), noninterest-bearing notes sold at a discount and redeemed by the accepting bank at maturity for full face value. Payment is guaranteed by the accepting bank.

Bear Someone who believes the market will decline. Bears are pessimists who sell rather than buy.

Bear Market A declining market.

Beta A measure of the average percentage change in the price of a stock relative to the percentage change of a market index. Usually beta is computed relative to the S&P index. The higher the beta, usually the more volatile the stock.

Blue Chip Stock A company distinguished by its ability to produce quality products and services and by its demonstrated ability to make money and pay dividends.

Bond An interest-bearing certificate or promissory note, usually issued by a corporation or government in multiples of $1,000 or $5,000, evidence of a debt on which the issuing company promises to pay the bondholders a specified amount of interest for a specified length of time and to repay the loan on the expiration date.

Book Value An accounting term used to convey a company's assets, determined by adding all assets, deducting debts, and then dividing the sum by the number of common shares outstanding. Book value may have little relationship to market value.

Bull Someone who believes that the market will go up. Bulls are optimists who buy rather than sell.

Bull Market An advancing market.

Buy Down A creative financing method that decreases the interest rate paid for the first three to five years on a home mortgage loan. The loan is subsidized by the developer or home builder for a period of several years. Interest payments will, however, jump to the prevailing rate when the subsidized period is over.

Call *See* Option.

Capital Gain/Capital Loss Profit or loss from the sale of a capital asset. A capital gain, under federal tax law, may be either short term (12 months or less) or long term (more than 12 months). Short-term gains are taxed at the reporting individual's full income tax rate. A long-term capital gain is subject to a lower tax.

Capitalization Total amount of the various securities issued by a corporation. This may include bonds, debentures, preferred and common stock, and surplus.

Cash Management Account (CMA) A multipurpose money management plan that is a combination of a brokerage account and a checking account earning money market rates. Checks can be written against the account while ready credit is provided in the form of a credit card that debits the amount of purchases from the account. Although CMA is a trademark of Merrill Lynch, similar plans linking savings with investment are available from other brokerage houses.

CEIT *See* Closed-End Investment Trust.

Certificate of Deposit (CD) Negotiable notes, bearing interest, issued by commercial banks and savings and loan associations. Most CDs have an original maturity of one to three months, but some extend to five and even seven years.

Chapter 13 Part of the 1979 revision of the Federal Bankruptcy Act; a Wage Earner Plan for the repayment of debts, which allows a credit user in serious financial difficulty to pay off credit obligations without declaring bankruptcy.

Clifford Trusts A short-term trust that shifts income to a beneficiary for a period of years with the remainder reverting to the creator. A person in a high tax bracket may want to divert income on some property to members of his or her family who are in much lower tax brackets. At the end of the trust term, the property, with any capital appreciation, may be returned to the original owner and the accumulated income paid to the beneficiary.

Closed-End Investment Trust (CEIT) An investment company that issues a fixed number of shares and does not redeem them. Shares, some of which are invested on the New York Stock Exchange, are bought and sold like other shares. Prices reflect supply and demand and can exceed or fall below net asset value.

Closing Costs Costs in addition to the price of a house. These usually include mortgage origination fee, title insurance, state and county transfer taxes, revenue stamps, and prepayable items such as taxes and insurance payments collected in advance and held in escrow.

Commercial Paper Unsecured promissory notes issued by corporations and finance companies to meet short-term financing needs. The maximum maturity for which commercial paper can be sold is 270 days.

Commodities Products such as soybeans, sugar, gold, coffee, and livestock traded at a price set in the future.

Common Stock Equity securities having last claim on the residual assets and earnings of a corporation.

Convertible A bond, debenture, or preferred share that may be exchanged by the owner for common stock or another security, usually of the same company, in accordance with the terms of the issue.

Corporate Bond Instrument of indebtedness issued by a corporation rather than a government agency. Corporate bonds have priority over common stock if there is a business failure.

Coupon Bond Bond with interest coupons attached. The coupons are clipped as they become due and are presented by the holder for payment of interest.

Creative Financing New and unconventional methods of home financing substantially different from traditional mortgages that offer a fixed interest rate and full amortization (transfer of equity) over a period of 20 to 30 years.

Debenture A promissory note backed by the general credit of a company and usually not secured by a mortgage or lien on any specific property.

Debt-to-Equity Ratio Relationship of long-term debt to common shareholders' equity.

Depreciation A bookkeeping entry representing the estimated decrease in value of property due to use, deterioration, or obsolescence over a period of time.

Dividend The payment designated by the board of directors to be distributed pro rata among the shares outstanding. On preferred shares, it is a fixed amount. On common shares, the dividend varies with the fortunes of the company and may be omitted if business is poor or the directors determine to withhold earnings to invest in plant and equipment.

Easement A right or interest that individuals or the public may have to use land owned by another. For example, an electric company may have easement rights for its power lines to cross another's property.

Electronic Banking Use of computer networks to permit bank transactions from remote locations. Automatic Teller Machines (ATMs) enable customers to make deposits and withdrawals in their checking, savings, and credit card accounts. Eventually, this capability will be extended to banking at home.

Elliott Wave Principle A system of empirically derived rules for interpreting action in the major stock markets. The system involves counting correctly the development of a five-wave advance in the market averages—three up, with two intervening down. Named after Ralph N. Elliott.

Equity The ownership interest of common and preferred stockholders in a company. Also, the value of a property that remains after all debts against the property are paid. A property owner's equity consists of his or her monetary interest in the property in excess of the mortgage indebtedness.

ERISA Employment Retirement Income Security Act of 1974, which sets federal guidelines for private pension plans.

Escrow The deposit of instruments and funds with instructions to a third and neutral party bonded by law to carry out the provisions of a real estate contract.

Eurodollars Deposits of U.S. dollars in banks outside the United States. The term is a misnomer in that dollar deposits are accepted in Hong Kong, the Middle East, and other centers around the world.

Fannie Mae (FNMA) Federal National Mortgage Association, an agency for buying mortgages from lenders and providing mortgage insurance for loans. Fannie Mae buys government-insured and -guaranteed mortgages and conventional mortgages when mortgage money is in short supply and sells them when the demand for mortgage money subsides.

Federal Agency Security A wide range of debt obligations, including short-, medium-, and long-term bills, certificates, and notes issued by the federal government. The Treasury is by far the largest issuer.

Fixed-Income Security A bond, debenture, preferred stock, certificate of deposit, and so on that guarantees a fixed rate of return over a fixed period of time. In most cases, the value moves down when the cost of money rises, and up when it falls.

Fixed-Rate Mortgage Mortgages having an interest rate and monthly payments that remain constant over the life of the loan.

Flexible Rate Mortgage. *See* Graduated-Payment Mortgage.

Floating Rate Mortgage *See* Adjustable Rate Mortgage.

Foreclosure A legal action as a result of which all rights and possession on the part of the mortgagor (borrower) are ended because of default in payments. The property then becomes the property of the mortgagee (lender).

Fundamental Analysis An approach to investing in which the selection of stocks is based on the determination of value. Industries and companies are analyzed with respect to such factors as sales, assets, earnings, products or services, markets and management, and the potential returns offered by competitive investments such as bonds and Treasury bills.

Futures Exchange-traded contracts specifying a future date of delivery or receipt of a certain amount of a specific, tangible, or intangible product. Commodities traded in future markets include agricultural products such as wheat, soybeans, and pork bellies. There are also futures in financial instruments, currency, and stock indexes.

Ginnie Mae (GNMA) Government National Mortgage Association—a wholly government-owned corporation—that provides financing for selected types of mortgages through mortgage purchases and commitments; also creates pools of mortgages and sells participation in these pools to private investors.

Glamor Stocks Stocks that are highly popular for a time to an extent not usually justified by either their performance or prospects.

Government Bonds Obligations of the U.S. government, regarded as the highest grade of securities issued.

Graduated-Payment Mortgage A mortgage in which the payments are relatively low in the early years of the loan. Payments are structured to rise at a set rate over a specified period, such as five or ten years. The payments then remain constant for the remainder of the loan period.

Growth Stocks Stocks of companies with great earnings potential or whose growth has exceeded the rate of growth of the economy.

Hedge Use of two nearly opposite-direction securities, instruments, or futures contracts as a means of attempting to reduce market risk. In commodities, one side of the hedge is in the cash market and the other in the futures market.

Income Stock Stock purchased for the major objective of maximizing current income.

Investment Company/Trust A company or trust that uses its capital to invest in other companies. There are two principal types: the closed-end and the open-end or mutual fund.

IRA Individual Retirement Account, a savings plan with tax-deferral advantages. Effective since 1982, any worker can start an IRA and obtain a tax deduction for contributions up to $2,000 annually. IRA permits investment through intermediaries such as mutual funds, insurance companies, and banks or directly in stocks and bonds through stockbrokers.

Joint Tenancy Joint ownership of a property by two or more persons in which all joint tenants have equal interest, equal rights. If one owner dies, his or her share goes to the survivor(s).

Keogh Plan Tax-advantaged, personal retirement program that can be established by a self-employed individual. Currently, annual contributions can be made up to 15 percent of a person's income up to a limit of $15,000. Such contributions and reinvestments are not taxed as they accumulate but only when withdrawn (presumably at retirement when taxable income may be less).

Kondratieff Theory A long-wave theory of economic and social trends observed in the 1920s by Nikolai Kondratieff, a Russian economist who documented that economic cycles of modern capitalist countries tend to follow a long rhythmic pattern of approximately half a century.

Land Contract A legal instrument that gives control, but not title, to land. This enables the buyer to use the property while buying it. The seller retains the title until paid in full.

Leverage Loosely, making money on borrowed money. More specifically, the use of borrowed funds to purchase real estate that will increase in value to the point that it can be sold to pay off the debt and other expenses and yield a profit.

Lien A legal claim against the property of another as security for the payment of a debt.

Liquidity Ability of a stock to absorb a large amount of buying and selling without substantially disturbing the price.

Liquidity Ratio Measure of how quickly a company can raise or provide cash. The ratio is derived by subtracting inventories from current assets and dividing by the current liabilities.

Margin The amount paid by the buyer when using his or her broker's credit to purchase securities. The percentage that can be borrowed on margin is regulated by the Federal Reserve.

Margin Account A type of account where a customer borrows money from a broker to pay for a percentage of the cost of securities. The margin is the money borrowed.

Market Order An order to buy or sell a stated amount of a security at the best possible price as soon as possible.

Medicare A health insurance program established under the Social Security Act to assist Americans 65 years or older in paying for health care. It has two parts: hospital insurance, known as Part A, and medical insurance, known as Part B. Part B is voluntary and requires payment of a small monthly premium.

Merger *See* Takeover.

Money Market Instruments Short-term, high-quality debt instruments such as Treasury bills, bankers' acceptances, certificates of deposit, commercial paper, and federal agency securities.

Mortgage A recorded note, recognized by law, securing the debt that provides the cash used to purchase real property. The property is held in the name of the buyer and may be repossessed in the case of default.

Moving Average Computation of, for example, a 30-week average by adding the stock's closing price of the current week to the closing prices of the previous 29 weeks and dividing by 30. As time passes, the weekly average becomes a "moving average" showing a smooth trend of prices.

Municipal Bonds Bonds issued by a state or political subdivision, such as county, town, or village. The term is also used for bonds issued by state agencies or authorities. In general, interest paid on municipal bonds is exempt from federal income tax and state and local taxes within the state of issue.

Mutual Fund An open-end investment company that continuously offers new shares to the public in addition to redeeming shares on demand as required by law. The terms *mutual fund* and *open-end investment fund* are used interchangeably.

NASDAQ National Association of Securities Dealers Automated Quotations; an automated information network that provides brokers and dealers with price quotations on securities traded over-the-counter.

No-Load Purchase of shares without payment of commission (load).

NOW Account Negotiated order of withdrawal (NOW)—a checking account that pays interest. A NOW certificate looks like a check but is not the legal equivalent of a check. Legally, a NOW is a negotiable order to withdraw money from a savings account.

NYSE New York Stock Exchange; the largest organized securities market in the United States, founded in 1792. The Exchange is a not-for-profit corporation governed by a board of directors.

Odd-Lot Trading Trading of an amount of stock less than the established 100-share unit or 10-share round lot. It is believed by some that the small odd-lot trader is usually wrong when buying aggressively at market highs and selling aggressively at market lows.

Operating Profit Margin Profit calculated as a percentage of sales before deducting depreciation, interest, and taxes. This calculation indicates how profitable the company's products are to manufacture and sell.

Option A right to buy (call) or sell (put) a fixed amount of a given stock within a limited period of time. The purchaser hopes that the stock's price will go up (if he or she bought a call) or down (if he or she bought a put) by a sufficient amount to provide a profit when the purchaser sells the option. Individuals may write (sell) as well as purchase options.

OTC *See* Over-the-Counter.

Over-the-Counter A market for securities made up of securities dealers who may or may not be members of a securities exchange. The over-the-counter market is conducted over the telephone and deals mainly in stock of companies without sufficient shares, stockholders, or earnings to warrant listing on an exchange.

Penny Stocks Low-priced issues, often highly speculative, selling at less than $1 per share. Many believe that penny stocks that reach a dollar should be sold and never bought. Some penny stocks develop into investment-caliber issues, mainly on the OTC market.

P/E Ratio Current market price of a stock divided by the annual corporate earnings per share. When a stock sells below its historical P/E range, it is probably undervalued if the corporate prospects are favorable.

Points One percent of the mortgage loan amount. Points are a onetime charge levied by the lender at closing in order to increase the return on the loan.

Portfolio Value The total value of all investment assets purchased by an investor.

Preferred Stock Stock that has a claim on a corporation's earnings, dividends, and assets ahead of common stock but behind debt obligations.

Price/Earnings Ratio *See* P/E Ratio.

Put *See* Option.

Random Walk Theory The theory that stock prices move at random and not in accord with predictable patterns of behavior. Hence, stock market analysis is pointless since nothing can be gained from studying trends, patterns, or the inherent strength or weakness of individual stocks.

Redemption Price Price at which a bond may be redeemed before maturity at the option of the issuing company. Redemption value also applies to the price the company must pay to call in certain types of preferred stock.

REIT (Real Estate Investment Trust) An organization similar to an investment company in some respects but concentrating its holdings in real estate investments. The yield is generally liberal since REIT's are required to distribute as much as 90 percent of their income.

Renegotiable Rate Mortgage (RRM) A mortgage in which the rate of interest increases or decreases at specified intervals over the life of the loan.

Repurchase Agreement (Repo) Where a bank contracts with a customer such as an investment house to sell securities from the bank's portfolio and repurchase them the next day at a price that includes a "profit" or interest to the customer.

Rollover Retaining the tax-deferred status of pension proceeds by a rollover (transfer) into an Individual Retirement Account.

Rollover Mortgage Renegotiation of an existing mortgage that is rolled over (replaced) by a new mortgage reflecting current market conditions.

Salary Reduction Plan Use of tax-sheltered annuities available only to employees of educational institutions and certain other nonprofit organizations. An employee is permitted to reduce current or next year's salary by an amount equal to that being contributed to the annuity plan. An appropriate reduction-in-salary agreement must be signed in advance.

SEPP Simplified Employee Pension Plan (SEPP)—established to allow employees to use an Individual Retirement Account rather than a qualified pension plan. The employer makes contributions in an employee's name into an IRA. The maximum contribution is 15 percent of the employee's pay, up to $15,000 per year. The employer can deduct the full amount of the IRA contribution from the company's taxes so long as the pension plan qualifies as nondiscriminatory.

Settlement Costs *See* Closing Costs.

Shared Appreciation Mortgage Below-market interest rates with lower monthly payments, in exchange for a share of the profits (appreciation in home's value) when the property is sold or transferred at a later date.

Short Sale A trading technique that involves selling borrowed stock in anticipation that the same number of shares will be repurchased later at a lower price. Investors sell stock short when they expect the price to fall.

Spread Purchase of one security, option, or contract against the sale of another in the same or related market. The speculator anticipates that the difference in price will change sufficiently to make the trade profitable.

Stock Index Futures Contracts are promises to buy or sell a standardized amount of a stock index by some specified date. The Chicago Mercantile Exchange offers contracts on Standard & Poor's 500; the New York Futures Exchange offers contracts based on the New York Stock Exchange Composite and Financial Indexes; and the Kansas City Board of Trade offers contracts on the Value Line Composite Index.

Stock Split An increase in the number of corporate shares outstanding by means of a reduction in par value. Although the number of shares is increased, the equity remains the same. Ordinarily, splits must be voted by the directors of a corporation and approved by its shareholders.

Straddle Purchase of both a put and a call option simultaneously on the same stock. This is a double stock option contract with identical exercise prices, which entitles the holder to demand (call) or deliver (put) the stock named in the contract on or before a fixed date.

Strategic Metals Metals and minerals critical to national defense—for example, antimony, beryllium, manganese, rhodium, uranium, and vanadium.

Super-NOW Account A high-yield checking account offered by many banks and thrift institutions, which establish the rate of interest paid. A minimum balance of $2,500 is required. The maximum interest is 5¼ percent if the balance falls below the minimum. There is no limitation on the number of checks that can be drawn against the account.

Sweep Account A bank account linked to a money market fund. The first $2,500 is funneled into a NOW account paying 5¼ percent interest, while amounts above the minimum amount are swept, sometimes daily, into a higher paying money fund. Checks are drawn first against the money market pool and then against the balance in the NOW account.

Takeover (Merger) A transaction in which one corporation acquires the assets and liabilities of another corporation, and the acquired corporation's legal existence is terminated. The takeover may be friendly or involve a proxy fight.

Tax Deferral Postponement of the payment of taxes until some time in the future when probably an individual will be taxed at a lower rate.

Tax Deferred Annuity Annuities are contracts sold by insurance companies providing guaranteed income, usually on retirement, in return for the money paid to them. The earnings in the account are accumulated tax free until payments start, at which time they are subject to taxation.

Tax Haven Countries, usually small geographically, which impose little or no income tax on noncitizens. Several types exist: no-tax havens with no or negligible internal taxes, low-tax havens, and special-purpose tax havens. Although tax havens, such as the Cayman Islands, offer a perfectly legal means of tax avoidance, it is not possible under U.S. law to carry on a legal, covert tax-haven operation.

Tax Shelter Any device of investment that permits an individual the legal right to avoid, reduce, or defer tax liabilities. This can involve individual investments such as in municipal or other tax-exempt bonds; or investments in real estate, oil and gas, and cattle ranching, in which the investor gains not only fully or partially tax-free returns but also, in many cases, enough excess deductions and credits to reduce his or her current tax bill.

Technical Analysis An approach to investing based on analysis of supply and demand. Technicians believe that everything influencing investors is precisely revealed in the behavior of stock prices and trading volume. "Only the market tells the story." Technicians study price movements, volume, trends, and patterns and chart these factors in an attempt to project future market activity.

Tenancy by the Entirety Joint ownership of property by husband and wife with right of survivorship (property goes to the survivor in the case of death of one of the parties).

Tenancy in Common Sharing of property by two or more co-buyers without the right of survivorship. The percentage of ownership may not be equal.

Tender Offer A public offer to buy shares from stockholders of one public corporation by another company usually at a price above that prevailing in the open market. Stockholders are asked to "tender" (surrender) their holdings for a stated value over a certain time period.

TIGRS "Treasury Investment Growth Receipts" on portfolios of stripped Treasury issues. These are bonds with their interest-rate coupons removed. Several Wall Street brokerage firms, such as Merrill Lynch, have bought coupon-bearing, long-term Treasury bonds and stripped the coupons. Each component is then sold separately. The bond becomes, in effect, a zero-coupon bond with the guarantee of the U.S. Treasury.

Title Insurance Coverage that protects the owner and the mortgagee against losses due to defects in the title that were not discovered in the title search.

Treasury Bills (T-Bills) Issued in three-month, six-month, and one-year maturities sold at Federal Reserve auctions to those bidders offering the highest price (i.e., the lowest interest cost to the U.S. Treasury).

Treasury Bonds Interest-bearing negotiable bonds, issued in $1,000 units with a maturity of ten years or longer. The only difference between Treasury bonds and Treasury notes is that bonds are issued in longer maturities.

Treasury Notes Notes issued by the U.S. Treasury at or very near face value and redeemed at face value. Notes have an original maturity of one to ten years. Currently, the Treasury issues two- and four-year notes on a regular cycle. Notes, like bills, are sold through auctions held by the Federal Reserve.

Trustee Person or institution designated by the trustor or assigned by a court to administer a trust.

Trustor Creator of a trust.

Unit Investment Trust A type of mutual fund sponsored by some of the larger brokerage firms. Once the trust is established, and sold in units of $1,000, no securities within the trust are bought or sold. Income earned on the trust is paid out to the trust certificate holders as it is earned. The principal amount is refunded when the certificates mature.

Universal Life Insurance An alternative life insurance policy in which the cash values are invested in a variety of high-yield government securities. The tax on earnings during lifetime is deferred until the policy is surrendered. If the policy is retained until the death of the insured, the proceeds will be received by the beneficiary tax-free.

Vacation Time Sharing Purchase of a share of the ownership of a vacation property in units of time, for example, two weeks in a year. Ownership may be fee simple, in which a person receives clear title and a deed to his or her share, a right-to-use arrangement giving a long-term lease, or simply a membership.

Warrant A certificate giving the holder the right to purchase securities at a stipulated price within a specified time limit or perpetually. Sometimes a warrant is issued with securities as an inducement to buy.

"Wild Card" Certificate Certificates of deposit, maturing in two and a half years or longer. Banks and thrift institutions are free to pay whatever interest they choose and to establish the required minimum deposit.

Wraparound Mortgage A variation of a second mortgage in which the seller keeps the original low rate mortgage. The buyer than makes payments to the seller, who forwards a portion to the lender holding the original mortgage. This "wraparound" offers a lower effective rate of interest on the total transaction.

Yankee CDs Certificates of deposit held in American branches of foreign banks.

Yield The dividends or interest paid by a company or institution expressed as a percentage of the current price. Also known as return.

Zero-Coupon Bond These pay no interest but are priced at a discount of their redemption price. They offer the promise of reward through capital gains, which are normally taxed at a lower rate than income received as interest.

ACKNOWLEDGMENTS

Note: In the preparation of this glossary the following sources were consulted for the purpose of compiling definitions of terms.

Amling, Frederick, and Droms, William G. *Personal Financial Planning.* Homewood, IL: Dow Jones-Irwin, 1982.
Beer, Edith Lynn. *Monarch's Dictionary of Investment Terms.* New York: Monarch Press, 1983.
Brownstone, David M., and Sartisky, Jacques. *Personal Financial Survival: A Guide for the 1980's and Beyond.* New York: Wiley, 1981.
Darst, David M. *The Handbook of the Bond and Money Markets.* New York: McGraw-Hill, 1981.
Fabozzi, Frank J., and Zarb, Frank G. *Handbook of Financial Markets: Securities, Options and Futures.* Homewood, IL: Dow Jones-Irwin, 1981.
Hardy, C. Colburn. *Dun and Bradstreet's Guide to $ Your Investments $.* 27th Edition. New York: Harper & Row, 1982.
Hughes, Alan. *A Home of Your Own for the Least Cash: The Home Buyer's Guide for Today.* Washington, DC: Acropolis, 1982.
The Language of Investing: Glossary. New York: New York Stock Exchange, 1981.
LeClair, Robert T., Leimberg, Stephen R., and Chasman, Herbert. *Money and Retirement: How to Plan for Lifetime Financial Security.* Reading, MA: Addison-Wesley, 1982.
Little, Jeffery B., and Rhodes, Lucien. *Understanding Wall Street.* Cockeysville, MD: Liberty, 1978.
Ludy, Andrew. *Condominium Ownership: A Buyer's Guide.* Landing, NJ: Landing Press, 1982.
The Mortgage Money Guide: Creative Financing for Home Buyers from the Federal Trade Commission. Washington, DC: Federal Trade Commission, 1982.
Nauheim, Ferd. *The Retirement Money Book.* Washington, DC: Acropolis, 1982.
Raphaelson, Elliot. *Planning Your Financial Future: Tax Shelters, Annuities, IRA's, Keoghs, Stocks and Other Investment or Retirement Opportunities.* New York: Wiley, 1982.
Rolo, Charles J. *Gaining on the Market: Your Complete Guide to Investment Strategy: Stocks, Bonds, Options, Mutual Funds and Gold.* Boston: Little, Brown, 1982.
Speraw, Linda. *How to Buy Your First Home.* New York: Facts on File, 1983.
Tannenhauser, Robert, and Tannenhauser, Carol. *Tax Shelters: A Complete Guide.* New York: New American Library, 1980.
Tewles, Richard, and Bradley, Edward. *The Stock Market.* 4th Edition. New York: Wiley, 1982.
Van Caspel, Venita. *Money Dynamics for the 1980's.* Reston, VA: Reston, 1980.

Directory of Pamphlet Resource Organizations

Action for Independent Maturity
1909 K St., NW
Washington, DC 20049

AFL-CIO Department of Community
   Service
815 Sixteenth St., NW
Washington, DC 20006

Alliance of American Insurers
20 N. Wacker Dr.
Chicago, IL 60606

American Association of Individual
   Investors
Dept. WD
612 N. Michigan Ave.
Chicago, IL 60611

American Association of Retired
   Persons
National Retired Teachers Association
215 Long Beach Blvd.
Long Beach, CA 90801

American Bankers Association
1120 Connecticut Ave., NW
Washington, DC 20036

American Bar Association
1155 E. 60 St.
Chicago, IL 60637

American Board of Trade
9 S. William St.
New York, NY 10004

American Council of Life Insurance
1850 K St., NW
Washington, DC 20006

American Express
Public Affairs and Communication
American Express Plaza
New York, NY 10004

American Institute for Economic
   Research
Great Barrington, MA 01230

American Institute of Real Estate Appraisers
430 N. Michigan Ave.
Chicago, IL 60611

American Land Development Association
1000 Sixteenth St., NW
Suite 604
Washington, DC 20036

American Rental Association
2920 23rd Ave.
Moline, IL 61265

American Society of Appraisers
Box 17265
Washington, DC 20041

American Society of Internal Medicine
1101 Vermont Ave., NW
Suite 500
Washington, DC 20005

American Stock Exchange
86 Trinity Place
New York, NY 10006

Associated Credit Bureaus, Inc.
16211 Park 10 Place
Box 218300
Houston, TX 77218

Association of Publicly Traded Investment Funds
Information Bureau
201 N. Charles St.
Baltimore, MD 21201

At Home Abroad, Inc.
Sutton Town House
405 E. 56 St.
New York, NY 10022

The Attorney General of Ohio
30 E. Broad St.
Columbus, OH 43215

Bank of America
Box 37128
San Francisco, CA 94137

Bankers Life
Bankers Life Company
Des Moines, IA 50307

Banyan Books
Box 431160
Miami, FL 33143

Board of Governors of the Federal Reserve System
20th and Constitution Ave., NW
Washington, DC 20551

Business and Professional Women's Foundation
2012 Massachusetts Ave., NW
Washington, DC 20036

The CHB Company
Box 184
Los Altos, CA 94022

Chicago Board of Trade
La Salle at Jackson
Chicago, IL 60604

Chicago Board Options Exchange
La Salle at Jackson
Chicago, IL 60604

Chicago Mercantile Exchange
444 West Jackson Blvd.
Chicago, IL 60606

Chicago Mercantile Exchange, Index and Option Market. *See* **Chicago Mercantile Exchange**

Chicago Mercantile Exchange, International Monetary Market. *See* **Chicago Mercantile Exchange**

Commodity Exchange, Inc.
4 World Trade Center
New York, NY 10048

Commodity Futures Trading Commission
2033 K St., NW
Washington, DC 20581

Consumer Credit Education Foundation
1000 Sixteenth St., NW
Washington, DC 20036

Consumer Credit Project, Inc.
261 Kimberly, Dept. T
Barrington, IL 60010

Council of Better Business Bureaus, Inc.
1150 Seventeenth St., NW
Washington, DC 20036

Credit Union National Association
Box 431
Madison, WI 53701

Deloitte, Haskins and Sells
1114 Ave. of the Americas
New York, NY 10036

Direct Mail Marketing Association
6 E. 43 St.
New York, NY 10017

Direct Selling Education Foundation
1730 M St., NW
Suite 610
Washington, DC 20036

Di$count America Guide
51 E. 42 St.
Suite 417
New York, NY 10017

Energy Advisor, Inc.
Box 481
Shrewsbury, MA 01545

The Family Housing Bureau
Chicago Title Insurance Company
111 W. Washington St.
Chicago, IL 60602

Federal Deposit Insurance Corporation
550 Seventeenth St., NW
Washington, DC 20429

Federal Reserve Bank of Boston
Bank and Information Center
600 Atlantic Ave.
Boston, MA 02106

Federal Reserve Bank of Chicago
Public Information Center
Box 834
Chicago, IL 60690

Federal Reserve Bank of New York
Public Information Dept.
33 Liberty St.
New York, NY 10045

Federal Reserve Bank of Philadelphia
Dept. of Consumer Affairs
Box 66
Philadelphia, PA 19105

Federal Reserve Bank of Richmond
Bank and Public Relations Dept.
Box 27622
Richmond, VA 23261

Federal Reserve Bank of San Francisco
Box 7702
San Francisco, CA 94120

Federal Trade Commission
Bureau of Consumer Protection
Washington, DC 20580

Federal Trade Commission, Bureau of Consumer Protection, Office of Consumer Education. *See* **Federal Trade Commission**

Fidelity Group
Box 832, Dept. JaR03182
82 Devonshire St.
Boston, MA 02103

Food Marketing Institute
1750 K St., NW
Washington, DC 20006

Futures Industry Association, Inc.
1919 Pennsylvania Ave., NW
Washington, DC 20006

General Motors Acceptance Corporation
767 Fifth Ave.
New York, NY 10022

Health Insurance Association of America
1850 K St., NW
Washington, DC 20006

Holiday Exchanges
Box 878
Belen, NM 87002

House Master of America
18 Hamilton St.
Bound Brook, NJ 08805

E. F. Hutton and Company
Box 10318
Des Moines, IA 50306

Inform, Inc.
25 Broad St.
New York, NY 10004

Information USA
1000 Connecticut Ave., NW, #9
Washington, DC 20036

Institute for Information Studies
200 Little Falls St.
Suite 104
Falls Church, VA 22046

Institute of Real Estate Management
430 N. Michigan Ave.
Chicago, IL 60611

Insurance Information Institute
110 William St.
New York, NY 10038

International Paper Company
Dept. 8
Box 954
Madison Square Station
New York, NY 10010

InterService Home Exchange
Box 87
Glen Echo, MD 20812

Investment Company Institute
1775 K St., NW
Washington, DC 20006

Kansas City Board of Trade
4800 Main St.
Suite 274
Kansas City, MO 64112

Kemper Insurance Companies
Long Grove, IL 60049

Lawyers Title Insurance Corporation
Box 27567
Richmond, VA 23261

League of Women Voters of the U.S.A.
1730 M St., NW
Washington, DC 20036

Life Care Society of America
Ferry and Iron Hill Rds.
Doylestown, PA 18901

Life Insurance Marketing and Research Association, Inc.
Box 208
Hartford, CT 06141

Main Hurdman
Publications Dept. WD
55 E. 52 St.
New York, NY 10055

Manpower Education Institute
127 E. 35 St.
New York, NY 10016

Manufactured Housing Institute
1745 Jefferson Davis Highway
Suite 511
Arlington, VA 22202

Merrill Lynch, Pierce, Fenner and Smith, Inc.
25 Broadway
New York, NY 10004

Merrill Lynch Service Center
Box 2021
Jersey City, NJ 07303

Minneapolis Grain Exchange
400 South St.
Minneapolis, MN 55415

Money Management Institute
2700 Sanders Rd.
Prospect Heights, IL 60070

Mortgage Bankers Association of America
1125 Fifteenth St., NW
Washington, DC 20005

National Association of Home Builders
Fifteenth and M Sts., NW
Washington, DC 20005

National Association of Housing Cooperatives
2501 M St., NW
Suite 451
Washington, DC 20037

National Association of Investment Clubs
1515 E. Eleven Mile Rd.
Royal Oak, MI 48067

National Association of Mature People
Box 26792
Oklahoma City, OK 73126

National Consumer Finance Association
1000 Sixteenth St., NW
Washington, DC 20036

National Foundation for Consumer Credit, Inc.
1819 H St., NW
Washington, DC 20006

National Independent Automobile Dealers Association
3700 National Dr.
Suite 208
Raleigh, NC 27612

National Insurance Consumer Organization
344 Commerce St.
Alexandria, VA 22314

National Society of Public Accountants
1010 N. Fairfax St.
Alexandria, VA 22314

New Orleans Commodity Exchange
308 Board of Trade Place
New Orleans, LA 70130

New York Cotton Exchange
4 World Trade Center
New York, NY 10048

New York Futures Exchange
20 Broad St.
New York, NY 10005

New York Life Insurance Company
51 Madison Ave.
New York, NY 10010

New York Mercantile Exchange
4 World Trade Center
New York, NY 10048

New York State Banking Department
Consumer Affairs Division
2 World Trade Center
New York, NY 10047

New York Stock Exchange
11 Wall St.
New York, NY 10005

No-Load Mutual Fund Association
Valley Forge, PA 19481

North Carolina Bar Association
1025 Wade Ave.
Raleigh, NC 27605

Pension Benefit Guaranty Corporation
2020 K St., NW
Washington, DC 20006

Pension Rights Center
1346 Connecticut Ave., NW
Washington, DC 20036

Phoenix Mutual Life Insurance
    Company
Hartford, CT 06115

The President's Committee on Employment of the Handicapped
Washington, DC 20210

Public Affairs Committee
381 Park Ave. South
New York, NY 10016

Real Estate Education Company
500 N. Dearborn St.
Chicago, IL 60610

Reymont Associates
6556 SW Maple
Boca Raton, FL 33433

Society of Real Estate Appraisers
645 N. Michigan Ave.
Chicago, IL 60611

Springhill Press
Box 1762
Silver Spring, MD 20902

Standard and Poor's Corporation
25 Broadway
New York, NY 10004

State of California-State and Consumer Services
Dept. of Consumer Affairs
1020 N St.
Sacramento, CA 95814

Travel Enterprises
3602 W. Glen Branch
Peoria, IL 61614

The Travelers Insurance Companies
One Tower Square
Hartford, CT 06115

U.S. Dept. of Agriculture
Washington, DC 20250

U.S. Dept. of Education
400 Maryland Ave., SW
Washington, DC 20202

U.S. Dept. of Health and Human Services, Health Care Financing Administration
Baltimore, MD 21235

U.S. Dept. of Health and Human Services, Social Security Administration
6401 Security Boulevard
Baltimore, MD 21235

U.S. Dept. of Housing and Urban Development
Washington, DC 20410

U.S. Dept. of Labor
Labor-Management Services Administration
Washington, DC 20216

U.S. Dept. of the Interior
Bureau of Land Management
Washington, DC 20240

U.S. Dept. of the Treasury, Internal Revenue Service
Washington, DC 20224

U.S. Dept. of the Treasury, U.S. Savings Bonds Division
Washington, DC 20226

U.S. Railroad Retirement Board
844 Rush St.
Chicago, IL 60611

U.S. Securities and Exchange Commission
Washington, DC 20549

Vacation Exchange Club
350 Broadway
New York, NY 10013

Vacation Horizons International
9333 N. Meridian St.
Box 80348, Dept. B
Indianapolis, IN 46280

Veterans Administration
Washington, DC 20420

Subject Index

Advisory newsletters, 178–183
Agriculture, yearbook, 35
Almanacs, as reference sources, 224
American Stock Exchange, 14
Annuities
    pamphlets on, 190
    see also Taxes and tax forms
Appraisals, pamphlets on, 190
Astrology and the stock market, 84
Auctions, 101
Audits. See Taxes and tax forms
Automobiles, 26, 30, 31, 37, 102–103
    see also Insurance

Bank credit, 55
Bank scandals, 40
Bank Secrecy Act of 1970, 27
Banking, 25, 28, 29, 40, 62–63
    international, 24, 27
    pamphlets on, 190–191
    Swiss, 44, 62–63
Bankruptcy, 46, 63–66
    pamphlets on, 190, 196–197
Bankruptcy Reform Act of 1978, 64

Banks. See Banking
Bartering, 57–59
BASIC programs. See Computers
Bear market, 85, 87
Bibliographies, 9–21
    futures markets, 16, 17
    insurance, 18
    investing, 10, 12, 13, 16, 17
    personal finance, 10, 11
    popular, 10–15
    professional/technical, 16–21
    stocks, 13, 14, 16
    taxes, 11, 12
Blacks
    magazines for, 167
    money problems of, 28
Bonds, 94–95
    pamphlets on, 191, 213
    see also Stock market, stocks
Borrowing, 26, 27, 28, 35, 53–55
    see also Investments; Student aid
British publications, 16
Brokers. See Homes; Stock
    market, stocks

247

Subject Index

Budgeting, 27, 29, 49
  pamphlets on, 191-192
Bull market, 86, 87
Business data, 10-12, 16-18, 20
  see also Investments; Stock market, stocks
Business libraries, 18-19
Business periodicals, 163-175

Certified Financial Planner Program, 12
Charging. See Credit
Chart services, as reference sources, 220-221
Checking accounts, 26, 63
  pamphlets on, 192
Children and money, 25, 34, 49-50, 62, 63
  books for, 24, 50, 63
  pamphlets on, 192
  see also Families; Student aid
Closed-end funds, 81
Coins, 24, 41, 44, 98, 101, 102
Collectibles, 24, 28, 41, 72, 101-103
College expenses
  pamphlets on, 192-193
  see also Student aid
College for Financial Planning, 12
College loans and programs. See Student aid
College personnel tax guides, 125
Commodities, 24, 27, 72, 89, 91, 93-94
Commodity Exchange (COMEX), 14
Commodity exchanges, 18
Commodity futures trading, 17, 21, 90-94, 187-188
Company information, as reference sources, 217-220
Complaints, consumer. See Consumers, redress
Computers, 51, 72-73, 142
Condominiums, co-ops, 25, 35, 108, 113-115
  pamphlets on, 193
Consumer complaints, 26

Consumer magazines, 163-172
Consumer Price Index, 33
Consumers, 23-66
  children, 49-50
  families, 45-46
  general money data, 23-29
  home money-making tips, 50-51
  and inflation, 38-45
  money-saving tips, 30-37
  publications for, 163-175, 193
  redress, 37-38
  women, 46-49
  see also Financial planning; Personal Finance
Contests and sweepstakes. See Lotteries
Contractors, 34
Corporate finance. See Business data
Counseling, financial, 46
  see also Consumers
Couponing, 59-60
Crashes. See Panics and crashes
Creative financing. See Mortgages
Credit, 23, 24, 26, 27, 28, 29, 42, 46, 53-55, 63
  pamphlets on, 193-196
  and women, 15, 55
Credit bureaus. See Credit
Credit cards. See Credit
Credit unions, pamphlets on, 192
Currency, 24, 44, 97
Cycles, stock market, 69

Data bases, 20
Debt, 46
  see also Bankruptcy; Borrowing
Deductions, tax. See Taxes and tax forms, deductions
Depressions, 38-39, 40
Diamonds. See Gems
Dictionaries, as reference sources, 224-225
Digests, newsletter, 185-186
Directories, as reference sources, 221-222
Disinflation, 73

Subject Index 249

Divorce, 26
   see also Men; Women
Dow Jones guides, 35, 56, 75, 91, 96, 141, 153
Dow Jones Industrial Average, 75, 84, 86
   see also Stock market, stocks
Dowbeaters, 75, 80
Duck clubs, movement, 42
Dun and Bradstreet, 13, 71

Earning money
   at home, 50, 51
   extra, 33
   second incomes, 32
   see also Investments; Moonlighting
Economic Recovery Tax Act of 1981, 132, 133, 134, 143
Electronic fund transfer, pamphlets on, 197
Elliott wave principle, 21, 88
Encyclopedias, 25-26
   as reference sources, 222-224
Energy savings, 35
Escrow, 106
Estate planning, 26, 27, 44, 149, 197
European Geological Laboratory, (EGL), 100
Exchange rates, 25

Fads, investing in, 25
Families, 26, 45-46, 69, 144
   see also Consumers; Estate planning
Fashion/beauty magazines, 165-166
Federal Reserve, 14, 29, 40, 69
   pamphlets on, 191
Federal Trade Commission, 29, 54
Financial planning, 11, 12, 27, 45-46, 141-161
Financial reports, 83
Financial traps, 24
Fine art, 101-102, 103
Fixed-income securities, as reference sources, 220
Flea market selling, 30

Forecasting. *See* Stock market, stocks
Foreclosure. *See* Mortgages
Foreign exchanges, 92
Frauds, rackets. *See* Redress by consumers
Free tax help. *See* Taxes and tax forms, free help
Funerals, 26
Futures, 27, 70, 77, 80, 90-94, 99
   bibliographies, 16, 17
   pamphlets on, 197-199

Games of chance. *See* Lotteries
Gardening magazines, 167
Gemological Institute of America (GIA), 100
Gems, 27, 28, 72, 97, 100-101
   pamphlets on, 199
Gift taxes. *See* Estate planning
Ginnie Maes, 119
Glossaries, as reference sources, 224-225
Gold, 25, 27, 28, 41, 42, 44, 72, 84, 96-99
   pamphlets on, 199
Grants. *See* Student aid
Growth companies, 85
Growth stocks, 78-86
   newsletters on, 183-184
   see also Stock market, stocks
Guides, as reference sources, 222-224

H and R Block guides, 37, 129
Handbooks, as reference sources, 222-224
Health insurance, 18, 159-161
Home businesses, 50-51
Homes, 25, 26, 27, 28, 35-36, 105-114
   condominiums, co-ops, 25, 35, 108, 113-115, 193
   contractors, 34
   mobile, 25, 115
   mortgages, 111-114
   recycling, 124
   resort time sharing, 116

Homes (cont.)
  retirement, 147-148, 149, 150
  see also Real estate

IRAs, 29, 80, 149, 150-152
  pamphlets on, 202-203
IRS, 14-15, 27, 125, 127, 128, 131, 134, 137-138
  publications of, 14, 15
  see also Taxes and tax forms
Income, increasing, 32-33
Income taxes. See Taxes and tax forms
Indexes. See Bibliographies
Indicators, stock. See Stock market, stocks
Individual investors, 12-13
  see also Personal finance
Industry reference sources, 217-220
Inflation, 10, 25, 28, 30, 33-34, 38-45, 57, 60, 68, 72, 74, 75, 82, 85, 91, 119, 120, 125
  pamphlets on, 200
Inheritance taxes. See Estate planning
Insurance, 26, 27, 28, 29, 157-159
  auto, 25, 158
  bibliographies, 18
  health, 18
  industry, 159
  life, 18, 23, 25, 35, 157
  Medicare, 159-161
  old age, 24
  pamphlets on, 200-202
  social security, 159-161
  survivors, 24
International banking. See Banking, international
International investments, 24, 83
Investment experts, 86
Investments, 23-29, 39, 40, 46-49, 67-74, 149
  bibliographies, 10, 12, 13, 16, 17
  international, 24, 83
  low-risk, 81
  money market, 69
  newsletters on, 177-188

oil and gas, 68
over-the-counter, 68
pamphlets on, 203
periodicals on, 170-172
reference sources, 217-225
see also Collectibles; Gems; Gold; Newsletters, investment; Stock market, stocks
Investors, strategies of, 86

Keogh accounts, 23, 80, 149, 150-152

Lawyers, hiring, 23
Liquidations, 82
Living rich, 23, 51, 52, 61-62, 70-71
Living single, 27, 130
Living together, 24
Loans. See Borrowing; Homes
Loopholes, tax. See Taxes and tax forms
Lotteries, 61-62
Love and money. See Psychology of money
Low-risk investments, 81

Magazines
  black concerns, 167
  business, 170-172
  career, 166
  consumer concerns, 168
  family, 164-165
  fashion, 165-166
  futures, 174
  garden, 167
  investment, 170-172
  money management, 169-170
  news, 168-169
  retirement/preretirement, 167-168
  stock market, 174-175
  women's, 164-165
Managing money. See Consumers
Marketplace, rights in, 26
Markets, financial, 70

Medicare, 159-161
Men
  legal rights of, 29
  magazines for, 167
Mergers, 82
  newsletter on, 181
Metals, strategic, 99-100
Mobile homes, 25, 115
Monetary policy, 26, 28
Money and consumers
  banks, 62-63
  bartering, 57-59
  borrowing, 53-55
  children, 49-50
  coupons, 59-60
  credit, 53-55
  debt, 63-66
  earning at home, 50-51
  family concerns, 45-46
  general data, 23-29
  inflation, 38-45
  lotteries, 61-62
  money-saving tips, 30-37
  psychology, 51-53
  redress, 37-38
  refunding, 59-60
  student aid, 55-57
  travel, 60-61
  unemployment, 63
  women, 46-49
Money making at home, 50-51
Money Management Institute, pamphlets on, 192
Money management pamphlets, 204
Money management, personal. *See* Personal finance
Money markets, 41, 69, 73-74, 96
Money-saving tips, 30-37
  pamphlets on, 204-206
Moonlighting, 34
Mortgages, 23, 29, 35, 111-114, 116-124
  pamphlets on, 202
Mutual funds, 23, 25, 84, 95-96
  newsletters on, 186-187
  pamphlets on, 206
Myths of the money market, 73-74

National Association of Securities Dealers (NASD), 68
National Association of Securities Dealers Quotation (NASDAQ), 68, 77
Natural resources. *See* Metals, strategic
New York Public Interest Research Group, 38
News magazines, 168-169
Newsletters, 10-11
  investment, 177-188
Newspapers, 172-175
  special topic, 173-175
No-load funds, 95
NOW accounts, 15
  pamphlets on, 206

Oil and gas investments, 68
Options, 25, 70, 80, 84, 90
  pamphlets on, 206-207
Over-the-counter securities, 68, 174
Overseas investments. *See* Investments, international

Pamphlet resources, 189-215
Panics and crashes, 43, 44
Paper money, 43
Penny capitalism, 32
Penny stocks, 94, 185
  newspapers on, 174-175
Pensions, pamphlets on, 207
Performance ratings, newsletters, 185-186
Periodicals. *See* Business periodicals
Personal finance, 12, 25-29, 141-146
  bibliographies, 10, 11
  magazines on, 169-170
  see also Consumers
Personal guides. *See* Consumers, general money data
Personal money management. *See* Financial planning
Personal relationships, 51
  see also Living single; Living together; Men; Women

Subject Index

Planetary influence on stocks, 84
Planning. *See* Financial planning
Popular interest bibliographies, 10–15
Preparing tax returns, 125–134
Print/nonprint sources, 19, 24
Probate. *See* Estate planning
Professional/technical bibliographies, 16–21
Property
  country, 121
  distressed, 122
  see also Homes; Real estate
Psychology of money, 51–53
Psychology, stock market, 89–90
Publications
  consumer, 163–175
  IRS, 15
  newsletters, investment, 177–188
  pamphlets, 189–215

Racetrack investing, 73
Real estate, 23, 24, 25, 26, 28, 39, 41, 42, 105–124
  pamphlets on, 207–209
  taxes, 138–139
Recessions, 41
Recycling homes, 124
Redemptions, 82
Redress by consumers, 37–38
Reference books. *See* Bibliographies
Reference sources, investments and securities, 217–225
Refunding, 59–60
Rehabilitating property, 118
Relationships. *See* Divorce; Families; Living together; Men; Women
Rental homes, 119
Renting, rents, 26, 50
Reporting services, newsletters, 178–183
Resort time sharing, 116
  pamphlets on, 213
Retirement planning, 24, 25, 26, 27, 28, 29, 35, 39, 145–152
  discounts, 61
  magazines on, 167–168
  pamphlets on, 210
  taxes, 130
Risks, 24, 68, 79, 85, 90

Salary traps, 26
Saving money tips, 26
Savings, 35, 41, 52
Savings and loan associations, 29, 63
Scholarships. *See* Student aid
Second incomes, 32, 33
Securities, 41, 68, 70, 76, 79, 126
  pamphlets on, 213
  reference sources, 217–225
Securities and Exchange Commission, 82
Selection guides. *See* Bibliographies
Self-help. *See* Consumers
Selling guides, 33
Shopping guides, 30–31, 37, 50
  see also Couponing
Silver, 25, 41, 42, 72, 96–99
Single living, 27, 109, 118
  taxes, 130
Social security, 26, 29, 42, 159–161
  pamphlets on, 210–211
Speculating, 14
Spin-offs, 82
"Squeezes," 31, 75
Stamps, 41, 101, 103
Standard of living, 32
Stock exchanges, 14, 18
  see also Stock market, stocks
Stock market, stocks, 13, 14, 21, 23, 24, 25, 26, 28, 29, 35, 67–90, 149
  bibliographies, 13, 14, 16
  bonds, 94–95
  growth, 78–86, 183–184
  low-priced, newsletters on, 184–185
  over-the-counter, 68, 174, 89
  pamphlets on, 211
  penny, 94, 174–175, 185
  planetary influence on, 84
  psychology of, 89–90
  strategy, 78–88
  technical analysis, 86–90
  see also Newsletters, investment

Stock quotations, 78
Strategic metals. *See* Metals, strategic
Student aid, 23, 28, 55–57
Super stocks, 79
Superintendent of Documents publications, 19–20
Swiss banks. *See* Banking

Tax cuts. *See* Estate planning
Tax law, 132–133
Tax shelters. *See* Taxes and tax forms, shelters
Taxes and tax forms, 10, 15, 26, 27, 28, 29, 35, 43, 59, 125–132
 annuities, 35, 149, 190
 audits, 23, 137–138
 bibliographies, 11, 12
 deductions, 133–134
 free help, 128
 havens, 24, 27, 29, 62, 137
 laws, 132–133
 loopholes, 132
 pamphlets on, 211–213
 preparing returns, 125–134
 shelters, 25, 28, 29, 110, 126; 134–136, 149, 211
 see also Estate planning; Financial planning; IRS; Real estate; Retirement planning
Teachers, taxes, 130
Technical analysis of stocks, 86–90
Teen spending, 50
 see also Children and money
Telephone companies. *See* Telephones
Telephones, 30, 31, 36, 37
Tenants' rights. *See* Renting, rents
Tender offers, 82
Time sharing. *See* Resort time sharing
Toll-free numbers, 31, 37

Trade clubs. *See* Bartering
Travel, 23, 60–61
 pamphlets on, 206
Treasury bills, pamphlets on, 213
Trusts, 156–157

Underground economy. *See* Bartering
Unemployment, 25, 57–58, 63
U.S. Reporting Requirements on International Currency Transactions, 69

Veterans benefits, 213–214

Wall Street, 20, 75, 76, 77, 82
 newsletter on, 183
 see also Stock market, stocks
Wealthy living, 23, 51, 52, 61–62, 70–71
Welfare, 24
Wills, trusts, 25, 26, 156–157
 pamphlets on, 214
 see also Estate planning
Winning money, 61–62
Women
 career magazines for, 166
 credit, 15, 55
 divorce, 15, 48
 guides for, 15
 investments, 46–49
 magazines for, 164–165
 marriage, 15
 pamphlets for, 214–215
 self-help, 46–49
 and stocks, 76–77
 working needs, 15, 166
 see also Men; Property

Author Index

Abert, Geoffry F. *After the Crash: How to Survive and Prosper During the Depression of the 1980's*, 38

Abrams, Don. *The Profit-Taker: The Proven Rapid Money-Maker in Good and Bad Markets*, 78

Abrecht, Stephen, and Locker, Michael. *CDE Stock Ownership Directory*, 221

Ackerman, Diane. *Getting Rich: A Smart Woman's Guide to Successful Money Management*, 46; *The Only Guide You'll Ever Need to Marry Money*, 46; *see also* Ackerman, Martin, and Ackerman, Diane

Ackerman, Martin, and Ackerman, Diane. *Living Rich: A Manual for Would-Be Big Spenders*, 23

Albin, Francis. *Consumer Economics and Personal Money Management*, 141

Aliber, Robert. *Your Money and Your Life: A Lifetime Approach to Money Management*, 67

Allen, Robert G. *Creating Wealth: How to Make it—And Keep It!*, 116; *Nothing Down: How to Buy Real Estate with Little or No Money Down*, 117

Amling, Frederick, and Droms, William G. *The Dow Jones-Irwin Guide to Personal Financial Planning*, 141

Anderson, B. Ray. *How to Save 50% or More on Your Income Tax—Legally*, 125; *How You Can Use Inflation to Beat the IRS*, 125

Anderson, Larry, jt. auth. *See* Hansen, George, and Anderson, Larry

Angwell, George. *Winning in the Commodities Market: A Money-Making Guide to Commodity Futures Trading*, 90

Ansbacher, Max G. *How to Profit from the Coming Bull Market*, 75

Appel, Gerald. *99 Ways to Make Money in a Depression*, 39; *The Stock Option and No Load Switch Fund Scalper's Manual*, 86

Author Index

Appelbaum, Judith. "The 1040 Form and All That," 10
Appleman, John. *How to Increase Your Money-Making Power in the 80's*, 30
Arenson, Karen. *The New York Times Guide to Making the New Tax Law Work for You*, 132; "What to Do with Money," 10
Assael, Michael. *Money Smarts*, 101
Auerbach, Sylvia. *An Insider's Guide to Auctions*, 101

Baker, Ruth. *Getting Rich in Real Estate Partnerships*, 117
Barash, Samuel. *How to Reduce Your Real Estate Taxes*, 138
Barnes, John. *More Money for Your Retirement*, 145
Barnes, Robert M. *Making High Profits in Uncertain Times*, 91
Barry, James A., Jr. *Financial Freedom: A Positive Strategy for Putting Your Money to Work*, 78
Bawly, Dan. *The Subterranean Economy*, 57
Beadle, Patricia. *Investing in the 80's: What to Buy and When*, 79
Beckhardt, Israel. *The Small Investor's Guide to Gold*, 96
Beer, Edith L. *Monarch's Dictionary of Investment Terms*, 224–225
Benge, Eugene J. *How to Lick Inflation Before It Licks You*, 39
Bercoon, Norman, jt. auth. *See* Ullman, James M., and Bercoon, Norman
Berg, Adriane. *Moneythink: Financial Planning Finally Made Easy*, 51
Bernstein, Allen. *Tax Guide for College Teachers and Other College Personnel (For Filing 1982 Tax Returns)*, 125
Bernstein, Jacob. *The Investor's Quotient: The Psychology of Successful Investing in Commodities and Stocks*, 89
Bettner, Jill. "What to Read on How to Invest During Shaky Times," 10
Bickley, John S., jt. auth. *See* Green, Thomas E., Osler, Robert W., and Bickley, John S.
Bierbrier, Doreen. *Living with Tenants: How to Happily Share Your House with Renters for Profit and Security*, 50
Bingham, Joan, and Riccio, Dolores. *The Smart Shopper's Guide to Food Buying and Preparation*, 30
Bladen, Ashby. *How to Cope with the Developing Financial Crisis*, 39
Blamer, Thomas, and Shulman, Richard. *Dow 3000: The Investment Opportunity of the 1980's*, 75
Block, Julian. *Tax Saving: A Year Round Guide*, 126
Blotnick, Srully. *Winning: The Psychology of Successful Investing*, 89
Blume, Marshall E. and Friedman, Jack F. *Encyclopedia of Investments*, 222
Boeckh, J. Anthony, and Coghlan, Richard. *The Stock Market and Inflation*, 75
Bohigan, Valerie. *Successful Flea Market Selling*, 30
Bondy, Susan. *How to Make Money Using Other People's Money*, 67
Bottom Line/Personal, Experts. *The Book of Inside Information*, 23
Bove, Alexander. *Joint Property: Everything You Must Know to Save Time, Trouble, and Money on Your Jointly Owned Property*, 105
Boyd, Brendan, jt. auth. *See* Engel, Louis, and Boyd, Brendan
Bradford, W. Murray, and Reed, Ronald. *Business Tax Deduction Master Guide: Strategies for Business and Professional People*, 126
Bradley, Edward S., jt. auth. *See*

Teweles, Richard J., and Bradley, Edward S.
Brealey, Richard A., and Pyle, Connie. *A Bibliography of Finance and Investment*, 16
Breckner, Steven K. *The Hard Money Book: An Insider's Guide to Successful Investment in Currency, Gold, Silver, and Precious Stones*, 97
Bridwell, Rodger. *The Battle for Financial Security: How to Invest in the Runaway 80's*, 68
Brien, Mimi. *Moneywise*, 47
Briles, Judith. *The Woman's Guide to Financial Savvy*, 47
Brock, Jeanne, jt. auth. See Ledford, Lowell, and Brock, Jeanne
Brosnahan, Tom. *Frommer's How to Beat the High Cost of Travel*, 60
Brosterman, Robert. *The Complete Estate Planning Guide: Updated to Include 1981 and 1982 Tax Changes*, 152
Brown, Fern. *The Great Money Machine: How Your Bank Works*, 62
Brown, Thomas E. *Layman's Guide to Oil and Gas Investments*, 68
Browne, Harry. *New Profits from the Monetary Crisis*, 39
Browne, Harry, and Coxon, Terry. *Inflation-Proofing Your Investments*, 39
Brownstone, David M., and Carruth, Gordon. *Where to Find Business Information: A Worldwide Guide for Everyone Who Needs the Answers to Business Questions*, 16
Brownstone, David M., and Franck, Irene M. *The VNR Investor's Dictionary*, 225
Brownstone, David M., and Sartisky, Jacques. *Personal Financial Survival: A Guide for the 1980's and Beyond*, 10, 142

Bruss, Robert. *The Smart Investor's Guide to Real Estate: Big Profits from Small Investments*, 117
Buckley, Julian, and Loll, Leo. *The Over-the-Counter Securities Market*, 68
Buechner, Robert. *Prosper through Tax Planning*, 126
Bullock, Paul. *How to Profit from Condominium Conversions*, 114
Burkett, Larry. *The Financial Planning Workbook*, 45
Burkett, Larry, and Procter, William. *How to Prosper in the Underground Economy*, 57
Burton, Robert H., and Petrello, George J. *Personal Finance*, 142
Burtt, George. *The Barter Way to Beat Inflation*, 57
Butcher, Lee. *The Condominium Book: Getting the Most for Your Money Revised for the 1980's*, 114

Cabot, Val. *Goldmining in Foreclosure Properties*, 117
Cahill, Thomas D. *How to Save Tax Dollars as a Homeowner*, 105
Callaghan, P. J. *How to Make a Will, How to Use Trusts*, 152
Cammack, Emerson, jt. auth. See Mehr, Robert, and Cammack, Emerson
Cantor, Gilbert. *How to Avoid Estate Taxes*, 152
Cappiello, Frank. *Finding the Next Super Stock*, 79
Cardiff, Gray E., and English, John. *The Coming Real Estate Crash*, 117
Carlucci, Rocco, jt. auth. See Gargiulo, Albert F., and Carlucci, Rocco
Carruth, Gordon, jt. auth. See Brownstone, David M., and Carruth, Gordon

Carter, Malcolm N., "There's Help Out There: Knowing You Don't Have to Do It Alone Can Make the Difference Between Success and Not Even Getting Started," 11

Casey, Douglas. *Crisis Investing: Opportunities and Profits in the Coming Great Depression*, 40; *International Investing: The Complete Databook to the World's Last Frontiers for Smart Money Management Overseas*, 24; *Strategic Investing: How to Profit from the Coming Inflationary Depression*, 40

Cassiday, Bruce. *The Complete Condominium Guide*, 114

Cavelti, Peter. *How to Invest in Gold*, 97

Cerami, Charles A. *More Profit, Less Risk: Your New Financial Strategy*, 68

Charell, Ralph. *How to Make Big Money in Low-Priced Stocks in the Coming Bull Market*, 86; *The Magic of Thinking Rich*, 51

Chasman, Herbert, jt. auth. *See* LeClair, Robert, Leimberg, Stephan, and Chasman, Herbert

Church, Albert M. *The Sophisticated Investor: How to Target Prime Investment Opportunities*, 79

Clark, Cathy. *Credit!*, 53

Clark, Doug. *The Greatest Banking Scandal in History: And How It Affects You*, 40

Clay, William. *The Dow Jones-Irwin Guide to Estate Planning*, 153

Cobleigh, Ira U. *Double Your Dollars in 600 Days*, 97

Cobleigh, Ira U., and Dorfman, Bruce K. *The Dowbeaters: How to Buy Stocks That Go Up*, 80; *The Roaring 80's on Wall Street: How to Make a Killing in the Coming Stock Market Boom*, 75

Coffee, Frank. *Everything You Need to Know about Creative Home Financing*, 111

Coghlan, Richard, jt. auth. *See* Boeckh, J. Anthony, and Coghlan, Richard

Cohen, Jerome. *Personal Finance*, 142

Cohen, Jerome B., Zinbarg, Edward, and Zeikel, Arthur. *Guide to Intelligent Investing*, 69

College for Financial Planning. *Financial Planning Bibliography: A Selected List, Resources*, 12

Colman, Carol. *Love and Money: What Your Finances Say about Your Personal Relationships*, 51

Coltman, Michael M. *Resort Condos and Timesharing: Buyer Beware!*, 116

Coman, Edwin. *Sources of Business Information*, 17

Consumer Group Inc., jt. auth. *See* Darack, Arthur, and Consumer Group Inc.

Consumer Guide. *How to Prosper in the 80's*, 41; *see also* Dickinson, Peter, and the Editors of Consumer Guide

Consumer Guide, and Dickinson, Peter. *Your Retirement: A Complete Planning Guide*, 145

Consumer Guide, with Dickinson, Peter A. *How to Make Money during Inflation/Recession*, 41

Consumer Reports. *The Consumers Union Report on Life Insurance: A Guide to Planning and Buying the Protection You Need*, 157

Cook, John A., and Wool, Robert. *All You Need to Know about Banks*, 62

Cook, Timothy, and Summers, Bruce. *Instruments of the Money Market*, 69

Cooley, Marilyn, jt. auth. *See* Schlayer, Mary E., with Cooley, Marilyn

Corrigan, Arnold. *How Your IRA Can Make You a Millionaire*, 150

Coslow, Samson. *How to Make Money on the Interest Rate Roller Coaster:*

A Proven Method for Profitable Investment in a Rising or Falling Market, 87
Cote, Norma, jt. auth. *See* Grant, Mary M., and Cote, Norma
Cox, Wesley. *Kiss Ma Bell Good-bye: How to Install Your Own Telephones, Extensions and Accessories*, 30
Coxon, Terry, jt. auth. *See* Browne, Harry, and Coxon, Terry
Crestol, Jack, and Schneider, Herman M. *Tax Planning for Investors: The Eighties Guide to Securities Investments and Tax Shelters*, 126
Crittenden, Alan. *How to Adjust to Adjustable Home Mortgages*, 112
Crumbley, Larry, and Crumbley, Tony. *The Financial Management of Your Coin/Stamp Estate*, 101
Crumbley, Tony, jt. auth. *See* Crumbley, Larry, and Crumbley, Tony
Cullen, Jean, jt. auth. *See* Gross, Robin, and Cullen, Jean
Cummings, Jack. *Cashless Investing in Real Estate*, 118; *Successful Real Estate Investing for the Single Person*, 118
Curtis, Richard. *How to Prosper in the Coming Apocalypse*, 41

Dacey, Norman F. *How to Avoid Probate—Updated!*, 153
Dames, Ralph T. *The Winning Option*, 90
Daniells, Lorna M. *Basic Investment Sources*, 17; *Business Information Sources*, 17
Darack, Arthur, and Consumer Group Inc. *Used Cars: How to Avoid Highway Robbery*, 30
Darst, David M. *The Handbook of the Bond and Money Markets*, 222
David, Ann. *Get Out and Stay Out of Debt*, 63

David, Carl. *Collecting and Care of Fine Art*, 101
Davids, Lewis E. *Dictionary of Insurance*, 225
Davidson, James D. *The Squeeze*, 31
Davis, Jerry. *Rehabbing for Profit*, 118
Davis, Joann, and Smith, Wendy. "Books on Money Matters: A Current Checklist," 11
Davis, Ken, and Taylor, Tom. *Kids and Cash: Solving a Parent's Dilemma*, 49
Day, Adrian. *Investing without Borders: The Best Opportunities around the World for the 80's*, 69
Dayton, Howard. *Your Money: Frustration or Freedom?*, 45
Diamond, William. *Bulls, Bears, and Massacres: A Proven System for Investing in the Stock Market*, 87
Dickinson, Peter, and the Editors of Consumer Guide. *Get More Money from . . . Social Security, Govt. Benefits, Medicare, Plus*, 159
Dickinson, Peter, jt. auth. *See* Consumer Guide, and Dickinson, Peter; Consumer Guide, with Dickinson, Peter A.
Dickson, David. *Tax Shelters for the Not-So-Rich*, 134
DiMattia, Susan S. "Business Books of 198-: A Selection of Recommended Books Published during the Past Year." 11, 12
Dirks, Ray. *Heads You Win, Tails You Win: The Dirks Investment Formula*, 80
Dissinger, Katherine. *Old, Poor, Alone and Happy: How to Live Nicely on Nearly Nothing*, 145
Dohrmann, Bernhard. *Grow Rich with Diamonds: Investing in the World's Most Precious Gems*, 100
Donald, Bruce. *Cutting College Costs: The Up-to-the-Minute Manual for 1983-1984*, 55

Donoghue, William, with Tilling, Thomas. *William Donoghue's Complete Money Market Guide: The Simple Low-Risk Way You Can Profit from Inflation and Fluctuating Interest Rates*, 95; *William E. Donoghue's No-Load Mutual Fund Guide*, 8, 95
Dooner, William, and Proctor, William. *How to Go from Rags to Riches in Real Estate: A Guide to Turning Depressed, Neglected, or Little-Known Property Investments into Millions in the 1980's*, 118
Dorfman, Bruce K., jt. auth. See Cobleigh, Ira U., and Dorfman, Bruce K.
Dorfman, John. *Consumer Tactics Manual: How to Get Action on Your Complaints*, 37; *Family Investment Guide: A Financial Handbook for Middle-Income People*, 69; *The Stock Market Directory*, 222
Dowd, Merle. *How to Live Better and Spend 20% Less*, 31
Downs, Hugh, and Roll, Richard J. *Hugh Downs' the Best Years Book: How to Plan for Fulfillment, Security and Happiness in the Retirement Years*, 146
Drach, Robert, jt. auth. See Herzfeld, Thomas, and Drach, Robert F.
Dreman, David. *The New Contrarian Investment Strategy: The Psychology of Stock Market Success*, 80
Drollinger, William C., and Drollinger, William C., Jr. *Tax Shelters and Tax-Free Income for Everyone*, 135
Drollinger, William C., Jr., jt. auth. See Drollinger, William C., and Drollinger, William C., Jr.
Droms, William G., jt. auth. See Amling, Frederick, and Droms, William G.
Drotning, Phillip. *You Can Buy a Home Now*, 105; see also Kaplan, Melvin J., and Drotning, Phillip, T.

Dunetz, Martin. *How to Finance Your Retirement*, 146
Dunn, Donald. "The First Risk in Investing: Reading About It," 12

Eder, G. *What's Behind Inflation and How to Beat It*, 41
Egan, Jack. *Your Complete Guide to IRA's and Keoghs: The Simple, Safe Tax-Deferred Way to Financial Security*, 150
Egan, Patricia B., and Maran, Marie Y. *This Way to Wall $treet*, 76
Engel, Louis, and Boyd, Brendan. *How to Buy Stocks*, 80
Engel, Louis, with Wyckoff, Peter. *How to Buy Stocks*, 80
English, John, jt. auth. See Cardiff, Gray E., and English, John

Fabozzi, Frank J., and Zarb, Frank G. *The Handbook of Financial Markets: Securities, Options and Futures*, 70
Farah, Vicker, jt. auth. See Horn, Frederick, and Farah, Vicker
Feinman, Jeffrey. *How You Can Profit from Today's Gold Rush*, 97
Feins, Judith, and Lane, Terry S. *How Much for Housing? New Perspectives on Affordability and Risk*, 106
Felix, Joseph. *It's Easier for a Rich Man to Enter Heaven than for a Poor Man to Remain on Earth*, 45
Fenwick, Daman. *Mobile Home Living: The Money-Saving Guide*, 115
Ferri, Robert, and Silverberg, Barry. *The Tax Organizer*, 126
Fierro, Robert D. *Tax Shelters in Plain English: New Strategies for the 1980's*, 135
Flaherty, Patrick F., and Ziegler, Richard. *Estate Planning for Everyone: The Whole Truth—from Planning to Probate*, 153
Flanagan, William G. *How to Beat the*

Author Index

Financial Squeeze: Don't Just Get Mad—Get Even, 31
Flynn, David H., jt. auth. *See* Pancheri, Michael, and Flynn, David H.
Fodor, R. V. *Nickels, Dimes and Dollars: How Currency Works*, 24
Franck, Irene M., jt. auth. *See* Brownstone, David M., and Franck, Irene M.
Freedman, Michael. *The Diamond Book: A Practical Guide for Successful Investing*, 100
Freeman, Kerry. *Chilton's Guide to Consumer's Auto Repairs and Prices: How to Save Money on Auto Repairs and Accessories*, 31
Friedman, Jack F., jt. auth. *See* Blume, Marshall E., and Friedman, Jack F.
Frost, Alfred, jt. auth. *See* Prechter, Robert, and Frost, Alfred
Fuhrman, Noah. *Seven Keys for Doubling Your Standard of Living (Without Increasing Your Income)*, 32

Gabriel, Richard. *How to Buy Your Own House When You Don't Have Enough Money*, 112
Gadow, Sandy. *All about Escrow: Or How to Buy the Brooklyn Bridge and Have the Last Laugh*, 106
Galanoy, Terry. *Charge It: Inside the Credit Card Conspiracy*, 53
Garber, Robert. *The Only Tax Book You'll Ever Need*, 127
Gargiulo, Albert F., and Carlucci, Rocco. *The "Questioned Stock" Manual: A Guide to Determining the True Worth of Old and Collectible Securities*, 76
Gargon, John. *The Complete Guide to Estate Planning*, 153
Gastineau, Gary. *The Stock Options Manual*, 90
Geczi, Michael L. *Futures: The Anti-Inflation Investment*, 91
Geisman, Miriam S., jt. auth. *See* Radics, Stephen P., Jr., and Geisman, Miriam S.
Genetski, Robert J., jt. auth. *See* Sprinkel, Beryl W., and Genetski, Robert J.
Georgi, Charlotte, jt. auth. *See* Wasserman, Paul, Georgi, Charlotte, and Woy, James
Gibbs, Gerald. *The Complete Guide to Credit and Loans: Everything You Should Know about Successful Borrowing*, 8, 53
Gieseking, Hal. *The Complete Handbook for Travelers*, 61
Gillies, Jerry. *MoneyLove: How to Get the Money You Deserve for Whatever You Want*, 51
Gilmore, Louis. *For Sale by Owner*, 106
Ginsberg, Linda. *Family Financial Survival*, 153
Girth, Marjorie. *Bankruptcy Options for the Consumer Debtor*, 64
Gitman, Lawrence J., and Joehnk, Michael D. *Fundamentals of Investing*, 70; "Resources: Financial News," 12
Glasner, Lynne, jt. auth. *See* Thypin, Marilyn, and Glasner, Lynne
Glubetich, Dave. *Double Your Money in Real Estate Every Two Years*, 118; *How to Grow a Money Tree: Earn 20 to 30 Percent and More with Safe Second Mortgages and Trust Deeds*, 118; *The Monopoly Game: The "How To" Book of Making Big Money with Rental Homes*, 119
Goldberg, Herb, and Lewis, Robert T. *Money Madne$$: The Psychology of Saving, Spending, Loving and Having Money*, 52
Goldberg, Philip, and Posner, Mitchell J. *The Strategic Metals Investment Handbook*, 99
Goldsmith, W. B. *BASIC Programs for Home Financial Management*, 142
Gollin, James. *The Star Spangled Dream*, 146

Author Index

Gordon, Marjorie. *A List of Worthwhile Life and Health Insurance Books*, 18

Gould, Bruce. *The Dow Jones-Irwin Guide to Commodities Trading*, 91

Grace, William J., Jr. *The ABC's of IRA's: The Complete Guide to Individual Retirement Accounts: The #1 Investment Strategy of the Eighties*, 151

Grant, Mary M., and Cote, Norma. *Directory of Business and Financial Services*, 18

Granville, Joseph. *Granville's New Strategy of Daily Stock Market Timing for Maximum Profit*, 87

Graver, Fred. *Get Out of Debt Now: How to Gain Control of Your Financial Affairs Once and for All*, 54

Green, Thomas E., Osler, Robert W., and Bickley, John S. *Glossary of Insurance Terms*, 225

Green, Timothy. *The New World of Gold: The Inside Story of the Mines, the Markets, the Politics, the Investors*, 97

Greene, Bill. *Think Like a Tycoon: Inflation Can Make You Rich*, 119; *Bill Greene's 101 New Loopholes: The Reagan Tax Package 1983-85*, 132; *Win Your Personal Tax Revolt*, 127

Greisman, Bernard. *J. K. Lasser's All You Should Know about IRA, Keogh, and Other Retirement Plans*, 151; *J. K. Lasser's How You Can Profit from the New Tax Laws*, 132

Gross, Robin, and Cullen, Jean. *Help: The Basics of Borrowing Money*, 54

Gupta, Udayan. "Market Publications: Guide Posts on the Investment Landscape," 13

Haft, Richard. *Investing in Securities: A Handbook for the '80's*, 70

Hale, Norman B., jt. auth. *See* Rugg, Donald D., and Hale, Norman B.

Hall, Craig. *Craig Hall's Book of Real Estate Investing*, 119

Hallman, G. Victor, and Rosenbloom, Jerry. *Personal Financial Planning*, 143

Halverson, Richard P. *Financial Freedom: Your New Guide to Economic Security and Success*, 24

Hancock, William. *Saving Money through 10-Year Trusts*, 156

Hansen, George, and Anderson, Larry. *How the IRS Seizes Your Dollars and How to Fight Back*, 127

Harden, Gerald, jt. auth. *See* Harden, Linda, and Harden, Gerald

Harden, Linda, and Harden, Gerald. *The Money Book for People Who Live Together*, 24

Hardy, C. Colburn. *ABC's of Investing Your Retirement Funds*, 146; "Bibliography" *Dun and Bradstreet's Guide to Your Investments*, 13; *Dun and Bradstreet's Guide to Your Investments*, 71; *The Investor's Guide to Technical Analysis*, 87; *Your Guide to a Financially Secure Retirement*, 146; *Your Money and Your Life: Planning Your Financial Future*, 147

Harkness, Richard M., jt. auth. *See* Silvers, William L., and Harkness, Richard M.

Harney, Kenneth. *Beating Inflation with Real Estate*, 120

Harrington, Geri. *The Medicare Answer Book: The Up-to-Date, Practical and Authoritative Guide to Medicare*, 159

Haskell, Richard. *Sell Your House through Creative Financing—Without a Broker*, 112

Hassan, Bernard. *The Beginning Investor*, 71

Hassay, Karen A., jt. auth. *See* Lee, Steven J., and Hassay, Karen A.

Hatfield, Weston. *The Weekend Real Estate Investor: The New, Low-Risk Team Approach That Transforms Everyday Opportunities into Big Profits*, 120

Hatton, Hap, and Torbet, Laura. *Helpful Hints for Hard Times: How to Live It Up While Cutting Down*, 32

Hayes, Mary Anne. *Ask the Coupon Queen: How to Buy Seventy-One Dollars and Seventy-One Cents Worth of Groceries for Seven Dollars and Nineteen Cents*, 59

Hazard, John. "Managing Your Money: Where to Research That Stock," 13; "A Reading List for Investors," 13

Heatter, Justin. *Buying a Condominium*, 114

Hefferlin, Jonathan. *Making Inflation Pay!: How Limited Funds in Gold, Silver, Coins, Stamps, Real Estate at the Right Time Can Win Big*, 41

Heil, Paula. *Your Personal Guide to Financial Fitness*, 25

Hemphill, Charles. *Wills and Trusts: A Legal and Financial Handbook for Everyone*, 154

Herrick, Tracy G. *Timing: How to Profitably Manage Money at Different Stages of Your Life*, 143

Herzfeld, Thomas. *The Investor's Guide to Closed-End Funds: The Herzfeld Hedge*, 81

Herzfeld, Thomas, and Drach, Robert F. *High-Return Low-Risk Investment*, 81

Hicks, Tyler G. *How to Borrow Your Way to Real Estate Riches Using Government Money*, 120; *How to Build a Second Income Fortune in Your Spare Time*, 32

Hirsh, Yale. *Mutual Funds Almanac*, 224

Holt, Robert. *Bonds: How to Double Your Money Quickly and Safely*, 94; *The Complete Book of Bonds: How to Buy and Sell Profitably*, 94

Holt, Thomas J. *How to Survive and Grow Richer in the Tough Times Ahead*, 71

Holzman, Robert. *A Survival Kit for Taxpayers: Staying on Good Terms with the I.R.S.*, 127; *Take It Off! Close to 2,363 Deductions Most People Overlook*, 133

Honigsberg, Peter. *The Unemployment Benefits Handbook*, 63

Horatio, Algernon. *The Penny Capitalist: How to Build a Small Fortune from Next to Nothing*, 32

Horn, Frederick, and Farah, Vicker. *Trading in Commodity Futures*, 91

Horowitz, David. *Fight Back! and Don't Get Ripped Off*, 38

Howard, Alfred, jt. auth. See Howard, Alice, and Howard, Alfred

Howard, Alice, and Howard, Alfred. *Turn Your Kitchen into a Gold Mine*, 50

Hubbard, L. Ron, and Winfrey, Dennis W. *How to Flourish, Prosper, and Survive the 80's Despite Everything: The Working Person's Financial Crash Course*, 32

Hudgeons, Marc. *The Official Investors Guide to Buying and Selling Gold, Silver and Diamonds*, 100

Huff, Charles, and Marinacci, Barbara. *Commodity Speculation for Beginners: A Guide to the Futures Market*, 91

Hughes, Alan. *A Home of Your Own for the Least Cash: The Home Buyer's Guide for Today*, 106

Hurley, Gale E. *Personal Money Management*, 143

Huskin, J., and Monsees, William. *How to Get Rich while You Sleep*, 71

Hyman, Henry. *The Where to Sell Anything and Everything Book*, 33

Income Opportunities. *Dollars on Your Doorstep: How to Run a Business from Your Own Home*, 50

Ingram, Rich, jt. auth. *See* Traister, Robert, and Ingram, Rich

Internal Revenue Service, Department of the Treasury, *A Selection of 1982 Internal Revenue Service Tax Information Publications*, 14; *Taxpayer's Guide to IRS Information and Assistance*, 15

Irwin, Robert. *How to Buy a Home at a Reasonable Price*, 107; *How to Buy and Sell Real Estate for Financial Security*, 120; *Riches in Real Estate: A Beginner's Guide to Group Investing*, 120; *The New Mortgage Game*, 112; *The $100,000 Decision: The Older American's Guide to Selling a Home and Choosing Retirement Housing*, 147; *The $125,000 Decision: The Older American's Guide to Selling a Home and Choosing Retirement Housing*, 147; *Smart Money Real Estate for the 80's: New Profits in Big Properties*, 120; *see also* Morris, Hal, and Irwin, Robert

J. K. Lasser Tax Institute. *J. K. Lasser's Financial Planning for Your Family*, 45; *J. K. Lasser's Your Estate and Gift Taxes*, 154

Jacobe, Dennis, and Kendall, James N. *How to Get the Money to Buy Your New Home*, 113

Jacobs, Vernon K. *The New Taxpayer's Counterattack*, 128

Jacobs, Vernon K., and Schoeneman, Charles. *The Taxpayer's Audit Survival Manual*, 137; *The Taxpayer's Internal Revenue Service Audit Survival Manual*, 137

Janik, Carolyn. *The House Hunt Game: A Guide to Winning*, 107; *Selling Your Home: A Guide to Getting the Best Price with or without a Broker*, 107

Jeddloh, James, and Perkins, Cheryl. *Real Estate Taxation: A Practical Guide*, 139

Jenkins, Emyl. *Why You're Richer Than You Think*, 102

Jensen, Ronald W. *Sell Your Home "By Owner" and Save the Commission*, 107

Jessup, L. F. *Law of Retirement*, 148

Joehnk, Michael D., jt. auth. *See* Gitman, Lawrence J., and Joehnk, Michael, D.

Johnson, Bert. *Bert Johnson's Credit Loopholes: An Instant Credit Guide*, 54; *Credit: Get It, Use It, Stretch It, Save It*, 54

Johnson, H. Webster. *How to Use the Business Library: With Sources of Business Information*, 18

Johnstad, Jack, and Johnstad, Lois. *The Power of Prosperous Thinking: A Practical and Inspirational Guide to Making, Managing, and Multiplying Your Money*, 33

Johnstad, Lois, jt. auth. *See* Johnstad, Jack, and Johnstad, Lois

Jorgensen, James. *Your Retirement Income*, 148

Joselow, Froma. *Get Your Money's Worth: The Book for People Who Are Tired of Paying More for Less*, 33

Joyce, Nancy, jt. auth. *See* Rogers, Mary, and Joyce, Nancy

Judd, Stanley H. *Think Rich*, 52

Juroe, David. *Money: How to Spend Less and Have More*, 52

Kahn, Arnold. *Family Security through Estate Planning*, 154

Kamensky, Dennis. *Winning on Your Income Taxes*, 128

Kandel, Myron. *How to Cash In on the Coming Stock Market Boom: The Smart Investor's Guide to Making Money*, 81

Kaplan, H. Roy. *Lottery Winners:*

How They Won and How Winning Changed Their Lives, 61

Kaplan, Melvin J., and Drotning, Phillip T. *How to Get Your Creditors Off Your Back without Losing Your Shirt*, 64

Kast, Sheilah. *Cut Your Own Taxes and Save: The Everything-You-Need-to-Know Guide for Your 1981 Tax Return*, 132

Kaufman, Daniel. *How to Get Out of Debt: Without Despair and Without a Lawyer*, 64

Kaye, Barry. *How to Save a Fortune on Your Life Insurance*, 157

Kendall, James N., jt. auth. *See* Jacobe, Dennis, and Kendall, James N.

Kennedy, David, jt. auth. *See* Steiner, Barry, and Kennedy, David

Kenton, Walter. *How Life Insurance Companies Rob You and What You Can Do about It*, 157

Kessler, A. D. *A Fortune at Your Feet: How You Can Get Rich, Stay Rich and Enjoy Being Rich with Creative Real Estate*, 121

Kettle, Brian. *Gold*, 98

Kiev, Phyllis. *The Woman's Guide to Buying Houses, Co-ops, and Condominiums*, 108

Kilgore, James E. *Dollars and Sense: Making Your Money Work for You and Your Family*, 45

Kimmel, Kenneth. *Real Estate: How to Double Your Money Every Two to Three Years with Income-Producing Properties*, 121

Kinevan, Marcos. *Personal Estate Planning: Financial and Legal Aspects of Accumulating, Protecting, and Disposing of Your Personal Estate*, 154

King, Norman. *The Money Market Book*, 96; *Turn Your House into a Money Factory*, 51

Kinsman, Robert. *The Robert Kinsman Guide to Tax Havens*, 137; *Your New Swiss Bank Book*, 62

Kirsch, Charlotte. *A Survivor's Manual to: Contingency Planning, Wills, Trusts, Guidelines for Guardians, Getting through Probate, Taxes, Life Insurance, Emotional Stability, Protection from Reckless Spending, Living on a Fixed Income, Reconciling Family Differences, Avoiding Con Artists*, 154

Klein, Howard. *Fad Money: How to Make Money from Fads, Crazes, and Trends*, 25

Koch, James. *Profits from Country Property: How to Select, Buy, Maintain, and Improve Your Country Property*, 121

Kornfeld, Leo L. et al., *How to Beat the High Cost of Learning: The Complete and Up-to-Date Guide to Student Financial Aid*, 55

Kosel, Janice. *Bankruptcy: Do It Yourself*, 65; *Chapter 13: The Federal Plan to Repay Your Debts*, 65

Kramer, J. J. *The Mobile Home Guide: Your Affordable Manufactured House*, 115

Kramer, Nancy, jt. auth. *See* Newman, Stephen, and Kramer, Nancy

Kratovil, Robert, and Kratovil, Ruth. *Buying, Owning and Selling a Home in the 1980's*, 108

Kratovil, Ruth, jt. auth. *See* Kratovil, Robert, and Kratovil, Ruth

Krefetz, Gerald. *The Smart Investor's Guide: How to Make Money in the Coming Bull Market*, 76

Ladley, Barbara, and Wilford, Jane. *Money and Finance: Sources of Print and Non-Print Materials*, 19

Laird, Joseph, jt. auth. *See* Sokoloff, Kiril, Laird, Joseph, and Mack, Thomas

Landau, Elaine. *The Smart Spending Guide for Teens*, 50

Lane, Paul. *The Dow Jones-Irwin Guide to College Financial Planning*, 56
Lane, Terry S., jt. auth. *See* Feins, Judith, and Lane, Terry S.
Lank, Edith. *Home Buying*, 108
Lapin, Lawrence. *The Home Owner's Guide to Making a Fortune*, 121
Larsen, David C. *Who Gets It when You Go? A Guide for Planning Your Will, Protecting Your Family's Future, Minimizing Inheritance Taxes, and Avoiding Probate*, 155
Larson, Martin. *The I.R.S. versus the Middle Class: Or How the Average Citizen Can Protect Himself from the Federal Tax Collector*, 128
Lasry, George. *Valuing Common Stock: The Power of Prudence*, 76
Lasser, J. K., Tax Institute. *See* J. K. Lasser Tax Institute
Laurins, Alex, jt. auth. *See* Tanner, Beverly, Pheffer, Marvin, and Laurins, Alex
LeBlanc, Rena, jt. auth. *See* LeBlanc, Terry, and LeBlanc, Rena
LeBlanc, Terry, and LeBlanc, Rena. *Suddenly Rich*, 61
LeClair, Robert, Leimberg, Stephan, and Chasman, Herbert, *Money and Retirement: How to Plan for Lifetime Financial Security*, 148
Ledford, Lowell, and Brock, Jeanne. *Ready or Not: Planning Your Successful Retirement*, 148
Lee, Barbara, with Morgenson, Gretchen. *The Woman's Guide to the Stock Market: How to Make Your Own Investment Plan*, 76
Lee, James S. *Buyer's Handbook for the Single-Family House*, 108
Lee, Steven J., and Hassay, Karen A. *Women's Handbook of Independent Financial Management*, 47
Leider, Robert. *Don't Miss Out: The Ambitious Student's Guide to Scholarships and Loans*, 56; *Your Own Financial Aid Factory: The Guide to Locating College Money*, 56
Leimberg, Stephan, jt. auth. *See* LeClair, Robert, Leimberg, Stephan, and Chasman, Herbert; *see also* Plotnick, Charles, and Leimberg, Stephan
Lesko, Matthew. *How to Get Free Tax Help*, 128
Levi, Donald, jt. auth. *See* Penson, John B., Jr., Levi, Donald, and Nixon, Claire
Levi, Maurice. *Economics Deciphered: A Layman's Survival Guide*, 25
Levin, Martin, et al. *You May Be Losing Your Inheritance: A Guide to Psychological, Financial, and Legal Hazards and What You Can Do about Them Now*, 155
Levine, Sumner. *The Dow Jones-Irwin Business and Investment Almanac*, 224
Levinson, Jay. *Earning Money without a Job*, 57; *555 Ways to Earn Extra Money*, 33
Levitt, Arthur, Jr. *How to Make Your Money Make Money: The Experts Explain Your Alternatives, the Risks, the Rewards*, 71
Lewis, Robert T., jt. auth. *See* Goldberg, Herb, and Lewis, Robert T.
Lichello, Robert. *How to Make $1,000,000 in the Stock Market—Automatically*, 81
Liebman, Walter H. "Buyer's Guide: When You Wish Upon a Stock," 14
Lindgren, Henry. *Great Expectations: The Psychology of Money*, 52
Lippett, Peter. *Estate Planning: After the Reagan Tax Cut*, 155; *Estate Planning: What Anyone Who Owns Anything Must Know*, 155
Little, Jeffrey B., and Rhodes, Lucien. *Understanding Wall Street*, 77
Locker, Michael, jt. auth. *See* Abrecht, Stephen, and Locker, Michael

Loll, Leo, jt. auth. *See* Buckley, Julian, and Loll, Leo

Long, Charles. *How to Survive without a Salary,* 58

Loosigan, Allan. *Foreign Exchange Futures: A Guide to International Currency Trading,* 92; *Interest Rate Futures,* 92

Lowry, Albert. *How You Can Become Financially Independent by Investing in Real Estate,* 122

Ludy, Andrew. *Condominium Ownership: A Buyer's Guide,* 114

Lumb, Fred A. *What Every Woman Should Know About Finances,* 47

McClintock, Mike. *Getting Your Money's Worth from Home Contractors,* 34

McConnally, Kevin. *How to Get More for Your Money,* 34

MacGregor, Malcolm. *Training Your Children to Handle Money,* 50

Mack, Thomas, jt. auth. *See* Sokoloff, Kiril, Laird, Joseph, and Mack, Thomas

Mackevich, Gene. *The Woman's Money Book: How to Make Your Money Grow,* 48

McLachlan, Christopher. *Inflation-Wise: How to Do Almost Everything for Less,* 33

McLean, Andrew J. *Foreclosures: How to Profitably Invest in Distressed Real Estate,* 122

McLendon, Gordon. *Get Really Rich in the Coming Super Metals Boom,* 99

McMillan, Lawrence G. *Options as a Strategic Investment,* 90

McQuown, Judith. *Playing the Takeover Market: How to Profit from Corporate Mergers, Spin-Offs, Tender Offers and Liquidations,* 82; *Tax Shelters That Work for Everyone: A Common Sense Guide to Keeping More of the Money You Earn,* 135

McWilliams, Bruce. *Penny Stocks: How the Small Investor Can Make Large Profits in the Penny Market,* 94

Maital, Shlamo. *Minds, Markets, and Money: Psychological Foundations of Economic Behavior,* 52

Majika, Paul. *You Can Save a Bundle on Your Car Insurance,* 158

Malabre, Alfred. *Investing for Profit in the Eighties: The Business Cycle System,* 82

Malcolm, Maurice. *How to Survive (And Make Money) in the Coming Real Estate Crunch,* 113

Malkiel, Burton. *A Random Walk Down Wall Street,* 82; *The Inflation Beater's Investment Guide: Winning Strategies for the 1980's,* 82

Mamis, Justin. *How to Buy: An Insider's Guide to Making Money in the Stock Market,* 88

Maran, Marie Y., jt. auth. *See* Egan, Patricia B., and Maran, Marie Y.

Marinacci, Barbara, jt. auth. *See* Huff, Charles, and Marinacci, Barbara

Marino, John. *How to Make Big Money in Real Estate,* 122

Mason, Alexander. *The Real Estate Broker's Inside Guide to Selling Your Own Home (And Keeping the Commission!),* 108

Mechanic, Sylvia. *Investment Bibliography: A Selected List of Books, Services, Newspapers, Periodicals and Financial Organizations,* 14

Mehr, Robert. *Fundamentals of Insurance,* 158

Mehr, Robert, and Cammack, Emerson. *Principles of Insurance,* 158

Meltzer, Bernard. *Bernard Meltzer Solves Your Money Problems: Borrowing, Buying and Investment Strategies to Profit from Inflation,* 72

Meltzer, Yale. *Putting Money to Work: An Investment Primer for the 80's,* 8, 72

Mendlowitz, Edward. *Successful Tax Planning,* 129

Merton, Henry. *Your Gold and Silver: An Easy Guide to Appraising Household Objects, Coins, Heirlooms and Jewelry,* 98

Metz, Robert. *Future Stocks: Investing for Profit in the Growth Stocks of the 1980's,* 77

Meyer, Martin. *Don't Bank on It: How to Make up to 22% or More on Your Savings—All Fully Insured,* 62

Michaels, Joseph. *Prime of Your Life,* 148

Michaels, Richard. *Moonlighter's Guide to a Sparetime Fortune,* 34

Miller, Nancy. *Managing Your Money,* 34

Miller, Theodore. *Make Your Money Grow,* 25

Milton, Arthur. *How Your Life Insurance Policies Rob You,* 158

Minkow, Robert, jt. auth. See Minkow, Rosalie, and Minkow, Robert

Minkow, Rosalie. *Money Management for Women,* 48

Minkow, Rosalie, and Minkow, Robert. *The Complete List of IRS Tax Deductions, 1983,* 134

Moffitt, Donald. *Your Money Matters: A Guide to Personal Finance from the Pages of the Wall Street Journal,* 143

Monsees, William, jt. auth. See Huskin, J., and Monsees, William

Moody, William J. *How to Probate an Estate: A Handbook for Executors and Administrators,* 156

Moore, Donald. *Money for College: How to Get It,* 57

Morgenson, Gretchen, jt. auth. See Lee, Barbara, with Morgenson, Gretchen

Morris, Hal. *Crisis Real Estate Investing: Increase and Protect Your Assets from Potential Disaster,* 122

Morris, Hal, and Irwin, Robert. *How to Stop Foreclosure: What to Do When Your "Balloon Is Due and You're Laid Off or Facing Other Financial Crises,"* 113

Mosburg, Lewis. *The Tax Shelter Coloring Book,* 135

Mosely, Norma F., jt. auth. See Phipps, Antony A., and Mosely, Norma F.

Mumford, Amy. *It Only Hurts between Paydays: A Practical, Exciting, and Fun Plan for Getting Control of Your Personal Finances,* 45

Murphy, Michael. *How to Buy a Home while You Can Still Afford To,* 108

Murzim, Howy, jt. auth. See Schiff, Irwin A., with Murzim, Howy

Nagan, Peter. *Fail-Safe Investing: How to Make Money with Less Than $10,000 . . . Without Losing Sleep,* 72

Naifeh, Steven, with Smith, Gregory. *The Bargain Hunter's Guide to Art Collecting,* 102

Natelson, Robert G. *How to Buy and Sell a Condominium,* 115

Nauheim, Fred. *Move Your Assets to Beat Inflation,* 42; *The Retirement Money Book: New Ways to Have More Income When You Retire,* 149

Nelson, Paula. *Where to Get Money for Everything: A Complete Guide to Today's Money Sources,* 55

Nelson, Wayne. *How to Buy Money: Investing Wisely for Maximum Return,* 72

Nessen, Robert L. *The Real Estate Book: A Complete Guide to Acquiring, Financing and Investing in a Home or Commercial Property,* 109

Author Index

Newman, Stephen, and Kramer, Nancy. *Getting What You Deserve: A Handbook for the Assertive Consumer*, 38

Nicholas, Ted. *How to Get Out of Debt*, 65

Nickerson, William. *How I Turned $1,000 into Five Million in Real Estate—In My Spare Time*, 122

Nielsen, Jackie, jt. auth. *See* Nielsen, Jens, and Nielsen, Jackie

Nielsen, Jens, and Nielsen, Jackie. *How to Save or Make Thousands when You Buy or Sell Your House*, 109

Niendorf, Robert, jt. auth. *See* Ward, David, and Niendorf, Robert

Nixon, Claire, jt. auth. *See* Penson, John B., Jr., Levi, Donald, and Nixon, Claire

O'Neill, Richard. *The Home Buyer's Guide for the 80's: A Complete Guide to Every Step You Need to Take for the Biggest and Best Investment You'll Ever Make*, 109

Osler, Robert W., jt. auth. *See* Green, Thomas E., Osler, Robert W., and Bickley, John S.

Pancheri, Michael, and Flynn, David H. *The IRA Handbook: A Complete Guide*, 152

Paris, Alexander. *The Coming Credit Collapse: An Update for the 1980's*, 42

Parker, Robert, jt. auth. *See* Sinclair, James E., and Parker, Robert

Pasquarelli, Michael, jt. auth. *See* VanMeer, Mary, and Pasquarelli, Michael

Paulsen, Gary. *Beat the System: A Survival Guide*, 58

Penson, John B., Jr., Levi, Donald, and Nixon, Claire. *Personal Finance*, 143

Perkins, Cheryl, jt. auth. *See* Jeddloh, James, and Perkins, Cheryl

Perkins, Gail, and Rhoades, Judith. *The Women's Financial Survival Handbook*, 48

Petersen, Kristelle. *The Single Person's Home Buying Handbook*, 109

Petrello, George J., jt. auth. *See* Burton, Robert H., and Petrello, George J.

Phalon, Richard. *Your Money: How to Make It Work Harder Than You Do*, 35

Pheffer, Marvin, jt. auth. *See* Tanner, Beverly, Pheffer, Marvin, and Laurins, Alex

Phillips, Carole. *The Money Workbook for Women: A Step-by-Step Guide to Managing Your Personal Finances*, 48

Phipps, Antony A., and Mosely, Norma F. *The Homebuying Guide*, 109

Pierce, Phyllis. *The Dow-Jones Investor's Handbook*, 223

Pike, William. *Why Stocks Go Up (and Down): A Guide to Sound Investing*, 77

Pinto, Robert J. *How to Save Taxes through Estate Planning*, 156

Pivar, William. *Get Rich on Other People's Money: Real Estate Investment Secrets*, 123

Plotnick, Charles, and Leimberg, Stephan. *Die Rich: Making It, Keeping It, and Passing It Along under the New Tax Laws*, 156

Pomeroy, Ruth. *Redbook's Guide to Buying Your First Home*, 110

Porter, Sylvia. *Sylvia Porter's New Money Book for the 80's*, 8, 25; *Sylvia Porter's 1983 Income Tax Book*, 129

Posner, Mitchell J., jt. auth. *See* Goldberg, Philip, and Posner, Mitchell J.

Post, William G. *How to Benefit from

the New Tax Laws: Immediate Gains and Long-Term Strategies, 132
Powers, Mark. Getting Starting in Commodity Futures Trading, 92
Powers, Mark, and Vogel, David. Inside the Financial Futures Markets, 92
Prechter, Robert, and Frost, Alfred. Elliott Wave Principle: Key to Stock Market Profits, 88
Price, Irving. How to Get Top Dollar for Your Home in Good Times or Bad, 110
Price, J. R., with Putney, Valerie. In This Corner—The IRS, 138
Pring, Martin. How to Forecast Interest Rates: A Guide to Profits for Consumers, Managers and Investors, 83; International Investing Made Easy: Proven Money Strategies with as Little as $5,000, 83; Technical Analysis Explained: An Illustrated Guide for the Investor, 88
Pritchard, Jeffrey. Heads You Win, Tails You Win: The Inside Secrets to Rare Coin Investing, 102
Prochnow, Herbert V. Bank Credit: An Indepth Study of Credit or Loan Practices by 30 Outstanding Banking Authorities, 55
Proctor, William, jt. auth. See Burkett, Larry, and Proctor, William; see also Dooner, William, and Proctor, William
Proulx, Annie. What'll You Take for It: Back to Barter, 58
Pugsley, John. The Alpha Strategy: The Ultimate Plan of Financial Self-Defense for the Small Investor, 83
Purcell, W. R., Jr. Understanding a Company's Finances: A Graphic Approach, 83
Putney, Valerie, jt. auth. See Price, J. R., with Putney, Valerie
Pyle, Connie, jt. auth. See Brealey, Richard A., and Pyle, Connie

Quinn, Jane B. Everyone's Money Book, 26

Radics, Stephen P., Jr., and Geisman, Miriam S. Your Home as a Tax Shelter: How to Save Taxes When You Buy, Hold, or Sell Your Home, 110
Rahney, Philip. Do-It-Yourself Family Money Kit: A Four Step Method to Building Financial Security, 26
Ramsey, Dan. How to Make Your First Quarter Million in Real Estate in Five Years, 123
Raphaelson, Elliot. "Low Cost Investment Information," 14; Planning Your Financial Future: Tax Shelters, Annuities, IRAs, Keoghs, Stocks and Other Investment or Retirement Opportunities, 149
Raskhodoff, Nicholas. The Complete Mobile Home Book: The Guide to Manufactured Homes, 115
Reed, John T. Aggressive Tax Avoidance for Real Estate Investors: How to Make Sure You Aren't Paying One More Cent in Taxes Than the Law Requires, 139
Reed, Ronald, jt. auth. See Bradford, W. Murray, and Reed, Ronald
Reilly, Jim. Bonds as Investments in the Eighties, 95
Reinach, Anthony. The Fastest Game in Town/Trading Commodity Futures, 92
Rejnis, Ruth. Her Home: A Woman's Guide to Buying Real Estate, 110; How to Buy Real Estate without Getting Burned, 111
Rhoades, Judith, jt. auth. See Perkins, Gail, and Rhoades, Judith
Rhodes, Lucien, jt. auth. See Little, Jeffrey B., and Rhodes, Lucien
Riccio, Dolores, jt. auth. See Bingham, Joan, and Riccio, Dolores

Rieder, Thomas. *Sun Spots, Stars, and the Stock Market*, 84
Rifenbark, Richard K. *How To Beat the Salary Trap: 8 Steps to Financial Independence*, 26
Righetti, Raymond. *Stock Market Strategy for Consistent Profits*, 84
Ritter, Lawrence S., and Silber, William J. *Money*, 26
Robertson, A. Haeworth. *The Coming Revolution in Social Security*, 160
Roethenmund, Robert. *The Swiss Banking Handbook: A Complete Manual for Practical Investors*, 63
Rogers, Harry. *The American Bankruptcy Kit*, 76
Rogers, Mary. *Women, Divorce and Money: Plain Talk about Money, Procedures, Settlement, Financial Survival for Women Who Are Divorced or Thinking about Divorce*, 48
Rogers, Mary, and Joyce, Nancy. *Women and Money*, 49
Roll, Richard, and Young, G. Douglas. *Getting Yours: Financial Success Strategies for Young Professionals in a Tougher Era*, 144
Roll, Richard J., jt. auth. See Downs, Hugh, and Roll, Richard J.
Rolo, Charles. *Gaining on the Market: Your Complete Guide to Investment Strategy: Stocks, Bonds, Options, Mutual Funds and Gold*, 84
Romero, George. *The Great Dollar Deception: Losing When You Think You're Winning* (Romero), 42
Rosefsky, Robert. *Financial Planning for the Young Family*, 144; *Money Talks: Bob Rosefsky's Complete Program for Financial Success*, 8, 27
Rosen, Lawrence R. *The Dow Jones-Irwin Guide to Interest: What You Should Know About the Time Value of Money*, 35
Rosenberg, Claude. *Stock Market Primer*, 84

Rosenberg, Jerome R. *Managing Your Own Money*, 27
Rosenberg, Jerry M. *Dictionary of Business and Management*, 225
Rosenbloom, Jerry, jt. auth. See Hallman, G. Victor, and Rosenbloom, Jerry
Rotchstein, Janice. *The Money Diet: How to Save Up to $360 in 28 Days*, 35
Rothchild, John. *Stop Burning Your Money: The Intelligent Homeowner's Guide to Household Energy Savings*, 35
Rubin, Richard L. *Your 1983/84 Tax Guide to Social Security Benefits*, 160
Rubinstein, David. *Invest for Retirement: A Conservative Investor's Guide*, 149
Ruff, Howard. *How to Prosper during the Coming Bad Years*, 42; *Howard Ruff from A to Z: A Timeless Money Making Odyssey through the First Four Years of America's Leading Financial Advisory Service*, 42; *Survive and Win in the Inflationary Eighties*, 43
Rugg, Donald D., and Hale, Norman B. *The Dow Jones-Irwin Guide to Mutual Funds*, 96
Rupprecht, Leslie P. *Business Literature*, 16
Rush, Richard. *Automobiles as an Investment*, 102; *Selling Collectibles for Profit and Capital Gains*, 103
Rutberg, Sidney. *Playboy's Investment and Financial Planning Guide for Singles: Making It and Keeping It in the Eighties*, 27

Sammons, Donna, jt. auth. See Wiltsee, Joseph L., and Sammons, Donna
Samtur, Susan J., and Tuleja, Tad. *Cashing in at the Checkout*, 59;

Coupon Magic: The Beginner's Kit of Tricks for Slashing Supermarket Costs, 60
Sarnoff, Paul. *The Smart Investor's Guide to the Money Market*, 96; *Trading in Gold: How to Buy, Sell, and Profit in the Gold Market*, 98
Sartisky, Jacques, jt. auth. *See* Brownstone, David M., and Sartisky, Jacques
Savage, Michael. *Everything You Always Wanted to Know about Taxes But Didn't Know How to Ask*, 130
Schandel, Susan, jt. auth. *See* Schandel, Terry, and Schandel, Susan
Schandel, Terry, and Schandel, Susan. *Tax Tactics for Teachers*, 130; *Tax Tactics for the Retired*, 130; *Tax Tactics for the Single or Divorced*, 130
Schiff, Irwin A., with Murzim, Howy. *How Anyone Can Stop Paying Income Taxes*, 130
Schlayer, Mary E., with Cooley, Marilyn. *How to Be a Financially Secure Woman*, 49
Schmeltz, L. *Playing the Stock Markets with Your Personal Computer*, 72
Schneider, Herman M., jt. auth. *See* Crestol, Jack, and Schneider, Herman M.
Schnepper, Jeff. *How to Pay Zero Taxes: Over 100 Ways to Reduce Your Taxes—To Nothing*, 134
Schoeneman, Charles, jt. auth. *See* Jacobs, Vernon K., and Shoeneman, Charles
Schultz, Harry. *Bear Market Investment Strategies*, 85; *Panics and Crashes: How You Can Make Money Out of Them*, 43; *see also* Sinclair, James, and Schultz, Harry
Schwarz, Edward W. *How to Use Interest Rate Futures Contracts*, 93
Scott, Jim. *How to Make Money in Penny Stocks: The Ultimate Solution for the Small Investor*, 94
Scott, William L. *Investing at the Racetrack*, 73
Segall, Mark, and Tobin, Margaret. *How to Make Love to Your Money*, 53
Seidler, Lee J. *Everything You Wanted to Know about Tax Shelters, but Were Afraid to Ask*, 135
Seldin, Maury. *Real Estate Investment for Profit through Appreciation*, 123
Seldin, Maury, and Swesnick, Richard. *Real Estate Investment Strategies*, 123
Self, Robert. *Long Distance for Less: How to Choose Between Ma Bell and Those "Other" Carriers*, 36
Shafer, Ronald, jt. auth. *See* Sumichrast, Michael, and Shafer, Ronald; *see also* Sumichrast, Michael, Shafer, Ronald, and Sumichrast, Marika
Sharpe, William. *Investments*, 73
Shepherd, William G. "Variety, New Risks, Complicate Decisions," 8
Shulman, Morton. *Anyone Can Make Big Money Buying Art*, 103; *How to Invest Your Money and Profit from Inflation*, 43
Shulman, Richard, jt. auth. *See* Blamer, Thomas, and Shulman, Richard
Shupp, Gary L., jt. auth. *See* Suthers, John W., and Shupp, Gary L.
Sideris, Georgia. "Free Booklets on Smart Money Management," 15
Silber, William J., jt. auth. *See* Ritter, Lawrence S., and Silber, William J.
Silverberg, Barry, jt. auth. *See* Ferri, Robert, and Silverberg, Barry
Silvers, William L., and Harkness, Richard M. *I Filed Bankruptcy and

Author Index

I'm Glad I Did, 66
Simm, Dyanne. *The Barter Book*, 58
Simon, Carl P., and Witte, Ann D. *Beating the System: The Underground Economy*, 59
Simon, Samuel, and Waz, Joseph. *Reverse the Charges: How to Save $$$ on Your Phone Bill*, 36
Simons, Alice, jt. auth. See Simons, Gustave, and Simons, Alice
Simons, Gustave, and Simons, Alice. *Money and Women*, 49
Simons, Myron. *How to Profit from Disinflation*, 73
Sinclair, James, and Schultz, Harry. *How You Can Profit from Gold*, 98
Sinclair, James E., and Parker, Robert. *The Strategic Metals War: The Current Crisis and Your Investment Opportunities*, 99
Sirico, Louis J. *How to Talk Back to the Telephone Company: Playing the Telephone Game to Win*, 36
Siverd, Bonnie, "Financial Supermarkets," 8
Skousen, Mark. *Tax Free*, 136; *Mark Skousen's Guide to Financial Privacy*, 27
Sloan, Irving J. *Income and Estate Tax Planning*, 149
Sloane, Martin. *The Nineteen Eighty-One Guide to Coupons and Refunds*, 60
Small, Linda. "Want to Curl Up with a Good Money Book? Our No-Frills Guide Tells Which Ones Are Worth It," 15
Smith, Adam. *Paper Money*, 43
Smith, Barbara, jt. auth. See Smith, Jerome, and Smith, Barbara
Smith, Charles. *The Mind of the Market: A Study of Stock Market Philosophies, Their Use and Implications*, 89
Smith, Gregory, jt. auth. See Naifeh, Steven, with Smith, Gregory
Smith, Jerome. *The Coming Currency Collapse: And What You Can Do about It*, 44
Smith, Jerome, and Smith, Barbara. *Silver Profits in the Eighties*, 98
Smith, Milton. *Money Today, More Tomorrow*, 144
Smith, Stuart, and Sprogen, Janet. *How You Can Get the Most from the New Tax Law*, 133
Smith, Thurman. *Investors Can Beat Inflation: A Practical Guide*, 85
Smith, Wendy, jt. auth. See Davis, Joann, and Smith, Wendy
Snyder, Earl. *Before You Invest: Questions and Answers on Real Estate*, 123
Sokoloff, Kiril. *The Paine Webber Handbook of Stock and Bond Analysis*, 223; *The Thinking Investor's Guide to the Stock Market*, 85
Sokoloff, Kiril, Laird, Joseph, and Mack, Thomas. *Investing in the Future: 10 New Industries and 75 Key Growth Companies That Are Changing the Face of Corporate America*, 85
Spencer, Phyllis. *Vacation Timesharing: Upper Income Holidays on Middle Income Budgets*, 116
Speraw, Linda. *How to Buy Your First Home*, 111
Spielman, Peter, and Zelman, Aaron. *The Life Insurance Conspiracy Made Elementary by Sherlock Holmes*, 158
Sprinkel, Beryl W., and Genetski, Robert J. *Winning with Money: A Guide for Your Future*, 28
Sprogen, Janet, jt. auth. See Smith, Stuart, and Sprogen, Janet
Sprouse, Mary L. *How to Survive a Tax Audit: What To Do before and after You Hear from the IRS*, 138

Starchild, Adam. *Building Wealth: A Layman's Guide to Trust Planning*, 157; *Everyman's Guide to Tax Havens*, 137

Steif, Bill. *What You've Got Coming in Social Security and Medicare*, 160

Stein, Ben, and Stein, Herbert. *Money Power: How to Make Inflation Make You Rich*, 44

Stein, Herbert, jt. auth. See Stein, Ben, and Stein, Herbert

Steiner, Barry, and Kennedy, David. *Perfectly Legal: 275 Foolproof Methods for Paying Less Tax*, 134

Steskal, T. J. *Understanding Medicare*, 160

Stigum, Marcia. *The Money Market: Myth, Realities and Practice*, 73

Stillman, Richard. *Money-Wise: The Prentice-Hall Book of Personal Money Management*, 144; *More for Your Money: Personal Finance Techniques to Cope with Inflation and the Energy Shortage*, 28

Stloukal, Robert. *The Greatest Real Estate Book in the World: The One Way You Can Make a Fortune in the 80's*, 113

Storer, Philip, and Williams, Brian. *The Tax Fighter's Guide*, 131

Stossel, John. *John Stossel's Shopping Smart: The Only Consumer's Guide You'll Ever Need*, 37

Strassels, Paul N. *Money in Your Pocket: Using the New Reagan Tax Laws*, 133

Strassels, Paul N., and Wool, Robert. *All You Need to Know about the IRS: A Taxpayer's Guide*, 131

Sullivan, Colleen. *High-Risk, High-Reward Investing: An Expert Guide to Twenty-five Growth Fields*, 85

Sumichrast, Marika, jt. auth. See Sumichrast, Michael, Shafer, Ronald, and Sumichrast, Marika

Sumichrast, Michael, and Shafer, Ronald. *The Complete Book of Home Buying: A Consumer's Guide to Housing in the 80's*, 111

Sumichrast, Michael, Shafer, Ronald, and Sumichrast, Marika. *Where Will You Live Tomorrow? The Complete Guide to Planning for Your Retirement Housing*, 149

Summers, Bruce, jt. auth. See Cook, Timothy, and Summers, Bruce

Suthers, John W., and Shupp, Gary L. *Fraud and Deceit: How to Stop Being Ripped Off*, 38

Sutton, Remar. *Don't Get Taken Every Time: The Insider's Guide to Buying Your Next Car*, 37

Swanson, Barbara M., jt. auth. See Swanson, Robert E., and Swanson, Barbara M.

Swanson, Robert E., and Swanson, Barbara M. *Tax Shelters: A Guide for Investors and Their Advisors*, 136

Swesnick, Richard, jt. auth. See Seldin, Maury, and Swesnick, Richard

Szuprowicz, Bohdan. *How to Invest in Strategic Metals*, 99

Tannenhauser, Carol, jt. auth. See Tannenhauser, Robert, and Tannenhauser, Carol

Tannenhauser, Robert, and Tannenhauser, Carol. *Tax Shelters: A Complete Guide*, 136

Tanner, Beverly, Pheffer, Marvin, and Laurins, Alex. *Shelter What You Make, Minimize the Take: Tax Shelters for Financial Planning*, 136

Tanzer, Milt. *Real Estate Investments and How to Make Them: The Only Guide You'll Ever Need*, 123

Tappan, William. *The Real Estate Acquisition Handbook: Money-Making Techniques for the Serious Investor*, 124

Taylor, Thomas J. *Get Rich on the*

Obvious: How to Turn Your Everyday Observations into Money, 77

Taylor, Tom, jt. auth. *See* Davis, Ken, and Taylor, Tom

Temple, Douglas. *Creative Home Financing: You Can Buy a House, Condominium or Co-Op in Today's Market*, 113; *Investing in Residential Income Property*, 124; *Real Estate Investment for the 80's: How to Build Financial Security in the Face of Inflation*, 124

Teweles, Richard J., and Bradley, Edward S. *The Stock Market*, 78

Thomason, James. *Common Sense about Your Family Dollars*, 46

Thorsell, Richard L. *Investing on Your Own: How to Find Winning Stocks in Your Own Backyard*, 78

Thypin, Marilyn, and Glasner, Lynne. *Checking and Balancing: (Banking)*, 63

Tilling, Thomas, jt. auth. *See* Donoghue, William, with Tilling, Thomas

Tobias, Andrew. *The Invisible Bankers: Everything the Insurance Industry Never Wanted You to Know*, 159; *The Only Investment Guide You'll Ever Need*, 74; "Want the Bottom Line on TV's Business Reporting?," 7

Tobin, Margaret, jt. auth. *See* Segall, Mark, and Tobin, Margaret

Torbet, Laura, jt. auth. *See* Hatton, Hap, and Torbet, Laura

Touhey, John C. *Stock Market Forecasting for Alert Investors*, 88

Train, John. *The Money Masters: Nine Great Investors, Their Winning Strategies and How You Can Apply Them*, 86

Traister, Robert, and Ingram, Rich. *Making Money with Your Microcomputer*, 51

Trowbridge, Keith W. *Resort Timesharing: How You Can Invest in Inflation-Proof Vacations for Life*, 116

Trower-Subira, George. *Black Folks' Guide to Making Big Money in America*, 28

Trubo, Richard. *The Consumer's Book of Hints and Tips*, 37

Tso, Lin. *Complete Investors Guide to Listed Options*, 90

Tuccille, Jerome. *Dynamic Investing: The System for Dynamic Profits—No Matter Which Way the Market Goes*, 86; *Everything the Beginner Needs to Know to Invest Shrewdly: A Step by Step Guide to the Basics of Financial Growth*, 74; *Inside the Underground Economy: Over Twenty Million Americans Are Avoiding Income Taxes—and May Be Getting Away with It*, 59; *Mind over Money: Why Most People Lose Money in the Stock Market and How You Can Become a Winner*, 89; *The New Tax Law and You*, 133; *The Optimist's Guide to Making Money in the 1980's: A Complete Program for Investing in the American Economic Miracle of the Next Decade*, 74

Tuleja, Tad, jt. auth. *See* Samtur, Susan J., and Tuleja, Tad; *see also* Tyndall, Carolyn, Tyndall, Roger, with Tuleja, Tad

Tyndall, Carolyn, Tyndall, Roger, with Tuleja, Tad. *And the Lucky Winner Is . . . A Complete Guide to Winning Contests and Sweepstakes*, 62

Tyndall, Roger, jt. auth. *See* Tyndall, Carolyn, Tyndall, Roger, with Tuleja, Tad

Ullman, James M., and Bercoon, Norman. *How to Build a Fortune with an IRA*, 152

Ungaro, Susan. *The H and R Block Family Financial Planning Workbook*, 37
United Business Services. *Successful Investing: A Complete Guide to Your Financial Future*, 74
U.S. Government Printing Office, Superintendent of Documents, *Subject Bibliography Index*, 19

VanArsdale, Mary G. *A Guide to Family Financial Counseling: Credit, Debt and Money Management*, 46
Van Caspel, Venita. *Money Dynamics for the 1980's*, 28; *The New Money Dynamics*, 28; *The Power of Money Dynamics*, 28
VanMeer, Mary, and Pasquarelli, Michael. *Free Attractions, USA*, 61
Vogel, David, jt. auth. *See* Powers, Mark, and Vogel, David
Vreeland, Richard. *Become Financially Independent: An Investment Plan That Really Works*, 74

Wade, Jack Warren. *When You Owe the IRS*, 131
Wagenheim, Kal. *Paper Gold: How to Hedge against Inflation by Investing in Postage Stamps*, 103
Walker, Glen. *Credit Where Credit Is Due: A Legal Guide to Your Credit Rights and How to Assess Them*, 55
Waller, Kal. *How to Recover Your Medical Expenses: A Comprehensive Guide to Understanding and Unscrambling Medicare*, 161
Ward, David, and Niendorf, Robert. *Consumer Finance: The Consumer Experience*, 145
Warfield, Gerald. *The Investor's Guide to Stock Quotations and Other Financial Listings*, 78
Wasserman, Paul, Georgi, Charlotte, and Woy, James. *Encyclopedia of Business Information Sources: A Detailed Listing of Primary Subjects of Interest to Managerial Personnel, with a Record of Sourcebooks, Periodicals, Organizations, Directories, Handbooks, Bibliographies, On-Line Data Bases and Other Sources of Information on Each Topic*, 20
Waz, Joseph, jt. auth. *See* Simon, Samuel, and Waz, Joseph
Webster, Jonathan, jt. auth. *See* Webster, Harriet, and Webster, Jonathan
Webster, Harriet, and Webster, Jonathan. *The Underground Marketplace: A Guide to New England and the Middle Atlantic States*, 59
Weinstein, Bob. *Winning the Battle with Your Money Hang-Ups*, 53
Weintz, Caroline, and Weintz, Walter. *The Discount Guide for Travelers over 55*, 61
Weintz, Walter, jt. auth. *See* Weintz, Caroline, and Weintz, Walter
Weir, Mary. *House Recycling: The Best Real Estate Opportunity for the 80's*, 124
Weiss, Martin. *The Great Money Panic: A Guide for Survival and Action*, 44
White, Robert. *The Duck Book: Investment for Survival in the 1980's*, 44
Whitman, Robert. *Simplified Guide to Estate Planning and Administration*, 156
Whitney, Victor. *How to Beat the Money Grabbers: The Essentials of Estate Planning*, 156
Wilford, Jane, jt. auth. *See* Ladley, Barbara, and Wilford, Jane
Williams, Brian, jt. auth. *See* Storer, Philip, and Williams, Brian
Williams, Gordon L. *Financial Survival in the Age of New Money*, 29

Author Index

Williams, Larry. *How to Prosper in the Coming Good Years*, 93

Wiltsee, Joseph L., and Sammons, Donna. *You Can Profit from the New Tax Law*, 133

Winfrey, Dennis W., jt. auth. *See* Hubbard, L. Ron, and Winfrey, Dennis W.

Wishard, Bill, and Wishard, Laurie. *Men's Rights: A Handbook for the 80's*, 29

Wishard, Laurie, jt. auth. *See* Wishard, Bill, and Wishard, Laurie

Witte, Ann D., jt. auth. *See* Simon, Carl P., and Witte, Ann D.

Wolenik, Robert. *Buying and Selling Currency for Profit*, 93; *How You Can Share in the Futures Being Made in Gold*, 99

Wool, Robert, jt. auth. *See* Cook, John A., and Wool, Robert; *see also* Strassels, Paul N., and Wool, Robert

Worley, H. Wilson. *Retirement Living Alternatives USA: The Inside Story*, 150

Woy, James. *Commodity Futures Trading: A Bibliographic Guide*, 21; *Investment Methods: A Bibliographic Guide*, 21; *see also* Wasserman, Paul, Georgi, Charlotte, and Woy, James

Wykoff, Gerald L. *Beyond the Glitter: Everything You Need to Know to Buy . . . Sell . . . Care for . . . and Wear Gems and Jewelry Wisely*, 101

Wyckoff, Peter, jt. auth. *See* Engel, Louis, with Wyckoff, Peter

Yarry, Mark. *The Fastest Game in Town: Commodities*, 93

Young, G. Douglas, jt. auth. *See* Roll, Richard, and Young, G. Douglas

Youngquist, Walter. *Investing in Natural Resources: 1980's Guide to Tomorrow's Needs*, 100

Zarb, Frank G., jt. auth. *See* Fabozzi, Frank J., and Zarb, Frank G.

Zeikel, Arthur, jt. auth. *See* Cohen, Jerome B., Zinbarg, Edward, and Zeikel, Arthur

Zelman, Aaron, jt. auth. *See* Spielman, Peter, and Zelman, Aaron

Zerden, Shelden. *Best Books on the Stock Market: An Analytical Bibliography*, 21

Ziegler, Richard, jt. auth. *See* Flaherty, Patrick F., and Ziegler, Richard

Zimmerman, Gary. *Managing Your Own Money: A Self-Teaching Guide*, 29

Zinbarg, Edward, jt. auth. *See* Cohen, Jerome B., Zinbarg, Edward, and Zeikel, Arthur

Zucker, Benjamin. *How to Buy and Sell Gems: Everyone's Guide to Rubies, Sapphires, Emeralds and Diamonds*, 101

Title Index

Note: Pamphlet titles listed in Chapter 10 (Pamphlet Resources), pp. 189–215, are not indexed here.

ABC's of Investing Your Retirement Funds (Hardy), 146
The ABC's of IRA's: The Complete Guide to Individual Retirement Accounts: The #1 Investment Strategy of the Eighties (Grace), 151
After the Crash: How to Survive and Prosper During the Depression of the 1980's (Abert), 38
Aggressive Tax Avoidance for Real Estate Investors: How to Make Sure You Aren't Paying One More Cent in Taxes Than the Law Requires (Reed), 139
All about Escrow: Or How to Buy the Brooklyn Bridge and Have the Last Laugh (Gadow), 106
All You Need to Know about Banks (Cook and Wool), 62
All You Need to Know about the IRS: A Taxpayer's Guide (Strassels and Wool), 131
The Alpha Strategy: The Ultimate Plan of Financial Self-Defense for the Small Investor (Pugsley), 83
The American Bankruptcy Kit (Rogers), 65
And the Lucky Winner Is . . . A Complete Guide to Winning Contests and Sweepstakes (Tyndall, Tyndall, with Tuleja), 62
Anyone Can Make Big Money Buying Art (Shulman), 103
Ask the Coupon Queen: How to Buy Seventy-One Dollars and Seventy-One Cents Worth of Groceries for Seven Dollars and Nineteen Cents (Hayes), 59
Automobiles as an Investment (Rush), 102

Bank Credit: An Indepth Study of Credit or Loan Practices by 30 Outstanding Banking Authorities (Prochnow), 55
Bankruptcy: Do It Yourself (Kosel), 65
Bankruptcy Options for the Consumer Debtor (Girth), 64
The Bargain Hunter's Guide to Art Collecting (Naifeh and Smith), 102
Barron's, 170
The Barter Book (Simm), 58
The Barter Way to Beat Inflation (Burtt), 57
Basic Investment Sources (Daniells), 17
BASIC Programs for Home Financial Management (Goldsmith), 142
The Battle for Financial Security: How to Invest in the Runaway 80's (Bridwell), 68
Bear Market Investment Strategies (Schultz), 85
Beat the System: A Survival Guide (Paulsen), 58
Beating Inflation with Real Estate (Harney), 120
Beating the System: The Underground Economy (Simon and Witte), 59
Become Financially Independent: An Investment Plan That Really Works (Vreeland), 74
Before You Invest: Questions and Answers on Real Estate (Snyder), 123
The Beginning Investor (Hassan), 71
Bernard Meltzer Solves Your Money Problems: Borrowing, Buying and Investment Strategies to Profit from Inflation (Meltzer), 72
Bert Johnson's Credit Loopholes: An Instant Credit Guide (Johnson), 54
Best Books on the Stock Market: An Analytical Bibliography (Zerden), 21
Better Homes and Gardens, 164
Better Investing, 169
Beyond the Glitter: Everything You Need to Know to Buy . . . Sell . . . Care for . . . and Wear Gems and Jewelry Wisely (Wykoff), 101
Bibliography and Information Source List: Financial Futures, 16
"Bibliography," Dun and Bradstreet's Guide to Your Investments (Hardy), 13
A Bibliography of Finance and Investment (Brealey and Pyle), 16
Bill Greene's 101 New Loopholes: The Reagan Tax Package 1983-85 (Greene), 132
Black Enterprise, 167
Black Folks' Guide to Making Big Money in America (Trower-Subira), 28
Bond Guide, 220
Bond Record, 220
Bond Survey, 220
Bonds as Investments in the Eighties (Reilly), 95
Bonds: How to Double Your Money Quickly and Safely (Holt), 94
The Book of Inside Information (Bottom Line/Personal, Experts), 23
"Books on Money Matters: A Current Checklist" (Davis and Smith), 11
The Bowser Report, 184
Bruce Gould on Commodities, 187
Bruce McDowell's Investment Newsletter, 178
Building Wealth: A Layman's Guide to Trust Planning (Starchild), 157
Bull and Bear, 174
Bulls, Bears, and Massacres: A Proven System for Investing in the Stock Market (Diamond), 87
"Business Books of 198-. A Selection of Recommended Books Published During the Past Year" (DiMattia), 11, 12
Business Information from Your Public Library, 10
Business Information Sources (Daniells), 17
Business Literature (Rupprecht), 16

Title Index

Business Tax Deduction Master Guide: Strategies for Business and Professional People (Bradford and Reed), 126
Business Week, 170
"Buyer's Guide: When You Wish Upon a Stock" (Liebman), 14
Buyer's Handbook for the Single-Family House (Lee), 108
Buying a Condominium (Heatter), 114
Buying and Selling Currency for Profit (Wolenik), 93
Buying, Owning and Selling a Home in the 1980's (Kratovil and Kratovil), 108

CDE Stock Ownership Directory (Abrecht and Locker), 221
The Cabot Market Letter, 179
Cashing in at the Checkout (Samtur and Tuleja), 59
Cashless Investing in Real Estate (Cummings), 118
Changing Times, 169
Chapter 13: The Federal Plan to Repay Your Debts (Kosel), 65
Charge It: Inside the Credit Card Conspiracy (Galanoy), 53
The Cheap Investor, 185
Checking and Balancing: (Banking) (Thypin and Glasner), 63
Chilton's Guide to Consumer's Auto Repairs and Prices: How to Save Money on Auto Repairs and Accessories (Freeman), 31
Collecting and Care of Fine Art (David), 101
The Coming Credit Collapse: An Update for the 1980's (Paris), 42
The Coming Currency Collapse: And What You Can Do about It (Smith), 44
The Coming Real Estate Crash (Cardiff and English), 117

The Coming Revolution in Social Security (Robertson), 160
Commodities: The Magazine of Futures Trading, 170
Commodity Futures Trading: A Bibliographic Guide (Woy), 21
Commodity Futures Trading Bibliography Cumulative through 1976 and Updates, 17
Commodity Speculation for Beginners: A Guide to the Futures Market (Huff and Marinacci), 91
Common Sense about Your Family Dollars (Thomason), 46
The Complete Book of Bonds: How to Buy and Sell Profitably (Holt), 94
The Complete Book of Home Buying: A Consumer's Guide to Housing in the 80's (Sumichrast and Shafer), 111
The Complete Condominium Guide (Cassiday), 114
The Complete Estate Planning Guide: Updated to Include 1981 and 1982 Tax Changes (Brosterman), 152
The Complete Guide to Credit and Loans: Everything You Should Know about Successful Borrowing (Gibbs), 8, 53
The Complete Guide to Estate Planning (Gargon), 153
The Complete Handbook for Travelers (Gieseking), 61
Complete Investors Guide to Listed Options (Tso), 90
The Complete List of IRS Tax Deductions (Minkow and Minkow), 134
The Complete Mobile Home Book: The Guide to Manufactured Homes (Raskhodoff), 115
The Condominium Book: Getting the Most for Your Money Revised for the 1980's (Butcher), 114
Condominium Ownership: A Buyer's Guide (Ludy), 114
Consensus: National Commodity Futures Weekly, 174

Consensus of Insiders, 179
The Conservative Investor, 179
Consumer Economics and Personal Money Management (Albin), 141
Consumer Finance: The Consumer Experience (Ward and Niendorf), 145
Consumer Reports, 168
Consumer Saturday, New York Times, 8
Consumer Tactics Manual: How to Get Action on Your Complaints (Dorfman), 37
The Consumer's Book of Hints and Tips (Trubo), 37
Consumer's Digest, 168
Consumers Guide to Mortgage Payments, 111
Consumers' Research, 168
The Consumers Union Report on Life Insurance: A Guide to Planning and Buying the Protection You Need (Consumer Reports), 157
Cosmopolitan, 166
Coupon Magic: The Beginner's Kit of Tricks for Slashing Supermarket Costs (Samtur with Tuleja), 60
Craig Hall's Book of Real Estate Investing (Hall), 119
Creating Wealth: How to Make It—And Keep It! (Allen), 116
Creative Home Financing: You Can Buy a House, Condominium or Co-Op in Today's Market (Temple), 113
Credit! (Clark), 53
Credit: Get It, Use It, Stretch It, Save It (Johnson), 54
Credit Week, 220
Credit Where Credit Is Due: A Legal Guide to Your Credit Rights and How to Assess Them (Walker), 55
Crisis Investing: Opportunities and Profits in the Coming Great Depression (Casey), 40
Crisis Real Estate Investing: Increase and Protect Your Assets from Potential Disaster (Morris), 122

Current Market Perspectives, 221
Cut Your Own Taxes and Save: The Everything-You-Need-to-Know Guide for Your 1981 Tax Return (Kast), 132
Cutting College Costs: The Up-to-the-Minute Manual for 1983-1984 (Donald), 55

Daily Action Stock Charts, 220
Daily Stock Price Record, 217-218
Dessauer's Journal of Financial Markets, 179
The Diamond Book: A Practical Guide for Successful Investing (Freedman), 100
Dictionary of Business and Management (Rosenberg), 225
Dictionary of Insurance (Davids), 225
Die Rich: Making It, Keeping It, and Passing It Along under the New Tax Laws (Plotnick and Leimberg), 156
Directory of American Savings and Loan Associations, 221
Directory of Business and Financial Services (Grant and Cote), 18
Directory of Obsolete Securities: Financial Stock Guidance Service, 221-222
The Directory of Toll-Free Phone Numbers, 31
The Discount Guide for Travelers over 55 (Weintz and Weintz), 61
Dividend Record, 218
Dividend Records, 219
Do-It-Yourself Family Money Kit: A Four Step Method to Building Financial Security (Rahney), 26
Dollars and Sense: Making Your Money Work for You and Your Family (Kilgore), 45
Dollars on Your Doorstep: How to Run a Business from Your Own Home (Income Opportunities), 50
Donoghue's Money Letter, 186
Don't Bank on It: How to Make up

Title Index

to 22% or More of Your Savings—All Fully Insured (Meyer), 62
Don't Get Taken Every Time: The Insider's Guide to Buying Your Next Car (Sutton), 37
Don't Miss Out: The Ambitious Student's Guide to Scholarships and Loans (Leider), 56
Double Your Dollars in 600 Days (Cobleigh), 97
Double Your Money in Real Estate Every Two Years (Glubetich), 118
The Dow-Jones Investor's Handbook (Pierce), 223
The Dow Jones-Irwin Business and Investment Almanac (Levine), 224
The Dow Jones-Irwin Guide to College Financial Planning (Lane), 56
The Dow Jones-Irwin Guide to Commodities Trading (Gould), 91
The Dow Jones-Irwin Guide to Estate Planning (Clay), 153
The Dow Jones-Irwin Guide to Interest: What You Should Know About the Time Value of Money (Rosen), 35
The Dow Jones-Irwin Guide to Mutual Funds (Rugg and Hale), 96
The Dow Jones-Irwin Guide to Personal Financial Planning (Amling and Droms), 141
Dow Theory Letters, 179
Dow 3000: The Investment Opportunity of the 1980's (Blamer and Shulman), 75
The Dowbeaters: How to Buy Stocks That Go Up (Cobleigh and Dorfman), 80
The Duck Book: Investment for Survival in the 1980's (White), 44
Dun and Bradstreet's Guide to Your Investments (Hardy), 71
Dun's Business Month, 170
Dynamic Investing: The System for Dynamic Profits—No Matter Which Way the Market Goes (Tuccille), 86
Dynamic Years, 167

Earning Money without a Job (Levinson), 57
Economics Deciphered: A Layman's Survival Guide (Levi), 25
Elliott Wave Principle: Key to Stock Market Profits (Prechter and Frost), 88
Encyclopedia of Business Information Sources: A Detailed Listing of Primary Subjects of Interest to Managerial Personnel, with a Record of Sourcebooks, Periodicals, Organizations, Directories, Handbooks, Bibliographies, On-Line Data Bases and Other Sources of Information on Each Topic (Wasserman, Georgi, and Woy), 20
Encyclopedia of Investments (Blume and Friedman), 222
Equity Research Associates, 183
Esquire, 167
Essence, 166
Estate Planning: After the Reagan Tax Cut (Lippett), 155
Estate Planning for Everyone: The Whole Truth—from Planning to Probate (Flaherty and Ziegler), 153
Estate Planning: What Anyone Who Owns Anything Must Know (Lippett), 155
Everybody's Money, 168
Everyman's Guide to Tax Havens (Starchild), 137
Everyone's Money Book (Quinn), 26
Everything the Beginner Needs to Know to Invest Shrewdly: A Step by Step Guide to the Basics of Financial Growth (Tucille), 74
Everything You Always Wanted to Know about Taxes but Didn't Know How to Ask (Savage), 130
Everything You Need to Know about Creative Home Financing (Coffee), 111
Everything You Wanted to Know about Tax Shelters, but Were Afraid to Ask (Seidler), 135

284 Title Index

Fact: The Money Management Magazine, 169
Fad Money: How to Make Money from Fads, Crazes, and Trends (Klein), 25
Fail-Safe Investing: How to Make Money with Less Than $10,000 . . . Without Losing Sleep (Nagan), 72
Family Circle, 164
Family Financial Survival (Ginsberg), 153
Family Investment Guide: A Financial Handbook for Middle-Income People (Dorfman), 69
Family Security through Estate Planning (Kahn), 154
The Fastest Game in Town: Commodities (Yarry), 93
The Fastest Game in Town/Trading Commodity Futures (Reinach), 92
50 Plus, 167
Fight Back! and Don't Get Ripped Off (Horowitz), 38
Financial Freedom: A Positive Strategy for Putting Your Money to Work (Barry), 78
Financial Freedom: Your New Guide to Economic Security and Success (Halverson), 24
The Financial Management of Your Coin/Stamp Estate (Crumbley and Crumbley), 101
Financial Planning Bibliography: A Selected List, Resources (College for Financial Planning), 12
Financial Planning for the Young Family (Rosefsky), 144
The Financial Planning Workbook (Burkett), 45
"Financial Supermarkets" (Siverd), 8
Financial Survival in the Age of New Money (Williams), 29
Financial Times, 172
The Financial War Room, 179
Financial World, 170
Finding the Next Super Stock (Cappiello), 79

"The First Risk in Investing: Reading about It" (Dunn), 12
555 Ways to Earn Extra Money (Levinson), 33
For Sale by Owner (Gilmore), 106
Forbes, 170
Ford Value Report, 179
Foreclosures: How to Profitably Invest in Distressed Real Estate (McLean), 122
Foreign Exchange Futures: A Guide to International Currency Trading (Loosigan), 92
Fortune, 170
A Fortune at Your Feet: How You Can Get Rich, Stay Rich and Enjoy Being Rich with Creative Real Estate (Kessler), 121
Fraud and Deceit: How to Stop Being Ripped Off (Suthers and Shupp), 38
Free Attractions, USA (VanMeer and Pasquarelli), 61
"Free Booklets on Smart Money Management" (Sideris), 15
Frommer's How to Beat the High Cost of Travel (Brosnahan), 60
Fundamentals of Insurance (Mehr), 158
Fundamentals of Investing (Gitman and Joehnk), 70
Future Stocks: Investing for Profit in the Growth Stocks of the 1980's (Metz), 77
Futures: The Anti-Inflation Investment (Geczi), 91

Gaining on the Market: Your Complete Guide to Investment Strategy: Stocks, Bonds, Options, Mutual Funds and Gold (Rolo), 84
Get More Money from . . . Social Security, Govt. Benefits, Medicare, Plus (Dickinson, and the Editors of Consumer Guide), 159

Title Index 285

Get Out and Stay Out of Debt (David), 63
Get Out of Debt Now: How to Gain Control of Your Financial Affairs Once and for All (Graver), 54
Get Really Rich in the Coming Super Metals Boom (McLendon), 99
The "Get Rich" Investment Guide, 70
Get Rich on Other People's Money: Real Estate Investment Secrets (Pivar), 123
Get Rich on the Obvious: How to Turn Your Everyday Observations into Money (Taylor), 77
Get Your Money's Worth: The Book for People Who Are Tired of Paying More for Less (Joselow), 33
Getting Rich: A Smart Woman's Guide to Successful Money Management (Ackerman), 46
Getting Rich in Real Estate Partnerships (Baker), 117
Getting Started in Commodity Futures Trading (Powers), 92
Getting What You Deserve: A Handbook for the Assertive Consumer (Newman and Kramer), 38
Getting Your Money's Worth from Home Contractors (McClintock), 34
Getting Yours: Financial Success Strategies for Young Professionals in a Tougher Era (Roll and Young), 144
The Ginnie Mae Manual, 119
Glamour, 156
Glossary of Insurance Terms (Green, Osler, and Bickley), 225
Gold (Kettle), 98
Goldmining in Foreclosure Properties (Cabot), 117
Good Housekeeping, 164
The Granville Market Letter, 180
Granville's New Strategy of Daily Stock Market Timing for Maximum Profit (Granville), 87
The Great Dollar Deception: Losing When You Think You're Winning (Romero), 42
Great Expectations: The Psychology of Money (Lindgren), 52
The Great Money Machine: How Your Bank Works (Brown), 62
The Great Money Panic: A Guide for Survival and Action (Weiss), 44
The Greatest Banking Scandal in History: And How It Affects You (Clark), 40
The Greatest Real Estate Book in the World: The One Way You Can Make a Fortune in the 80's (Stloukal), 113
Grow Rich with Diamonds: Investing in the World's Most Precious Gems (Dohrmann), 100
Growth Fund Guide, 186
Growth Stock Outlook, 184
A Guide to Family Financial Counseling: Credit, Debt And Money Management (VanArsdale), 46
Guide to Intelligent Investing (Cohen, Zinbarg, and Zeikel), 69

The H and R Block Family Financial Planning Workbook (Ungaro), 37
The Handbook of Financial Markets: Securities, Options and Futures (Fabozzi and Zarb), 70
The Handbook of the Bond and Money Markets (Darst), 222–223
The Hard Money Book: An Insider's Guide to Successful Investment in Currency, Gold, Silver, and Precious Stones (Breckner), 97
Harry Browne's Special Reports, 187
Heads You Win, Tails You Win: The Dirks Investment Formula (Dirks), 80
Heads You Win, Tails You Win: The Inside Secrets to Rare Coin Investing (Pritchard), 102
Helpful Hints for Hard Times: How to

Live It Up While Cutting Down (Hatton and Torbet), 32
Help: The Basics of Borrowing Money (Gross and Cullen), 54
Her Home: A Woman's Guide to Buying Real Estate (Rejnis), 110
High-Return Low-Risk Investment (Herzfeld and Drach), 81
High-Risk, High-Reward Investing: An Expert Guide to Twenty-five Growth Fields (Sullivan), 85
High Technology Growth Stocks, 184
High Technology Investments, 184
The Home Buyer's Guide for the 80's: A Complete Guide to Every Step You Need to Take for the Biggest and Best Investment You'll Ever Make (O'Neill), 109
Home Buying (Lank), 108
A Home of Your Own for the Least Cash: The Home Buyer's Guide for Today (Hughes), 106
The Home Owner's Guide to Making a Fortune (Lapin), 121
The Homebuying Guide (Phipps and Mosely), 109
House and Garden, 167
The House Hunt Game: A Guide to Winning (Janik), 107
House Recycling: The Best Real Estate Opportunity for the 80's (Weir), 124
How Anyone Can Stop Paying Income Taxes (Schiff with Murzim), 130
How I Turned $1,000 into Five Million in Real Estate—In My Spare Time (Nickerson), 122
How Life Insurance Companies Rob You and What You Can Do about It (Kenton), 157
How Much for Housing? New Perspectives on Affordability and Risk (Feins and Lane), 106
How the IRS Seizes Your Dollars and How to Fight Back (Hansen and Anderson), 127
How to Adjust to Adjustable Home Mortgages (Crittenden), 112

How to Avoid Estate Taxes (Cantor), 152
How to Avoid Probate—Updated! (Dacey), 153
How to Be a Financially Secure Woman (Schlayer and Cooley), 49
How to Beat the Financial Squeeze: Don't Just Get Mad—Get Even (Flanagan), 31
How to Beat the High Cost of Learning: The Complete and Up-to-Date Guide to Student Financial Aid (Kornfeld et al.), 55
How to Beat the Money Grabbers: The Essentials of Estate Planning (Whitney), 156
How to Beat the Salary Trap: 8 Steps to Financial Independence (Rifenbark), 26
How to Benefit from the New Tax Laws: Immediate Gains and Long-Term Strategies (Post), 132
How to Borrow Your Way to Real Estate Riches Using Government Money (Hicks), 120
How to Build a Fortune with an IRA (Ullman and Bercoon), 152
How to Build a Second Income Fortune in Your Spare Time (Hicks), 32
How to Buy a Home at a Reasonable Price (Irwin), 107
How to Buy a Home while You Can Still Afford To (Murphy), 108
How to Buy: An Insider's Guide to Making Money in the Stock Market (Mamis), 88
How to Buy and Sell a Condominium (Natelson), 115
How to Buy and Sell Gems: Everyone's Guide to Rubies, Sapphires, Emeralds and Diamonds (Zucker), 101
How to Buy and Sell Real Estate for Financial Security (Irwin), 120
How to Buy Money: Investing Wisely for Maximum Return (Nelson), 72
How to Buy Real Estate without Getting Burned (Rejnis), 111

How to Buy Stocks (Engel and Boyd), 80
How to Buy Stocks (Engel with Wyckoff), 80
How to Buy Your First Home (Speraw), 111
How to Buy Your Own House When You Don't Have Enough Money (Gabriel), 112
How to Cash In on the Coming Stock Market Boom: The Smart Investor's Guide to Making Money (Kandel), 81
How to Cope with the Developing Financial Crisis (Bladen), 39
How to Finance Your Retirement (Dunetz), 146
How to Flourish, Prosper, and Survive the 80's Despite Everything: The Working Person's Financial Crash Course (Hubbard and Winfrey), 32
How to Forecast Interest Rates: A Guide to Profits for Consumers, Managers and Investors (Pring), 83
How to Get Free Tax Help (Lesko), 128
How to Get More for Your Money (McConnally), 34
How to Get Out of Debt (Nicholas), 65
How to Get Out of Debt: Without Despair and Without a Lawyer (Kaufman), 64
How to Get Rich while You Sleep (Huskin and Monsees), 71
How to Get the Money to Buy Your New Home (Jacobe and Kendall), 113
How to Get Top Dollar for Your Home in Good Times or Bad (Price), 110
How to Get Your Creditors Off Your Back without Losing Your Shirt (Kaplan and Drotning), 64
How to Go from Rags to Riches in Real Estate: A Guide to Turning Depressed, Neglected, or Little-Known Property Investments into Millions in the 1980's (Dooner and Proctor), 118
How to Grow a Money Tree: Earn 20 to 30 Percent and More with Safe Second Mortgages and Trust Deeds (Glubetich), 118
How to Increase Your Money-Making Power in the 80's (Appleman), 30
How to Invest in Gold (Cavelti), 97
How to Invest in Strategic Metals (Szuprowicz), 99
How to Invest Your Money and Profit from Inflation (Shulman), 43
How to Lick Inflation Before It Licks You (Benge), 39
How to Live Better and Spend 20% Less (Dowd), 31
How to Make a Will, How to Use Trusts (Callaghan), 152
How to Make Big Money in Low-Priced Stocks in the Coming Bull Market (Charell), 86
How to Make Big Money in Real Estate (Marino), 122
How to Make Love to Your Money (Segall and Tobin), 53
How to Make Money during Inflation/Recession (Consumer Guide, with Dickinson), 41
How to Make Money in Penny Stocks: The Ultimate Solution for the Small Investor (Scott), 94
How to Make Money on the Interest Rate Roller Coaster: A Proven Method for Profitable Investment in a Rising or Falling Market (Coslow), 67
How to Make Money Using Other People's Money (Bondy), 67
How to Make $1,000,000 in the Stock Market—Automatically (Lichello), 81
How to Make Your First Quarter Million in Real Estate in Five Years (Ramsey), 123
How to Make Your Money Make Money: The Experts Explain Your Alternatives, the Risks, the Rewards (Levitt), 71
How to Pay Zero Taxes: Over 100 Ways to Reduce Your Taxes—To Nothing (Schnepper), 134

How to Probate an Estate: A Handbook for Executors and Administrators (Moody), 156
How to Profit from Condominium Conversions (Bullock), 114
How to Profit from Disinflation (Simons), 73
How to Profit from the Coming Bull Market (Ansbacher), 75
How to Prosper during the Coming Bad Years (Ruff), 42
How to Prosper in the Coming Apocalypse (Curtis), 41
How to Prosper in the Coming Good Years (Williams), 93
How to Prosper in the 80's (Consumer Guide), 41
How to Prosper in the Underground Economy (Burkett and Procter), 57
How to Recover Your Medical Expenses: A Comprehensive Guide to Understanding and Unscrambling Medicare (Waller), 161
How to Reduce Your Real Estate Taxes (Barash), 138
How to Save a Fortune on Your Life Insurance (Kaye), 157
How to Save 50% or More on Your Income Tax—Legally (Anderson), 125
How to Save or Make Thousands when You Buy or Sell Your House (Nielsen and Nielsen), 109
How to Save Tax Dollars as a Homeowner (Cahill), 105
How to Save Taxes through Estate Planning (Pinto), 156
How to Stop Foreclosure: What to Do When Your "Balloon Is Due and You're Laid Off or Facing Other Financial Crises" (Morris and Irwin), 113
How to Survive and Grow Richer in the Tough Times Ahead (Holt), 71
How to Survive (And Make Money) in the Coming Real Estate Crunch (Malcolm), 113
How to Survive without a Salary (Long), 58
How to Talk Back to the Telephone Company: Playing the Telephone Game to Win (Sirico), 36
How to Use Interest Rate Futures Contracts (Schwarz), 93
How to Use the Business Library: With Sources of Business Information (Johnson), 18
How You Can Become Financially Independent by Investing in Real Estate (Lowry), 122
How You Can Get the Most from the New Tax Law (Smith and Sprogen), 133
How You Can Profit from Gold (Sinclair and Schultz), 98
How You Can Profit from Today's Gold Rush (Feinman), 97
How You Can Share in the Futures Being Made in Gold (Wolenik), 99
How You Can Use Inflation to Beat the IRS (Anderson), 125
How Your IRA Can Make You a Millionnaire (Corrigan), 150
How Your Life Insurance Policies Rob You (Milton), 158
Howard Ruff from A to Z: A Timeless Money Making Odyssey through the First Four Years of America's Leading Financial Advisory Service (Ruff), 42
Hugh Downs' the Best Years Book: How to Plan for Fulfillment, Security and Happiness in the Retirement Years (Downs and Roll), 146
The Hulbert Financial Digest, 185

I Filed Bankruptcy and I'm Glad I Did (Silvers and Harkness), 66
The IRA Handbook: A Complete Guide (Pancheri and Flynn), 152
IRA's: Your Complete New Money Guide: How to Open Your IRA,

Title Index

Manage It, Switch It, Withdraw It and Get the Best, Safest Yields, 151
The I.R.S. versus the Middle Class: Or How the Average Citizen Can Protect Himself from the Federal Tax Collector (Larson), 128
Income and Estate Tax Planning (Sloan), 149
Income Investor, 180
Industrial Manual and News Reports, 219
Industry Surveys, 218
The Inflation Beater's Investment Guide: Winning Strategies for the 1980's (Malkiel), 82
Inflation-Proofing Your Investments (Browne and Coxon), 39
Inflation-Wise: How to Do Almost Everything for Less (McLachlan), 33
Inside the Financial Futures Markets (Powers and Vogel), 92
Inside the Underground Economy: Over Twenty Million Americans Are Avoiding Income Taxes—and May Be Getting Away with It (Tuccille), 59
Insider Indicator, 180
The Insiders, 180
An Insider's Guide to Auctions (Auerbach), 101
Instruments of the Money Market (Cook and Summers), 69
Interest Rate Futures (Loosigan), 92
International Investing Made Easy: Proven Money Strategies with as Little as $5,000 (Pring), 83
International Investing: The Complete Databook to the World's Last Frontiers for Smart Money Management Overseas (Casey), 24
International Investment Letter, 180
Invest for Retirement: A Conservative Investor's Guide (Rubinstein), 149
Investing at the Racetrack (Scott), 73
Investing for Profit in the Eighties: The Business Cycle System (Malabre), 82
Investing in Natural Resources: 1980's Guide to Tomorrow's Needs (Youngquist), 100
Investing in Residential Income Property (Temple), 124
Investing in Securities: A Handbook for the '80's (Haft), 70
Investing in the 80's: What to Buy and When (Beadle), 79
Investing in the Future: 10 New Industries and 75 Growth Companies That Are Changing the Face of Corporate America (Sokoloff, Laird, and Mack), 85
Investing on Your Own: How to Find Winning Stocks in Your Own Backyard (Thorsell), 78
Investing without Borders: The Best Opportunities around the World for the 80's (Day), 69
Investment Bibliography: A Selected List of Books, Services, Newspapers, Periodicals and Financial Organizations (Mechanic), 14
Investment Companies, 1982 (Wiesenberg Investment Companies), 224
Investment Methods: A Bibliographic Guide (Woy), 64
Investment Quality Trends, 180
The Investment Reporter, 181
Investments (Sharpe), 73
Investors Can Beat Inflation: A Practical Guide (Smith), 85
The Investor's Guide to Closed-End Funds: The Herzfeld Hedge (Herzfeld), 81
The Investor's Guide to Stock Quotations and Other Financial Listings (Warfield), 78
The Investor's Guide to Technical Analysis (Hardy), 87
Investor's Intelligence, 185
The Investor's Quotient: The Psychology of Successful Investing in Commodities and Stocks (Bernstein), 89
The Invisible Bankers: Everything the Insurance Industry Never Wanted You to Know (Tobias), 159

Title Index

It Only Hurts between Paydays: A Practical, Exciting, and Fun Plan for Getting Control of Your Personal Finances (Mumford), 45
It's Easier for a Rich Man to Enter Heaven than for a Poor Man to Remain on Earth (Felix), 45

J. K. Lasser's All You Should Know about IRA, Keogh, and Other Retirement Plans (Greisman), 151
J. K. Lasser's Financial Planning for Your Family (J. K. Lasser's Tax Institute), 45
J. K. Lasser's How You Can Profit from the New Tax Laws (Greisman), 132
J. K. Lasser's Your Estate and Gift Taxes (J. K. Lasser's Tax Institute), 154
J. K. Lasser's Your Income Tax, 128
John Stossel's Shopping Smart: The Only Consumer's Guide You'll Ever Need (Stossel), 37
The Johnson Survey, 181
Joint Property: Everything You Must Know to Save Time, Trouble, and Money on Your Jointly Owned Property (Bove), 105
Junior Growth Stocks, 184

Kids and Cash: Solving a Parent's Dilemma (Davis and Taylor), 49
Kiplinger Washington Letter, 170
Kiss Ma Bell Good-bye: How to Install Your Own Telephones, Extensions and Accessories (Cox), 30

Ladies' Home Journal, 164
Law of Retirement (Jessup), 148
Layman's Guide to Oil and Gas Investments (Brown), 68

The Life Insurance Conspiracy Made Elementary by Sherlock Holmes (Spielman and Zelman), 158
A List of Worthwhile Life and Health Insurance Books (Gordon), 18
Living Rich: A Manual for Would-be Big Spenders (Ackerman and Ackerman), 23
Living with Tenants: How to Happily Share Your House with Renters for Profit and Security (Bierbrier), 50
Long Distance for Less: How to Choose between Ma Bell and Those "Other" Carriers (Self), 36
Lottery Winners: How They Won and How Winning Changed Their Lives (Kaplan), 61
Love and Money: What Your Finances Say about Your Personal Relationships (Colman), 51
"Low Cost Investment Information" (Raphaelson), 14
Low Priced Stock Digest, 185

McCalls, 164
Mademoiselle, 165
The Magic of Thinking Rich (Charell), 51
Make Your Money Grow (Miller), 25
Making High Profits in Uncertain Times (Barnes), 91
Making Inflation Pay!: How Limited Funds in Gold, Silver, Coins, Stamps, Real Estate at the Right Time Can Win Big (Hefferlin), 41
Making Money with Your Microcomputer (Traister and Ingram), 51
Managing Your Money (Miller), 34
"Managing Your Money: Where to Research That Stock" (Hazard), 13
Managing Your Own Money (Rosenberg), 27
Managing Your Own Money: A Self-Teaching Guide (Zimmerman), 29
Mark Skousen's Guide to Financial Privacy (Skousen), 27

Title Index 291

Market Logic, 181
"Market Publications: Guide Posts on the Investment Landscape" (Gupta), 13
The Medicare Answer Book: The Up-to-Date, Practical and Authoritative Guide to Medicare (Harrington), 159
Men's Rights: A Handbook for the 80's (Wishard and Wishard), 29
Mergers and Acquisitions Journal, 181
Merrill-Lynch Market Letter, 181
The Mind of the Market: A Study of Stock Market Philosophies, Their Use and Implications (Smith), 89
Mind over Money: Why Most People Lose Money in the Stock Market and How You Can Become a Winner (Tucille), 89
Minds, Markets, and Money: Psychological Foundations of Economic Behavior (Maital), 52
The Mobile Home Guide: Your Affordable Manufactured House (Kramer), 115
Mobile Home Living: The Money-Saving Guide (Fenwick), 115
Modern Maturity, 167
Monarch's Dictionary of Investment Terms (Beer), 224
Money, 169
Money (Ritter and Silber), 26
Money and Finance: Sources of Print and Non-Print Materials (Ladley and Wilford), 19
Money and Retirement: How to Plan for Lifetime Financial Security (LeClair, Leimberg, and Chasman), 148
Money and Women (Simons and Simons), 49
The Money Book for People Who Live Together (Harden and Harden), 24
The Money Diet: How to Save Up to $360 in 28 Days (Rotchstein), 35
Money Dynamics for the 1980's (Van Caspel), 28
Money for College: How to Get It (Moore), 57

Money: How to Spend Less and Have More (Juroe), 52
Money in Your Pocket: Using the New Reagan Tax Laws (Strassels), 133
MoneyLove: How to Get the Money You Deserve for Whatever You Want (Gillies), 51
Money Madne$$: The Psychology of Saving, Spending, Loving and Having Money (Goldberg and Lewis), 52
Money Management for Women (Minkow), 48
The Money Market Book (King), 96
The Money Market: Myth, Realities and Practice (Stigum), 73
Money Market Safety Ratings, 187
The Money Masters: Nine Great Investors, Their Winning Strategies and How You Can Apply Them (Train), 86
Money Power: How to Make Inflation Make You Rich (Stein and Stein), 44
Money Smarts (Assael), 101
Money Talks: Bob Rosefsky's Complete Program for Financial Success (Rosefsky), 8, 27
Moneythink: Financial Planning Finally Made Easy (Berg), 51
Money Today, More Tomorrow (Smith), 144
Moneywise (Brien), 47
Money-Wise: The Prentice-Hall Book of Personal Money Management (Stillman), 144
The Money Workbook for Women: A Step-by-Step Guide to Managing Your Personal Finances (Phillips), 48
The Monopoly Game: The "How To" Book of Making Big Money with Rental Homes (Glubetich), 119
Moody's Handbook of Common Stocks, 223
Moonlighter's Guide to a Sparetime Fortune (Michaels), 34
More for Your Money: Personal Finance Techniques to Cope with In-

flation and the Energy Shortage (Stillman), 28
More Money for Your Retirement, (Barnes), 145
More Profit, Less Risk: Your New Financial Strategy (Cerami), 68
Move Your Assets to Beat Inflation (Nauheim), 42
Ms. The New Magazine for Women, 166
The Mutual Fund Specialist, 187
Mutual Funds Almanac (Hirsch), 224

National Investor News, 174
The National OTC Stock Exchange, 174
Nation's Business, 170
The New Contrarian Investment Strategy: The Psychology of Stock Market Success (Dreman), 80
The New Money Dynamics (Van Caspel), 28
The New Mortgage Game (Irwin), 112
New Profits from the Monetary Crisis (Browne), 39
The New Tax Law and You (Tucille), 133
The New Taxpayer's Counterattack (Jacobs), 128
New Woman, 166
The New World of Gold: The Inside Story of the Mines, the Markets, the Politics, the Investors (Green), 97
The New York Times, 172
The New York Times Guide to Making the New Tax Law Work for You (Arenson), 132
Newsletter Digest, 186
Newsweek, 168
The Nicholson Report, 181
Nickels, Dimes and Dollars: How Currency Works (Fodor), 24
The 1980 Yearbook of Agriculture: Cutting Energy Costs, 35
The Nineteen Eighty-One Guide to Coupons and Refunds (Sloane), 60

1983 H and R Block Income Tax Workbook, 129
99 Ways to Make Money in a Depression (Appel), 39
Nothing Down: How to Buy Real Estate with Little or No Money Down (Allen), 117

OTC Chart Manual, 221
OTC Growth Stock Watch, 184
The Official Investors Guide to Buying and Selling Gold, Silver and Diamonds (Hudgeons), 100
Old, Poor, Alone and Happy: How to Live Nicely on Nearly Nothing (Dissinger), 145
The $100,000 Decision: The Older American's Guide to Selling a Home and Choosing Retirement Housing (Irwin), 147
The $125,000 Decision: The Older American's Guide to Selling a Home and Choosing Retirement Housing (Irwin), 147
The Only Guide You'll Ever Need to Marry Money (Ackerman), 46
The Only Investment Guide You'll Ever Need (Tobias), 74
The Only Tax Book You'll Ever Need (Garber), 127
The Optimist's Guide to Making Money in the 1980's: A Complete Program for Investing in the American Economic Miracle of the Next Decade (Tucille), 74
Options as a Strategic Investment (McMillan), 90
The Outlook, 182
The Over-the-Counter Securities Market (Buckley and Loll), 68

The Paine Webber Handbook of Stock and Bond Analysis (Sokoloff), 223
Panics and Crashes: How You Can

Make Money Out of Them (Schultz), 43
Paper Gold: How to Hedge against Inflation by Investing in Postage Stamps (Wagenheim), 103
Paper Money (Smith), 43
Parents, 164
Pay Less Tax, 129
The Penny Capitalist: How to Build a Small Fortune from Next to Nothing (Horatio), 32
The Penny Stock Journal, 175
Penny Stock News, 175
Penny Stock Preview, 185
Penny Stocks: How the Small Investor Can Make Large Profits in the Penny Market (McWilliams), 94
Perfectly Legal: 275 Foolproof Methods for Paying Less Tax (Steiner and Kennedy), 134
Personal Estate Planning: Financial and Legal Aspects of Accumulating, Protecting, and Disposing of Your Personal Estate (Kinevan), 154
Personal Finance (Burton and Petrello), 142
Personal Finance (Cohen), 142
Personal Finance (Penson, Levi, and Nixon), 143
"Personal Finance: Peddling Advice to the Middle Class," 8
Personal Finance—The Inflation Survival Letter, 182
Personal Financial Planning (Hallman and Rosenbloom), 143
Personal Financial Survival: A Guide for the 1980's and Beyond (Brownstone and Sartisky), 10, 142
Personal Money Management (Hurley), 143
The Peter Dag Investment Letter, 182
Planning Your Financial Future: Tax Shelters, Annuities, IRAs, Keoghs, Stocks and Other Investment or Retirement Opportunities (Raphaelson), 149
Playboy's Investment and Financial Planning Guide for Singles: Making It and Keeping It in the Eighties (Rutberg), 27
Playing the Stock Markets with Your Personal Computer (Schmeltz), 72
Playing the Takeover Market: How to Profit from Corporate Mergers, Spin-Offs, Tender Offers and Liquidations (McQuown), 82
The Power of Money Dynamics (Van Caspel), 28
The Power of Prosperous Thinking: A Practical and Inspirational Guide to Making, Managing, and Multiplying Your Money (Johnstad and Johnstad), 115
The Predictor, 182
Prentice-Hall Federal Tax Handbook, 1983, 129
The Primary Trend, 182
Prime of Your Life (Michaels), 148
Principles of Insurance (Mehr and Cammack), 158
The Professional Tape Reader, 182
The Profit-Taker: The Proven Rapid Money-Maker in Good and Bad Markets (Abrams), 78
Profits from Country Property: How to Select, Buy, Maintain, and Improve Your Country Property (Koch), 121
Prosper through Tax Planning (Buechner), 126
Putting Money to Work: An Investment Primer for the 80's (Meltzer), 8, 72

The "Questioned Stock" Manual: A Guide to Determining the True Worth of Old and Collectible Securities (Gargiulo and Carlucci), 76

A Random Walk Down Wall Street (Malkiel), 82
Rating the Stock Selectors, 186

"A Reading List for Investors" (Hazard), 13
Ready or Not: Planning Your Successful Retirement (Ledford and Brock), 148
The Real Estate Acquisition Handbook: Money-Making Techniques for the Serious Investor (Tappan), 124
The Real Estate Book: A Complete Guide to Acquiring, Financing and Investing in a Home or Commercial Property (Nessen), 109
The Real Estate Broker's Inside Guide to Selling Your Own Home (And Keeping the Commission!) (Mason), 108
Real Estate: How to Double Your Money Every Two to Three Years with Income-Producing Properties (Kimmel), 121
Real Estate Investment for Profit through Appreciation (Maury), 123
Real Estate Investment for the 80's: How to Build Financial Security in the Face of Inflation (Temple), 124
Real Estate Investment Strategies (Seldin and Swesnick), 123
Real Estate Investments and How to Make Them: The Only Guide You'll Ever Need (Tanzer), 123
Real Estate Taxation: A Practical Guide (Jeddloh and Perkins), 139
Redbook, 164
Redbook's Guide to Buying Your First Home (Pomeroy), 110
Rehabbing for Profit (Davis), 118
Resort Condos and Timesharing: Buyer Beware! (Coltman), 116
Resort Timesharing: How You Can Invest in Inflation-Proof Vacations for Life (Trowbridge), 116
"Resources: Financial News" (Gitman and Joehnk), 12
Retirement Life, 167
Retirement Living Alternatives USA: The Inside Story (Worley), 150
The Retirement Money Book: New Ways to Have More Income When You Retire (Nauheim), 149
Reverse the Charges: How to Save $$$ on Your Phone Bill (Simon and Waz), 36
Riches in Real Estate: A Beginner's Guide to Group Investing (Irwin), 120
The Roaring 80's on Wall Street: How to Make a Killing in the Coming Stock Market Boom (Cobleigh and Dorfman), 75

SIE Performance Review, 186
Saving Money through 10-Year Trusts (Hancock), 156
Savvy: The Magazine for Executive Women, 166
Security Dealers of North America, 222
A Selection of 1982 Internal Revenue Service Tax Information Publications (Internal Revenue Service, Department of the Treasury), 14
Self, 165
Sell Your Home "By Owner" and Save the Commission (Jensen), 107
Sell Your House through Creative Financing—Without a Broker (Haskell), 112
Selling Collectibles for Profit and Capital Gains (Rush), 103
Selling Your Home: A Guide to Getting the Best Price with or without a Broker (Janik), 107
Seven Keys for Doubling Your Standard of Living (Without Increasing Your Income) (Fuhrman), 32
Shelter What You Make, Minimize the Take: Tax Shelters for Financial Planning (Tanner, Pheffer, and Laurins), 136
Silver Profits in the Eighties (Smith and Smith), 98
Simplified Guide to Estate Planning and Administration (Whitman), 156

The Single Person's Home Buying Handbook (Petersen), 109
The Singlinger Digest, 183
The Small Investor's Guide to Gold (Beckhardt), 96
The Smart Investor's Guide: How to Make Money in the Coming Bull Market (Krefetz), 76
The Smart Investor's Guide to Real Estate: Big Profits from Small Investments (Bruss), 117
The Smart Investor's Guide to the Money Market (Sarnoff), 96
Smart Money Real Estate for the 80's: New Profits in Big Properties (Irwin), 120
The Smart Shopper's Guide to Food Buying and Preparation (Bingham and Riccio), 30
The Smart Spending Guide for Teens (Landau), 50
The Sophisticated Investor: How to Target Prime Investment Opportunities (Church), 79
Sources of Business Information (Coman), 17
The Squeeze (Davidson), 31
Standard and Poor's Ratings Guide: Including Corporate Bonds, Commercial Paper, Municipal Bonds, International Securities, 223
The Star Spangled Dream (Gollin), 146
Stock Guide, 218
The Stock Market (Teweles and Bradley), 78
The Stock Market and Inflation (Boeckh and Coghlan), 75
The Stock Market Directory, (Dorfman) 222
Stock Market Encyclopedia of the S&P "500," 218
Stock Market Forecasting for Alert Investors (Touhey), 88
Stock Market Primer (Rosenberg), 84
Stock Market Strategy for Consistent Profits (Righetti), 84
The Stock Option and No Load Switch Fund Scalper's Manual (Appel), 86

The Stock Options Manual (Gastineau), 90
Stock Reports, 219
Stock Summary, 219
Stop Burning Your Money: The Intelligent Homeowner's Guide to Household Energy Savings (Rothchild), 35
Strategic Investing: How to Profit from the Coming Inflationary Depression (Casey), 40
The Strategic Metals Investment Handbook (Goldberg and Posner), 99
The Strategic Metals War: The Current Crisis and Your Investment Opportunities (Sinclair and Parker), 99
Subject Bibliography Index (Superintendent of Documents, Government Printing Office), 19
The Subterranean Economy (Bawly), 57
Successful Flea Market Selling (Bohigan), 30
Successful Investing: A Complete Guide to Your Financial Future (United Business Services), 74
Successful Real Estate Investing for the Single Person (Cummings), 118
Successful Tax Planning (Mendlowitz), 129
Suddenly Rich (LeBlanc and LeBlanc), 61
Sun Spots, Stars, and the Stock Market (Rieder), 84
A Survival Kit for Taxpayers: Staying on Good Terms with the I.R.S. (Holzman), 127
Survive and Win in the Inflationary Eighties (Ruff), 43
A Survivor's Manual to: Contingency Planning, Wills, Trusts, Guidelines for Guardians, Getting through Probate, Taxes, Life Insurance, Emotional Stability, Protection from Reckless Spending, Living on a Fixed Income, Reconciling Family

Title Index

Differences, Avoiding Con Artists (Kirsch), 154
The Swiss Banking Handbook: A Complete Manual for Practical Investors (Roethenmund), 63
Switch Fund Advisory, 187
Sylvia Porter's New Money Book for the 80's (Porter), 8, 25
Sylvia Porter's 1983 Income Tax Book (Porter), 129
Systems and Forecasts, 183

Take It Off! Close to 2,363 Deductions Most People Overlook (Holzman), 133
The Tax Fighter's Guide (Storer and Williams), 131
Tax Free (Skousen), 136
Tax Guide for College Teachers and Other College Personnel (For Filing 1982 Tax Returns) (Bernstein), 125
The Tax Organizer (Ferri and Silverberg), 126
Tax Planning for Investors: The Eighties Guide to Securities Investments and Tax Shelters (Crestol and Schneider), 126
Tax Saving: A Year Round Guide (Block), 126
The Tax Shelter Coloring Book (Mosburg), 135
Tax Shelters: A Complete Guide (Tannenhauser and Tannenhauser), 136
Tax Shelters: A Guide for Investors and Their Advisors (Swanson and Swanson), 136
Tax Shelters and Tax-Free Income for Everyone (Drollinger and Drollinger), 135
Tax Shelters for the Not-So-Rich (Dickson), 134
Tax Shelters in Plain English: New Strategies for the 1980's (Fierro), 135
Tax Shelters That Work for Everyone: A Common Sense Guide to Keeping More of the Money You Earn (McQuown), 135
Tax Tactics for Teachers (Schandel and Schandel), 130
Tax Tactics for the Retired (Schandel and Schandel), 130
Tax Tactics for the Single or Divorced (Schandel and Schandel), 130
The Taxpayer's Audit Survival Manual (Jacobs and Schoeneman), 137
Taxpayer's Guide to IRS Information and Assistance (Internal Revenue Service, Department of the Treasury), 15
The Taxpayer's Internal Revenue Service Audit Survival Manual (Jacobs and Schoeneman), 137
Technical Analysis Explained: An Illustrated Guide for the Investor (Pring), 88
"The 1040 Form and All That" (Ackerman), 10
"There's Help Out There: Knowing You Don't Have to Do It Alone Can Make the Difference Between Success and Not Even Getting Started" (Carter), 11
Think Like a Tycoon: Inflation Can Make You Rich (Greene), 119
Think Rich (Judd), 52
The Thinking Investor's Guide to the Stock Market (Sokoloff), 85
This Way to Wall $treet (Egan and Maran), 76
Time, 168
Timing: How To Profitably Manage Money at Different Stages of Your Life (Herrick), 143
Toll-Free Digest: A New Enlarged Directory of Over 17,000 Toll-Free Listings, 37
Trading in Commodity Futures (Horn and Farah), 91
Trading in Gold: How to Buy, Sell and Profit in the Gold Market (Sarnoff), 98
Training Your Children to Handle Money (MacGregor), 50
Trendline, 220–221

Title Index 297

Turn Your House into a Money Factory (King), 51
Turn Your Kitchen into a Gold Mine (Howard and Howard), 50

The Underground Marketplace: A Guide to New England and the Middle Atlantic States (Webster and Webster), 59
Understanding a Company's Finances: A Graphic Approach (Purcell), 83
Understanding Medicare (Steskal), 160
Understanding Wall Street (Little and Rhodes), 77
The Unemployment Benefits Handbook (Honigsberg), 63
United Mutual Fund Selector, 187
U.S. News & World Report, 168
Used Cars: How to Avoid Highway Robbery (Darack, Arthur, and Consumer Group Inc.), 30

The VNR Investor's Dictionary (Brownstone and Franck), 225
Vacation Timesharing: Upper Income Holidays on Middle Income Budgets (Spencer), 116
Value Line, 219
Valuing Common Stock: The Power of Prudence (Lasry), 76
"Variety, New Risks, Complicate Decisions" (Shepherd), 8
Vogue, 165

The Wag Letter, 183
Wall Street Journal, 172
Wall Street Prophets, 183
The Wall Street Review of Books, 20
Wall Street Transcript, 172
"Want the Bottom Line on TV's Business Reporting?" (Tobias), 7
"Want to Curl Up with a Good Money Book? Our No-Frills Guide Tells Which Ones Are Worth It" (Small), 15
The Weekend Real Estate Investor: The New Low-Risk Team Approach That Transforms Everyday Opportunities into Big Profits (Hatfield), 120
What Every Woman Should Know about Finances (Lumb), 47
"What to Do with Money" (Arenson), 10
"What to Read on How to Invest During Shaky Times" (Bettner), 10
What You've Got Coming in Social Security and Medicare (Steif), 160
What'll You Take for It: Back to Barter (Proulx), 58
What's Behind Inflation and How to Beat It (Eder), 41
What's It Worth? 1983 Investors Guide: Silver Bullion and Coins, 98
When You Owe the IRS (Wade), 131
Where to Find Business Information: A Worldwide Guide for Everyone Who Needs the Answers to Business Questions (Brownstone and Carruth), 16
Where to Get Money for Everything: A Complete Guide to Today's Money Sources (Nelson), 55
The Where to Sell Anything and Everything Book (Hyman), 33
Where Will You Live Tomorrow? The Complete Guide to Planning for Your Retirement Housing (Sumichrast, Shafer, and Sumichrast), 149
Who Gets It When You Go? A Guide for Planning Your Will, Protecting Your Family's Future, Minimizing Inheritance Taxes, and Avoiding Probate (Larsen), 155
Why Stocks Go Up (and Down): A Guide to Sound Investing (Pike), 77
Why You're Richer Than You Think (Jenkins), 102
Wiesenberger Investment Companies

Service. Investment Companies, 1982, 224
William Donoghue's Complete Money Market Guide: The Simple Low-Risk Way You Can Profit from Inflation and Fluctuating Interest Rates (Donoghue with Tilling), 95
William E. Donoghue's No-Load Mutual Fund Guide (Donoghue with Tilling), 8, 95
Wills and Trusts: A Legal and Financial Handbook for Everyone (Hemphill), 154
Win Your Personal Tax Revolt (Greene), 127
Winning in the Commodities Market: A Money-Making Guide to Commodity Futures Trading (Angwell), 90
Winning on Your Income Taxes (Kamensky), 128
The Winning Option (Dames), 90
Winning the Battle with Your Money Hang-Ups (Weinstein), 53
Winning: The Psychology of Successful Investing (Blotnick), 89
Winning with Money: A Guide for Your Future (Sprinkel and Genetski), 28
Woman's Day, 164
The Woman's Guide to Buying Houses, Co-ops, and Condominiums (Kiev), 108
The Woman's Guide to Financial Savvy (Briles), 47
The Woman's Guide to the Stock Market: How to Make Your Own Investment Plan (Lee with Morgenson), 76
The Woman's Money Book: How to Make Your Money Grow (Mackevich), 48
Women and Money (Rogers and Joyce), 49
Women, Divorce and Money: Plain Talk about Money, Procedures, Settlement, Financial Survival for Women Who Are Divorced or Thinking about Divorce (Rogers), 48
The Women's Financial Survival Handbook (Perkins and Rhoades), 48
Women's Handbook of Independent Financial Management, (Lee and Hassay), 47
Working Mother, 166
Working Woman, 166
The World Almanac Consumer Information Kit, 29

You Can Buy a Home Now (Drotning), 105
You Can Profit from the New Tax Law (Wiltsee and Sammons), 133
You Can Save a Bundle on Your Car Insurance (Majika), 158
You May Be Losing Your Inheritance: A Guide to Psychological, Financial, and Legal Hazards and What You Can Do about Them Now (Levin et al.), 155
Your Complete Guide to IRA's and Keoghs: The Simple, Safe Tax-Deferred Way to Financial Security (Egan), 150
Your Federal Income Tax: For Individuals: For Use in Preparing 1982 Returns, 131
Your Gold and Silver: An Easy Guide to Appraising Household Objects, Coins, Heirlooms, and Jewelry (Merton), 98
Your Guide to a Financially Secure Retirement (Hardy), 146
Your Home as a Tax Shelter: How to Save Taxes When You Buy, Hold, or Sell Your Home (Radics and Geisman), 110
Your Money and Your Life: A Lifetime Approach to Money Management (Aliber), 67
Your Money and Your Life: Planning Your Financial Future (Hardy), 147

Your Money: Frustration or Freedom? (Dayton), 45
Your Money: How to Make It Work Harder Than You Do (Phalon), 35
Your Money Matters: A Guide to Personal Finance from the Pages of the Wall Street Journal (Moffitt), 143
Your New Swiss Bank Book (Kinsman), 62
Your 1983/84 Guide to Social Security Benefits (Rubin), 160
Your Own Financial Aid Factory: The Guide to Locating College Money (Leider), 56
Your Personal Guide to Financial Fitness (Heil), 25
Your Retirement: A Complete Planning Guide (Consumer Guide and Dickinson), 145
Your Retirement Income (Jorgensen), 148

The Zweig Forecast, 183

NO LONGER THE PROPERTY
OF THE
UNIVERSITY OF R.I. LIBRARY